· MILET ·
BILINGUAL VISUAL
DICTIONARY
ENGLISH · ARABIC

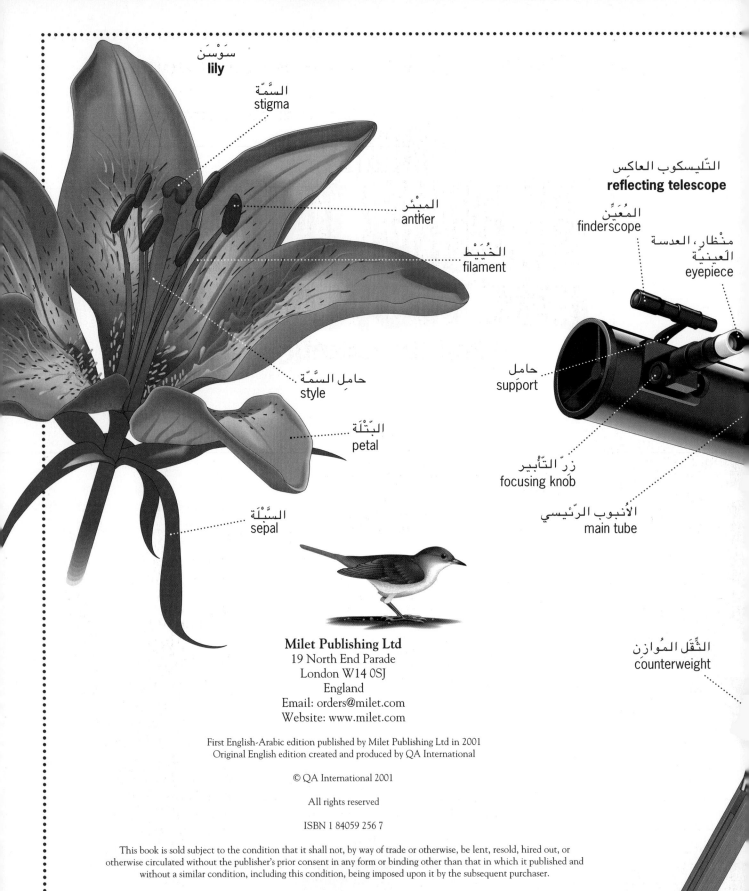

سَوْسَن
lily

السَّمَّة
stigma

المِبْئَر
anther

الخُيَيْط
filament

حامِلِ السَّمَّة
style

البَتْلَة
petal

السَّبْلَة
sepal

التِّليسكوب العاكِس
reflecting telescope

المُعَيِّن
finderscope

مِنْظار، العدسة العَينِيَّة
eyepiece

حامِل
support

زِرّ التَّبْئير
focusing knob

الأُنبوب الرَّئيسي
main tube

الثَّقَل المُوازِن
counterweight

Milet Publishing Ltd
19 North End Parade
London W14 0SJ
England
Email: orders@milet.com
Website: www.milet.com

First English-Arabic edition published by Milet Publishing Ltd in 2001
Original English edition created and produced by QA International

ISBN 1 84059 256 7

Dual language typesetting by Typesetters Ltd
Printed and bound in Slovakia

...rbeil • Ariane Archambault

· MILET ·
BILINGUAL VISUAL
DICTIONARY
ENGLISH • ARABIC

Authors
Jean-Claude Corbeil, Ariane Archambault
Director of Computer Graphics
François Fortin
Art Directors
Jean-Louis Martin, François Fortin
Graphic Designer
Anne Tremblay
Computer Graphic Designers
Marc Lalumière, Jean-Yves Ahern,
Rielle Lévesque, Anne Tremblay, Jacques Perrault,
Jocelyn Gardner, Christiane Beauregard,
Michel Blais, Stéphane Roy, Alice Comtois,
Benoît Bourdeau
Computer Programming
Yves Ferland, Daniel Beaulieu
Data Capture
Serge D'Amico
Page Make-up
Lucie Mc Brearty, Pascal Goyette
Technical Support
Gilles Archambault
Production
Tony O'Riley

Arabic translation by Mohamed Mahmoud

Editorial Note: For objects whose English terms are
different in North America and Britain,
we have used both terms: the North American term
followed by the British term. In the
index, these dual terms are listed alphabetically
by the first term.

Translation Note: In cases where there is no direct
Arabic term for an object, the translator has
used an approximate term or a descriptive term.
In cases where the English term is commonly
use...   ...term,
...of

SKY

solar system..6
Sun..8
Moon..9
comet...10
solar eclipse..10
lunar eclipse..10
reflecting telescope...............................11
refracting telescope..............................11

EARTH

Earth coordinate system.........................12
structure of the Earth............................12
earthquake..13
cave...13
coastal features...................................14
volcano...15
glacier..16
mountain...17
the continents......................................18
seasons of the year...............................20
structure of the biosphere......................20
elevation zones and vegetation................20
climates of the world.............................21
weather..22
meteorological measuring instruments.......23
cartography...24
compass card......................................27
ecology...28

PLANT KINGDOM

plant and soil.......................................34
soil profile...34
germination...34
mushroom...35
structure of a plant...............................36
flowers...38
tree..40
conifer..43

FRUITS AND VEGETABLES

fleshy fruits: berry fruits........................44
fleshy stone fruits.................................45
fleshy pome fruits.................................46
fleshy fruits: citrus fruits........................47
tropical fruits.......................................48
vegetables...49

GARDENING

gardening..54

ANIMAL KINGDOM

insects and spider.................................56
butterfly..57
honeybee..58
amphibians..60
crustaceans...61
fish..62
reptiles...64
cat...66
dog..66
horse..67
farm animals..68
types of jaws.......................................70
major types of horns..............................71
major types of tusks..............................71
types of hoofs......................................71
wild animals...72
bird..74
examples of birds..................................76

HUMAN BODY

human body, anterior view.......................78
human body, posterior view.....................79
skeleton..80
human anatomy....................................81
eye: the organ of sight...........................82
hand: the organ of touch.........................82
ear: the organ of hearing........................83
nose: the organ of smell.........................84
mouth: the organ of taste.......................84
human denture......................................85

ARCHITECTURE

traditional houses.................................86
mosque...87
castle...88
gothic cathedral....................................89
downtown..90

HOUSE

house...92
window...94
bed..95
seats..96
table and chairs....................................97
lights...98
lighting...99
glassware..100
dinnerware...100
silverware..101
kitchen utensils...................................102
cooking utensils...................................104
kitchen appliances...............................105
refrigerator..106
cooking appliances..............................107

DO-IT-YOURSELF

carpentry tools....................................108
electric tools.......................................110
painting upkeep...................................111

CLOTHING

men's clothing.....................................112
women's clothing.................................114
sweaters..117
gloves and stockings............................118
shoes..119
sportswear...120

PERSONAL ARTICLES

hairdressing..122
dental care...122
glasses..123
leather goods......................................123
umbrella...123

COMMUNICATIONS

communication by telephone...................124
photography..125
television..126

video..127
stereo system 128
portable sound systems 129

ROAD TRANSPORTATION

car...130
trucking..134
motorcycle 135
bicycle 136

RAIL TRANSPORTATION

diesel-electric locomotive 138
types of freight cars.............................138
highway crossing 140
high-speed train 140

MARITIME TRANSPORTATION

four-masted bark 141
hovercraft 141
cruise liner 142
harbor...142

AIR TRANSPORTATION

plane 144
helicopter 145
airport..146

SPACE TRANSPORTATION

space shuttle.......................................148
spacesuit 149

SCHOOL

school supplies.....................................150

school equipment..................................152
geometry 156
drawing 157

MUSIC

traditional musical instruments 158
keyboard instrument 159
musical notation...................................160
stringed instruments 162
wind instruments 164
percussion instruments 166
symphony orchestra...............................167

TEAM GAMES

baseball 168
football...170
soccer 172
volleyball 174
field hockey 175
ice hockey 176
basketball..178
tennis...180

WATER SPORTS

swimming...182
sailboard 184

WINTER SPORTS

skating..185
skiing 186

GYMNASTICS

gymnastics...188

CAMPING

tents 190
sleeping equipment 191
camping equipment................................192

INDOOR GAMES

card games...194
dominoes 194
dice 194
chess..195
backgammon...196
checkers 196
video entertainment system 197
game of darts..197

MEASURING DEVICES

measure of time 198
measure of temperature..........................199
measure of weight 200

ENERGY

oil 202
hydroelectric energy 204
nuclear energy......................................206
solar energy 208
wind energy 209

HEAVY MACHINERY

fire prevention 210
heavy vehicles 212
heavy machinery....................................214

SYMBOLS

common symbols 216
safety symbols 216
protection 216

5

المَنْظُومة الشَّمْسية
SOLAR SYSTEM

الأجْرام السَّماوية :الكَواكِب السَّيَّارة والأقْمار
planets and moons

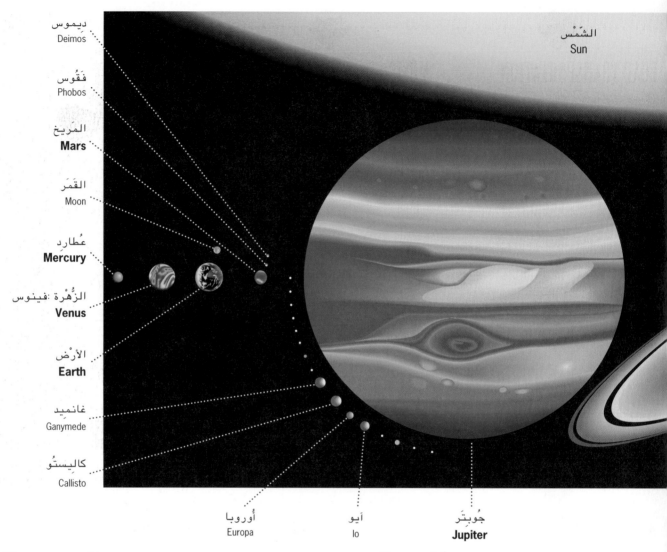

ديموس
Deimos

فَقُوس
Phobos

المَرِّيخ
Mars

القَمَر
Moon

عُطارد
Mercury

الزُّهْرة :فينوس
Venus

الأرْض
Earth

غانميد
Ganymede

كاليسْتُو
Callisto

الشَّمْس
Sun

أُوروبا
Europa

آيو
Io

جُوبِتَر
Jupiter

أفْلاك الكَواكِب السَّيَّارة
orbits of the planets

نِطاق الكُوَيْكبات السَّيَّارة
asteroid belt

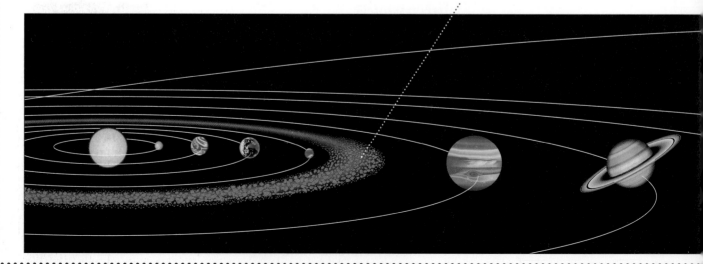

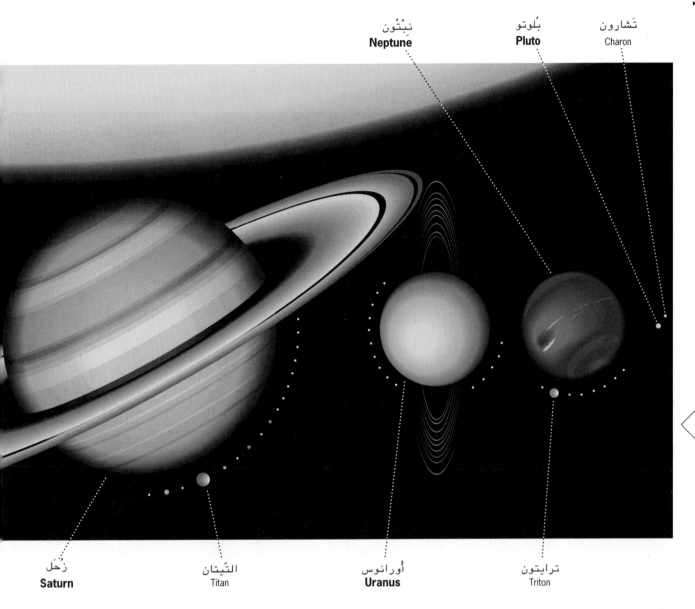

نِبْتُون
Neptune

بُلوتو
Pluto

تَشارون
Charon

زُحَل
Saturn

التَّيتان
Titan

أُورانوس
Uranus

ترايتون
Triton

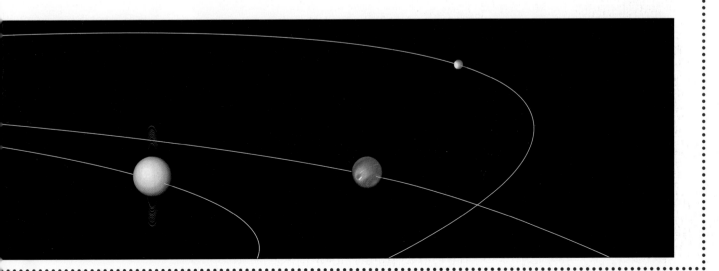

الشَّمْس
SUN

بِنْية الشَّمْس
structure of the Sun

نِطاق الإشْعاع
radiation zone

نِطاق الانْكِسار أو الانْعِكاس
convection zone

سَطْح الشَّمّس
Sun's surface

هَالَة
corona

نُتوء
prominence

بُقْعَة شَمسية
sunspot

قَلْب أو بُؤرة
core

شَطِرُ أو انْشِطار
flare

القَمَر
MOON

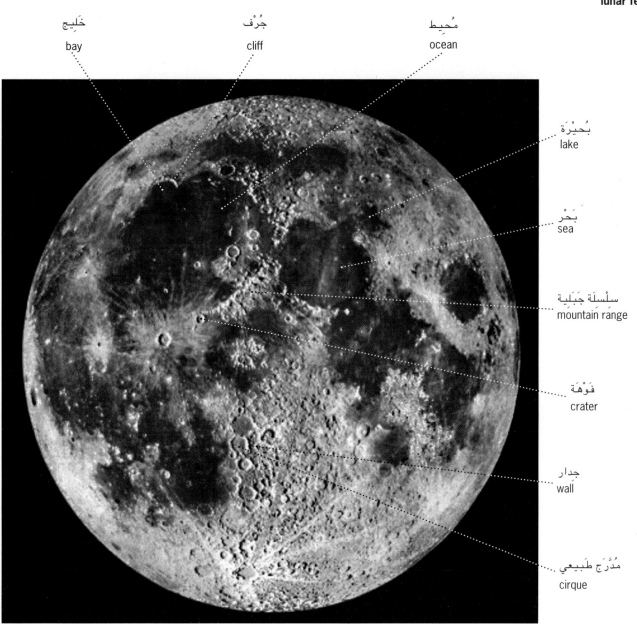

خَلِيج
bay

جُرُف
cliff

مُحيط
ocean

بُحَيرَة
lake

بَحْر
sea

سِلْسِلَة جَبَلية
mountain range

فَوْهَة
crater

جِدار
wall

مُدَرَّج طَبِيعي
cirque

9

مَنازِل القَمَر
PHASES OF THE MOON

الهِلال الجَديد
new crescent

البَدْر
waxing gibbous Moon

المُحاق
waning gibbous Moon

الهِلال القَديم
old crescent

القَمَر الجَديد
new Moon

الرُّبْع الأوَّل
first quarter

البَدْر
full Moon

الرُّبْع الأخِير
last quarter

النَّجْم المُذَنَّب
COMET

ذُؤابَة
coma

رَأْس
head

نَواة
nucleus

الذَّنَب الغازيّ
gas tail

الذَّنَب الغُباريّ
dust tail

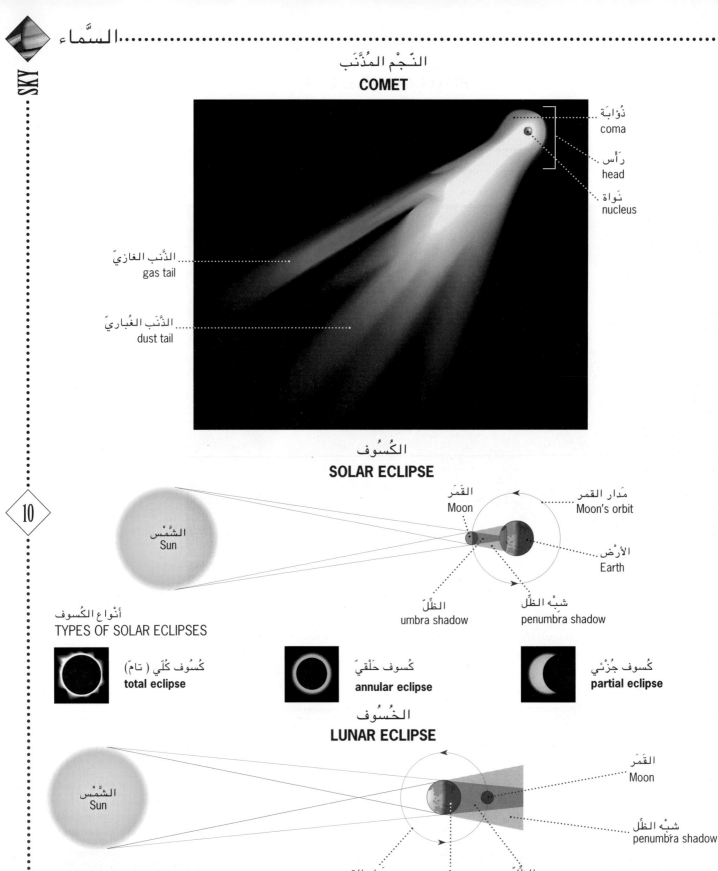

الكُسُوف
SOLAR ECLIPSE

القَمَر
Moon

مَدار القمر
Moon's orbit

الشَّمْس
Sun

الأَرْض
Earth

الظِّلّ
umbra shadow

شِبْه الظِّلّ
penumbra shadow

أَنْواع الكُسُوف
TYPES OF SOLAR ECLIPSES

كُسُوف كُلّي (تامّ)
total eclipse

كُسوف حَلْقيّ
annular eclipse

كُسوف جُزْئي
partial eclipse

الخُسُوف
LUNAR ECLIPSE

القَمَر
Moon

الشَّمْس
Sun

شِبْه الظِّلّ
penumbra shadow

مَدار القمر
Moon's orbit

الأَرْض
Earth

الظِّلّ
umbra shadow

أَنْواع الخُسُوف
TYPES OF LUNAR ECLIPSES

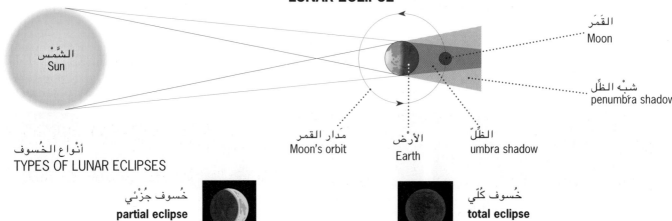

خُسوف جُزْئي
partial eclipse

خُسُوف كُلّي
total eclipse

التِّلِسْكُوب العَاكِس
REFLECTING TELESCOPE

المُعَيَّن
finderscope

مِنْظار
eyepiece

الأنْبُوب الرَّئِيسي
main tube

زِرّ التَّأْبِير
focusing knob

مِيْزان ضَبْط الانْحِدار الزَّاوي
declination setting scale

مِلْزَم السَّمْت
azimuth clamp

مِيْزان ضَبْط المَيْل التَّصاعُدي الزَّاوي
right ascension setting scale

مِلْزَم الارْتِفاع
altitude clamp

ضَبْط السَّمْت الدَّقيق
azimuth fine adjustment

ضَبْط السَّمْت الدَّقيق
altitude fine adjustment

مَقْطَع عَرْضي للتِّليسكوب العاكس
cross section of a reflecting telescope

مِنْظار
eyepiece

الأنْبُوب الرَّئِيسي (العَدَسة الرّئِيسية)
main tube

المِرآة الرَّئِيسية
main mirror

المِرآة المُسَطَّحَة
flat mirror

ضَوْء
light

التِّليسْكُوب الانْكِساريّ
REFRACTING TELESCOPE

حامِل او مِسْنَد
support

حامِل المِنْظار
eyepiece holder

المِرآة العَينية العاكِسَة
star diagonal

العَدَسة الشَّيئِية
objective lens

وِقاء النَّدى
dew shield

مِمْسَك، حامِل، مِسْنَد
cradle

الثَّقَل المُوازِن
counterweight

مِفْرَع
fork

حامِل ثُلاثيّ القَوائِم
tripod

رَفّ الأدَوات الإضافيّة
tripod accessories shelf

مَقْطَع عَرْضي للتِّليسكوب الانْكِساري
cross section of a refracting telescope

العَدَسة الشَّيئِية
objective lens

مِنْظار
eyepiece

الأنْبُوب الرَّئِيسي
main tube

ضَوْء
light

العَدَسة الشَّيئِية
objective lens

اِحداثي الارض
EARTH COORDINATE SYSTEM

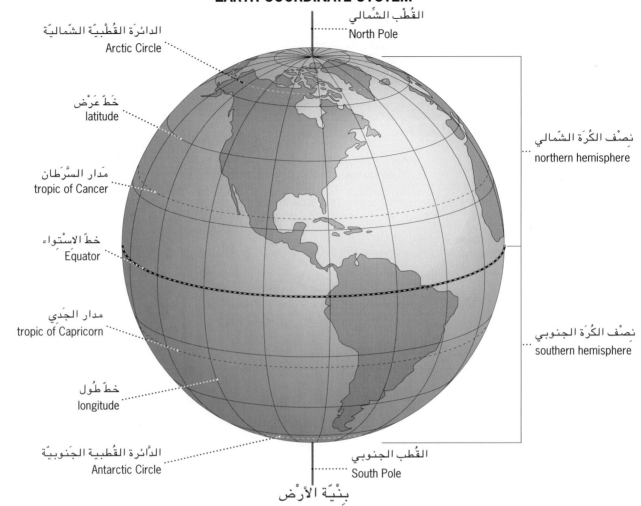

القُطْب الشِّمالي
North Pole

الدائِرَة القُطْبِيَّة الشِّمالِيَّة
Arctic Circle

خَطّ عَرْض
latitude

مَدار السَّرَطان
tropic of Cancer

خطّ الاسْتِواء
Equator

مَدار الجَدي
tropic of Capricorn

خطّ طُول
longitude

الدّائِرة القُطْبية الجَنوبِيّة
Antarctic Circle

نِصْف الكُرَة الشِّمالي
northern hemisphere

نِصْف الكُرَة الجَنوبي
southern hemisphere

القُطْب الجَنوبي
South Pole

بِنْيّة الأَرْض
STRUCTURE OF THE EARTH

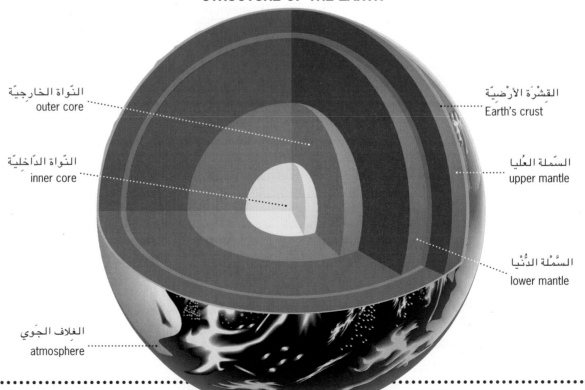

النّواة الخارجيّة
outer core

النّواة الدّاخليّة
inner core

القِشْرَة الأرْضِيّة
Earth's crust

السَّمْلة العُليا
upper mantle

السَّمْلة الدُّنْيا
lower mantle

الغِلاف الجَوّي
atmosphere

الهَزَّة الأَرْضِية
EARTHQUAKE

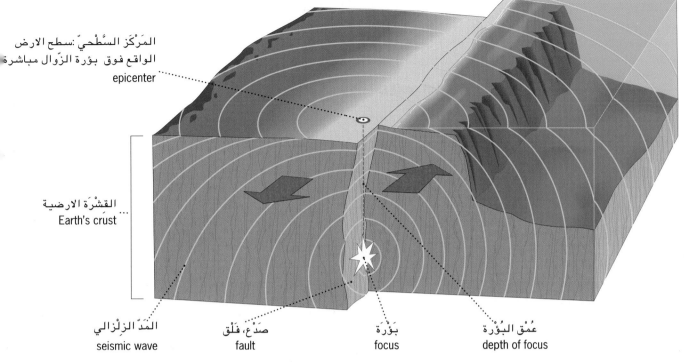

المَرْكَز السَّطْحيّ :سطح الارض
الواقع فوق بـؤرة الزّوال مباشرة
epicenter

القِشْرَة الارضية
Earth's crust

المَدّ الزِلْزالي
seismic wave

صَدْع، فَلْق
fault

بَؤْرَة
focus

عُمْق البُؤْرة
depth of focus

كَهْف
CAVE

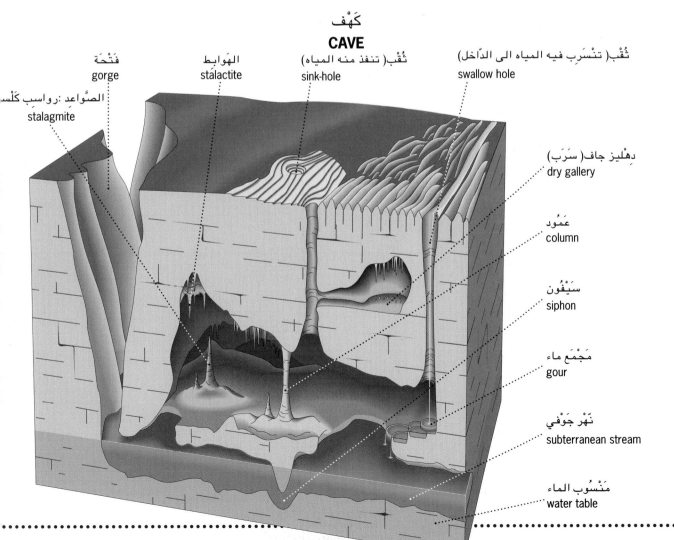

فَتْحَة
gorge

الصَّواعِد :رواسب كَلْس
stalagmite

الهَوابِط
stalactite

ثُقْب(تنفذ منه المياه)
sink-hole

ثُقْب(تنْسَرِب فيه المِياه الى الدّاخل)
swallow hole

دِهْليز جاف(سَرَب)
dry gallery

عَمُود
column

سَيْفُون
siphon

مَجْمَع ماء
gour

نَهْر جَوْفي
subterranean stream

مَنْسُوب الماء
water table

مَعالِم السَّاحِل
COASTAL FEATURES

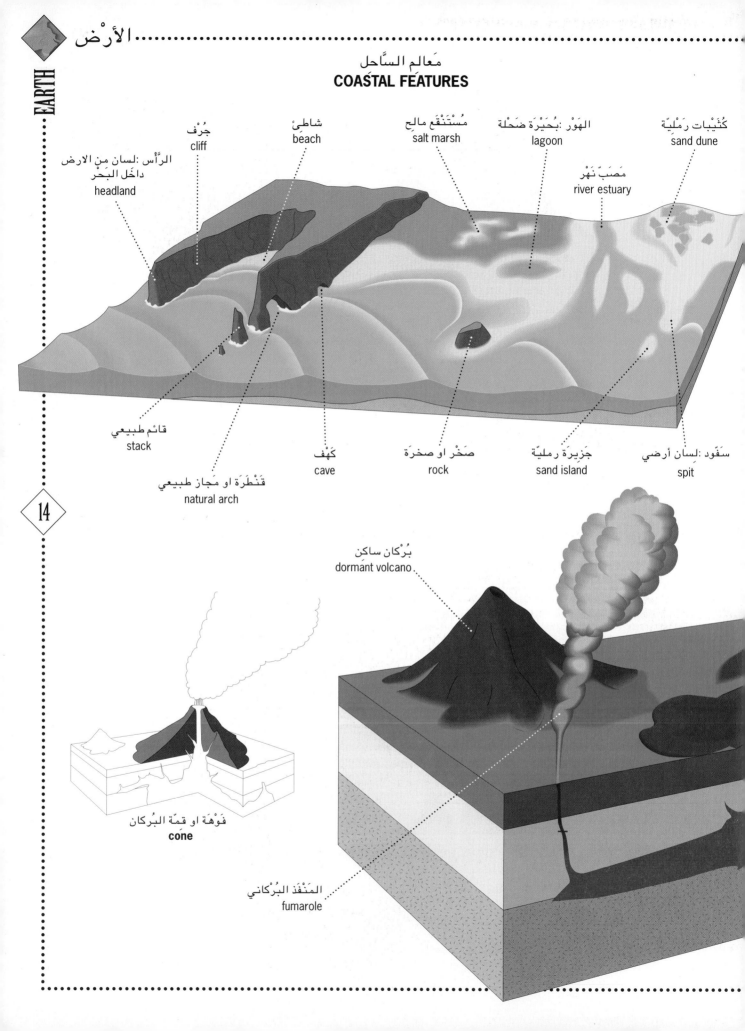

الرَّأْس :لِسان من الارض
داخِل البَحْر
headland

جُرْف
cliff

شاطِئ
beach

مُسْتَنْقَع مالِح
salt marsh

الهَوْر :بُحَيْرَة ضَحْلَة
lagoon

كُثَيْبات رَمْلِيّة
sand dune

مَصَبّ نَهْر
river estuary

قائم طبيعي
stack

قَنْطَرَة او مَجاز طبيعي
natural arch

كَهْف
cave

صَخْر او صخرَة
rock

جَزيرَة رملِيّة
sand island

سَفّود :لِسان أرضي
spit

14

بُرْكان ساكِن
dormant volcano

فَوْهَة او قمّة البُرْكان
cone

المَنْفَذ البُرْكاني
fumarole

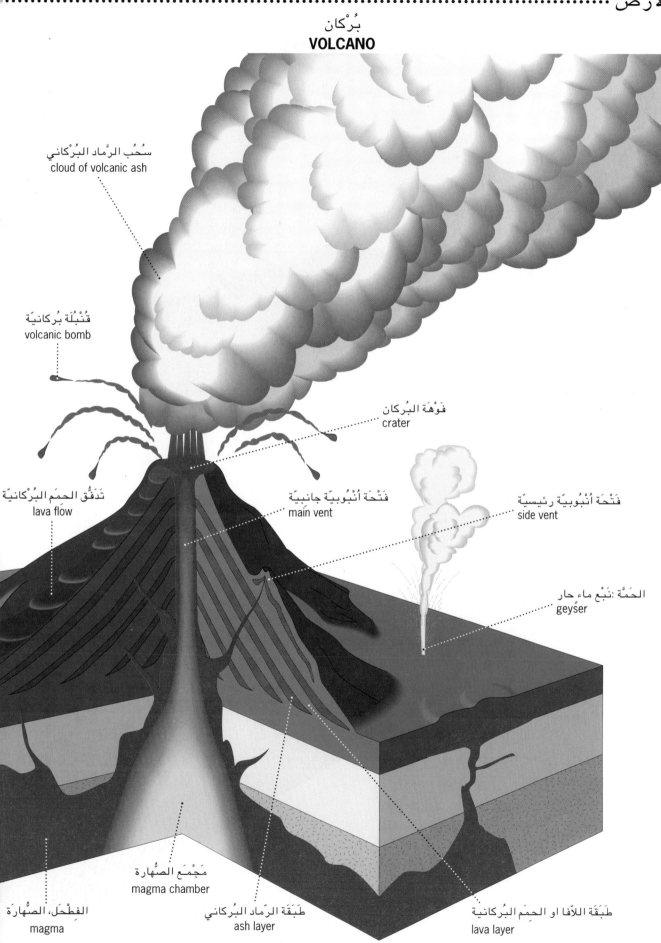
بُرْكان
VOLCANO

سُحُب الرَّماد البُرْكاني
cloud of volcanic ash

قَنْبُلَة بُرْكانيّة
volcanic bomb

فَوْهَة البُركان
crater

تَدَفُّق الحمَم البُرْكانيّة
lava flow

فَتْحَة اُنْبُوبيّة جانبيّة
main vent

فَتْحَة اُنْبُوبيّة رئيسيّة
side vent

الحَمَّة : نَبْع ماء حار
geyser

مَجْمَع الصُّهارة
magma chamber

طَبَقَة الرَّماد البُرْكاني
ash layer

طَبَقَة اللاّفا او الحمَم البُركانية
lava layer

الفِطْحَل، الصُّهارَة
magma

مَجْلَدَة : نهر الجَليد
GLACIER

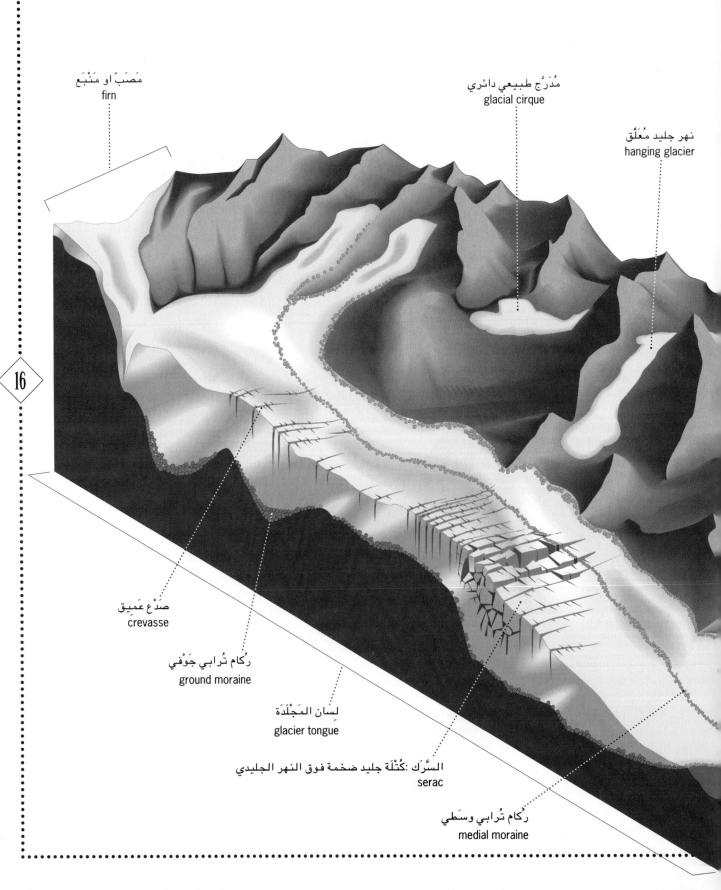

مَصَبّ او مَنْبَع
firn

مُدَرَّج طبيعي دائري
glacial cirque

نهر جليد مُعَلَّق
hanging glacier

صَدْع عَميق
crevasse

رُكام تُرابي جَوْفي
ground moraine

لِسان المَجْلَدَة
glacier tongue

السَّرَك : كُتْلَة جليد ضخمة فوق النهر الجليدي
serac

رُكام تُرابي وسَطي
medial moraine

جَبَل
MOUNTAIN

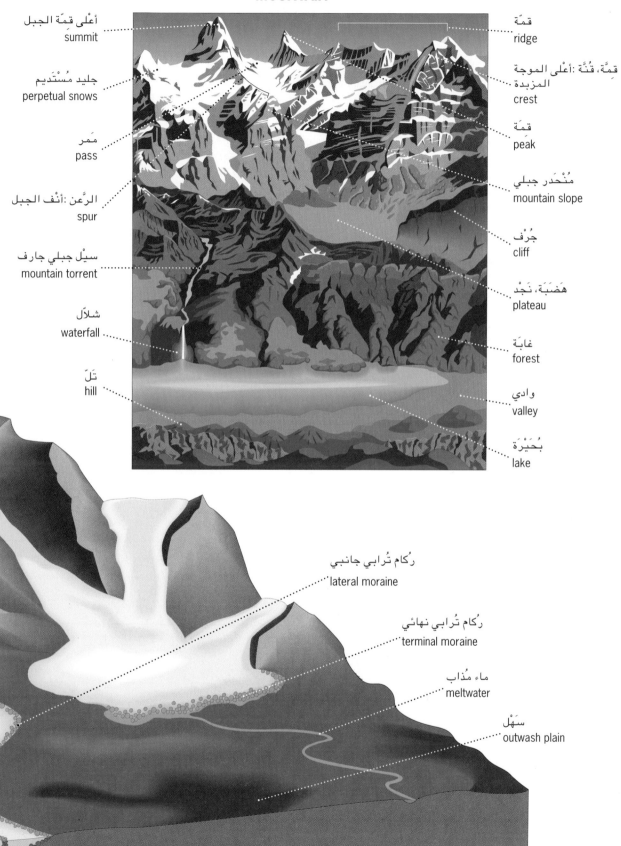

أعْلى قمّة الجبل
summit

جَليد مُسْتَديم
perpetual snows

مَمَر
pass

الرَّعن :أنْف الجبل
spur

سيْل جبلي جارف
mountain torrent

شلاّل
waterfall

تَلّ
hill

قمّة
ridge

قِمّة، قُنَّة :أعْلى الموجة المزبدة
crest

قمَة
peak

مُنْحَدر جبلي
mountain slope

جُرْف
cliff

هَضَبَة، نَجْد
plateau

غابَة
forest

وادي
valley

بُحَيْرة
lake

17

رُكام تُرابي جانبي
lateral moraine

رُكام تُرابي نهائي
terminal moraine

ماء مُذاب
meltwater

سَهْل
outwash plain

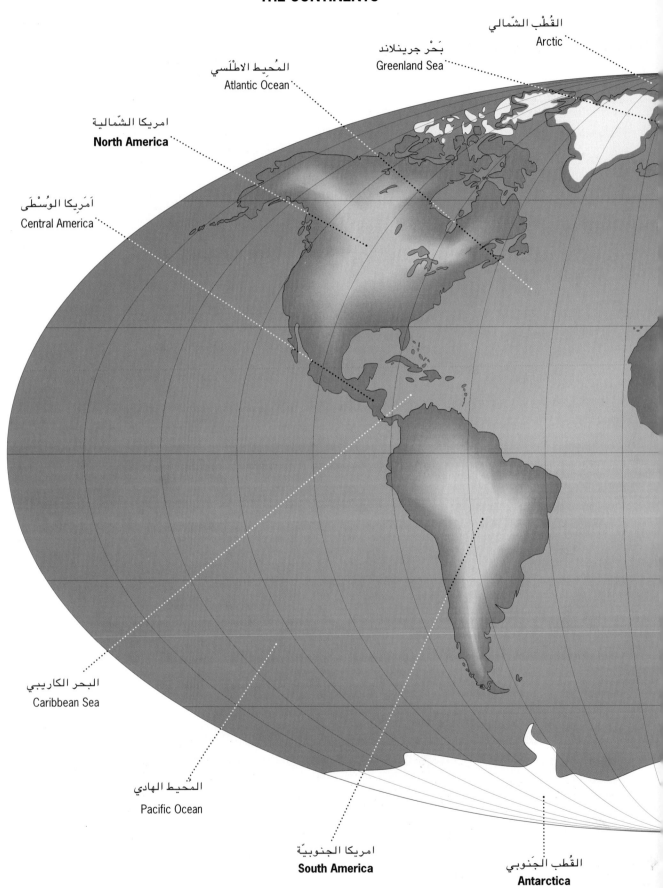

القارات
THE CONTINENTS

القُطْب الشّمالي
Arctic

بَحْر جرينلاند
Greenland Sea

المُحيط الاطْلَسي
Atlantic Ocean

امريكا الشّمالية
North America

أَمَريكا الوُسْطَى
Central America

البَحر الكاريبي
Caribbean Sea

المُحيط الهادي
Pacific Ocean

امريكا الجنوبيّة
South America

القُطب الجنَوبي
Antarctica

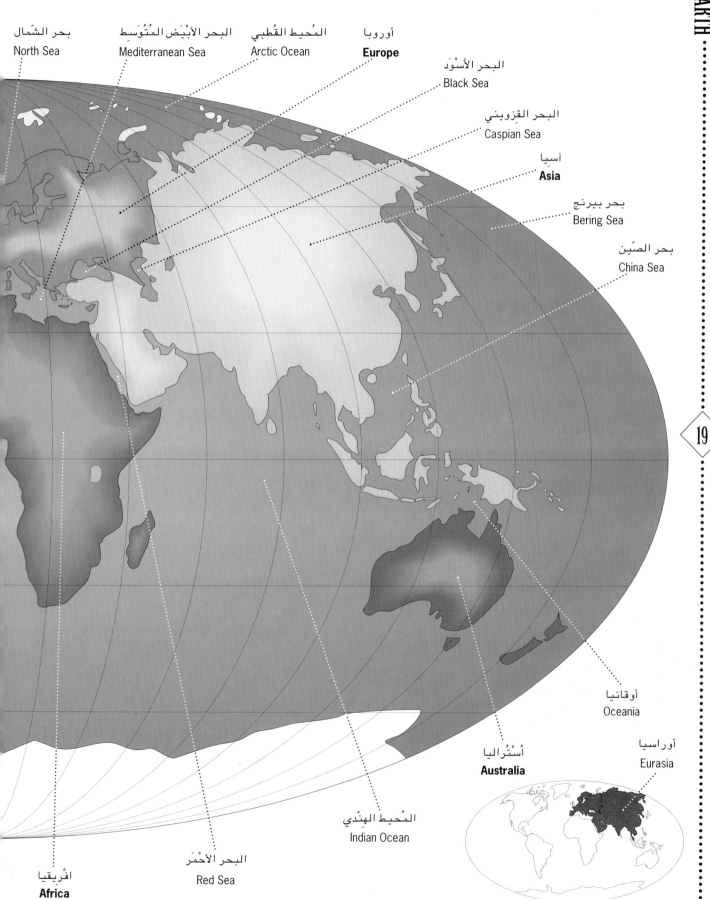

بحر الشّمال
North Sea

البحر الأبْيَض المُتَوَسِط
Mediterranean Sea

المُحيط القُطبي
Arctic Ocean

أوروبا
Europe

البحر الأسْوَد
Black Sea

البحر القزويني
Caspian Sea

أسِيا
Asia

بحر بيرنج
Bering Sea

بحر الصّين
China Sea

أوقانيا
Oceania

أوراسيا
Eurasia

أُسْتُراليا
Australia

المُحيط الهِنْدي
Indian Ocean

البحر الأحْمَر
Red Sea

افْريقيا
Africa

الأرْض

فُصول السَّنة
SEASONS OF THE YEAR

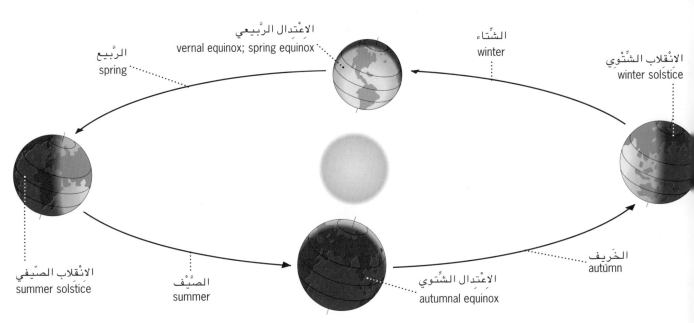

الاعْتدال الرَّبيعي
vernal equinox; spring equinox

الشِّتاء
winter

الرَّبيع
spring

الانْقلاب الشِّتْوي
winter solstice

الانْقلاب الصَّيفي
summer solstice

الصَّيْف
summer

الاعْتدال الشِّتْوي
autumnal equinox

الخَريف
autumn

بنْيّة(دورة)الغلاف الحَيَويّ
STRUCTURE OF THE BIOSPHERE

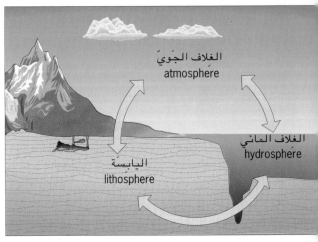

الغلاف الجَويّ
atmosphere

الغلاف المائي
hydrosphere

اليابِسة
lithosphere

التَّضاريس
ELEVATION ZONES AND VEGETATION

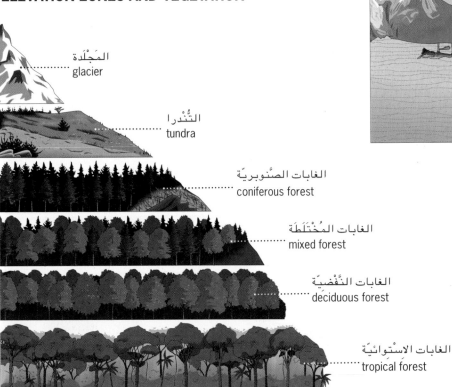

المَجلَدة
glacier

التُّنْدرا
tundra

الغابات الصَّنوبريّة
coniferous forest

الغابات المُخْتَلَطَة
mixed forest

الغابات النَّفْضيّة
deciduous forest

الغابات الاسْتوائيّة
tropical forest

مَناخات العالَم
CLIMATES OF THE WORLD

المناخات الاسْتوائيّة
tropical climates

 المناخ الاسْتوائيّ
tropical rain forest

مناخ السّافنا الاسْتوائي
tropical savanna

 سهُول
steppe

المناخ الصّحْراوي
desert

المناخات المُعْتَدِلَة
temperate climates

 صيف مُمطِر طويل
humid - long summer

صيف مُمطِر قصير
humid - short summer

 المناخ البحري
marine

المناخات القُطْبيّة
polar climates

 التُّنْدُرا القُطْبيّة
polar tundra

المناخ القُطبيّ المُتَجَمِّد
polar ice cap

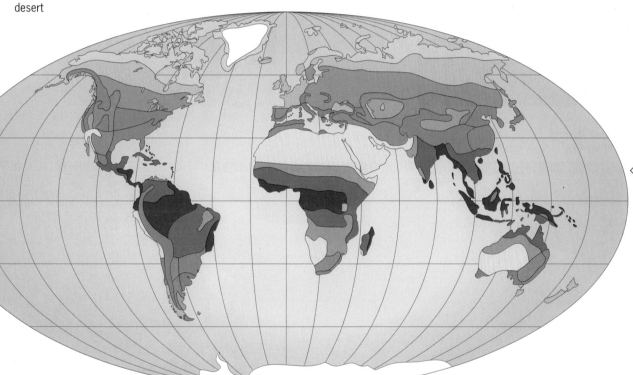

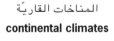
المناخات شبْه الاسْتوائية
subtropical climates

مناخ البحر الابْيَض المُتوسط شبْه الاسْتوائيّ
Mediterranean subtropical

شبْه الاستوائي المُمطِر
humid subtropical

شبْه الاستوائي الجاف
dry subtropical

المناخات القاريّة
continental climates

 المناخ القاريّ الجاف
dry continental - arid

المناخ القاريّ شبه الجاف
dry continental - semiarid

مناخات المُرْتَفعات
highland climates

 مناخات المُرْتَفعات
highland climates

المناخات شبْه القُطبيّة
subarctic climates

 المناخات شبْه القُطبيّة
subarctic climates

الجَوّ، الطَّقْس
WEATHER

ضَباب، سَدِيم
mist

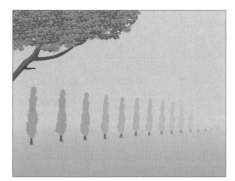

ضَباب
fog

النَّدى
dew

صَقِيع(مكْسُو بالجليد)
glazed frost

سماء عاصفة(هبوب)
stormy sky

قوْس قُزَح
rainbow

سُحُب، سَحاب
cloud

مَطَر
rain

قَطْرَة مطر
raindrop

البَرْق
lightning

أجْهِزَة القِياسات الجَويَّة
METEOROLOGICAL MEASURING INSTRUMENTS

مِقياس اتجاه الرِّيْح
MEASURE OF WIND DIRECTION

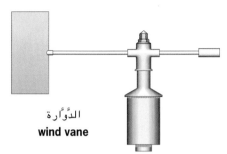

الدَّوَّارة
wind vane

مِقياس قوّة الرياح
MEASURE OF WIND STRENGTH

المِرْياح :مِقياس شِدّة الرّياح او سُرْعَتها
anemometer

قِياس الرُّطُوبَة
MEASURE OF HUMIDITY

هَيْجروف(المِرطاب الاوتامتيكي)
hygrograph

قِياس هُطُول المطر
MEASURE OF RAINFALL

مُسَجِّل منْسوب المطر
rain gauge recorder

وُحْدة تسْجيل
recording unit

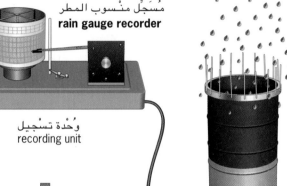

وِعاء تَجْميع
collecting vessel

صَنْدوق ارْصاد جويّ
instrument shelter

قِياس منْسوب المطر المُباشِر
direct-reading rain gauge

وِعاء تجميع
collecting funnel

أُنْبوب قِياس
measuring tube

شَريط تثْبيت
tightening band

وِعاء
container

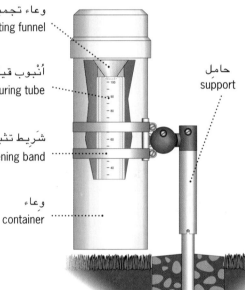

حامِل
support

قِياس الضَغْط الجويّ
MEASURE OF AIR PRESSURE

مِقياس الحَرارَة
MEASURE OF TEMPERATURE

مِقياس الحَرارَة الأدْنَى
minimum thermometer

مِقياس الحَرارَة الأعْلَى
maximum thermometer

البارومتر الزِّئْبقي
mercury barometer

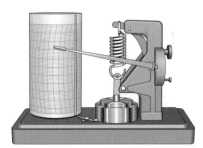

البارُوغراف
barograph

عِلْم الخَرائِط
CARTOGRAPHY

نِصْفا الكُرة الارضية
hemispheres

نِصْف الكُرة الشّمالي
Northern hemisphere

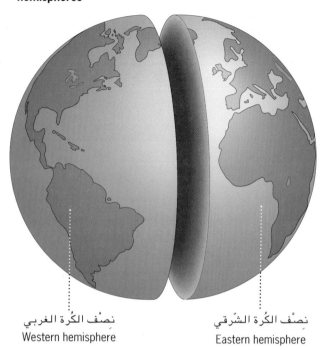

نِصْف الكُرة الغربي
Western hemisphere

نِصْف الكُرة الشّرقي
Eastern hemisphere

نِصْف الكُرة الجنوبي
Southern hemisphere

24

الشَّبَكَة المُتسامتة
GRID SYSTEM

خُطوط العَرْض
lines of latitude

خُطوط الطّول
lines of longitude

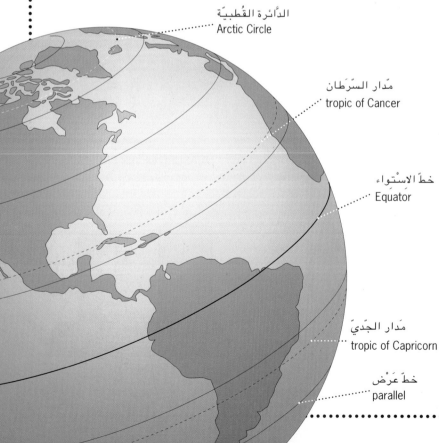

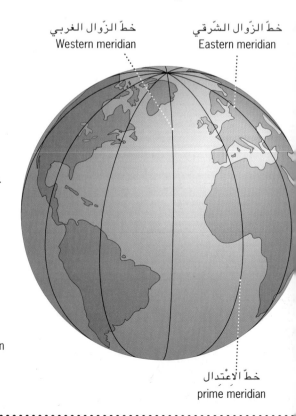

الدَّائرة القُطبيَّة
Arctic Circle

مَدار السّرَطان
tropic of Cancer

خطّ الاسْتِواء
Equator

مَدار الجّدي
tropic of Capricorn

خطّ عَرْض
parallel

خطّ الزّوال الغربي
Western meridian

خطّ الزّوال الشّرقي
Eastern meridian

خطّ الاعْتِدال
prime meridian

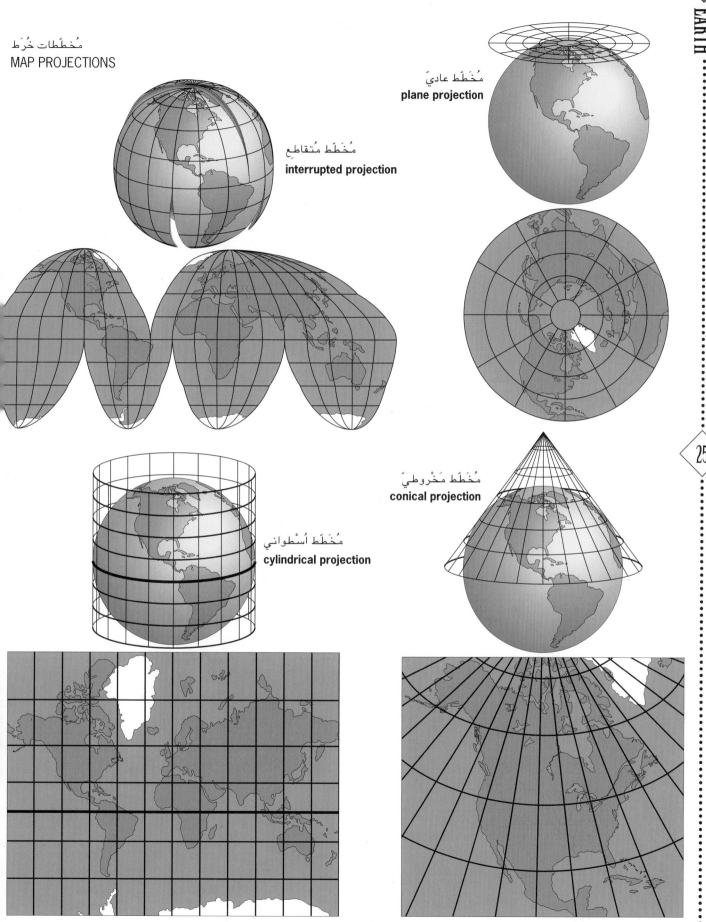

مُخطّطات خُرَط
MAP PROJECTIONS

مُخَطّط عاديّ
plane projection

مُخَطّط مُتقاطِع
interrupted projection

مُخَطّط أُسْطواني
cylindrical projection

مُخَطّط مَخْروطيّ
conical projection

علْم الخَرائط
CARTOGRAPHY

خارطة سِياسيّة
political map

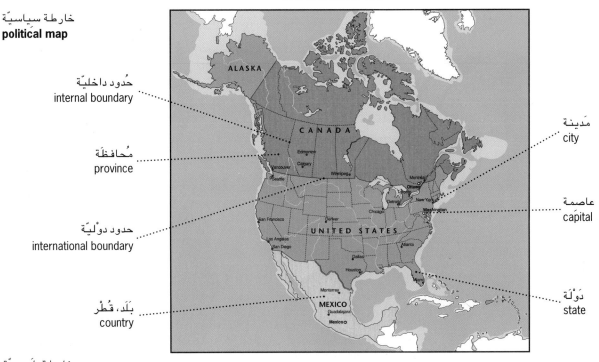

حُدود داخليّة
internal boundary

مُحافظَة
province

حدود دوْليّة
international boundary

بلَد، قُطْر
country

مَدينة
city

عاصمة
capital

دَوْلَة
state

خارطة طَبيعيّة
physical map

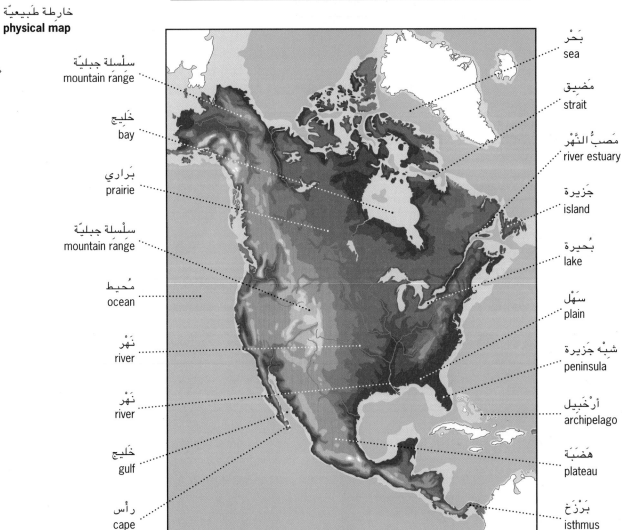

سلْسلة جبليّة
mountain range

خَليج
bay

بَراري
prairie

سلْسلة جبليّة
mountain range

مُحيط
ocean

نَهْر
river

نَهْر
river

خَليج
gulf

رأْس
cape

بَحْر
sea

مَضيق
strait

مَصبُّ النَّهْر
river estuary

جَزيرة
island

بُحيرة
lake

سَهْل
plain

شبْه جَزيرة
peninsula

أرْخَبيل
archipelago

هَضَبَة
plateau

بَرْزَخ
isthmus

خارِطَة طرق
road map

الطَّريق السَّريع
highway

رَقَم الطَّريق السَّريع
highway number

اسْتِراحَة
rest area

مَحَطّة خَدَمات
service area

الطَّريق السَّريع الدّائِريّ
belt highway

طريق ثانَوي
secondary road

شارِع
road

رَقَم شارِع
road number

مَطار
airport

مكان سياحي جاذب
point of interest

حَديقَة عامَة
national park

طريق سياحي
scenic route; tourist route

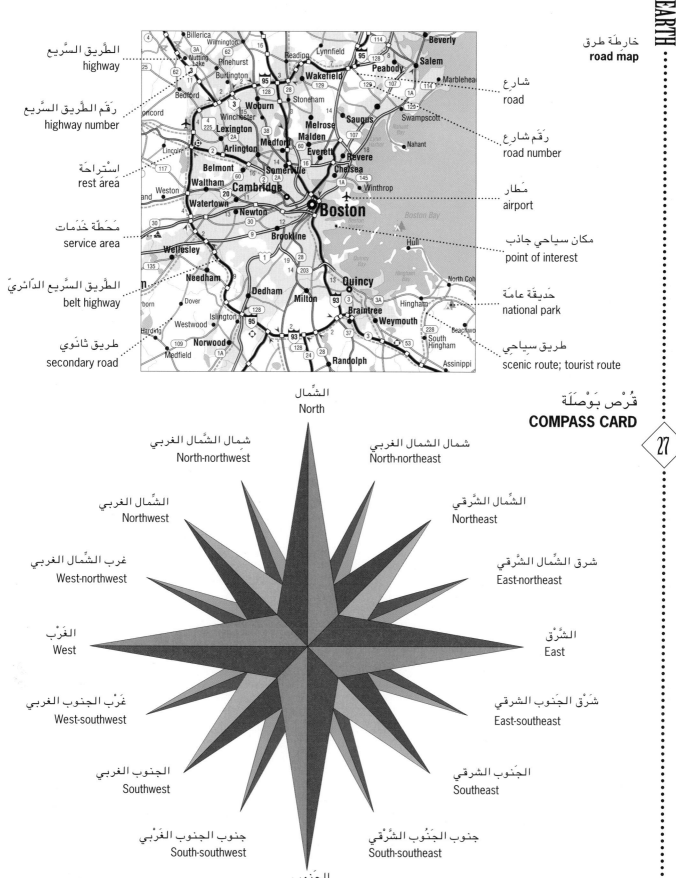

قُرْص بَوْصَلَة
COMPASS CARD

الشِّمال
North

شَمال الشَّمال الغربي
North-northwest

شمال الشَّمال الغربي
North-northeast

الشِّمال الغربي
Northwest

الشِّمال الشَّرقي
Northeast

غرب الشِّمال الغربي
West-northwest

شرق الشِّمال الشَّرقي
East-northeast

الغَرْب
West

الشَّرْق
East

غَرْب الجَنوب الغربي
West-southwest

شَرْق الجَنوب الشرقي
East-southeast

الجَنوب الغربي
Southwest

الجَنوب الشرقي
Southeast

جنوب الجَنوب الغَرْبي
South-southwest

جنوب الجَنوب الشَّرْقي
South-southeast

الجَنوب
South

الاِيكُوْلوجيا :عِلْم التَّبَيُّؤ
ECOLOGY

الدَّفيئَة
greenhouse effect

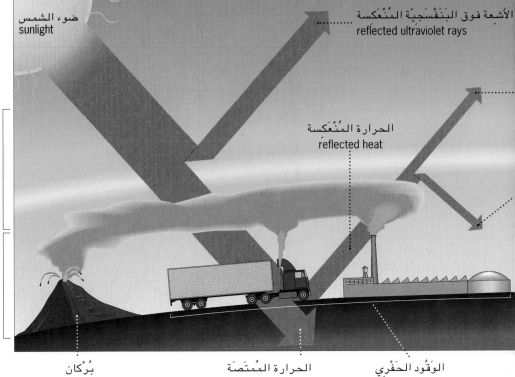

ضوء الشمس
sunlight

الأشعة فوق البَنَفْسَجِيَّة المُنْعَكسة
reflected ultraviolet rays

الحرارة المُنْعَكسة
reflected heat

طَبَقَة الغِلاف الجويّ العُلْيا
stratosphere

طَبَقَة الغِلاف الجويّ السُفْلَى
troposphere

بُرْكان
volcano

الحرارة المُمتَصَة
absorbed heat

الوَقُود الحَفْري
fossil fuels

28

دورة الطعام(او الغذاء)
food chain

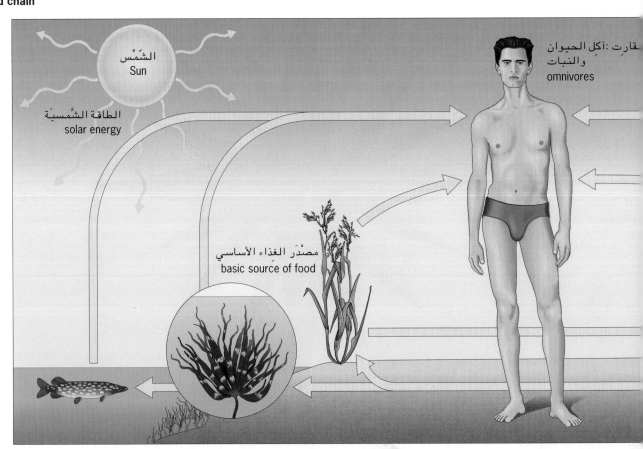

الشَّمْس
Sun

الطاقة الشَّمْسِيَة
solar energy

قارت :آكل الحيوان والنبات
omnivores

مصْدَر الغِذاء الأساسي
basic source of food

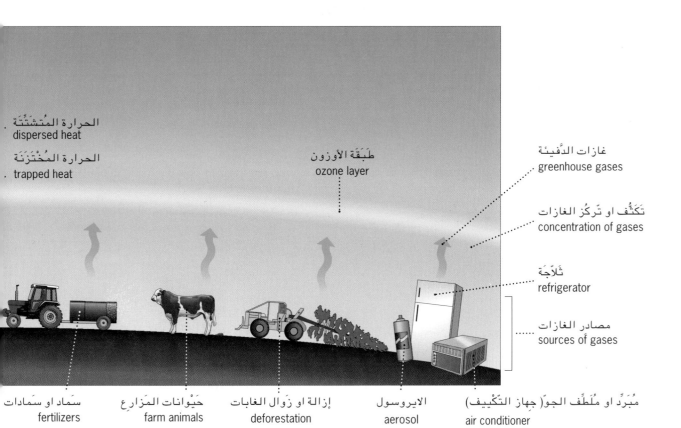

الحَرارة المُتشتِّتَة
dispersed heat

الحَرارة المُخْتَزِنَة
trapped heat

طَبَقة الأوزون
ozone layer

غازات الدَّفيئة
greenhouse gases

تَكَثُّف او تَّركُز الغازات
concentration of gases

ثَلَّاجَة
refrigerator

مَصادر الغازات
sources of gases

سَماد او سَمادات
fertilizers

حَيَوانات المَزارِع
farm animals

إزالة او زَوال الغابات
deforestation

الايروسول
aerosol

مُبَرِّد او مُلَطِّف الجوّ(جهاز التَّكْييف)
air conditioner

29

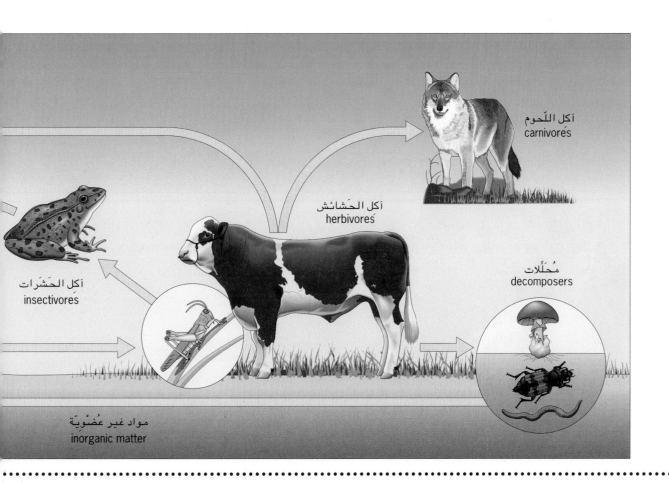

آكِل اللّحوم
carnivores

آكل الحَشائش
herbivores

آكل الحَشَرات
insectivores

مُحَلِّلات
decomposers

مواد غير عُضْوِيّة
inorganic matter

الاِيكُوْلوجيا: عِلْم التَّبَيُّؤ
ECOLOGY

تَلَوُّث الهَواء
atmospheric pollution

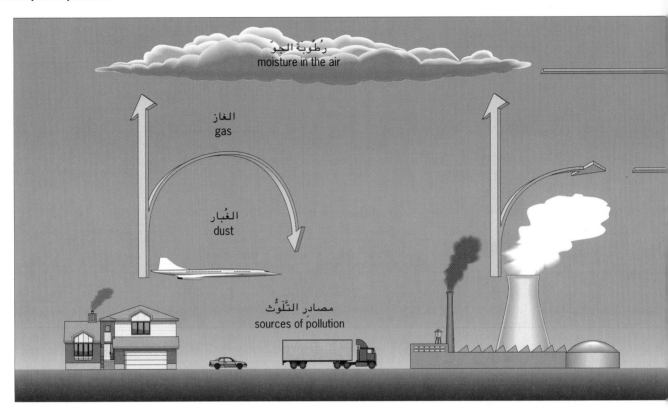

رُطُوبة الجوّ
moisture in the air

الغاز
gas

الغُبار
dust

مَصادِر التَّلَوُّث
sources of pollution

دورة الماء
water cycle

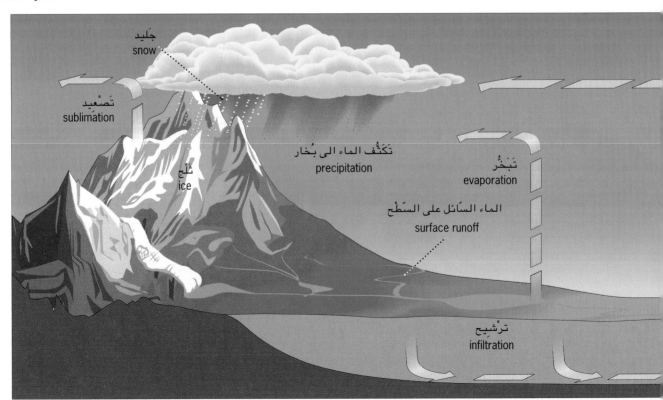

جَليد
snow

تَصْعِيد
sublimation

ثَلْج
ice

تَكَثُّف الماء الى بُخار
precipitation

تَبَخُّر
evaporation

الماء السّائِل على السّطْح
surface runoff

تَرْشِيح
infiltration

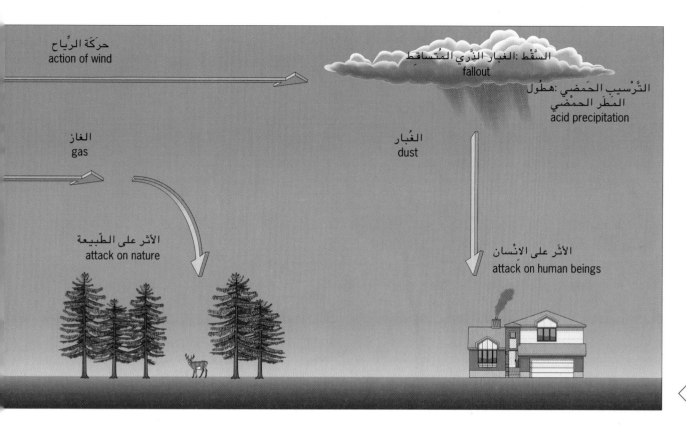

حَرَكَة الرِّياح
action of wind

السَّقْط :الغُبار الذَرِي المُتَساقِط
fallout

التَّرْسيب الحَمْضي :هُطول
المَطَر الحَمْضي
acid precipitation

الغاز
gas

الغُبار
dust

الأثَر على الطّبيعة
attack on nature

الأثَر على الانْسان
attack on human beings

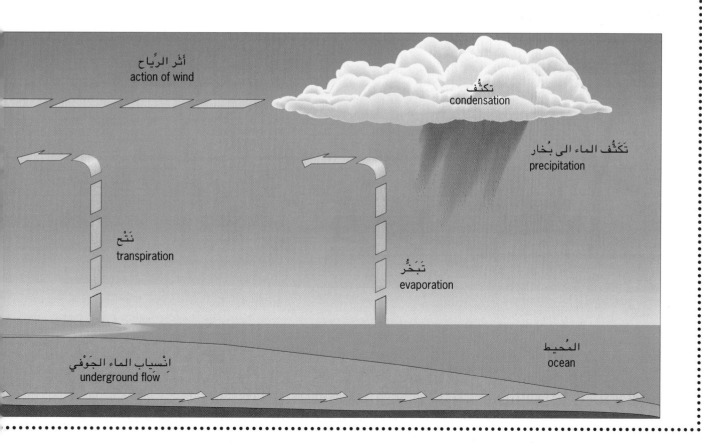

أثَر الرِّياح
action of wind

تكَثُّف
condensation

تَكَثُّف الماء الى بُخار
precipitation

نَتْح
transpiration

تَبَخُّر
evaporation

المُحيط
ocean

انْسياب الماء الجَوْفي
underground flow

الايكُوْلوجيا : علْم التَّبَيُّؤ
ECOLOGY

تلوُّث الطّعام على الارض
food pollution on ground

المطر الحَمْضي
acid rain

تلوُّث المَزارِع
farm pollution

تلوُّث صِناعي
industrial pollution

تلوُّث الطعام في الماء
food pollution in water

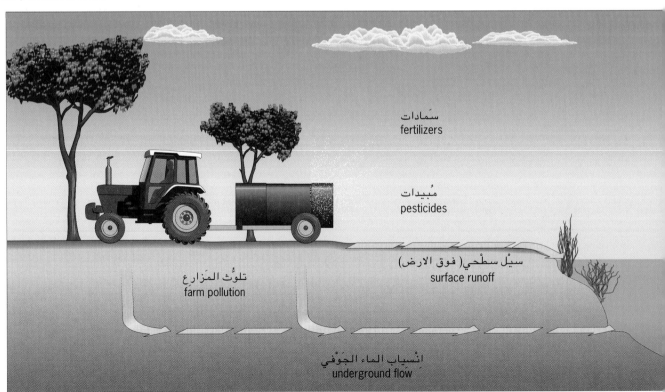

سَمادات
fertilizers

مُبيدات
pesticides

سيْل سطْحي (فوق الارض)
surface runoff

تلوُّث المَزارِع
farm pollution

انْسِياب الماء الجَوْفي
underground flow

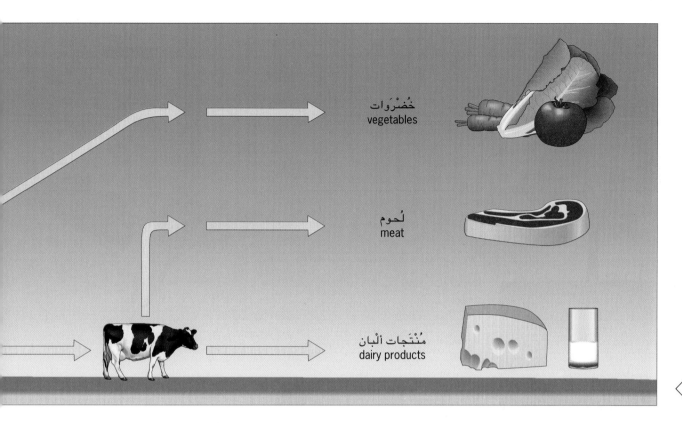

خُضْرَوات
vegetables

لُحوم
meat

مُنْتَجات ألْبان
dairy products

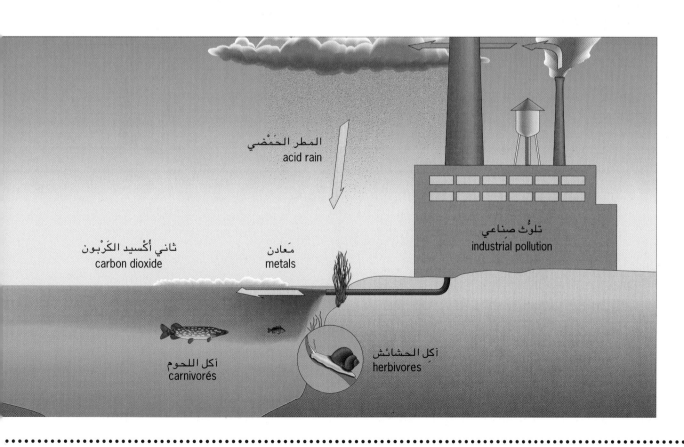

المطر الحَمْضي
acid rain

تلوُّث صِناعي
industrial pollution

ثاني أُكْسيد الكَرْبون
carbon dioxide

مَعادن
metals

أكل اللحوم
carnivorés

آكل الحشائش
herbivores

النبات والتُّرْبَة
PLANT AND SOIL

طَبَقات التُّرْبَة
SOIL PROFILE

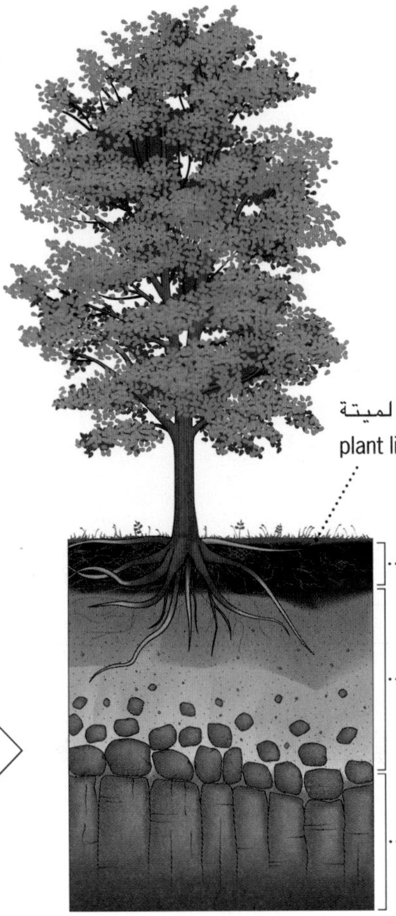

الانْبات
GERMINATION

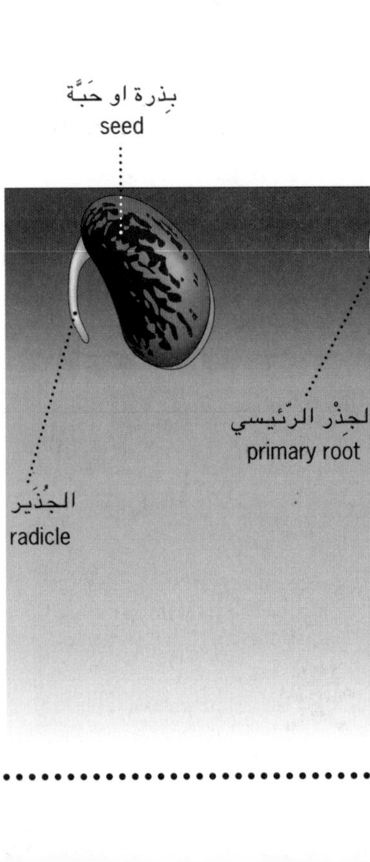

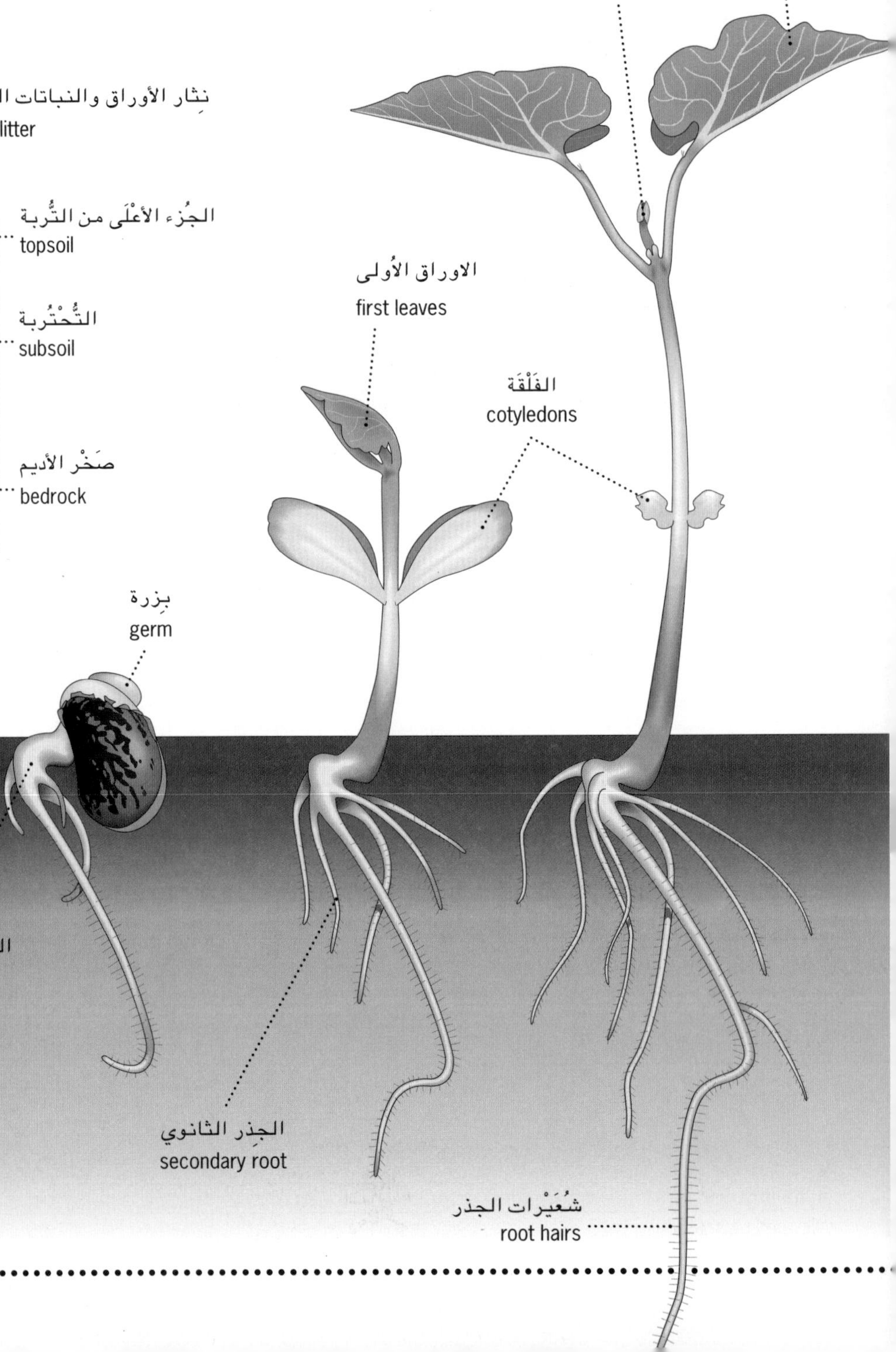

نِثار الأوراق والنباتات الميتة
plant litter

الجُزء الأعْلَى من التُّربة
topsoil

التُّحْتُربة
subsoil

صَخْر الأديم
bedrock

وَرَقَة
leaf

بُرْعُم طَرَفي او نِهائي
terminal bud

الاوراق الأُولى
first leaves

الفَلْقَة
cotyledons

بِزرة
germ

بِذرة او حَبَّة
seed

الجَذْر الرّئيسي
primary root

الجُذَير
radicle

الجِذر الثانوي
secondary root

شُعَيْرات الجذر
root hairs

الفُطْر
MUSHROOM

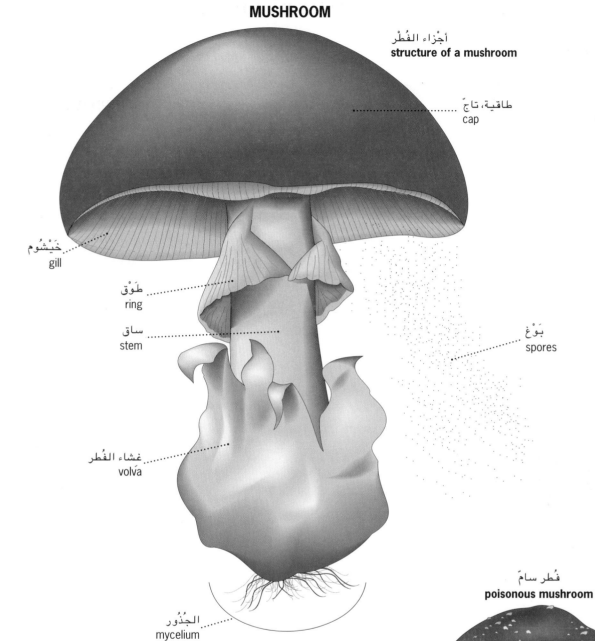

أجْزاء الفُطْر
structure of a mushroom

طاقية، تاجّ
cap

خَيْشُوم
gill

طَوْق
ring

ساق
stem

بَوْغ
spores

غشاء الفُطْر
volva

الجُذُور
mycelium

فُطر سامّ
poisonous mushroom

فُطر صالِح للأكْل
edible mushroom

فُطْر زِراعي
cultivated mushroom

فُطر قاتِل
deadly mushroom

فُطر مُدَمِّر
destroying angel

فُطر الغاريقُون
fly agaric

مَملَكة النّبات

اجْزاء النّبات
STRUCTURE OF A PLANT

أوراق مُرَكَّبة
COMPOUND LEAVES

البُرْعم النّهائي
terminal bud

بُرعم مُزْهِر
flower bud

زَهْرَة
flower

ثُلاثِية الصَّفَق
trifoliolate

البُرعم الجانبي
(نام من ابط النّبات)
axillary bud

بُرْعم جديد
shoot

غُصَيْن
twig

مَخْروطيّة ذات اِبَر
pinnatifid

ورقة
leaf

البيعُقْدي :الواقِع بين عُقْدَتي ساق
internode

العُجْرَة
leaf node

ساق
stem

ورقة البِذْرَة
seed leaf

نْفَرِجة كراحة اليد
palmate

أدْنَى ساق النبات
collar

الجَذُور
root system

الجِذْر الثانوي
secondary root

الجِذْر الرّئيسي
primary root

النَّصْل
blade

حاشِية الورقة
margin

الأسْلَة
tip

رأس الشُّعَيرة
root cap

شُعَيْرات الجذر
root hairs

الجُذَير
radicle

36

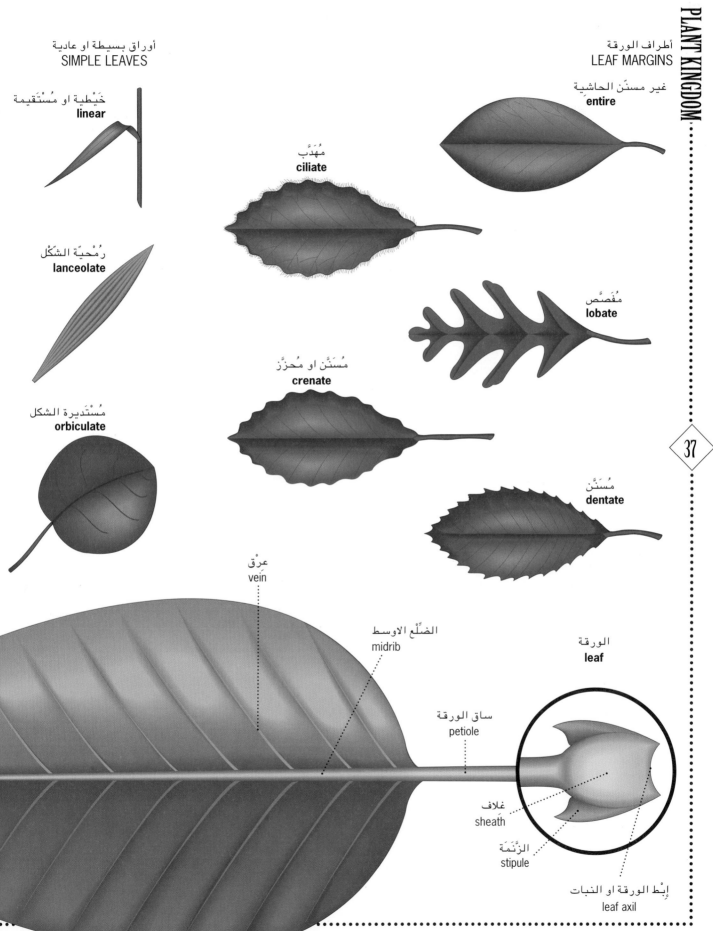

أوراق بسيطة او عادية
SIMPLE LEAVES

خَيْطية او مُسْتَقيمة
linear

رُمْحيّة الشّكل
lanceolate

مُسْتَديرة الشّكل
orbiculate

أطراف الورقة
LEAF MARGINS

غير مسنّن الحاشية
entire

مُهَدَّب
ciliate

مُفَصَّص
lobate

مُسَنَّن او مُحزَّز
crenate

مُسَنَّن
dentate

عِرْق
vein

الضِّلْع الاوسط
midrib

ساق الورقة
petiole

الورقة
leaf

غِلاف
sheath

الزَّنَمَة
stipule

إبْط الورقة او النبات
leaf axil

الأزْهار، الزُّهور
FLOWERS

أجْزاء الزَّهْرة
structure of a flower

السَّمَة
stigma

الخُيَيْط
filament

البَتْلَة
petal

السَّبْلَة
sepal

كُرْسي الزَّهْرة، القُرص
receptacle

المِبئَر
anther

حامل السَّمَة
style

مبيَض
ovary

بُذَيْرَة، بيَيْضَة
ovule

سُويقة، زُنَيْد
pedicel

التُّوَيْج
corolla

السَّداة
stamen

المدَّمَة
pistil

الكَأس
calyx

بعض أنْواع الأزهار
EXAMPLES OF FLOWERS

البَنَفْسَج
violet

السُّحْلَبيَة
orchid

التُّوليب
tulip

الخَشْخاش
poppy

الوَرْد
rose

البَقُونيَة
begonia

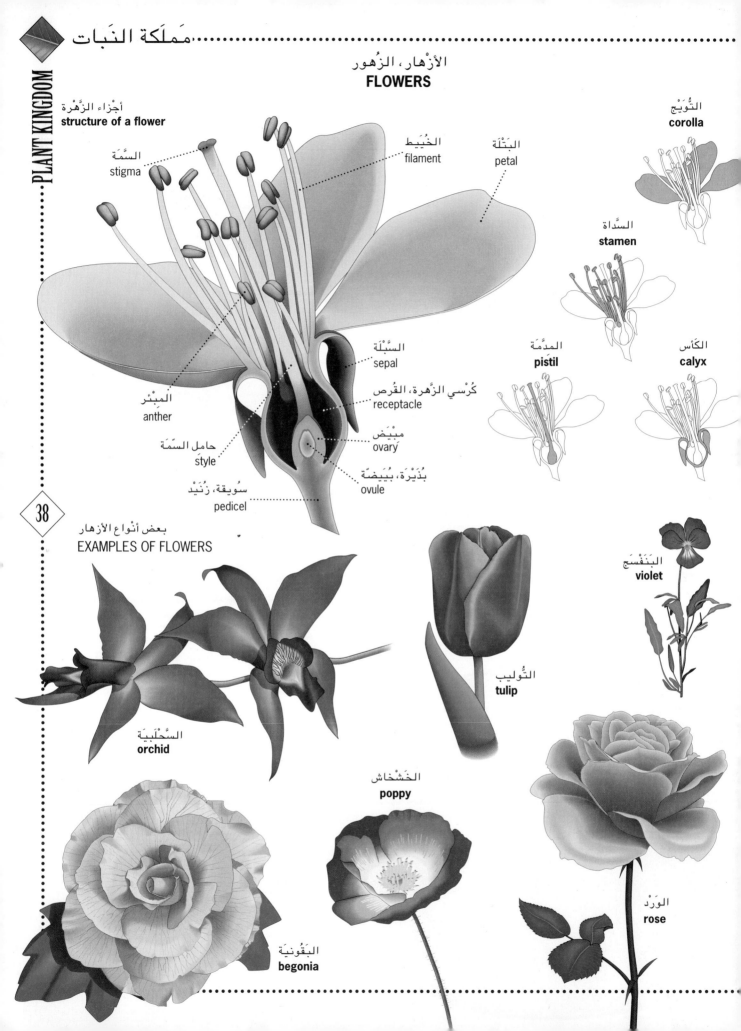

السَّوْسَن
lily

عبَّاد الشَّمْس
sunflower

سوْسَن الوادي
lily of the valley

الزَّعْفَران
crocus

القُرُنْفُل
carnation

النَّرْجس
daffodil

39

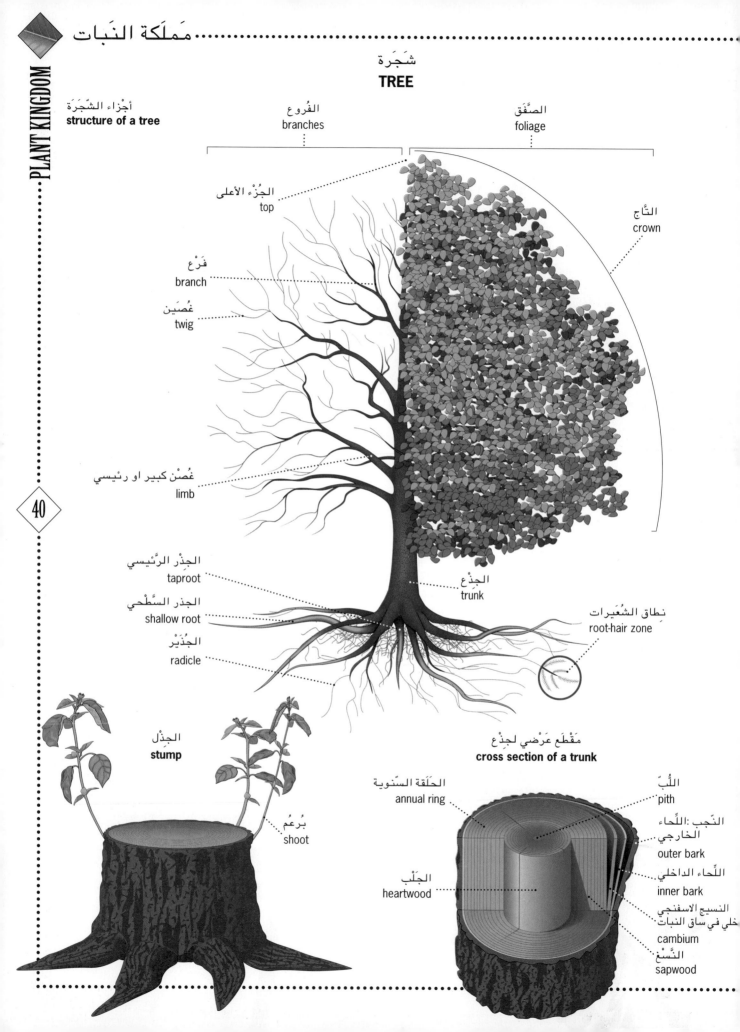

شَجَرة
TREE

أجْزاء الشّجَرَة
structure of a tree

الفُروع
branches

الصَّفَق
foliage

الجُزْء الأعلى
top

التَّاج
crown

فَرْع
branch

غُصَين
twig

غُصْن كبير او رئيسي
limb

الجِذْر الرَّئيسي
taproot

الجذر السَّطْحي
shallow root

الجُذَيْر
radicle

الجِذْع
trunk

نِطاق الشُّعَيرات
root-hair zone

الجِذْل
stump

بُرعُم
shoot

مَقْطَع عَرْضي لجِذْع
cross section of a trunk

الحَلَقة السّنوية
annual ring

الجَلْب
heartwood

اللُّبّ
pith

النَّجب :اللِّحاء
الخارجي
outer bark

اللِّحاء الداخلي
inner bark

النسيج الاسفنجي
خلي في ساق النبات
cambium

النَّسْغ
sapwood

بعض انواع الأشْجار
EXAMPLES OF TREES

الحَوْر
poplar

البَلُّوط، السِّنديان
oak

القَيقَب
maple

نخيل الزَيت
palm tree

الغَرَب
weeping willow

البَتُولا
birch

الصَّنوبَر
CONIFER

اللّاركس
larch

الصَّنوبَر المِظلّي
umbrella pine

كوْز الصنوبر
cone

ثِمار الصنوبر
pine seeds

بعض انواع الاوراق
TYPES OF LEAVES

فرع
branch

إبَر التَّنوب
fir needles

كوْز الصنوبر الأنْثى
female cone

أوْراق حَرْشَفيّة
cypress scalelike leaves

ابر الصنوبر
pine needles

كوْز الصنوبر الذَّكر
male cone

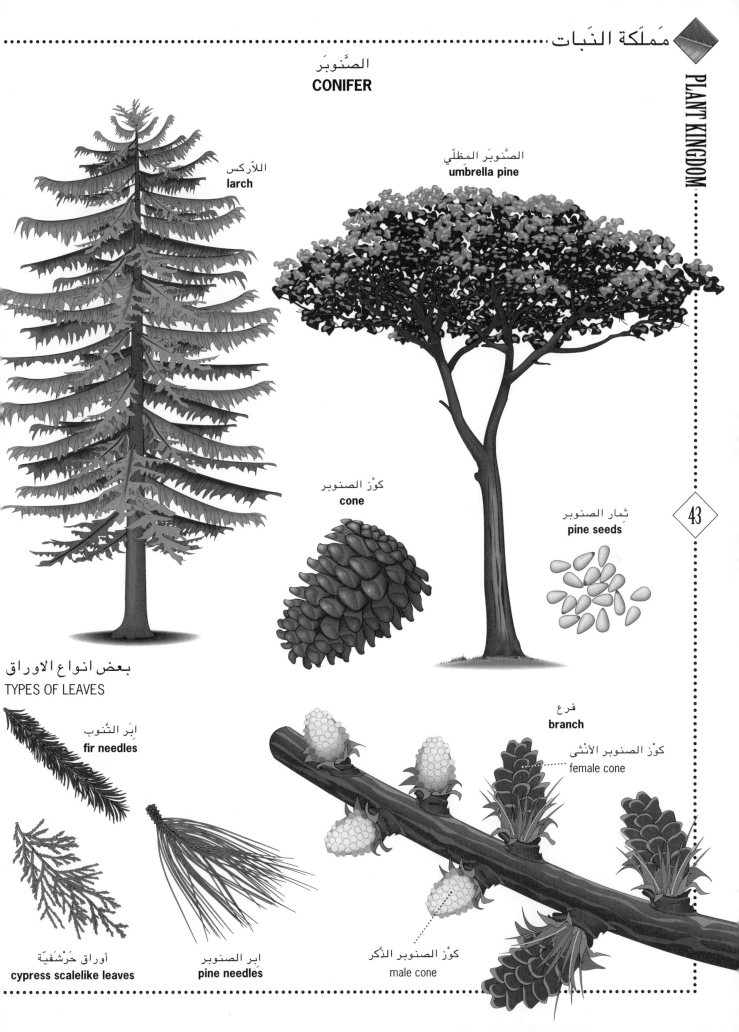

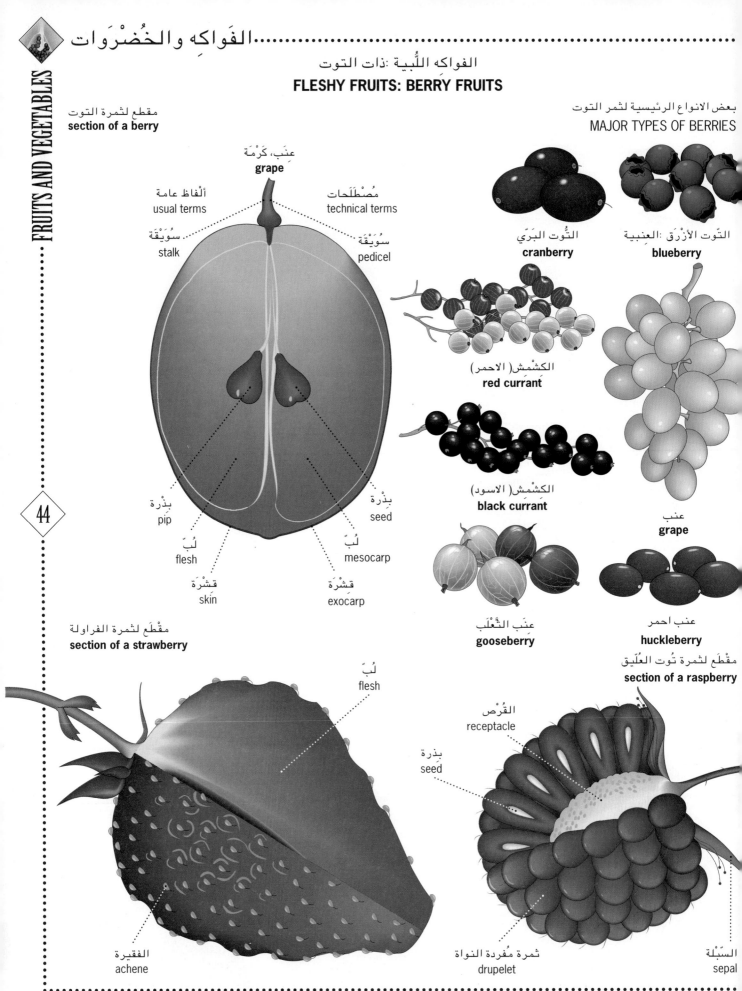

الفواكه اللُّبية: ذات التوت
FLESHY FRUITS: BERRY FRUITS

مقطع لثمرة التوت
section of a berry

بعض الانواع الرئيسية لثمر التوت
MAJOR TYPES OF BERRIES

عِنَب، كَرْمَة
grape

ألْفاظ عامة
usual terms

مُصْطَلَحات
technical terms

سُوَيْقَة
stalk

سُوَيْقَة
pedicel

التُّوت البَرّي
cranberry

التّوت الأزْرَق: العنبية
blueberry

الكشْمِش (الاحمر)
red currant

بِذْرَة
pip

بِذْرَة
seed

الكِشْمِش (الاسود)
black currant

لُبّ
flesh

لُبّ
mesocarp

عنب
grape

قِشْرَة
skin

قِشْرَة
exocarp

عِنَب الثَّعْلَب
gooseberry

عنب احمر
huckleberry

مقْطَع لثمرة الفراولة
section of a strawberry

مقْطَع لثمرة تُوت العُلّيق
section of a raspberry

لُبّ
flesh

القُرْص
receptacle

السَّبْلَة
sepal

بِذْرَة
seed

الفُقَيْرة
achene

ثمرة مُفردة النواة
drupelet

السَّبْلَة
sepal

44

الفواكه اللُّبِّية ذات النوى
FLESHY STONE FRUITS

مقْطَع عرضي لفاكهة لبِّية ذات نواة
section of a stone fruit

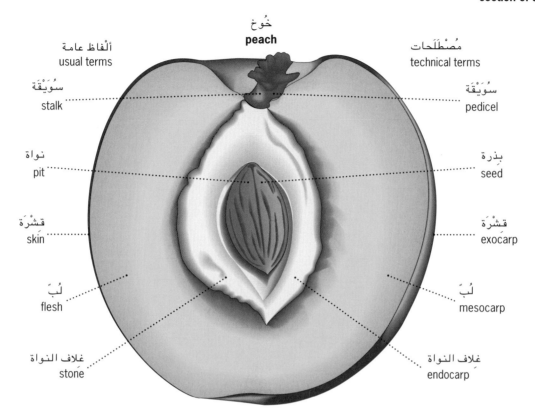

ألْفاظ عامة
usual terms

خُوخ
peach

مُصْطَلَحات
technical terms

سُوَيْقَة
stalk

سُوَيْقَة
pedicel

نواة
pit

بِذرة
seed

قِشْرَة
skin

قِشْرَة
exocarp

لُبّ
flesh

لُبّ
mesocarp

غِلاف النواة
stone

غلاف النواة
endocarp

بعض الانواع الرئيسية للفواكه اللبِّية
MAJOR TYPES OF STONE FRUITS

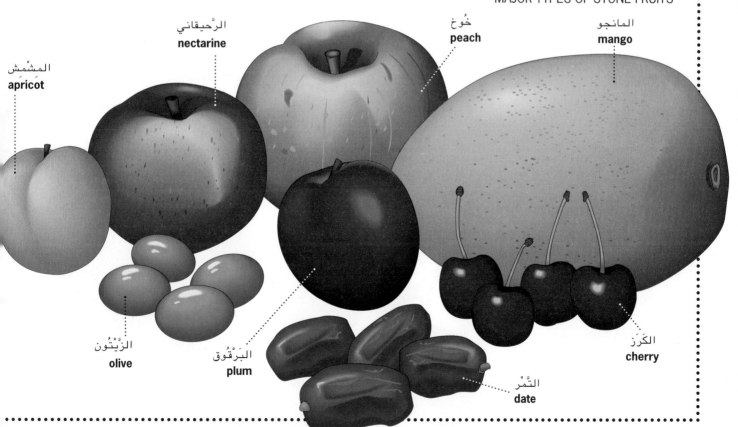

الرَّحيقاني
nectarine

خُوخ
peach

المانجو
mango

المشْمِش
apricot

الزَّيْتُون
olive

البَرقُوق
plum

التَّمْر
date

الكَرَز
cherry

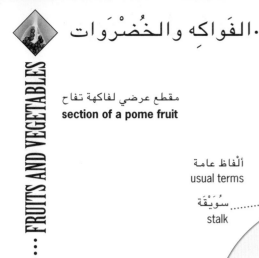

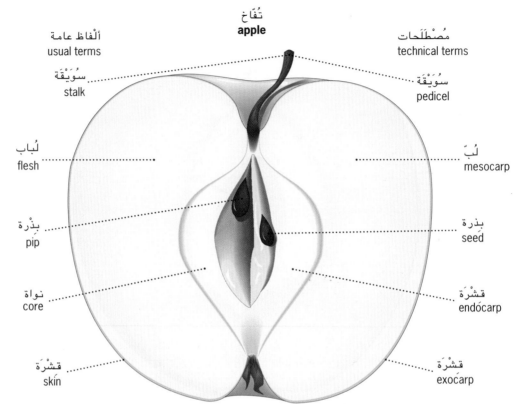

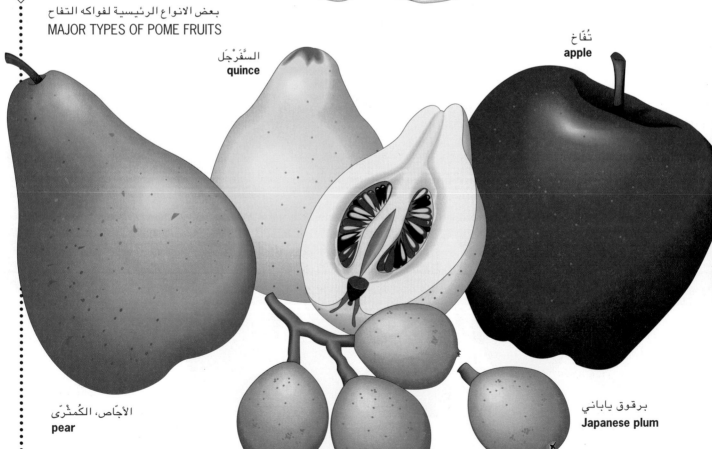

الفوكِه التُّفاحيّة
FLESHY POME FRUITS

مقطع عرضي لفاكهة تفاح
section of a pome fruit

تُفَّاح
apple

ألْفاظ عامة
usual terms

مُصْطَلَحات
technical terms

سُوَيْقَة
stalk

سُوَيْقَة
pedicel

لُباب
flesh

لُبّ
mesocarp

بِذْرة
pip

بِذْرة
seed

نواة
core

قِشْرَة
endócarp

قِشْرَة
skin

قِشْرَة
exocarp

بعض الانواع الرئيسية لفواكه التفاح
MAJOR TYPES OF POME FRUITS

السَّفَرْجَل
quince

تُفَّاح
apple

الأجَّاص، الكُمثْرَى
pear

برقوق ياباني
Japanese plum

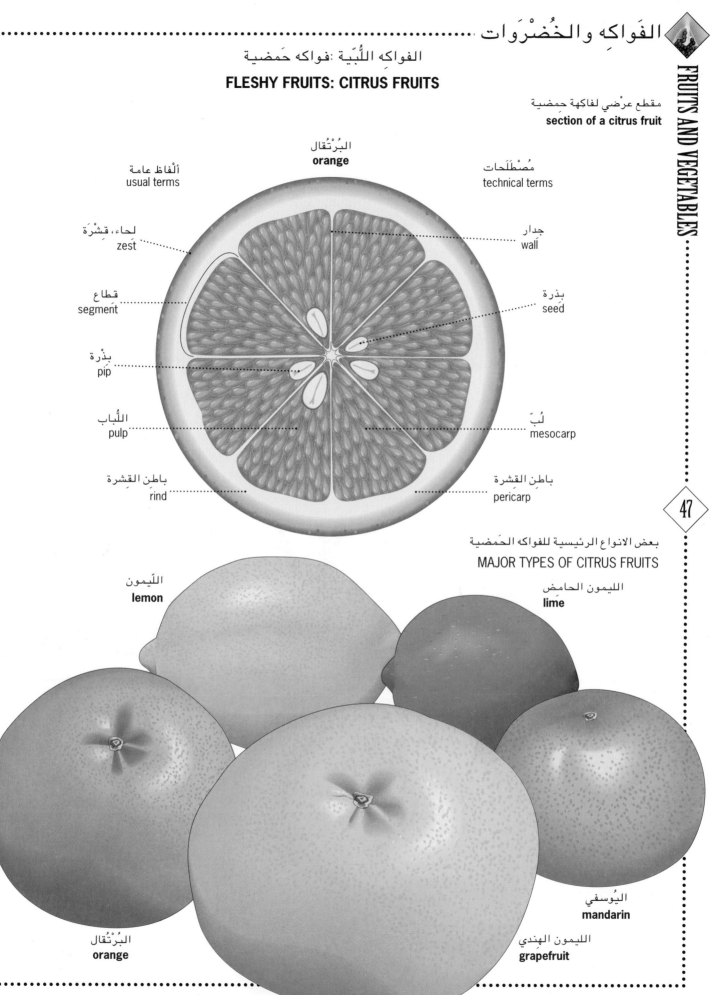

الفَواكِه اللُّبّية: فواكه حَمضية
FLESHY FRUITS: CITRUS FRUITS

مقطع عرْضي لفاكِهة حمضية
section of a citrus fruit

البُرْتُقال
orange

أَلْفاظ عامة
usual terms

مُصْطَلَحات
technical terms

لِحاء، قِشْرَة
zest

جِدار
wall

قِطاع
segment

بَذْرة
seed

بَذْرة
pip

اللُّبّاب
pulp

لُبّ
mesocarp

باطِن القِشرة
rind

باطِن القشرة
pericarp

بعض الانواع الرئيسية للفَواكه الحَمضية
MAJOR TYPES OF CITRUS FRUITS

اللّيمون
lemon

الليمون الحامِض
lime

اليُوسفي
mandarin

البُرْتُقال
orange

الليمون الهِندي
grapefruit

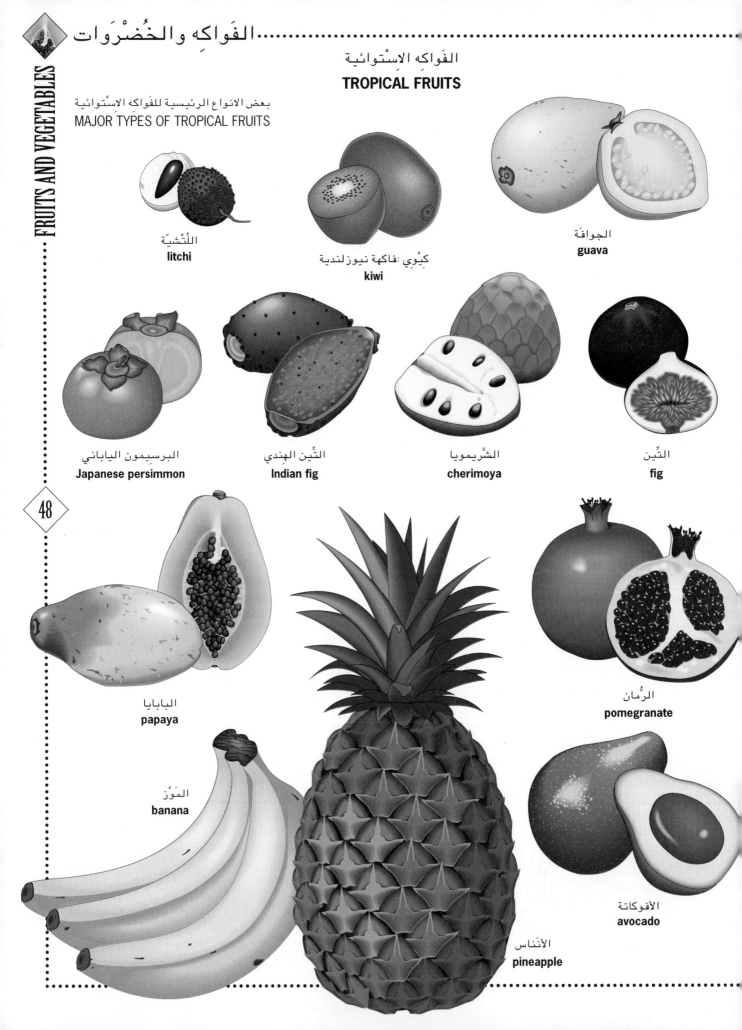

الفَواكِه الاسْتوائية
TROPICAL FRUITS

بعض الانواع الرئيسية للفَواكِه الاسْتوائية
MAJOR TYPES OF TROPICAL FRUITS

اللِّتْشِيّة
litchi

كِيْوِي: فاكهة نيوزلندية
kiwi

الجوافَة
guava

البرسيمون الياباني
Japanese persimmon

التِّين الهِندي
Indian fig

الشَّريمويا
cherimoya

التِّين
fig

48

البابايا
papaya

الرُّمان
pomegranate

المَوْز
banana

الأفوكاتة
avocado

الأنَناس
pineapple

الخُضْرَوات
VEGETABLES

الخُضْرَوات الزَّهْريّة
INFLORESCENT VEGETABLES

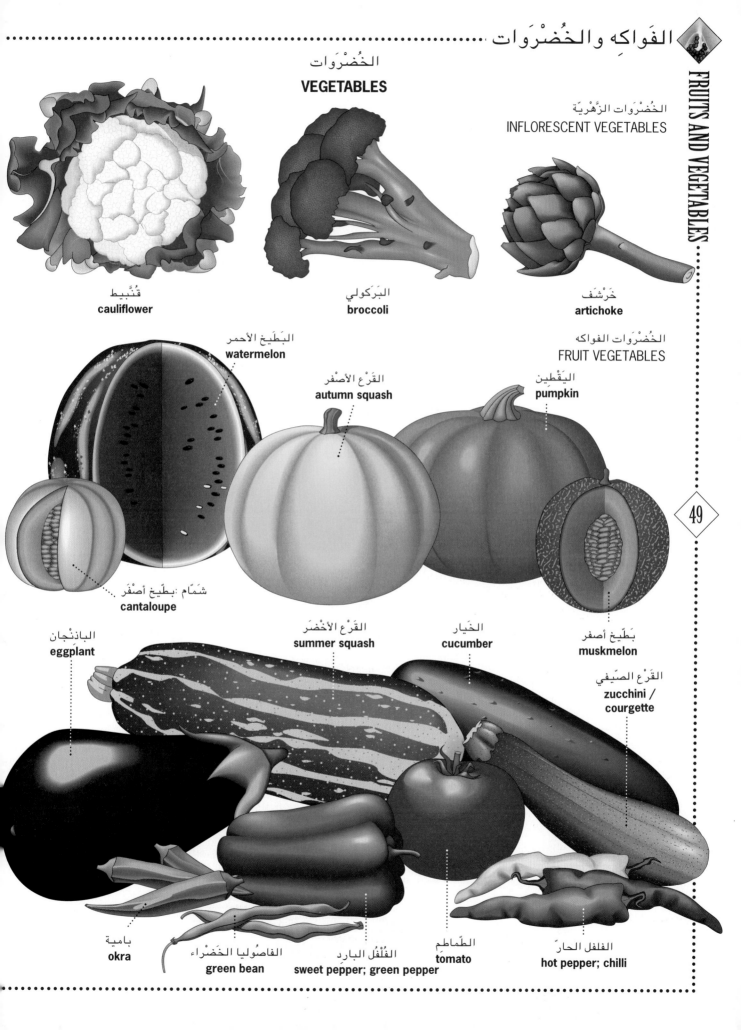

قُنَّبِيط
cauliflower

البَرَكولي
broccoli

خَرْشَف
artichoke

البَطِّيخ الأحمر
watermelon

القَرْع الأصْفَر
autumn squash

الخُضْرَوات الفواكه
FRUIT VEGETABLES

اليَقْطِين
pumpkin

شَمّام ؛ بطّيخ أصْفَر
cantaloupe

البَاذِنْجان
eggplant

القَرْع الأخْضَر
summer squash

الخَيار
cucumber

بَطّيخ أصفر
muskmelon

القَرْع الصّيْفي
**zucchini /
courgette**

بامية
okra

الفاصُوليا الخَضْراء
green bean

الفُلْفُل البارِد
sweet pepper; green pepper

الطَّماطِم
tomato

الفلفل الحارّ
hot pepper; chilli

49

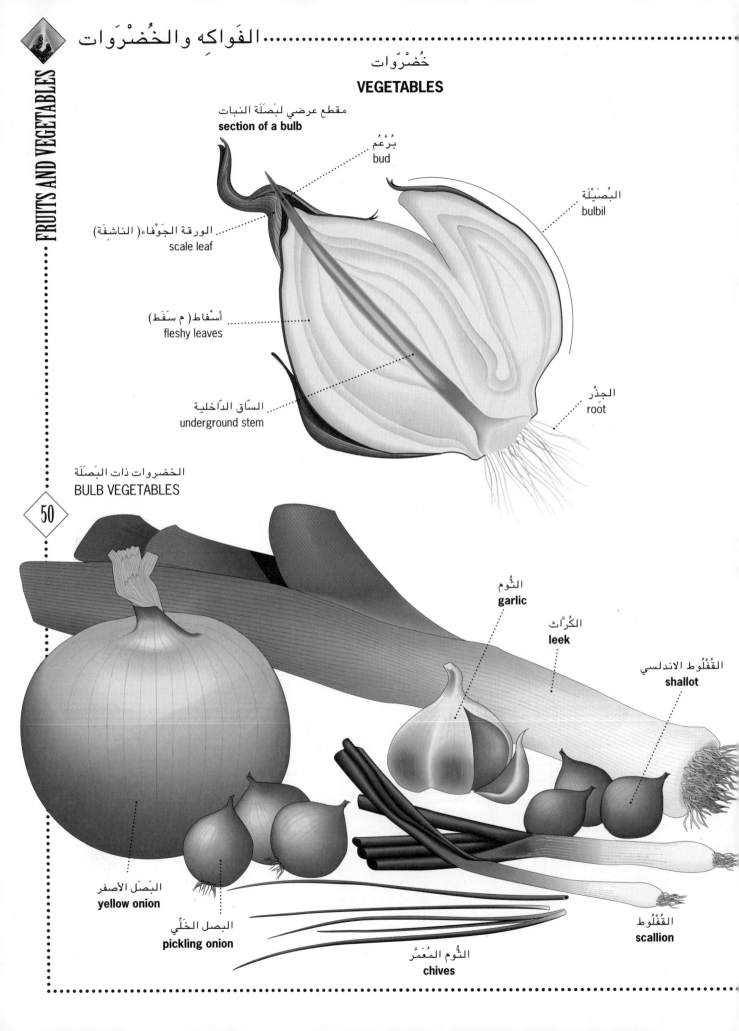

خُضْرّوات
VEGETABLES

مقطع عرضي لبَصلَة النبات
section of a bulb

بُرْعُم
bud

البُصَيْلَة
bulbil

الورقة الجَوْفاء(الناشِفَة)
scale leaf

أسْفاط(م سَفَط)
fleshy leaves

السّاق الدّاخلية
underground stem

الجذْر
root

الخضروات ذات البَصلَة
BULB VEGETABLES

الثُّوم
garlic

الكُرّاث
leek

القُفْلُوط الاندلسي
shallot

البَصَل الأصفر
yellow onion

البصل الخَلِّي
pickling onion

الثُّوم المُعَمَّر
chives

القُفْلُوط
scallion

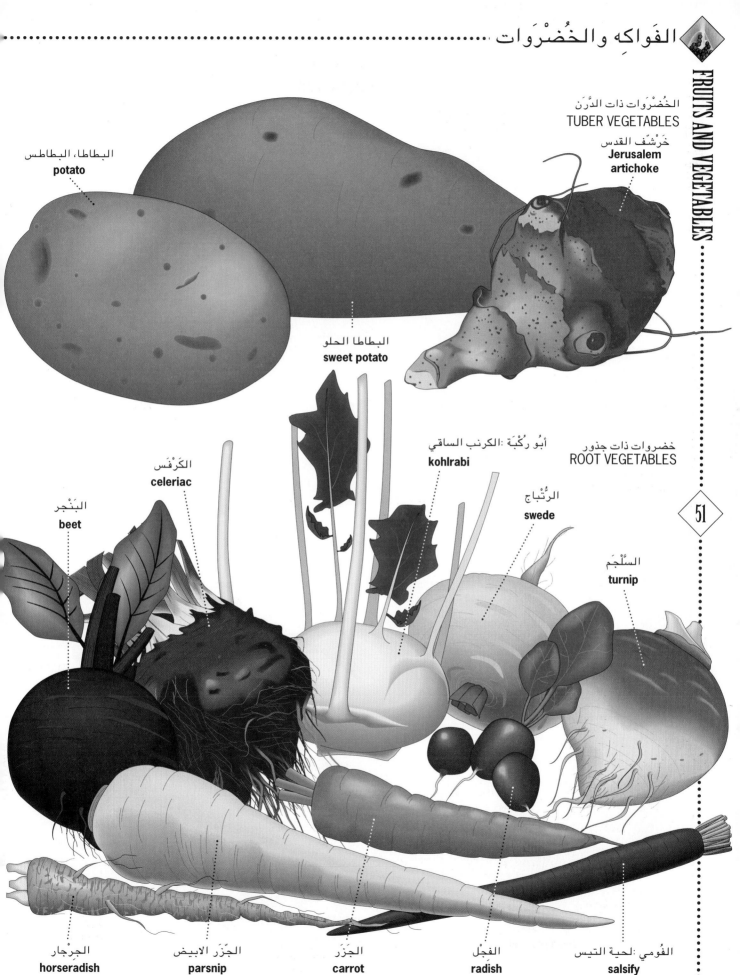

الخُضرَوات ذات الدَرَن
TUBER VEGETABLES

خَرْشّف القدس
Jerusalem artichoke

البطاطا، البطاطس
potato

البطاطا الحلو
sweet potato

أبُو رُكْبَة :الكرنب الساقي
kohlrabi

خضروات ذات جذور
ROOT VEGETABLES

الكَرْفَس
celeriac

الرُتْباج
swede

البَنْجر
beet

السَّلْجَم
turnip

الجِرْجار
horseradish

الجَزَر الابيض
parsnip

الجَزَر
carrot

الفِجْل
radish

الفُومي :لحية التيس
salsify

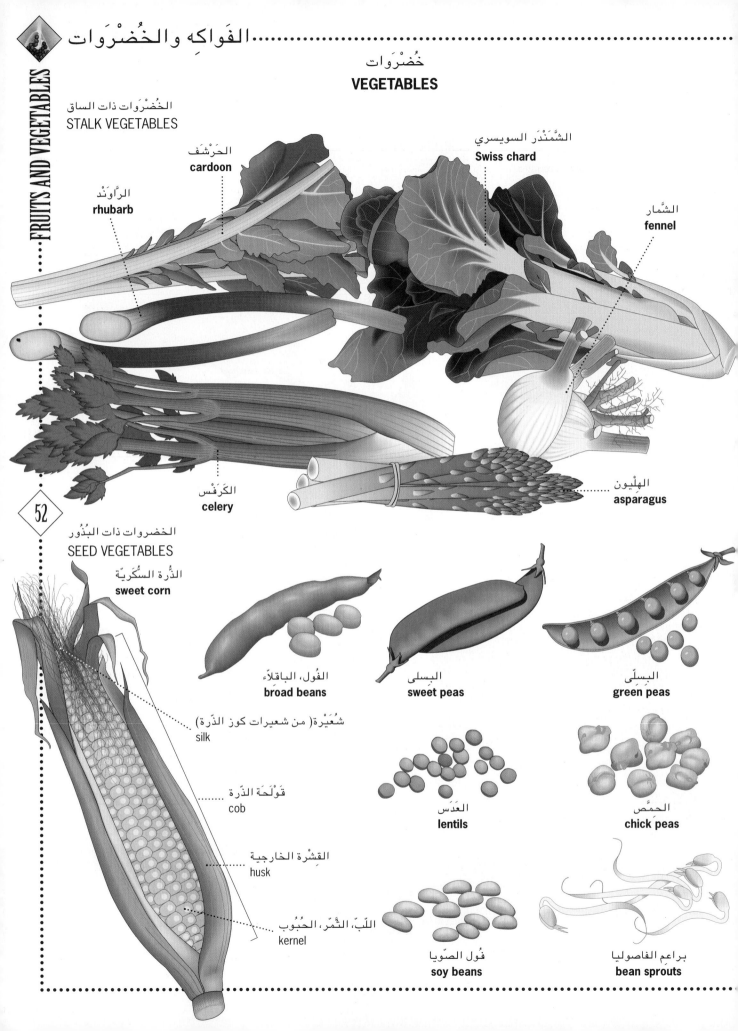

خُضْرَوات
VEGETABLES

الخُضْرَوات ذات الساق
STALK VEGETABLES

الحَرْشَف
cardoon

الرَّاوَنْد
rhubarb

الشَّمَنْدَر السويسري
Swiss chard

الشَّمار
fennel

الكَرَفْس
celery

الهِلْيون
asparagus

52

الخضروات ذات البُذُور
SEED VEGETABLES

الذُّرة السكُريّة
sweet corn

شُعَيْرة (من شعيرات كوز الذّرة)
silk

قَوْلَحَة الذّرة
cob

القِشْرة الخارجية
husk

اللّبّ، الثَّمَر، الحُبُوب
kernel

الفُول، الباقلاّء
broad beans

البِسلى
sweet peas

البِسلَّى
green peas

العَدَس
lentils

الحمَّص
chick peas

فُول الصّويا
soy beans

براعِم الفاصوليا
bean sprouts

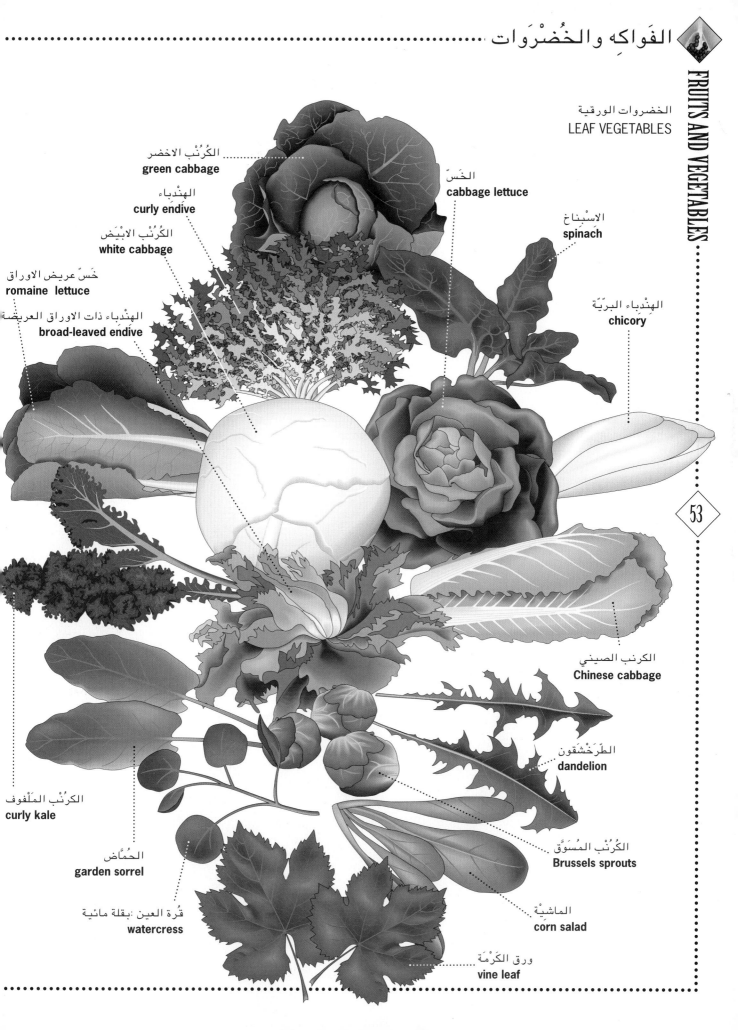

الخضروات الورقية
LEAF VEGETABLES

الكُرُنْب الاخضر
green cabbage

الهنْدِباء
curly endive

الكُرُنْب الابْيَض
white cabbage

خَسّ عريض الاوراق
romaine lettuce

الهنْدِباء ذات الاوراق العريضة
broad-leaved endive

الخَسّ
cabbage lettuce

الاسْبِناخ
spinach

الهِنْدِباء البرّيّة
chicory

الكرنب الصيني
Chinese cabbage

الطَرَخْشَقون
dandelion

الكُرُنْب المَلْفوف
curly kale

الحُمّاض
garden sorrel

قُرّة العين : بقلة مائية
watercress

الكُرُنْب المُسَوَّق
Brussels sprouts

الماشيْة
corn salad

ورق الكَرْمَة
vine leaf

البَسْتَنَة
GARDENING

المالِج
trowel

المِذْراة
hand fork

مِسْلَفة
hand cultivator

مِشْذاب، مِنجَل
pruning shears

جَزازَة العُشْب
lawnmower

التحكُّم في السُّرعة
speed control

مِفْتاح المحرك
ignition key

المِرَشَّة
watering can

مِقْبَض، مِقْوَد
handle

مقبض الأمان
safety handle

صنْدوق العُشْب
grassbox

المُحَرِّك
starter

الماكينة
motor

المحراف
deflector

غطاء
casing

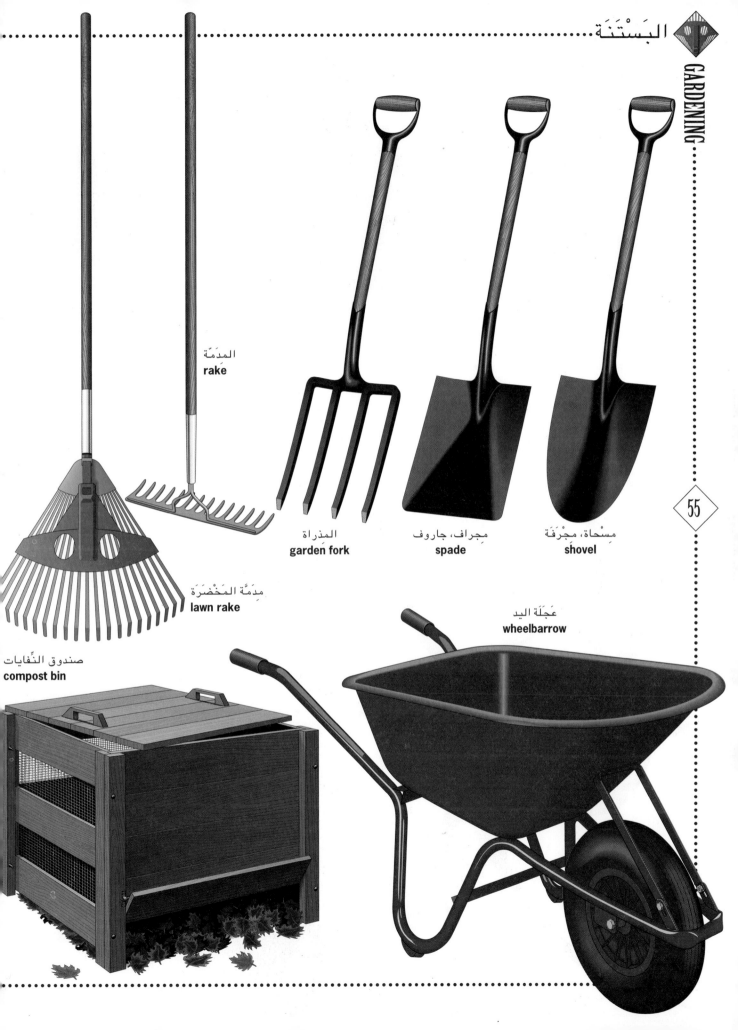

المِدَمَّة
rake

المِذراة
garden fork

مِجراف، جاروف
spade

مِسْحاة، مِجْرَفَة
shovel

مِدَمَّة المَخْضَرَة
lawn rake

عَجَلَة اليد
wheelbarrow

صندوق النِّفايات
compost bin

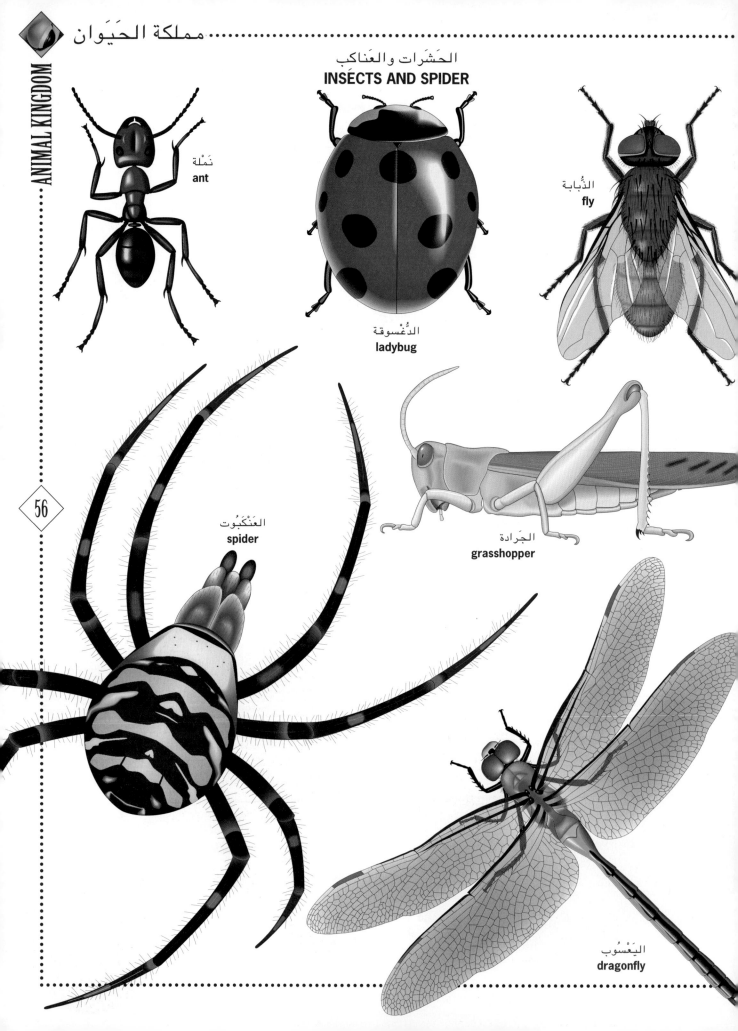

مملكة الحَيَوان

الحَشَرات والعَناكب
INSECTS AND SPIDER

نَمْلة
ant

الدُّعْسوقة
ladybug

الذُّبابة
fly

العَنْكَبُوت
spider

الجَرادة
grasshopper

اليَعْسُوب
dragonfly

56

الفَراشَة
BUTTERFLY

اليُسْرُوع
caterpillar

الرَأس
head

العين البسيطة
simple eye

الفَكّ
mandible

الرِّجل الزّاحفة
walking leg

الرجل البطنية
proleg

الجناح الأمامي
forewing

الخادرة
chrysalis

وَريد الجناح
wing vein

خَلية
cell

الصَّدْر، الزّور
thorax

الرّأس
head

قَرْن اسْتِشعار
antenna

الجناح الخلفي
hind wing

57

اللامِس: عضو اللّمس
labial palp

العَيْن المُرَكَّبَة
compound eye

خرطوم الحشرة
proboscis

الرِّجْل الأماميّة
foreleg

الرجل الوُسْطى
middle leg

بُرْثُن
claw

البَطْن
abdomen

الرِّجل الخَلْفية
hind leg

النَّحْلَة
HONEYBEE

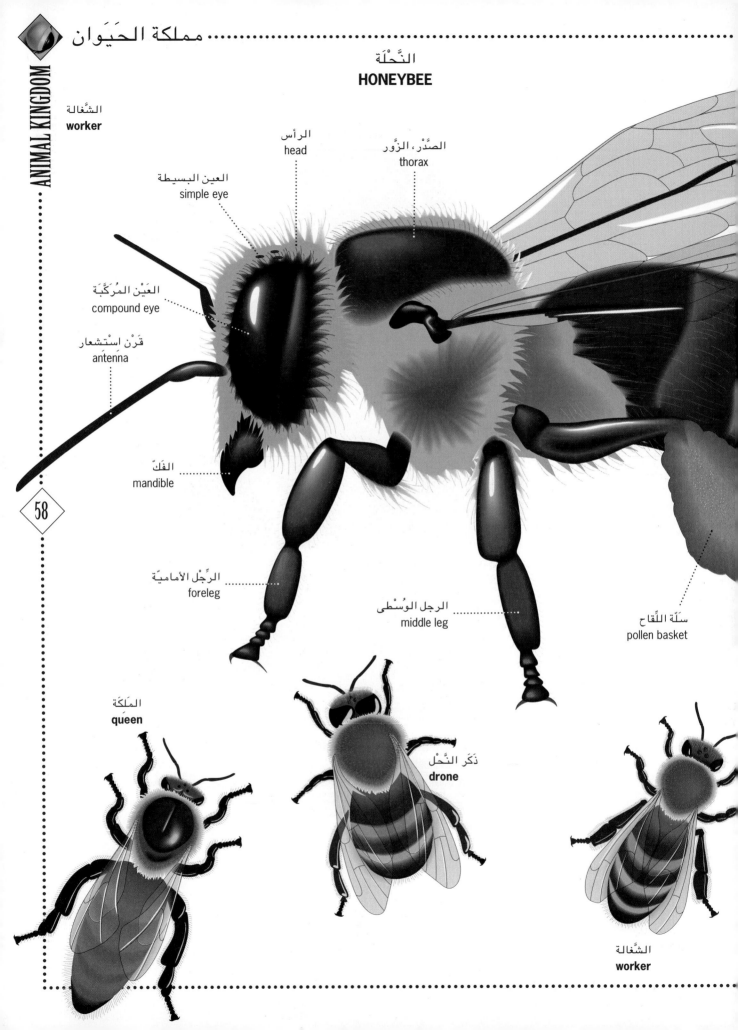

الشَّغالة
worker

الرَّأس
head

العين البسيطة
simple eye

الصَّدْر، الزُّور
thorax

العَيْن المُرَكَّبَة
compound eye

قَرْن اِسْتِشعار
antenna

الفَكّ
mandible

58

الرِّجْل الأماميّة
foreleg

الرجل الوُسْطى
middle leg

سَلَّة اللِّقاح
pollen basket

المَلِكَة
queen

ذَكَر النَّحْل
drone

الشَّغالة
worker

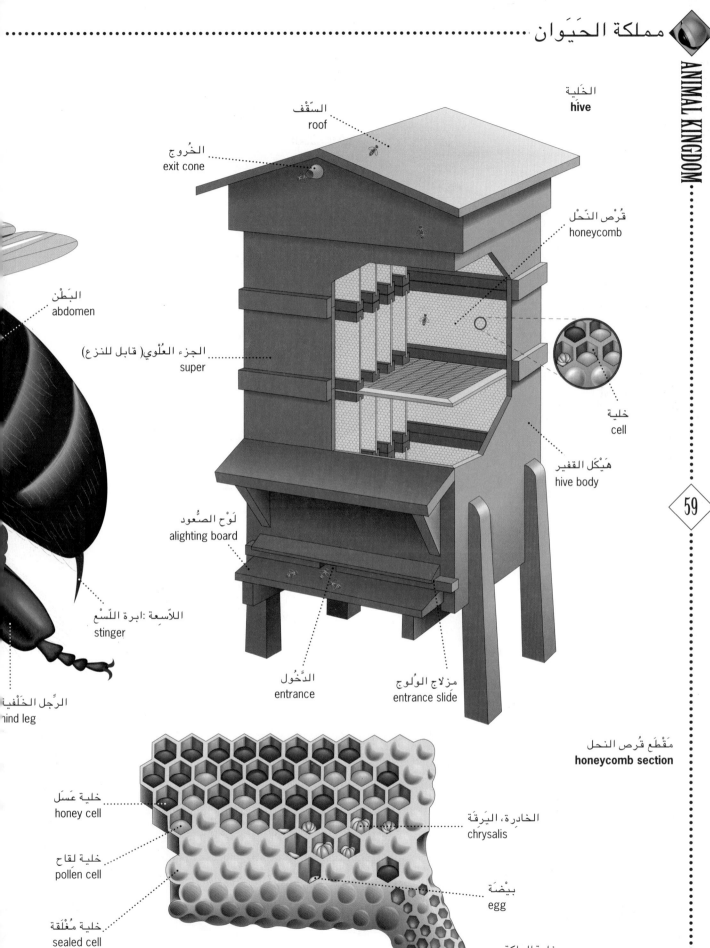

الخَلِية
hive

السّقْف
roof

الخُروج
exit cone

قُرْص النّحْل
honeycomb

البَطْن
abdomen

الجزء العُلْوي(قابل للنزع)
super

خلية
cell

هَيْكَل القفير
hive body

لَوْح الصُّعود
alighting board

اللاّسِعة :ابرة اللّسْع
stinger

الرِّجل الخَلْفية
hind leg

الدَّخُول
entrance

مزلاج الوُلوج
entrance slide

59

مَقْطَع قُرص النحل
honeycomb section

خلية عَسَل
honey cell

خلية لقاح
pollen cell

خلية مُغْلَقة
sealed cell

الخادِرة، اليَرقَة
chrysalis

بيْضَة
egg

خلية الملكة
queen cell

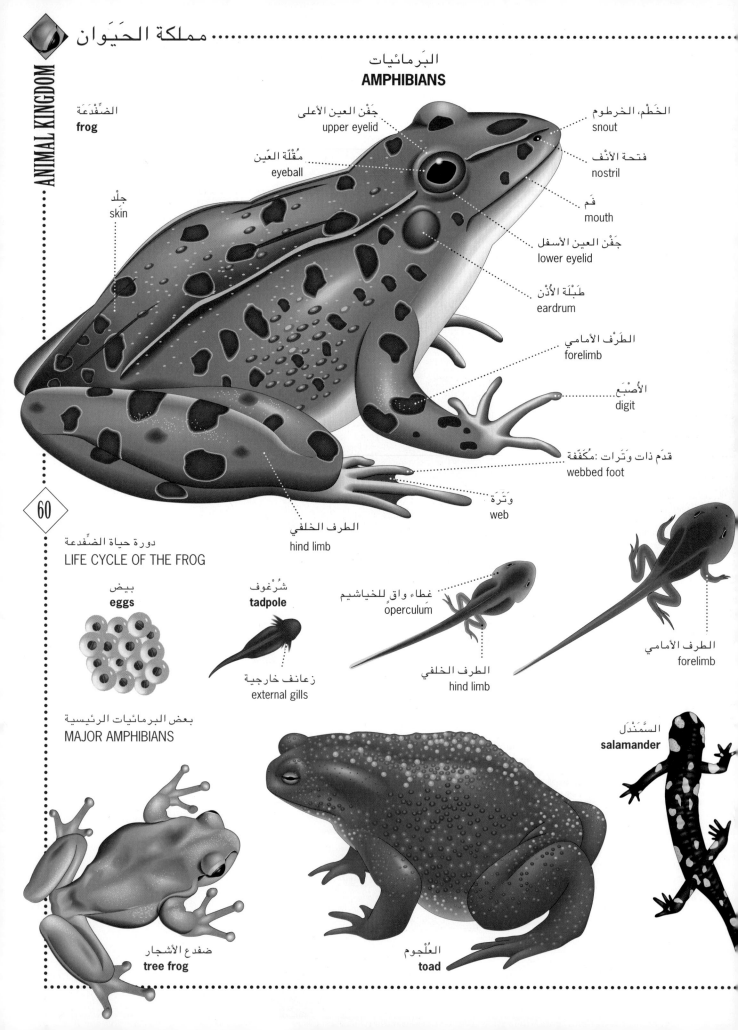

البَرمائيات
AMPHIBIANS

الضِّفْدَعَة
frog

جَفْن العين الأعلى
upper eyelid

الخَطْم، الخرطوم
snout

فتحة الأَنْف
nostril

مُقْلَة العَين
eyeball

فَم
mouth

جِلْد
skin

جَفْن العين الأسفل
lower eyelid

طَبْلَة الأُذُن
eardrum

الطَرْف الأمامي
forelimb

الأُصْبَع
digit

قدَم ذات وَتَرات: مُكَفَّفة
webbed foot

وَتَرَة
web

الطرف الخلفي
hind limb

60

دورة حياة الضِّفدعة
LIFE CYCLE OF THE FROG

بيض
eggs

شُرْغوف
tadpole

غِطاء واقٍ للخياشيم
operculum

الطرف الأمامي
forelimb

زعانف خارجية
external gills

الطرف الخلفي
hind limb

بعض البَرمائيات الرئيسية
MAJOR AMPHIBIANS

السَّمَنْدَل
salamander

ضفدع الأشجار
tree frog

العُلْجوم
toad

القِشْريات
CRUSTACEANS

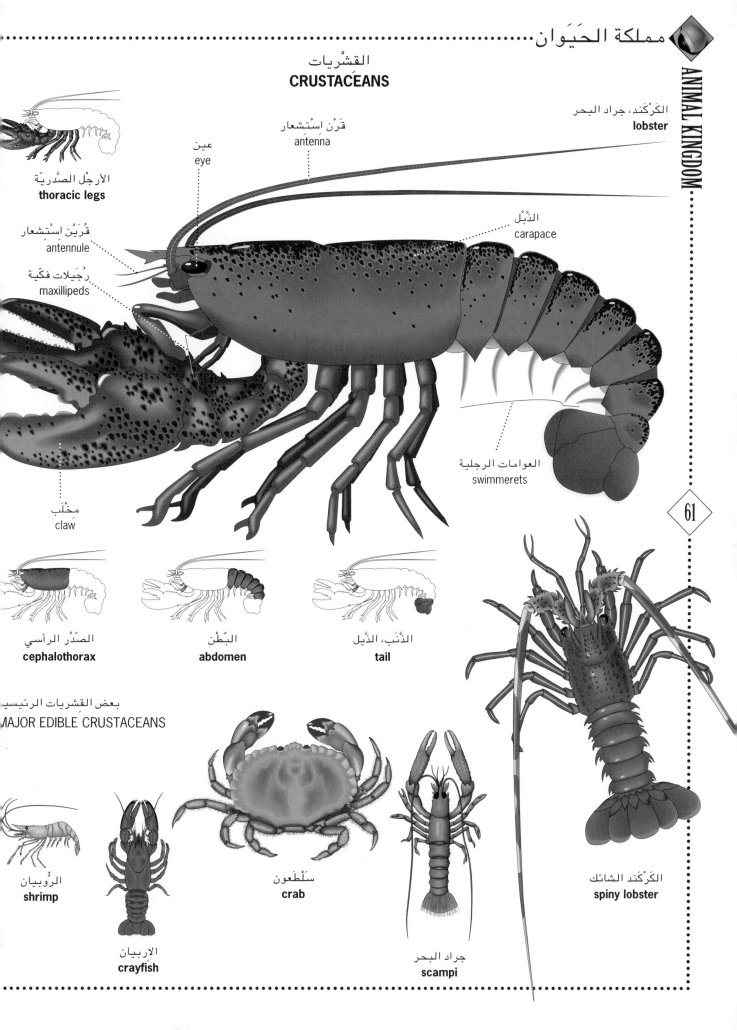

الأرْجُل الصَّدريّة
thoracic legs

قُرَيْن اِسْتِشعار
antennule

رُجَيلات فكّية
maxillipeds

مِخْلَب
claw

عين
eye

قَرْن اِسْتِشعار
antenna

الكَرْكَند، جراد البحر
lobster

الذَّبْل
carapace

العوامات الرجلية
swimmerets

الصَّدْر الرأسي
cephalothorax

البَّطْن
abdomen

الذَّنَب، الذَّيل
tail

بعض القِشْريات الرئيسيـ
MAJOR EDIBLE CRUSTACEANS

الرُّوبيان
shrimp

الاربيان
crayfish

سَلْطَعون
crab

جراد البحر
scampi

الكَرْكَند الشائك
spiny lobster

61

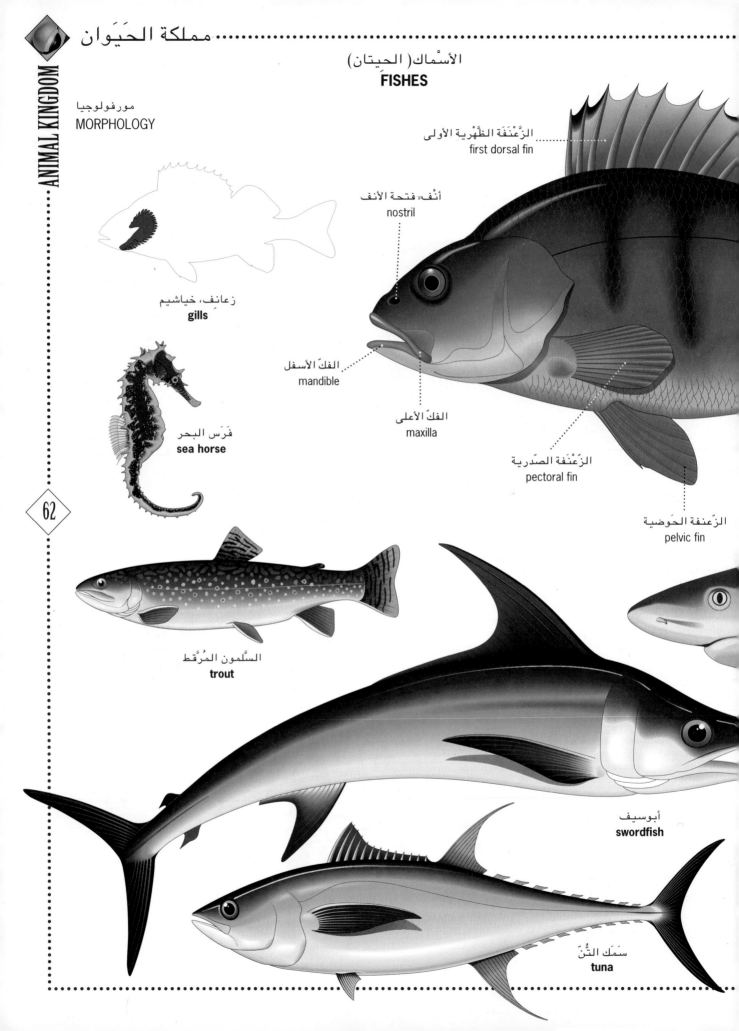

مملكة الحَيَوان

الأسْماك(الحيتان)
FISHES

مورفولوجيا
MORPHOLOGY

الزَّعْنَفَة الظَّهْرية الأولى
first dorsal fin

أنْف، فتحة الأنف
nostril

زعانف، خياشيم
gills

فَرَس البحر
sea horse

الفكّ الأسفل
mandible

الفكّ الأعلى
maxilla

الزّعْنَفَة الصّدرية
pectoral fin

الزّعنفة الحَوضية
pelvic fin

62

السَّلمون المُرَّقط
trout

أبوسيـف
swordfish

سَمَك التُّنَ
tuna

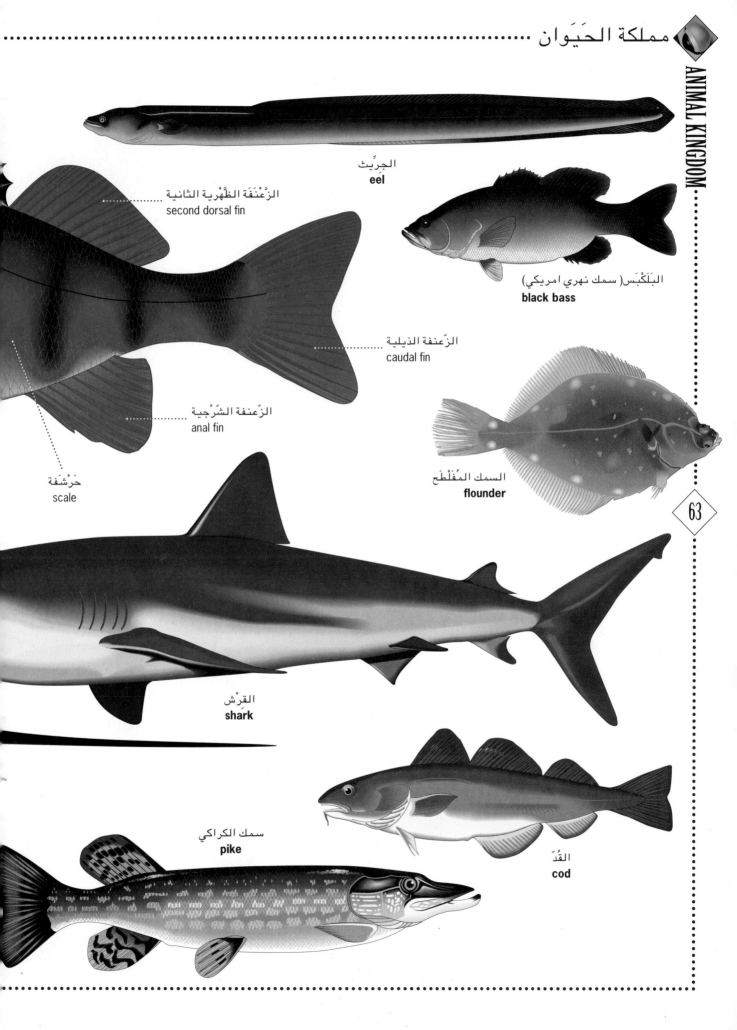

الجِرِّيث
eel

الزَّعْنَفَة الظَّهْرية الثانية
second dorsal fin

البَلَكْبَس (سمك نهري امريكي)
black bass

الزّعنفة الذيلية
caudal fin

الزّعنفة الشّرّجية
anal fin

السمك المُفَلْطَح
flounder

حَرْشَفَة
scale

63

القِرْش
shark

سمك الكراكي
pike

القُدّ
cod

مملكة الحَيَوان

الزَّواحِف
REPTILES

السُّلحفاة
turtle

طبْلة الأُذن
eardrum

الرَّقَبَة
neck

جَفْن
eyelid

عين
eye

مِنْقار صُلْب
horny beak

حَرْشَفَة
scale

قَوْقَعة
shell

ذَبْل
carapace

صَدْرّة السُّلْحفاة
plastron

رِجْل
leg

بُرْثُن
claw

64

رأس ثُعْبان سامّ
venomous snake's head

الفكّ الأعلى المُتحرّك
movable maxillary

حامِل السُّم
venom-conducting tube

قناة السُّم
venom canal

ناب، شوْكة، مخْلَب
fang

غُدّة السّم
venom gland

المِزمار
glottis

سِنّ
tooth

الكوبرا
cobra

التِّمساح
crocodile

قِراب اللِّسان
tongue sheath

لسان مُتفرِّع
forked tongue

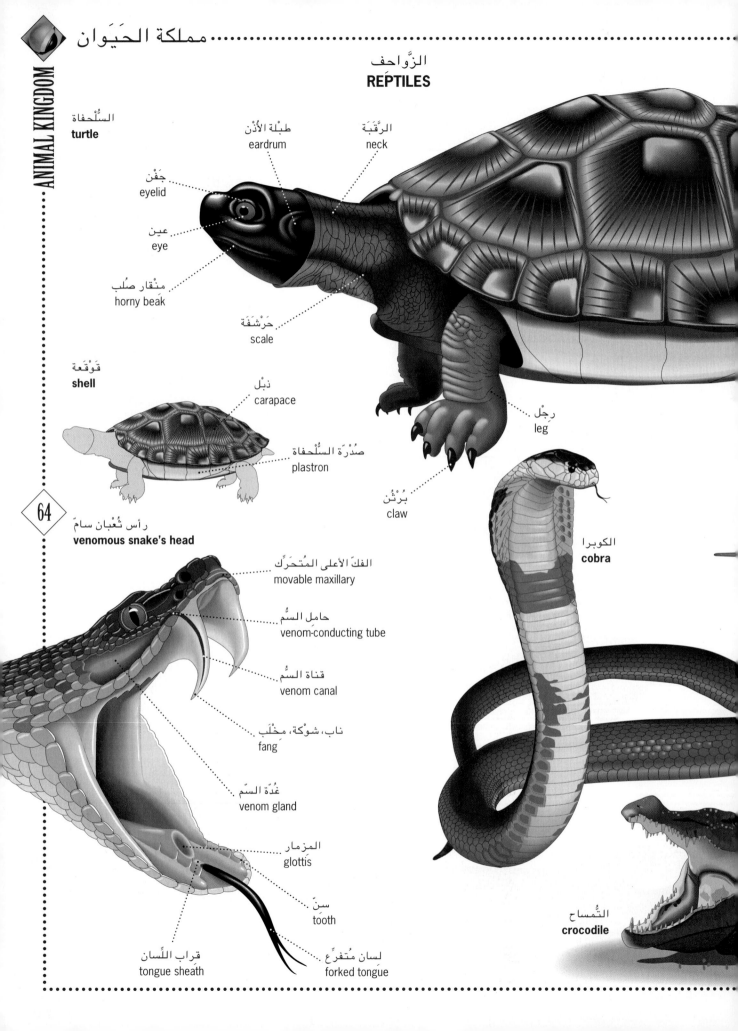

قَوْقَعة
shield

ذَيْل
tail

الحِرْباء
chameleon

السِّحْلية
lizard

ذات الجُلْجُل
rattlesnake

مملكة الحَيَوان

القطّ، الهِرّ
CAT

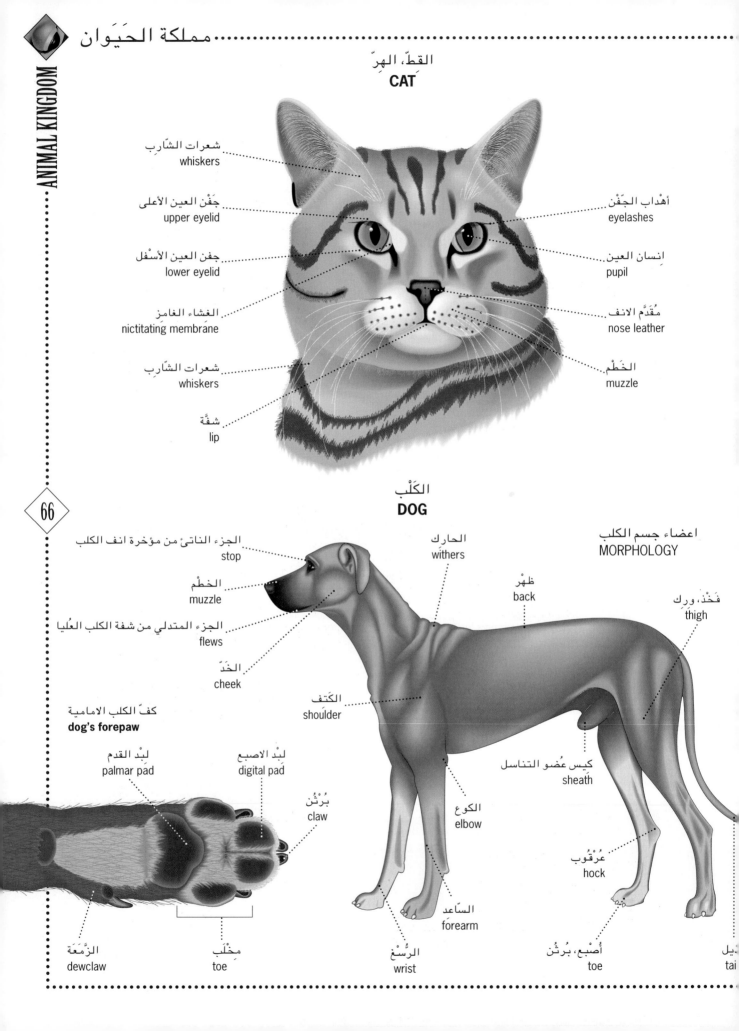

شعرات الشّارب
whiskers

جَفْن العين الأعلى
upper eyelid

جفن العين الأسْفل
lower eyelid

الغِشاء الغامِز
nictitating membrane

شعرات الشّارب
whiskers

شفَّة
lip

أهْداب الجَفْن
eyelashes

اِنسان العين
pupil

مُقَدَّم الانف
nose leather

الخَطْم
muzzle

الكَلْب
DOG

اعضاء جسم الكلب
MORPHOLOGY

الجزء الناتئ من مؤخرة انف الكلب
stop

الخطْم
muzzle

الجزء المتدلي من شفة الكلب العُليا
flews

الخَدّ
cheek

الحارك
withers

ظهْر
back

فَخْذ، ورك
thigh

كفّ الكلب الامامية
dog's forepaw

لبْد القدم
palmar pad

لبْد الاصبع
digital pad

بُرْثُن
claw

الكَتف
shoulder

كيس عُضو التناسل
sheath

الكوع
elbow

عُرْقُوب
hock

الزُّمَعَة
dewclaw

مِخْلَب
toe

السّاعد
forearm

الرُّسْغ
wrist

أصْبع، بُرثُن
toe

يل
tai

الحُصان، الجواد، الفَرَس
HORSE

النّاصية
forelock

الأنْف
nose

فتحة الأنْف
nostril

الخطْم
muzzle

الشّقّة
lip

العُرْف
mane

أعلى كاهِل الفرس :الحارك
withers

ظهر
back

حَقْو، أحد جانبي
مؤخرة الصلبْ
loin

الذيل، الذنب
tail

جانب، كَشْح
flank

الكَفَل
croup

العُنُق، الرّقَبَة
neck

الكَتف
shoulder

الصّدر
chest

الذُّراع
arm

الكُوع
elbow

الرُّكْبَة
knee

الجَسْأة
chestnut

مفْصل فوق الحافر
fetlock joint

أدنى الرُسْغ
coronet

نُتُوء يحمل خصلة شعَر فوق الحافر
fetlock

البَطْن
belly

كِيس عُضو التناسل
sheath

الفَخِذ، الورك
thigh

أدنى الورك
gaskin

الرُّسْغ
pastern

الحافِر
hoof

العُرقوب
hock

القَصَبَة
cannon

67

حيوانات المَزارِع
FARM ANIMALS

الفَرُّوج
chick

الدَّجاجة
hen

الدِّيك
rooster; cock

وِزَّة، أوزَة
goose

البَطّ
duck

الدِّيك الرُّومي
turkey

البَقَرَة
cow

العِجل
calf

68

الحَمَل
lamb

ضَأْن، خَروف، نَعجة
sheep

الماعِزَة
goat

الخِنزير
pig

أُنْثى الخِنْزِير
sow

الثَّور
ox

أنواع الأفكاك
TYPES OF JAWS

فكّ القوارض
rodent's jaw

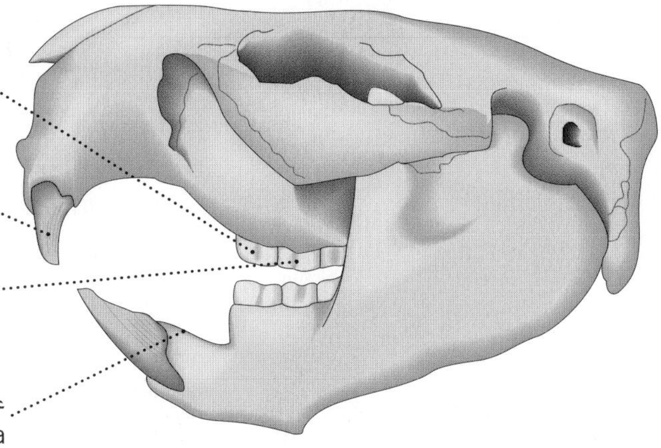

القُنْدُس، السَّمُور
beaver

قَبْطاحِن
premolar

القاطِعة(ج قواطِع)
incisor

ضِرْس
molar

عَظم القاطعة
diastema

فكّ آكل اللَّحوم
carnivore's jaw

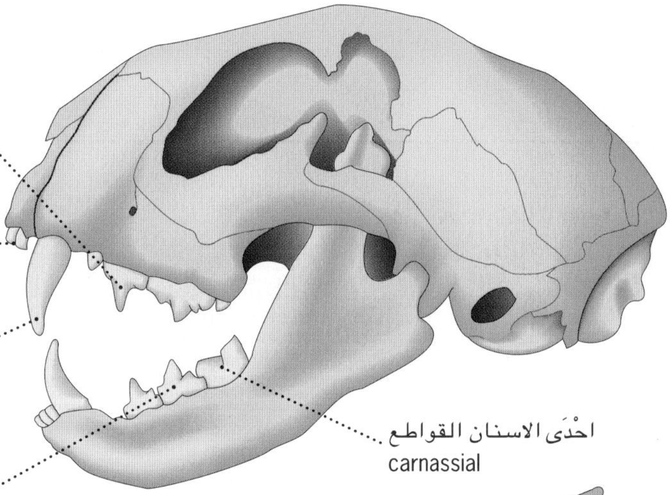

الأسَد
lion

قَبْطاحِن
premolar

القاطِعة(ج قواطِع)
incisor

نابّ
canine

احْدَى الاسنان القواطع
carnassial

ضِرْس
molar

70

فكّ آكل الحشائش
herbivore's jaw

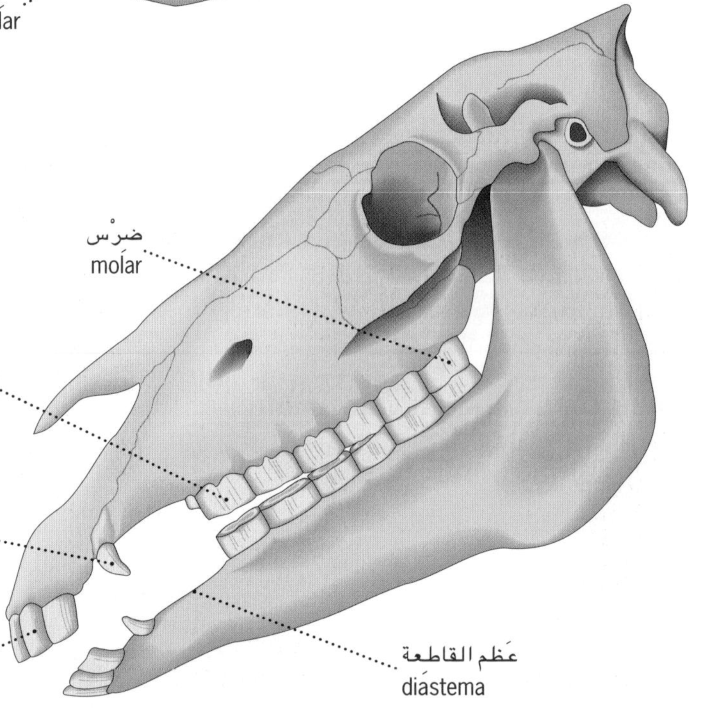

الحِصان
horse

ضِرْس
molar

قَبْطاحِن
premolar

نابّ
canine

القاطِعة(ج قواطِع)
incisor

عَظم القاطعة
diastema

بعض أنواع القُرون الرّئيسية
MAJOR TYPES OF HORNS

قَرْن المَفلُون
horns of mouflon

قرن الزّراف
horns of giraffe

قرن وَحيد القرن
horns of rhinoceros

بعض انواع الأنياب الرّئيسية
MAJOR TYPES OF TUSKS

أنياب الفَظّ
tusks of walrus

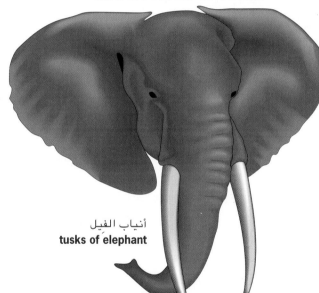

أنياب الفيل
tusks of elephant

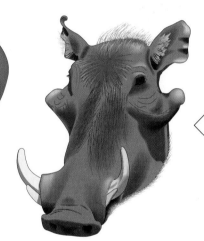

أنياب الخنزير الوَحْشي الافريقي
tusks of wart hog

بعض انواع الحوافر
TYPES OF HOOFS

حافِر ذو اصبع واحد
one-toe hoof

حافِر ذو اصبعين
two-toed hoof

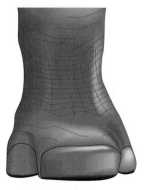

حافِر ذو ثلاثة اصابع
three-toed hoof

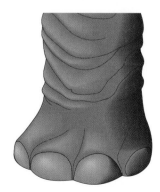

حافِر ذو أرْبَعَة اصابع
four-toed hoof

مملكة الحَيَوان

الحيوانات الوَحْشية
WILD ANIMALS

الزَّراف
giraffe

الدُّب القُطْبي
polar bear

النَّسْناس،السَّعْدان
monkey

الأسَد
lion

الدّوْلفين
dolphin

عجل البحر
whale

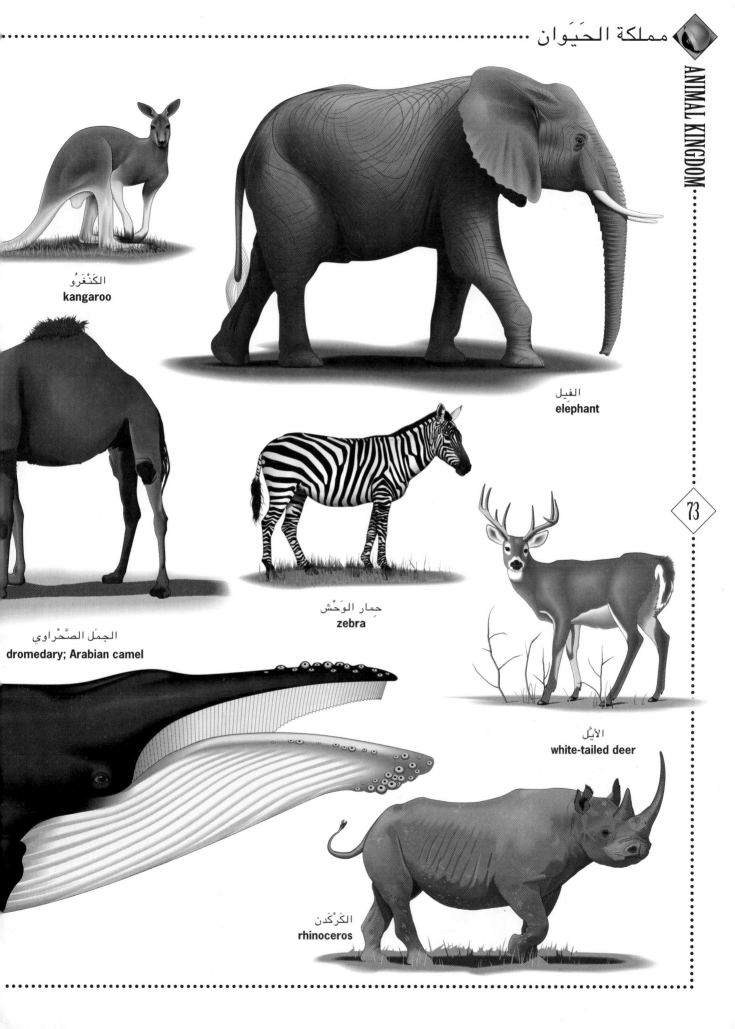

الكَنْغَرُو
kangaroo

الفِيل
elephant

الجمَل الصَّحْراوي
dromedary; Arabian camel

حِمار الوَحْش
zebra

الأيَّل
white-tailed deer

الكَرْكَدَن
rhinoceros

الطائر(ج الطّير)
BIRD

انواع المناقير الرّئيسية
PRINCIPAL TYPES OF BILLS

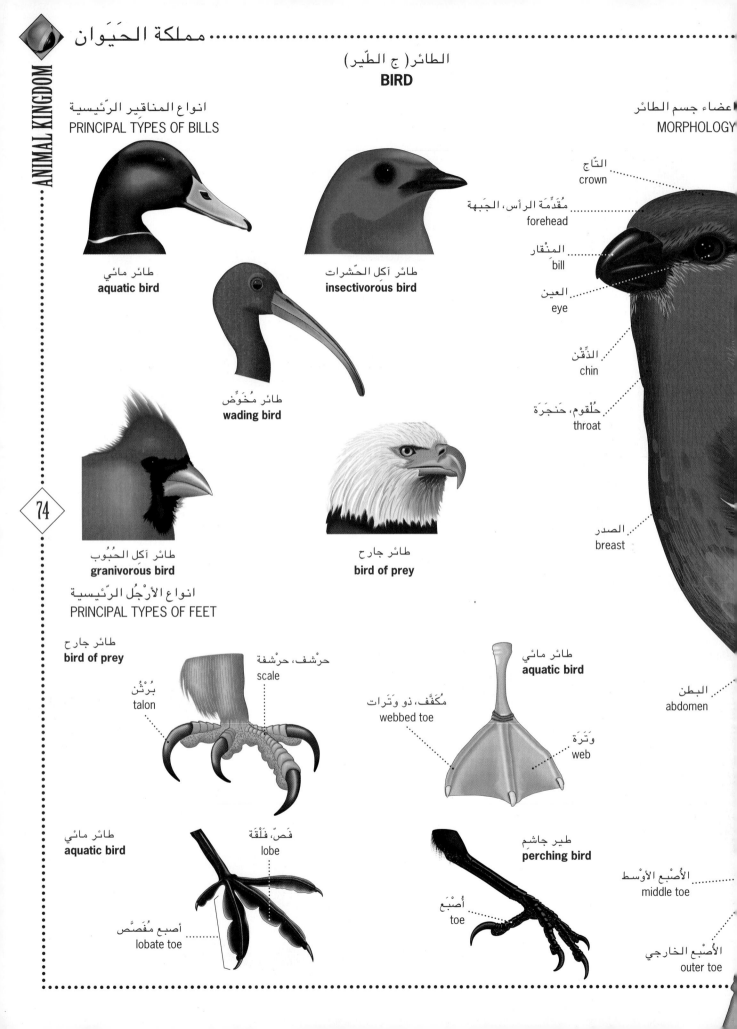

طائر مائي
aquatic bird

طائر آكل الحَشرات
insectivorous bird

طائر مُخَوِّض
wading bird

طائر آكل الحُبُوب
granivorous bird

طائر جارح
bird of prey

انواع الأرْجُل الرّئيسية
PRINCIPAL TYPES OF FEET

طائر جارح
bird of prey

حرْشف، حرْشفة
scale

بُرْثُن
talon

طائر مائي
aquatic bird

مُكَفَّف، ذو وَتَرات
webbed toe

وَتَرَة
web

طائر مائي
aquatic bird

فَصّ، فَلْقَة
lobe

طير جاشم
perching bird

أُصبع
toe

أصبع مُفَصَّص
lobate toe

عضاء جسم الطائر
MORPHOLOGY

التّاج
crown

مُقَدِّمَة الرأس، الجَبهة
forehead

المنْقار
bill

العين
eye

الذَّقْن
chin

حُلْقوم، حَنجَرَة
throat

الصدر
breast

البطن
abdomen

الأُصْبع الأوْسط
middle toe

الأصبع الخارجي
outer toe

74

عُشّ الطائر
bird's nest

بيت الطائر
birdhouse

جِهاز إطْعام الطَّير
bird feeder

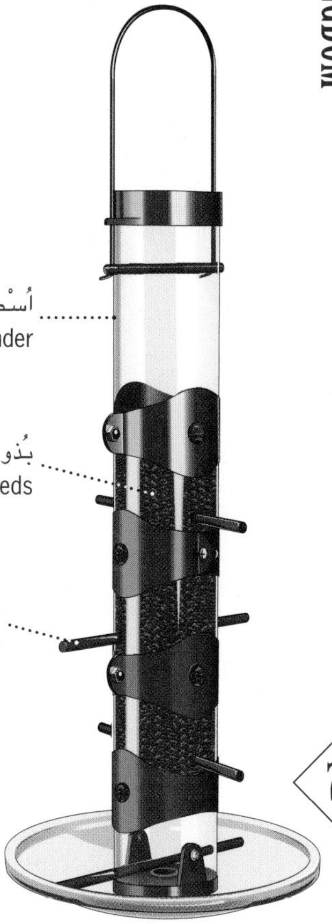

أُسْطُوانة
cylinder

بُذور، حُبُوب
seeds

مَجْثَم
perch

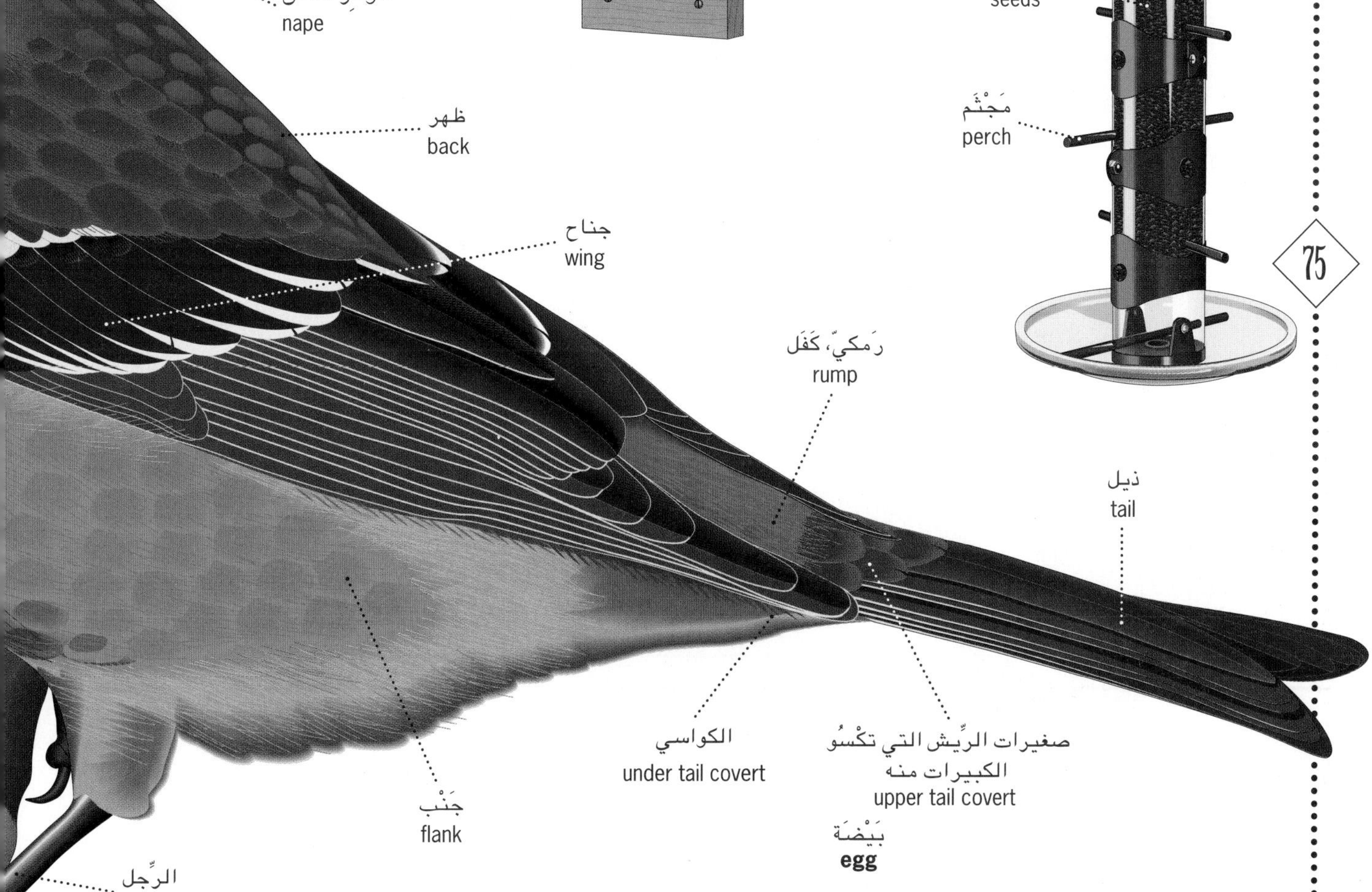

مُؤخِر العُنُق
nape

ظهر
back

جناح
wing

رَمكيّ، كَفَل
rump

ذيل
tail

75

الرِّجِل
foot

اصبع خلفي
hind toe

مِخْلَب
claw

جَنْب
flank

الكواسي
under tail covert

صغيرات الرِّيش التي تكْسُو
الكبيرات منه
upper tail covert

بَيْضَة
egg

نواة
blastodisc

فضاء هوائي
air space

صفار البيض
yolk

القشرة
shell

الآح، الزُّلال
albumen

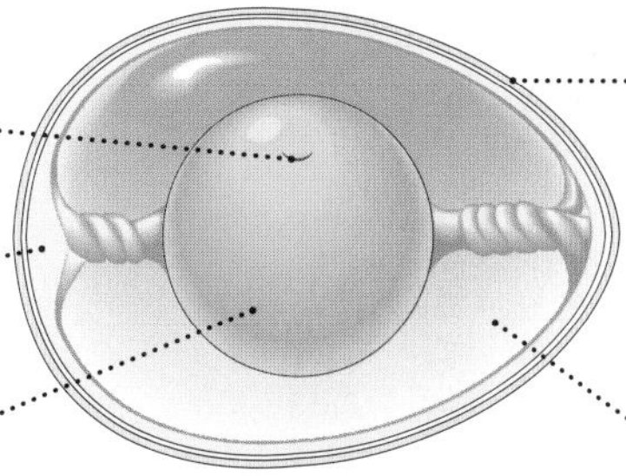

بعض انواع الطُّيور
EXAMPLES OF BIRDS

الغُراب
crow

البَبغاء
parrot

اللقْلاق
stork

السُّنونو، الخُطَاف
swallow

76

النَّحّام
flamingo

النَّعام
ostrich

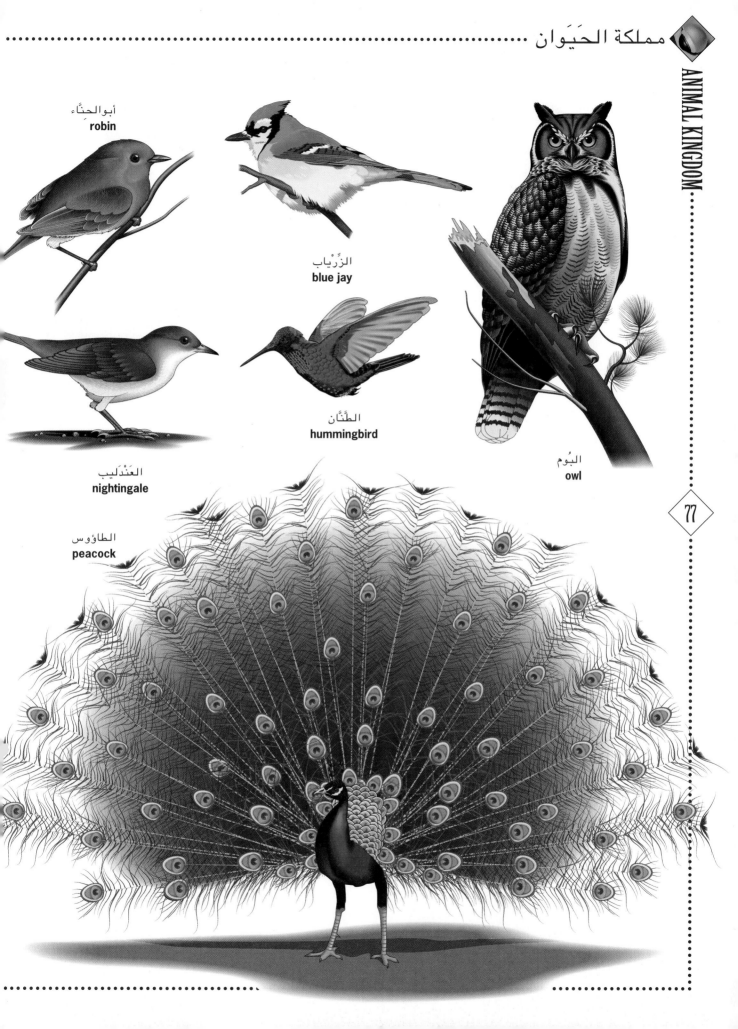

أبوالحِنَّاء
robin

الزِّرْياب
blue jay

الطَّنَّان
hummingbird

البُوم
owl

العَنْدَليب
nightingale

الطاوُوس
peacock

جسْم الاِنْسان، مَنْظَر امامي
HUMAN BODY, ANTERIOR VIEW

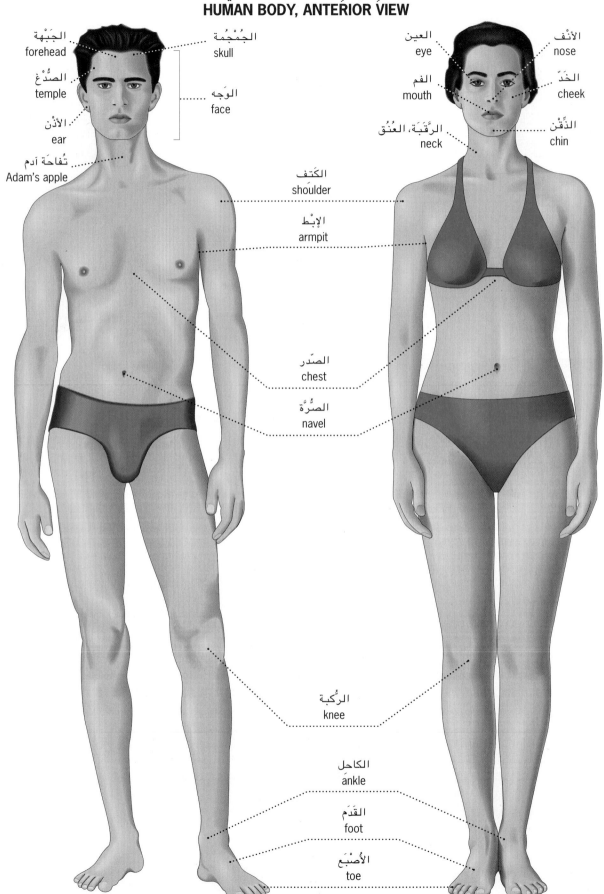

الجَبْهة
forehead

الجُمْجُمة
skull

العين
eye

الأَنْف
nose

الصُّدْغ
temple

الوَجه
face

الخَدّ
cheek

الفم
mouth

الأُذْن
ear

الذَّقْن
chin

تُفاحَة آدم
Adam's apple

الرَّقَبة، العُنُق
neck

الكَتِف
shoulder

الإِبْط
armpit

الصّدر
chest

الصُّرَّة
navel

الرُّكْبة
knee

الكاحِل
ankle

القَدَم
foot

الأُصْبَع
toe

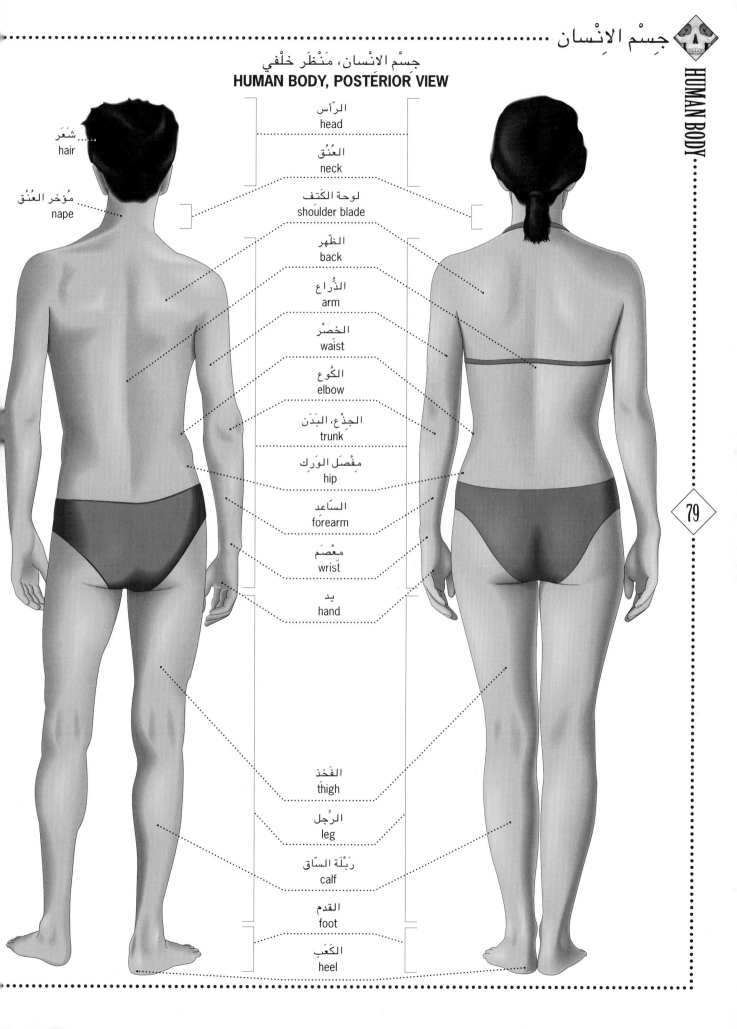

جِسْم الاِنْسان، مَنْظَر خلْفي
HUMAN BODY, POSTERIOR VIEW

شَعَر
hair

مُؤَخِر العُنُق
nape

الرَّأْس
head

العُنُق
neck

لوحة الكَتف
shoulder blade

الظّهر
back

الذُّراع
arm

الخصْر
waist

الكُوع
elbow

الجذْع، البَدَن
trunk

مِفْصَل الوَرِك
hip

السّاعد
forearm

مِعْصَم
wrist

يد
hand

الفَخذ
thigh

الرِّجل
leg

رَبْلَة السّاق
calf

القدم
foot

الكَعَب
heel

الهَيْكَل العَظْمي
SKELETON

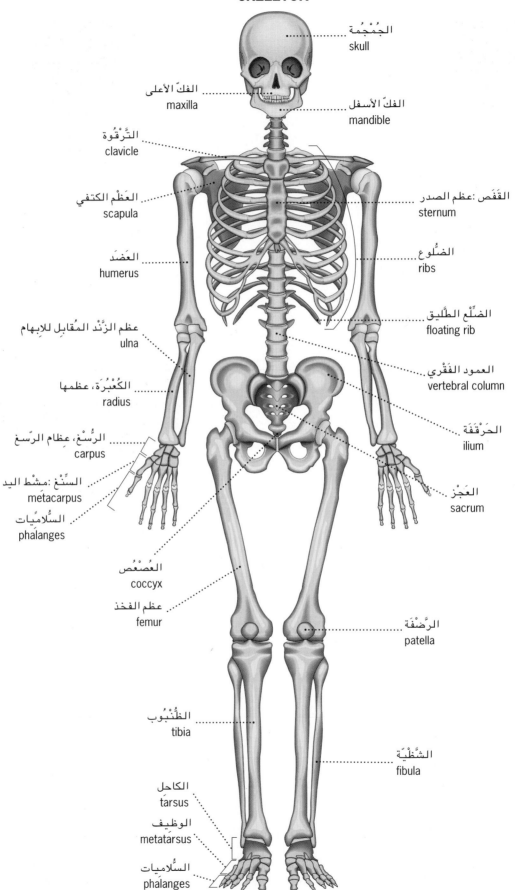

الجُمْجُمة
skull

الفكّ الأعلى
maxilla

الفكّ الأَسْفل
mandible

التَّرْقُوة
clavicle

العَظْم الكتفي
scapula

القَفَص :عظم الصدر
sternum

العَضَد
humerus

الضُّلوع
ribs

الضِّلع الطَّليق
floating rib

عظم الزَّنْد المُقابِل للابِهام
ulna

العمود الفَقْري
vertebral column

الكُعْبُرَة، عظمها
radius

الحَرْقَفَة
ilium

الرُّسْغ، عِظام الرّسغ
carpus

العَجْز
sacrum

السِّنْع :مشْط اليد
metacarpus

السُّلامِيّات
phalanges

العُصْعُص
coccyx

عظم الفخذ
femur

الرّضْفَة
patella

الظُّنْبُوب
tibia

الشَّظِيّة
fibula

الكاحِل
tarsus

الوَظيف
metatarsus

السُّلاميات
phalanges

جِسْم الانْسان
HUMAN ANATOMY

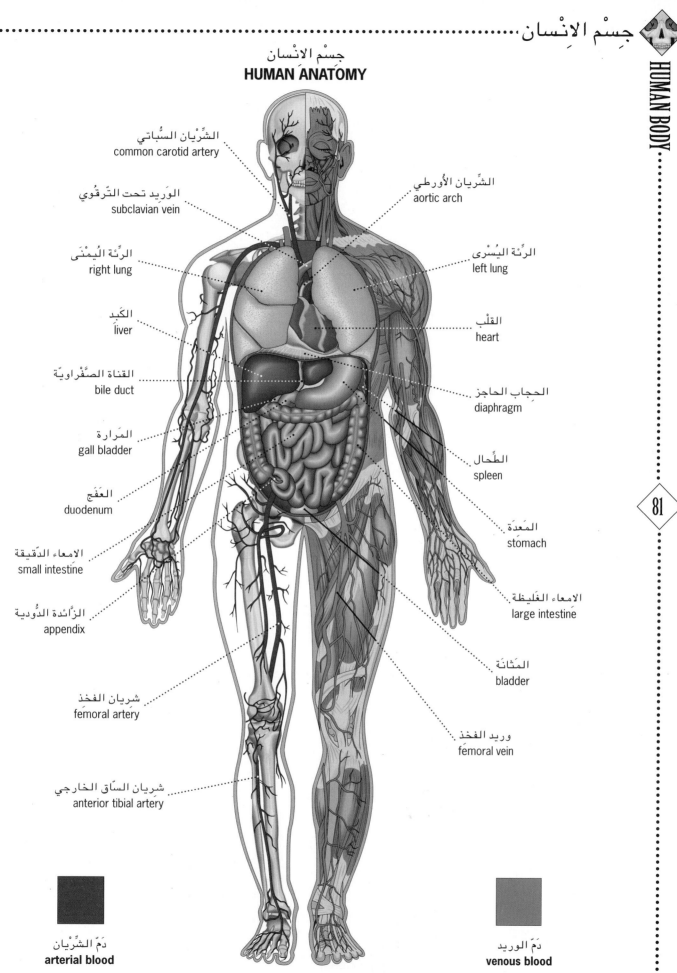

الشِّرْيان السُّباتي
common carotid artery

الشِّرْيان الأُورطي
aortic arch

الوَريد تحت التَّرقُوي
subclavian vein

الرِّئة اليُسْرى
left lung

الرِّئة اليُمْنَى
right lung

القلْب
heart

الكَبِد
liver

الحِجاب الحاجِز
diaphragm

القَناة الصَّفْراويّة
bile duct

الطُّحال
spleen

المَرارة
gall bladder

المَعِدة
stomach

العَفَج
duodenum

الامعاء الغَليظة
large intestine

الامعاء الدّقيقة
small intestine

المَثانة
bladder

الزّائدة الدُّودِية
appendix

شِريان الفخِذ
femoral artery

وريد الفخِذ
femoral vein

شريان السّاق الخارجي
anterior tibial artery

دَمّ الشِّرْيان
arterial blood

دَمّ الوريد
venous blood

العَيْن :عُضو النَّظَر
EYE: THE ORGAN OF SIGHT

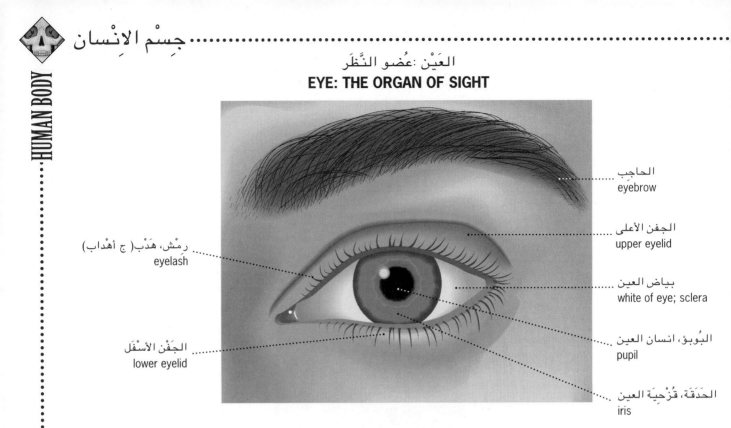

الحاجِب
eyebrow

الجَفن الأعلى
upper eyelid

رِمْش، هَدْب(ج أهْداب)
eyelash

بياض العين
white of eye; sclera

البُوبؤ، انسان العَين
pupil

الجَفْن الأسْفَل
lower eyelid

الحَدَقَة، قُزْحِيَة العين
iris

اليَد :عضو اللَّمْس
HAND: THE ORGAN OF TOUCH

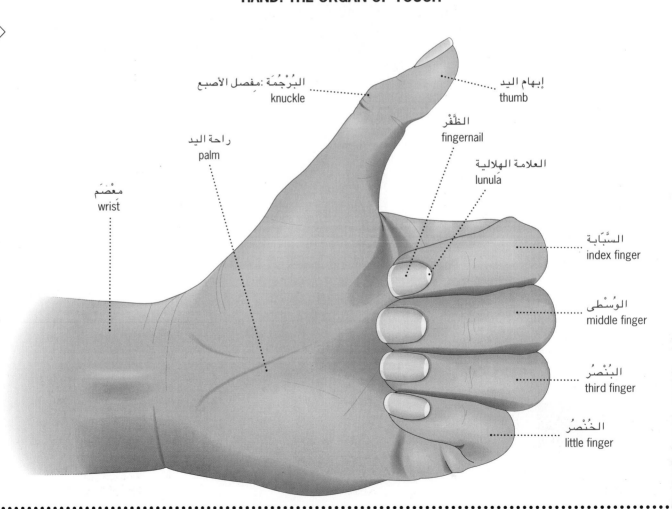

البُرْجُمَة :مِفصل الأصبع
knuckle

إبهام اليد
thumb

الظَّفْر
fingernail

راحة اليد
palm

العلامة الهلالية
lunula

مِعْصَم
wrist

السَّبَّابة
index finger

الوُسْطى
middle finger

البُنْصُر
third finger

الخُنْصُر
little finger

الأذْن :جهاز السَّمْع
EAR: THE ORGAN OF HEARING

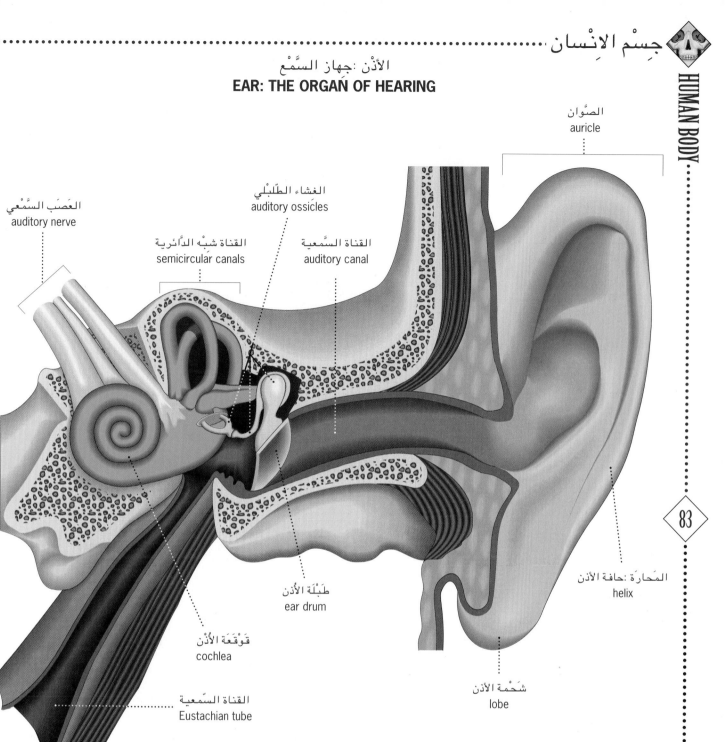

الصَّوان
auricle

العَصَب السَّمْعي
auditory nerve

الغشاء الطَّبْلي
auditory ossicles

القناة شبْه الدَّائرية
semicircular canals

القناة السَّمعية
auditory canal

المَحارة :حافة الأذن
helix

طَبْلَة الأُذن
ear drum

قَوْقَعَة الأُذن
cochlea

القناة السَّمعية
Eustachian tube

شَحْمة الأذن
lobe

أجْزاء الأذْن
PARTS OF THE EAR

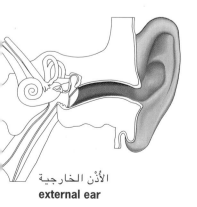

الأذن الخارجية
external ear

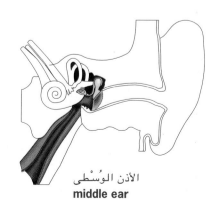

الأذن الوُسْطى
middle ear

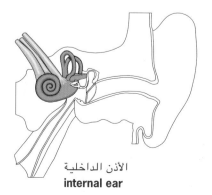

الأذن الداخلية
internal ear

الأنْف :عُضو الشَّمّ
NOSE: THE ORGAN OF SMELL

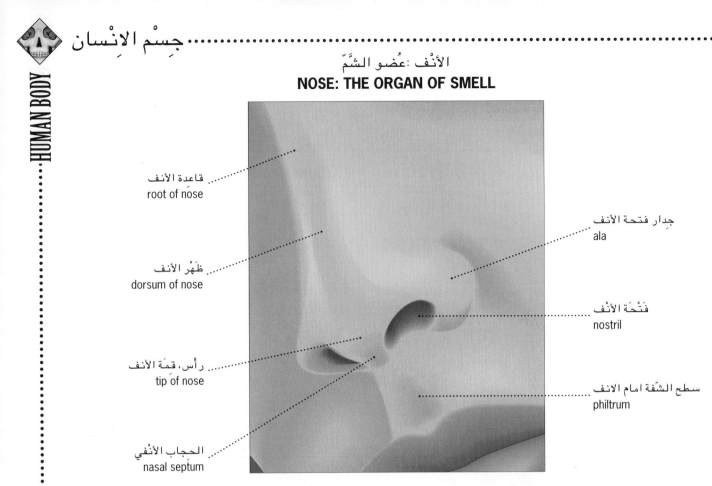

قاعدة الأنف
root of nose

ظَهْر الأنف
dorsum of nose

رأْس، قمَة الأنف
tip of nose

الحِجاب الأنْفي
nasal septum

جِدار فتحة الأنف
ala

فَتْحَة الأنف
nostril

سطح الشّفة امام الانف
philtrum

الفَمّ :عُضو الذَّوْق
MOUTH: THE ORGAN OF TASTE

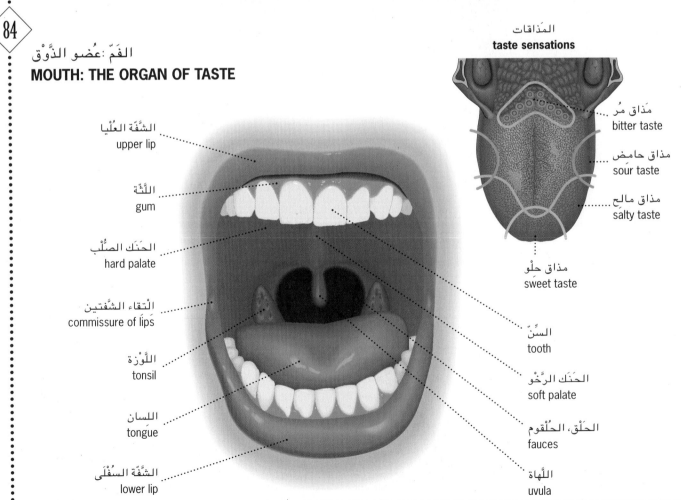

المَذاقات
taste sensations

مَذاق مُر
bitter taste

مذاق حامض
sour taste

مذاق مالح
salty taste

مذاق حلْو
sweet taste

الشَّفة العُلْيا
upper lip

اللَّثَّة
gum

الحَنَك الصُّلْب
hard palate

الْتِقاء الشَّفتين
commissure of lips

اللَّوْزة
tonsil

اللسان
tongue

الشَّفة السُفْلَى
lower lip

السِّنّ
tooth

الحَنَك الرَّخْو
soft palate

الحَلْق، الحُلْقوم
fauces

اللَّهاة
uvula

أسْنان الانْسان
HUMAN DENTURE

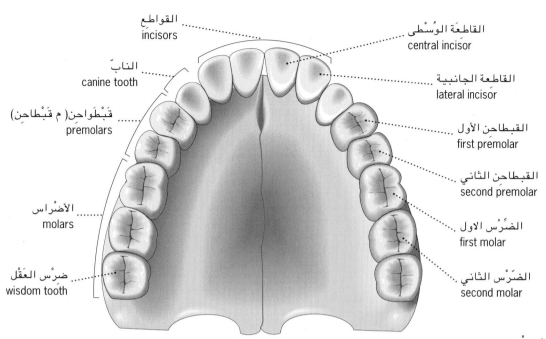

القواطِع
incisors

القاطِعَة الوُسْطى
central incisor

النابّ
canine tooth

القاطِعة الجانبية
lateral incisor

قَبْطَواحِن(م قَبْطاحِن)
premolars

القبطاحِن الأوّل
first premolar

القبطاحِن الثاني
second premolar

الأضْراس
molars

الضِّرْس الأول
first molar

ضِرْس العَقْل
wisdom tooth

الضِّرْس الثاني
second molar

مقْطَع عرْضي لِضِرْس
cross section of a molar

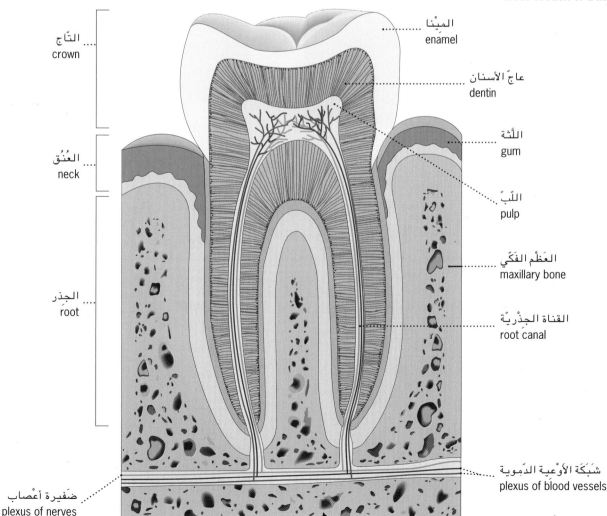

التّاج
crown

المينا
enamel

عاجّ الأسْنان
dentin

العُنُق
neck

اللَّثة
gum

اللّبّ
pulp

الجِذر
root

العَظْم الفَكّي
maxillary bone

القناة الجِذْريّة
root canal

شَبَكَة الأوْعية الدّمویة
plexus of blood vessels

ضَفيرة أعْصاب
plexus of nerves

المِعْمار

منازِل تَقْليديّة
TRADITIONAL HOUSES

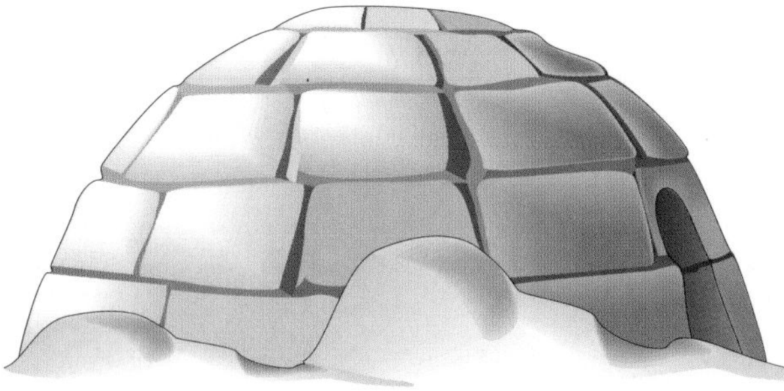

الكُوخ القُبِّي
igloo

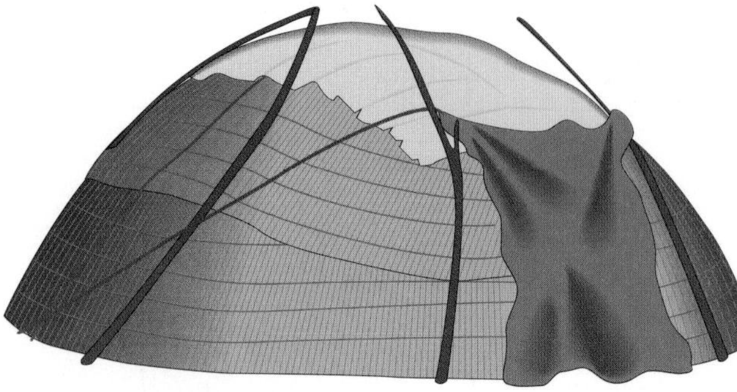

الوَغَم
wigwam

كُوخ من الخَشَب
log cabin

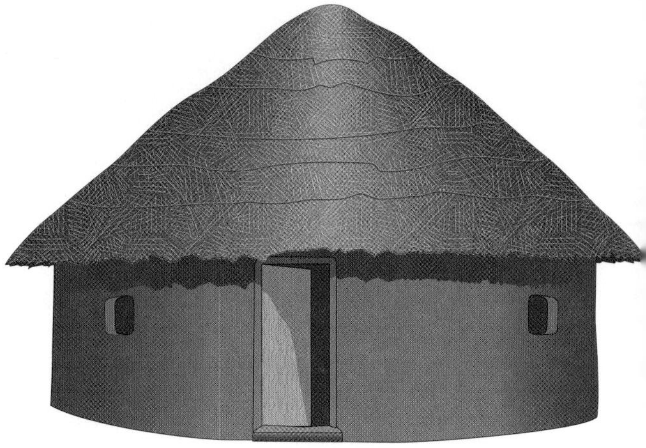

كُوخ من الطِّين
mud hut

بَيْت قائم على ركائز
house on stilts

التِّبية
tepee

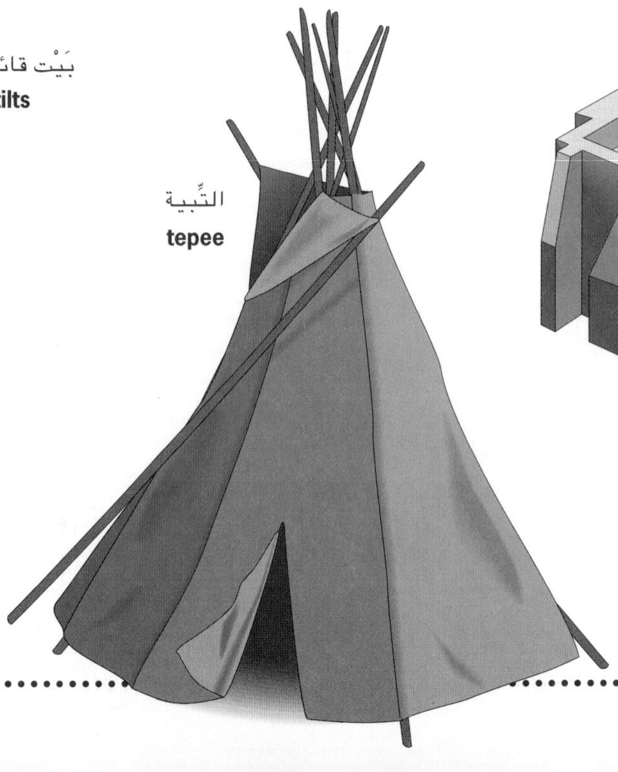

قُطْيّة، كُوخ
hut

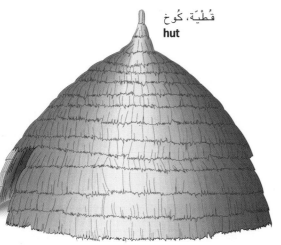

اليُوْرَتَة
yurt

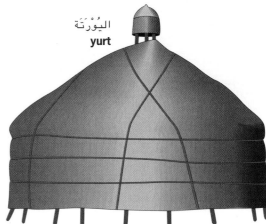

المَسْجِد، الجامِع
MOSQUE

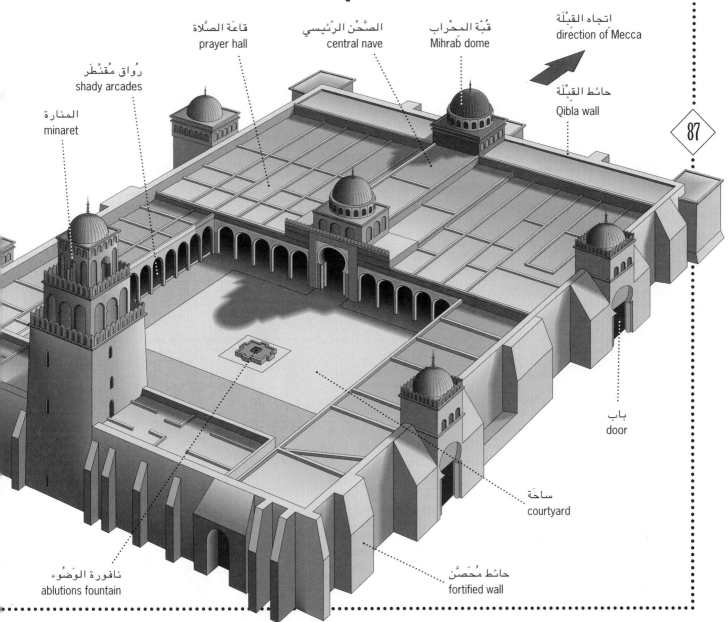

قاعَة الصَّلاة
prayer hall

الصَّحْن الرّئيسي
central nave

قُبّة المحْراب
Mihrab dome

اتجاه القِبْلَة
direction of Mecca

رُواق مُقنْطَر
shady arcades

حائط القِبْلَة
Qibla wall

المنارة
minaret

87

باب
door

ساحَة
courtyard

نافورة الوَضُوء
ablutions fountain

حائط مُحصَّن
fortified wall

المِعْمار

القَلْعَة
CASTLE

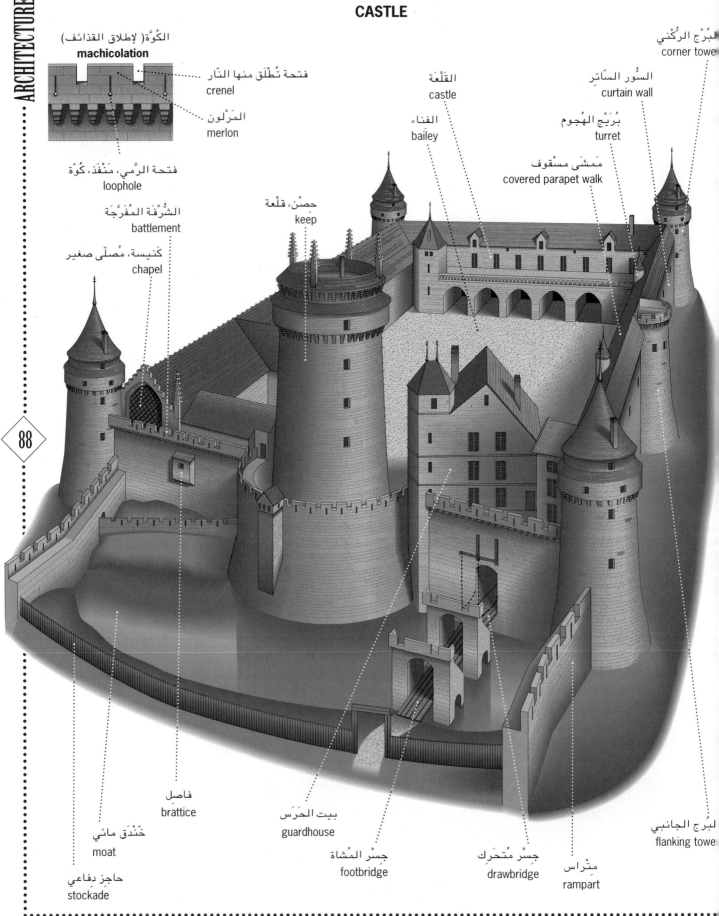

الكُوّة(لإطلاق القذائف)
machicolation

فتحة تُطْلَق منها النّار
crenel

المَرْلون
merlon

فتحة الرَّمي، مَنْفَذ، كُوّة
loophole

الشُّرْفَة المُفَرَّجَة
battlement

كَنيسة، مُصلّى صغير
chapel

حِصْن، قلْعة
keep

القَلْعَة
castle

الفِناء
bailey

لبُرْج الرُكْني
corner tower

السُّور السَّاتِر
curtain wall

بُرَيْج الهُجوم
turret

مَمْشَى مسْقوف
covered parapet walk

فاصِل
brattice

بيت الحَرَس
guardhouse

خَنْدَق مائي
moat

جِسْر المُشاة
footbridge

جسْر مُتَحَرِك
drawbridge

مِتْراس
rampart

لبُرج الجانبي
flanking tower

حاجِز دِفاعي
stockade

88

الكاتدْرائيّة القُوطيّة
GOTHIC CATHEDRAL

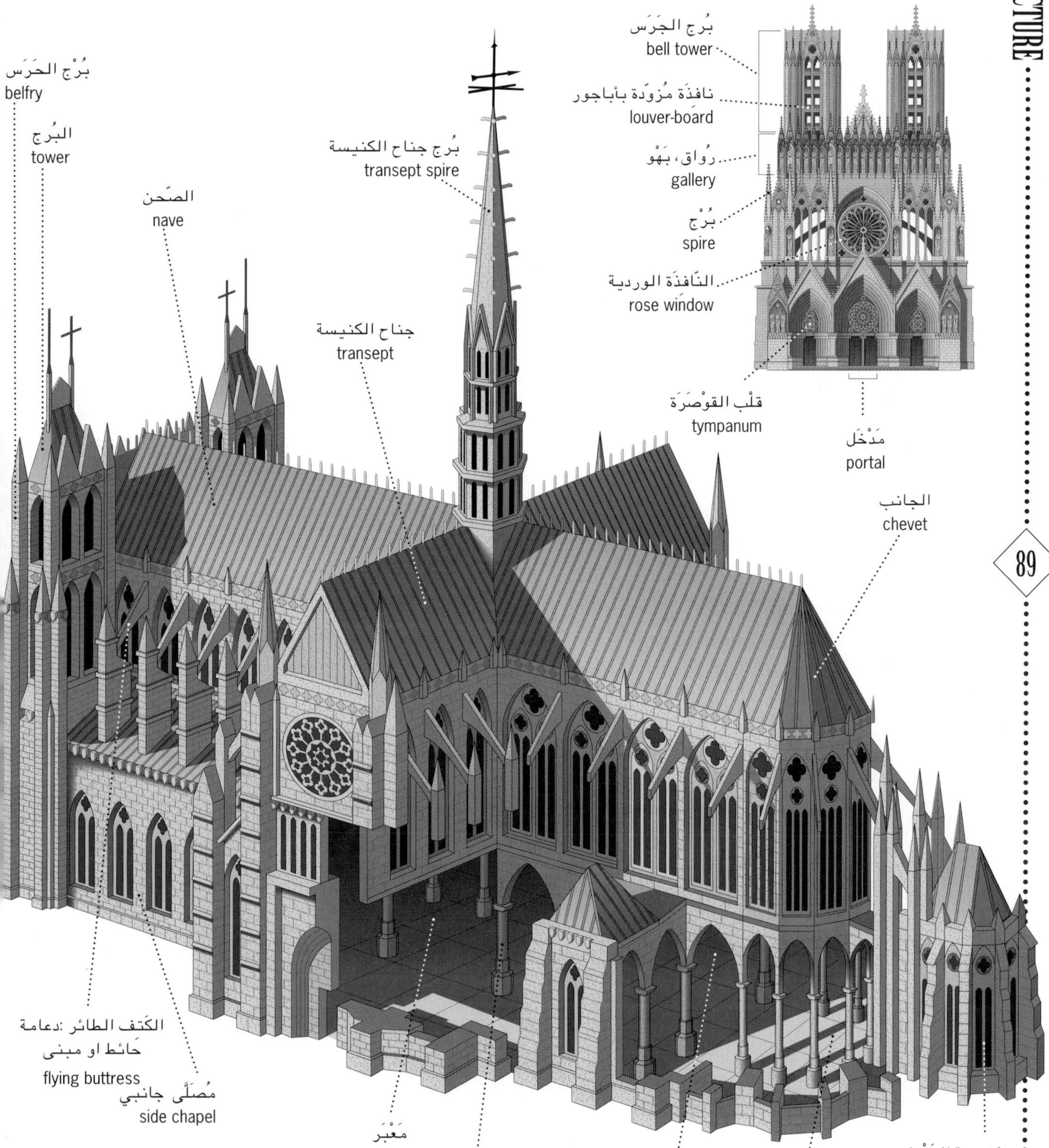

الواجهة
facade

بُرج الجَرَس
bell tower

نافذَة مُزوّدة بأباجور
louver-board

رُواق، بَهْو
gallery

بُرْج
spire

النّافذَة الوردية
rose window

قلْب القوْصَرَة
tympanum

مَدْخَل
portal

الجانب
chevet

بُرْج الحَرَس
belfry

البُرج
tower

الصّحن
nave

بُرج جناح الكنيسة
transept spire

جناح الكنيسة
transept

الكَتف الطائر: دعامة حَائط او مبنى
flying buttress

مُصلَّى جانبي
side chapel

مَعْبَر
crossing

عَمود، دعامَة
pillar

جوقَة المُنْشِدين
choir

ممشَى مسقُوف
ambulatory

كنيسة العَذْراء
Lady chapel

وَسَط المَدينة
DOWNTOWN

ساحَة
square

حَديقة، ساحة
park

كاتِدْرائيّة
cathedral

مَرْكَز الاحْتِفالات
convention center

مَحَطّة قطار
railroad station

بِناية مكاتب
office tower

فَضاء وسيط
median strip

البِلانِتُوريم
planetarium

خطّ سِكّة حديد
railroad

دائرة تنْظيم السَّير(للمشاة والسيارات)
traffic island

الجادّة
boulevard / high street

شارع، طريق
street

مُدرَّج تسليم وتسلُّم البضائع
delivery ramp

الطريق الحُرّة
freeway / dual carriageway

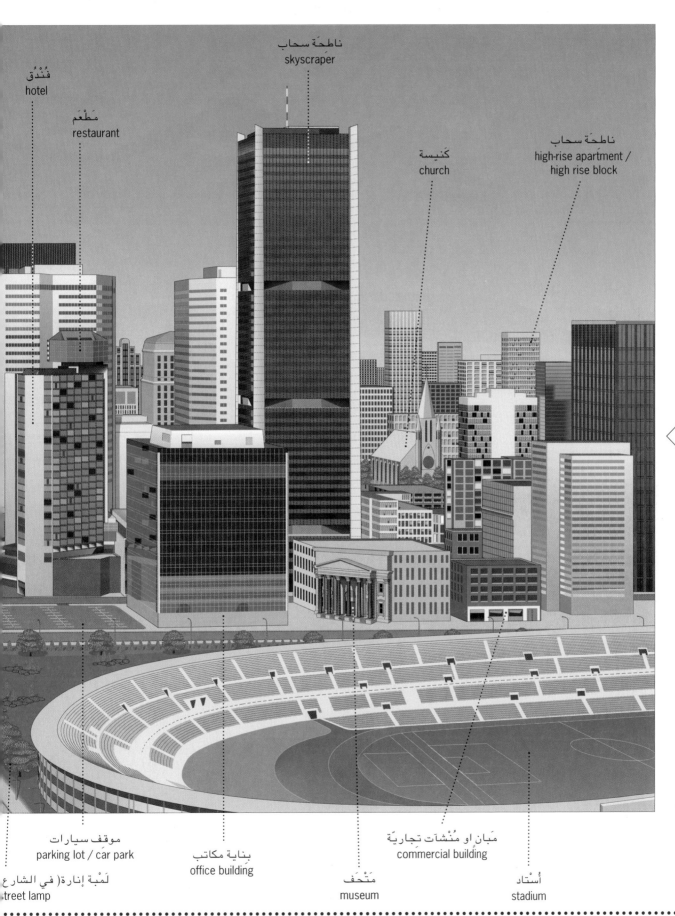

ناطِحَة سحاب
skyscraper

فُنْدُق
hotel

مَطْعَم
restaurant

كَنيسة
church

ناطِحَة سحاب
high-rise apartment /
high rise block

موقف سيارات
parking lot / car park

بِناية مكاتب
office building

مَبان او مُنْشآت تجاريّة
commercial building

أُسْتاد
stadium

لَمْبة إنارة(في الشارع
treet lamp

مَتْحَف
museum

بَيْت، مَنْزِل
HOUSE

البيت من الخارج
exterior of a house

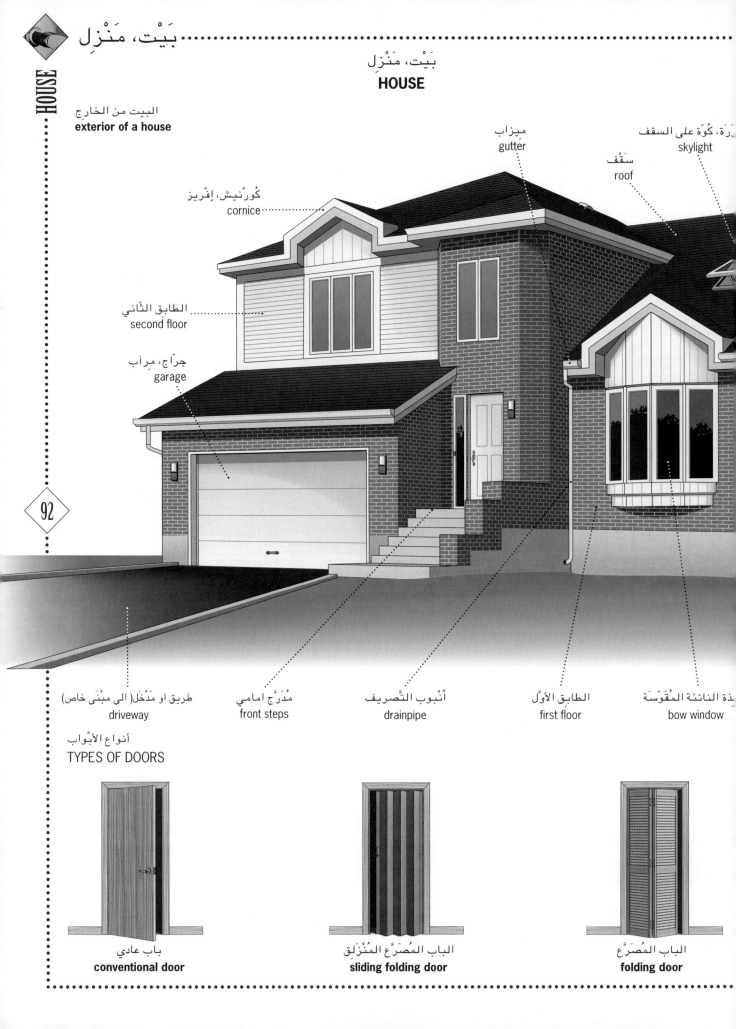

ميزاب
gutter

ـرَة، كُوّة على السقف
skylight

سَقْف
roof

كُورْنيش، إفْريز
cornice

الطابِق الثَّاني
second floor

جرّاج، مِرآب
garage

طريق او مَدْخَل(الى مبنَى خاص)
driveway

مُدَرَّج امامي
front steps

أُنْبوب التَّصْريف
drainpipe

الطابِق الأوَّل
first floor

ـذة النّاتِئة المُقَوَّسَة
bow window

92

أنواع الأبْواب
TYPES OF DOORS

بَاب عادي
conventional door

البَاب المُصَرَّع المُنْزَلِق
sliding folding door

البَاب المُصَرَّع
folding door

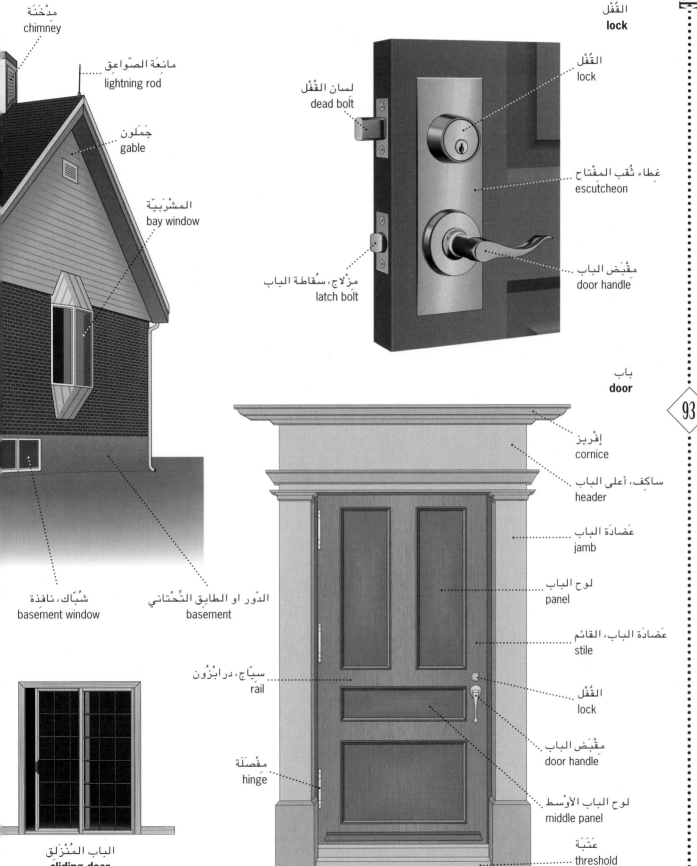

مِدْخَنَة
chimney

مانِعَة الصّواعِق
lightning rod

جَمَلون
gable

المِشْرَبِيَّة
bay window

شُبّاك، نافِذة
basement window

الدّور او الطابِق التَّحْتاني
basement

الباب المُنْزَلِق
sliding door

القُفْل
lock

القُفْل
lock

لِسان القُفْل
dead bolt

غِطاء ثُقب المِفْتاح
escutcheon

مِزْلاج، سُقاطة الباب
latch bolt

مِقْبَض الباب
door handle

باب
door

إِفْريز
cornice

ساكِف، أعلى الباب
header

عَضادَة الباب
jamb

لَوح الباب
panel

عَضادَة الباب، القائِم
stile

القُفْل
lock

مِقْبَض الباب
door handle

لَوح الباب الأَوْسَط
middle panel

عَتَبَة
threshold

سِيّاج، درابْزُون
rail

مِفْصَلَة
hinge

شُبّاك
WINDOW

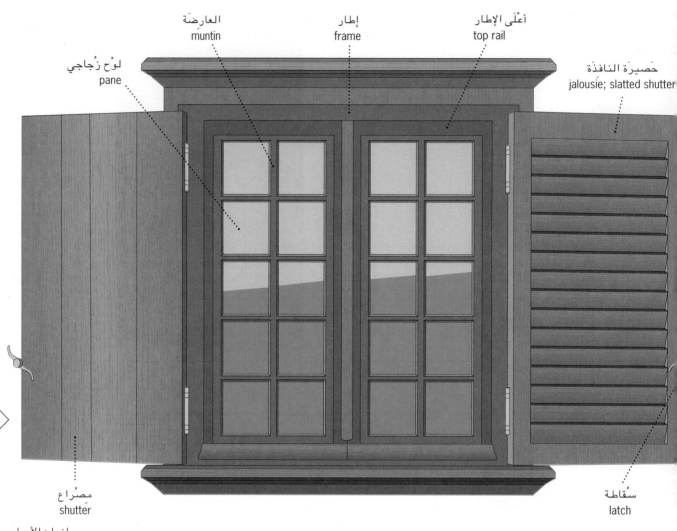

العارِضَة
muntin

إطار
frame

أعْلَى الإطار
top rail

لوْح زُجاجي
pane

حَصيرَة النافِذَة
jalousie; slatted shutter

مِصْراع
shutter

سُقّاطة
latch

انواع الأبواب
TYPES OF WINDOWS

شُبّاك فرنْسي :نافِذة تنْفَتِح كما ينْفَتِح الباب
**casement window
(inward opening)**

شُبّاك انْجليزِي
**casement window
(outward opening)**

شُبّاك أفقي ذو مِحْوَر
horizontal pivoting window

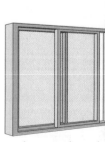

شُبّاك مُنْزَلِج او مُنْزلِق
sliding window

الشُّبّاك المُصَرَّع المُنْزلِق
sliding folding window

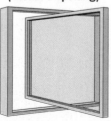

الشُّبّاك الرأسي :المنزلِق صعوداً او هُبوطاً
vertical pivoting window

الشباك المُؤطَر
sash window

نافِذة ذات اباجور
louvred window

سَرير
BED

أجْزاء
parts

اللَّوحة الرَأسيّة :مِسْنَد قائمتيْ السَّرير
headboard

لوح الأقْدام :مِسْنَد قائمتيْ السَّ
footboard

مقبَض
handle

كِيس المخَدّة
pillow protector

حَشْية، مَرْتَبَة
mattress

غِطاء
mattress cover

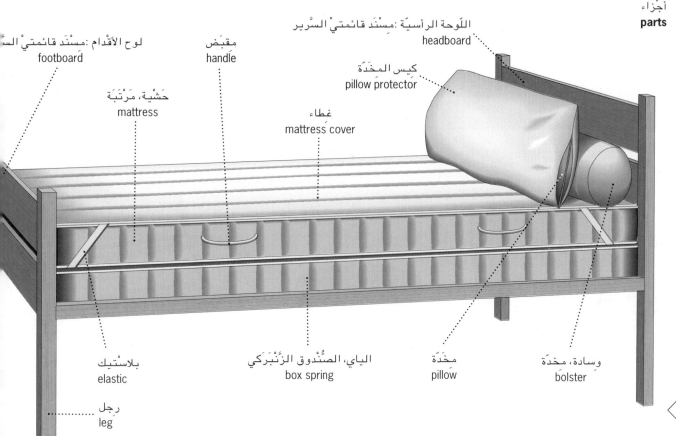

بلاسْتيك
elastic

اليَاي، الصُّنْدوق الزَّنْبَرَكي
box spring

مخَدّة
pillow

وِسادة، مخدّة
bolster

رِجل
leg

95

بياضات :أغْطِيّة السَّرير المَصنوعة من الكِتّان
linen

كِيس وِسادة مُزَخْرَف
sham / flat-border pillowcase

كِيس وِسادة
pillowcase

لِحاف
comforter / eiderdown

بَطانيّة
blanket

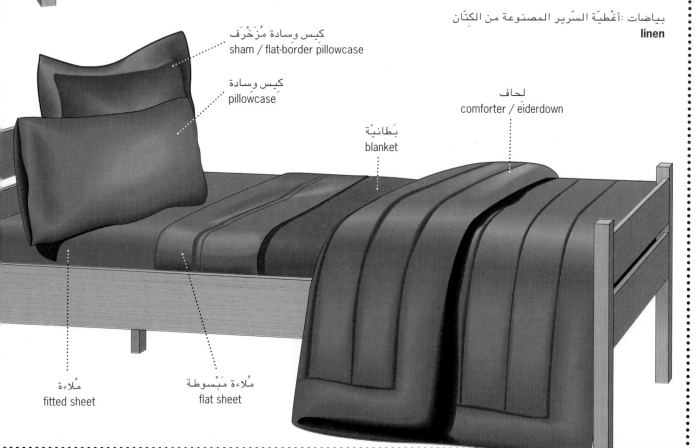

مُلاءة
fitted sheet

مُلاءة مَبْسوطة
flat sheet

مَقاعِد
SEATS

أَرِيكَة
sofa / settee

كُرْسي مُزْدَوَج
loveseat / settee

كرسي ذو ذُراعين
armchair

مَقْعَد، كرسي الأقدام
footstool

دَكَّة، مقعد
bench

كرسي البارات
bar stool

مقعَد
stool

الشِّيزْلُوْنج
chaise longue

كرسي قابِل للطي
folding chair

الكرسي الهَزّاز
rocking chair

الكراسي المُتراصّة
stacking chairs

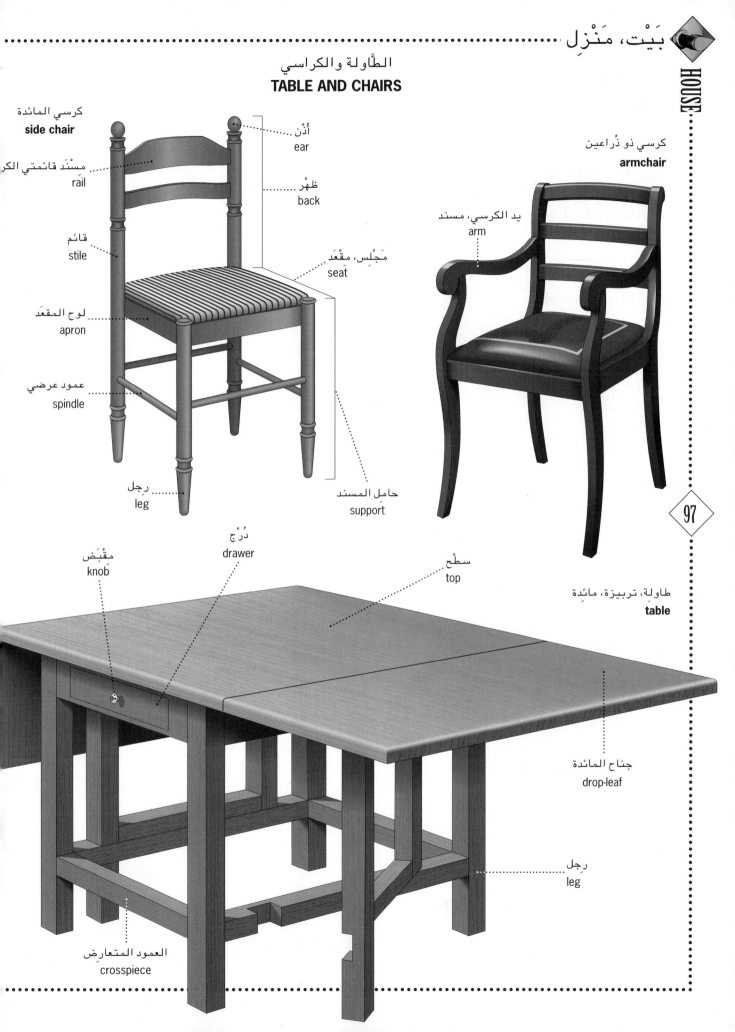

الطَّاولة والكراسي
TABLE AND CHAIRS

كرسي المائدة
side chair

أُذْن
ear

مِسْنَد قائمتي الكر
rail

ظهْر
back

قائم
stile

مَجْلِس، مقْعَد
seat

لوح المقعَد
apron

عمود عرضي
spindle

رِجل
leg

حامل المسند
support

كرسي ذو ذُراعين
armchair

يد الكرسي، مسند
arm

97

طاولة، تربيزة، مائدة
table

دُرْج
drawer

مقْبَض
knob

سطْح
top

جناح المائدة
drop-leaf

رِجل
leg

العمود المتعارِض
crosspiece

أضواء، أنْوار، مصابيح
LIGHTS

كَشَّاف
track lighting

خطّ انْطلاق، مَسْلك
track

مُحَوِّل
transformer

لمبة توضع على الأرْض
floor lamp

النُّور المُثبت على السقف
ceiling fixture

لمْبة الطَّاولة
table lamp

كُمَّة، ظلَّة
shade

اللمبة المعلَّقة
hanging pendant

حامل
stand

النُّور المُثبت على الحائط
wall fixture

إضاءة، إنارة
LIGHTING

لمبة وهّاجة
incandescent lamp

غاز خامل
inert gas

سُليك مُضيّ
filament

سلك كهربائي
lead-in wire

قاعدة
base

نُقْطَة التوصيل
contact

اللمبة التُنْجسْتِينية الهلوقنية
tungsten-halogen lamp

بروس، دَبوس
pin

قاعدة
base

مِصْباح، لمبة
bulb

قاعدة لولبية
screw base

قاعدة تشبه الحربة
bayonet base

المصباح الفَلوري، المُسْتَشْعِع
fluorescent tube

قاعدة البروس
pin base

غاز
gas

الغطاء الفسفوري، الوامض
phosphorescent coating

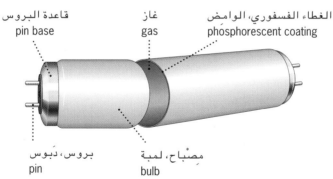

بروس، دَبوس
pin

بروس، دَبوس
pin

مِصْباح، لمبة
bulb

المصباح الاقْتِصادي(موفِّر للاستهلاك الكهربي)
energy saving bulb

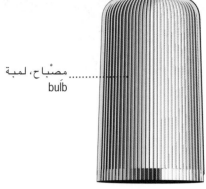

مصْباح، لمبة
bulb

المصباح المضئ، الانبوب المضئ
fluorescent tube

صُندوق، حاوية
housing

قاعدة
base

قابِس اوروبي
European plug

بروس، دَبوس
cover

بروس، دَبوس
pin

قابِس امريكي
American plug

بروس، دَبوس
pin

أرضي
grounding terminal

مفتاح
switch

منفذ، بريزة
outlet

99

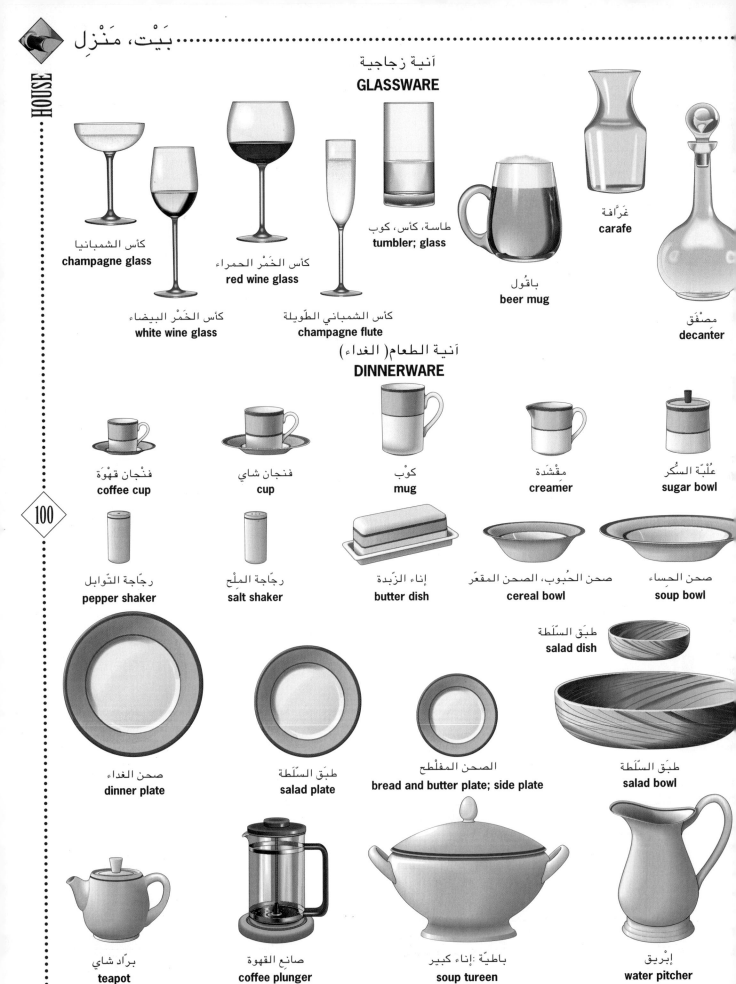

آنية زجاجية
GLASSWARE

كَأس الشمبانيا
champagne glass

كأس الخَمْر البيضاء
white wine glass

كأس الخَمْر الحمراء
red wine glass

كأس الشمباني الطّويلة
champagne flute

طاسة، كَأس، كوب
tumbler; glass

باقُول
beer mug

غَرَّافة
carafe

مصْفَق
decanter

آنية الطعام (الغداء)
DINNERWARE

فنْجان قهْوَة
coffee cup

فنْجان شاي
cup

كوْب
mug

مقْشَدة
creamer

عُلْبة السُكَّر
sugar bowl

رجَّاجة التَّوابل
pepper shaker

رجَّاجة المِلْح
salt shaker

إناء الزّبدة
butter dish

صحن الحُبُوب، الصحن المقعَّر
cereal bowl

صحن الحساء
soup bowl

طبَق السّلَطة
salad dish

صحن الغداء
dinner plate

طبَق السّلَطة
salad plate

الصحن المفلْطح
bread and butter plate; side plate

طبَق السّلَطة
salad bowl

برَّاد شاي
teapot

صانع القهوة
coffee plunger

باطيّة :إناء كبير
soup tureen

إبريق
water pitcher

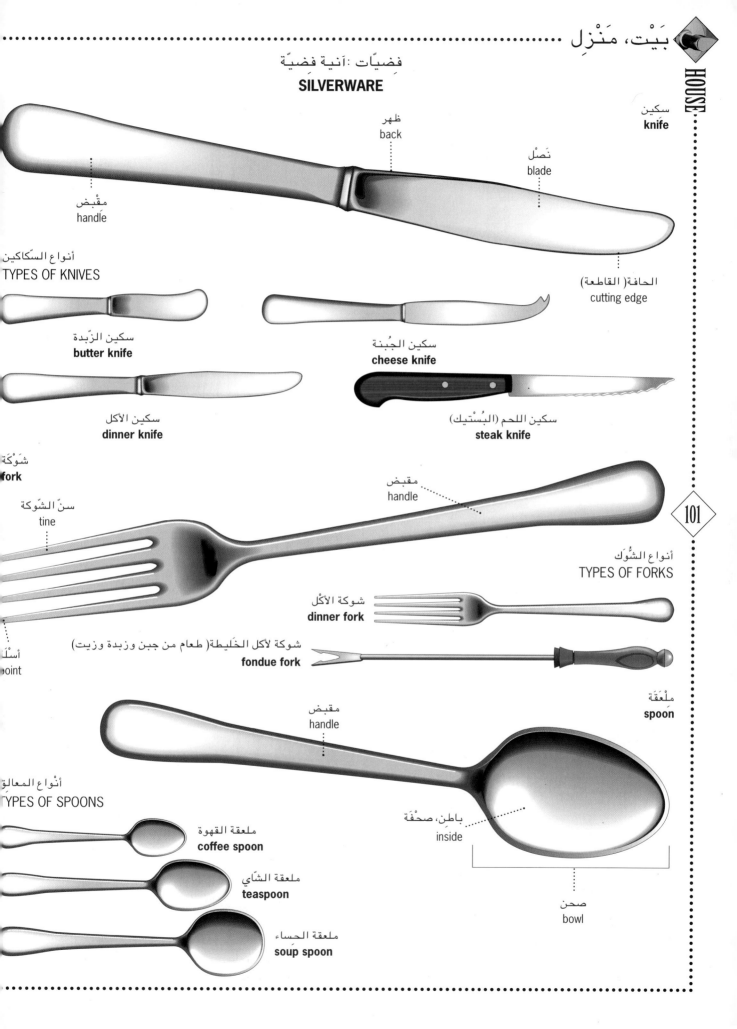

فِضيّات: آنية فِضيّة
SILVERWARE

سكّين
knife

ظهر
back

نَصْل
blade

مِقْبض
handle

الحافة (القاطعة)
cutting edge

أنواع السّكاكين
TYPES OF KNIVES

سكّين الزّبدة
butter knife

سكّين الجُبنة
cheese knife

سكّين الأكل
dinner knife

سكّين اللحم (البُسْتيك)
steak knife

شَوْكَة
fork

سنّ الشّوكة
tine

مِقبض
handle

أسْنا
point

أنواع الشُّوَك
TYPES OF FORKS

شوكة الأكّل
dinner fork

شوكة لأكل الخَليطة (طعام من جبن وزبدة وزيت)
fondue fork

مِلْعَقَة
spoon

مِقبض
handle

أنْواع المعالق
TYPES OF SPOONS

باطِن، صحْفَة
inside

صحن
bowl

ملعقة القهوة
coffee spoon

ملعقة الشّاي
teaspoon

ملعقة الحساء
soup spoon

101

بَيْت، مَنْزِل

أدوات المَطْبَخ
KITCHEN UTENSILS

مِغْرَفَة
ladle

هرّاسَة البطاطس
potato masher

ملعقة الصيدلاني
spatula

مِخْفَقَة
whisk

مِخْفَقَة، خفاقة البيض
egg beater

ملاعق القياس
measuring spoons

كسّارة البُنْدُق
nutcracker

المِبرام
lever corkscrew

مِفتاح الزُّجاجات
bottle opener

مِقْشَرَة
peeler

شُوْبَك
rolling pin

مفتاح العُلَب
can opener

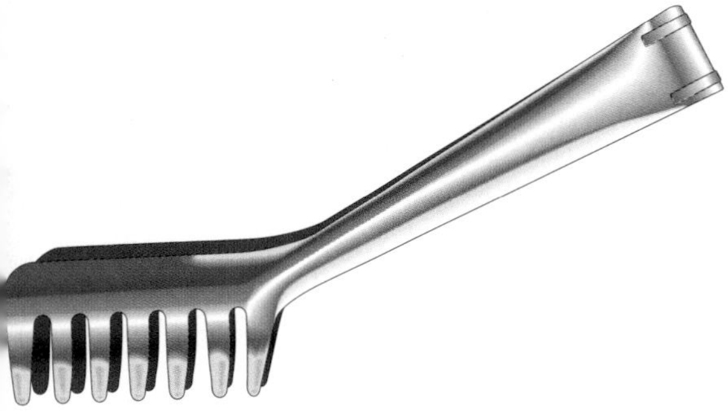

ملْقاط
spaghetti tongs

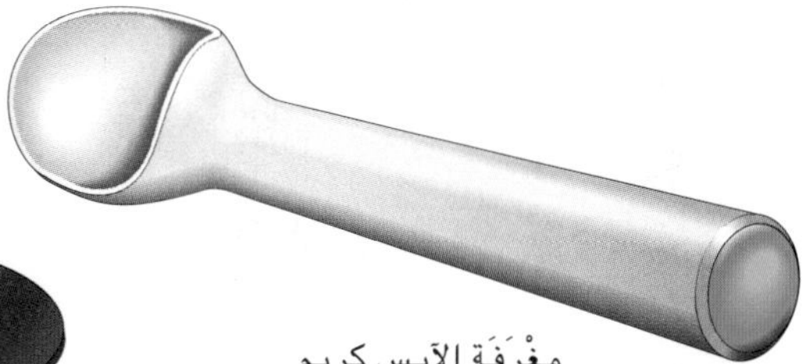

مغْرَفَة الآيس كريم
ice–cream scoop

قمْع
funnel

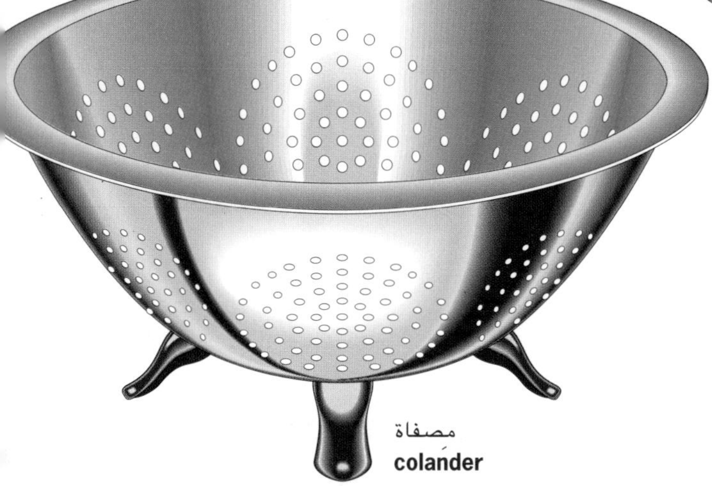

مصفاة
colander

عصّارة الليمون
lemon squeezer

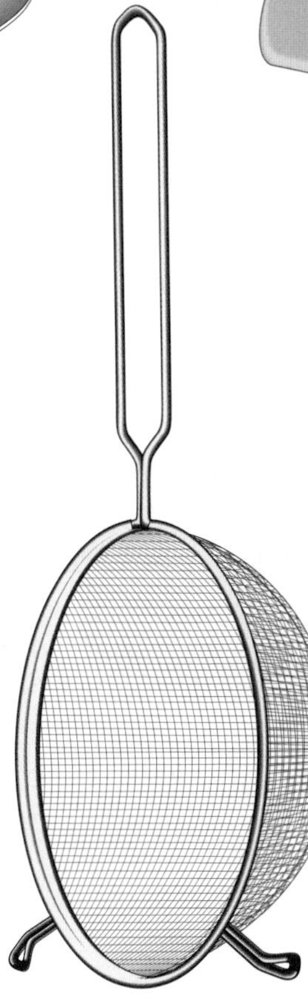

حافظ السلطة
salad spinner

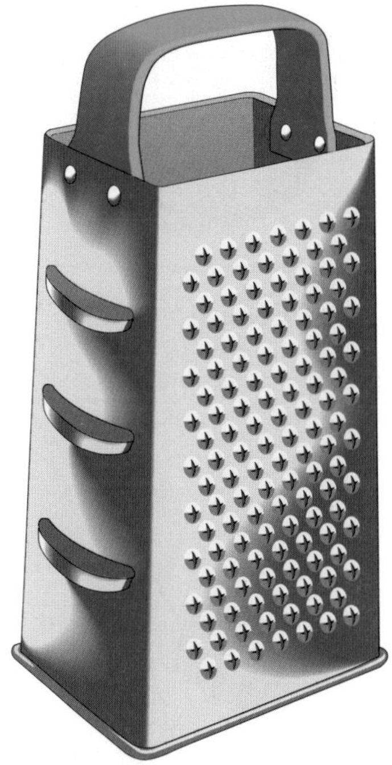

مصفاة، راووق
strainer

مقْشرة
grater

آنِيات الطّبْخ
COOKING UTENSILS

مِقلاة
sauté pan

مِقلاة
frying pan

جِهاز المُذوَّبَة
fondue set

كِسْرولة، طُنْجَرَة
stockpot; casserole

الوُك
wok

قِدْر المذوَّبَة
fondue pot

مَوْقِد
burner

سخّان مزدوج
double boiler

طُنْجَرَة الخُضَر
vegetable steamer

طُنْجَرَة
saucepan

آنِيات التَّحْمير
او الشّيّ
roasting pans

طابِخ الضّغْط
pressure cooker

صِمام الامان
safety valve

مُنَظِّم الضغط
pressure regulator

104

أَجْهِزَة المطبخ
KITCHEN APPLIANCES

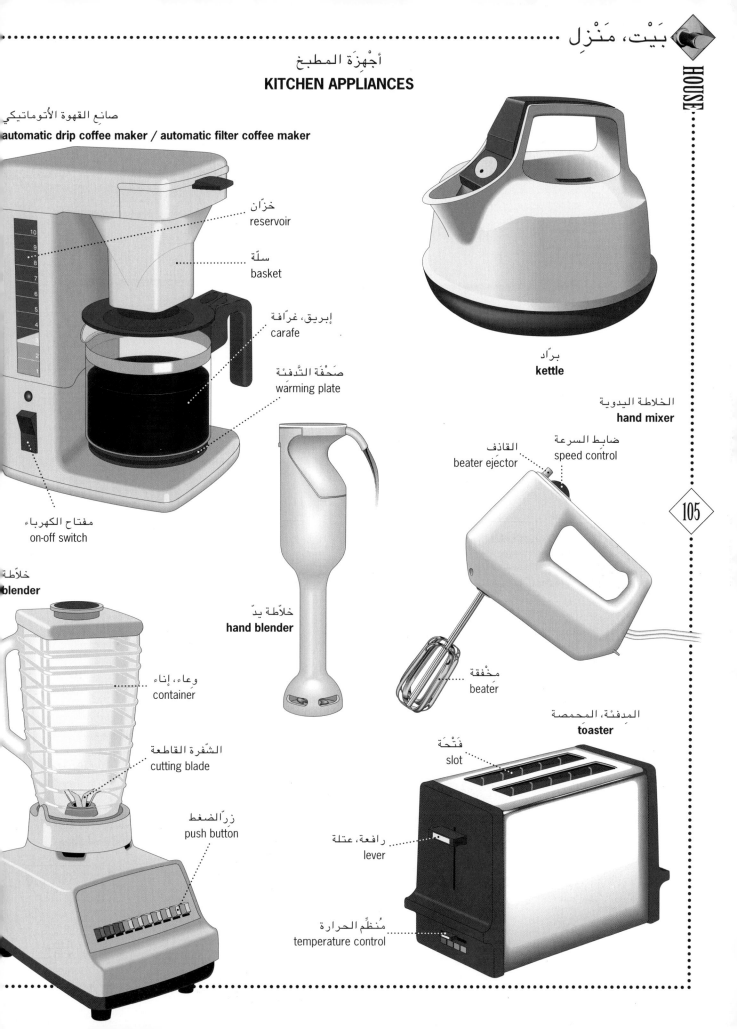

صانِع القهوة الأُتوماتيكي
automatic drip coffee maker / automatic filter coffee maker

خزّان
reservoir

سلّة
basket

إبريق، غرَافة
carafe

صَحْفَة التَّدفِئة
warming plate

مفتاح الكهرباء
on-off switch

برّاد
kettle

الخلاطة اليدوية
hand mixer

القاذف
beater ejector

ضابِط السرعة
speed control

مِخْفَقة
beater

خلّاطة
blender

خلّاطة يدّ
hand blender

وعاء، إناء
container

الشّفرة القاطعة
cutting blade

زرّ الضغط
push button

المدِفئة، المحمصة
toaster

فَتْحَة
slot

رافِعة، عتلة
lever

مُنظِّم الحرارة
temperature control

105

ثلاّجَة
REFRIGERATOR

حافظة الواح الثَّلْج
ice cube tray

المُجمِّدة
freezer compartment

مضْبِط الثَّرموستات
thermostat control

حافظة البيض
egg tray

خزانة مُنْتَجات الألْبان
dairy compartment

خِرانة الزِّبْدة
butter compartment

طَسْت الخضروات
crisper

المُثَلَّجَة
refrigerator compartment

حاجِز واقٍ
guard rail

جزانة اللحوم
meat tray

غِطاء زُجاجي
glass cover

رفّ
shelf

باب الثلاّجة
storage door

HOUSE

أَجْهِزة الطّبْخ
COOKING APPLIANCES

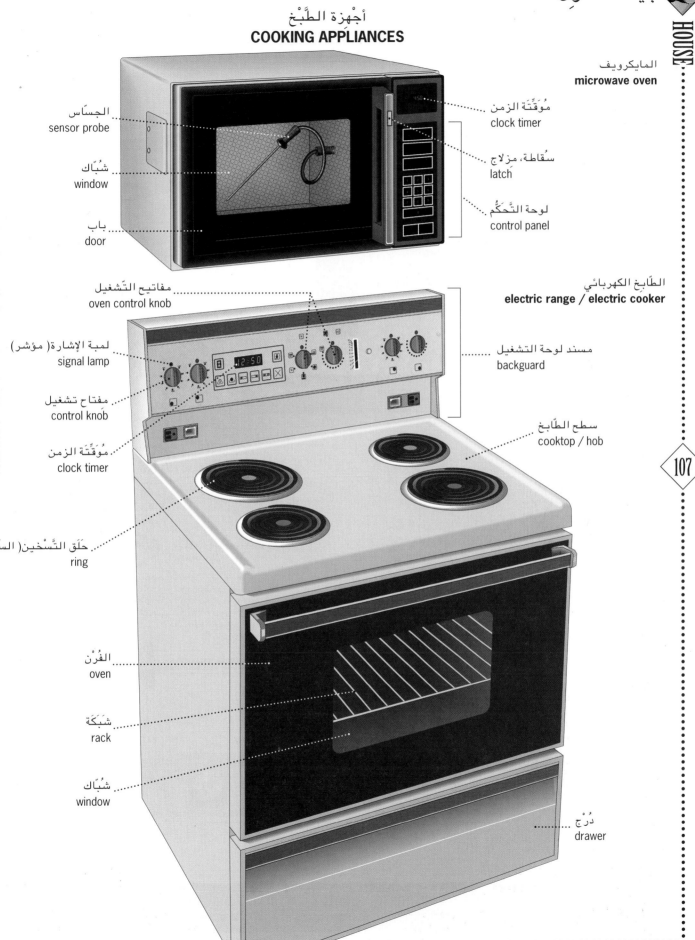

المايكرويف
microwave oven

الجسّاس
sensor probe

شُبّاك
window

باب
door

مُوَقِّتَة الزمن
clock timer

سُقاطة، مزلاج
latch

لوحة التَّحَكُّم
control panel

الطّابخ الكهربائي
electric range / electric cooker

مفاتيح التّشغيل
oven control knob

لمبة الإشارة(مؤشر)
signal lamp

مفتاح تشغيل
control knob

مُوَقِّتَة الزمن
clock timer

مسند لوحة التشغيل
backguard

سطح الطّابخ
cooktop / hob

حَلَق التَّسْخين(السّ
ring

107

الفُرْن
oven

شَبَكَة
rack

شُبّاك
window

دُرْج
drawer

أدوات النِّجارة
CARPENTRY TOOLS

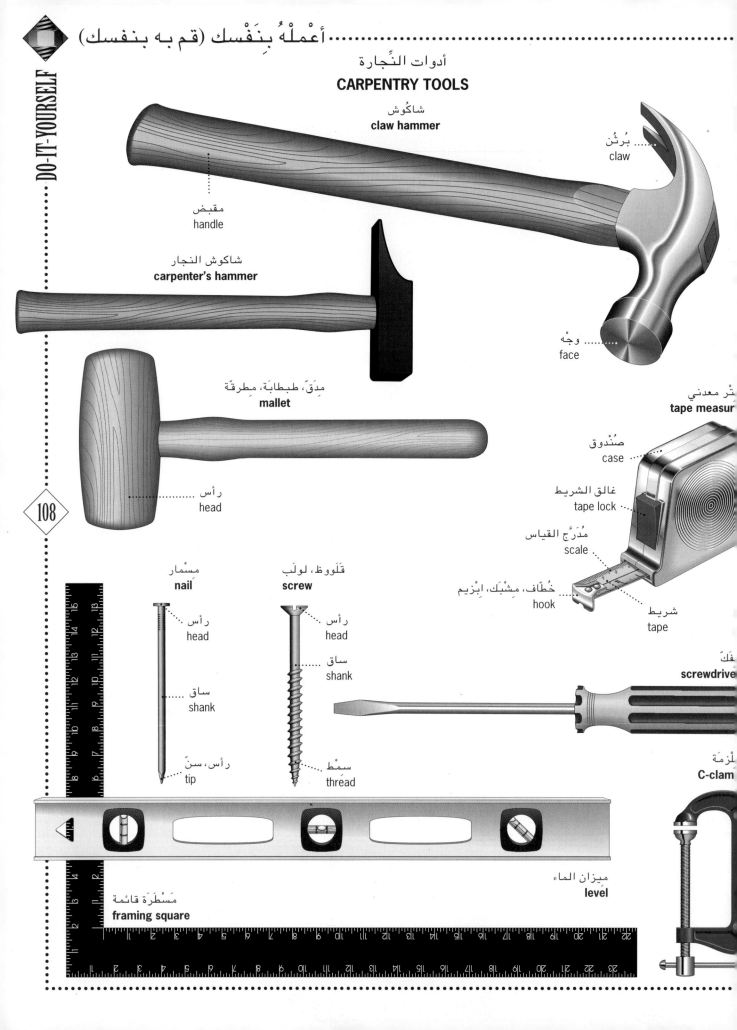

شاكُوش
claw hammer

بُرْثُن
claw

مقبض
handle

شاكوش النجار
carpenter's hammer

وجْه
face

مِدَقّ، طبطابَة، مِطرقّة
mallet

رأْس معدني
tape measur

صُنْدوق
case

غالِق الشريط
tape lock

مُدَرَّج القياس
scale

خُطَّاف، مِشْبَك، ابْزيم
hook

شريط
tape

رأْس
head

مسْمار
nail

ق﮹لَووظ، لولَب
screw

رأْس
head

ساق
shank

ساق
shank

فَكّ
screwdrive

رأْس، سنّ
tip

سمْط
thread

مِلزَمَة
C-clam

ميزان الماء
level

مَسطَرَة قائمة
framing square

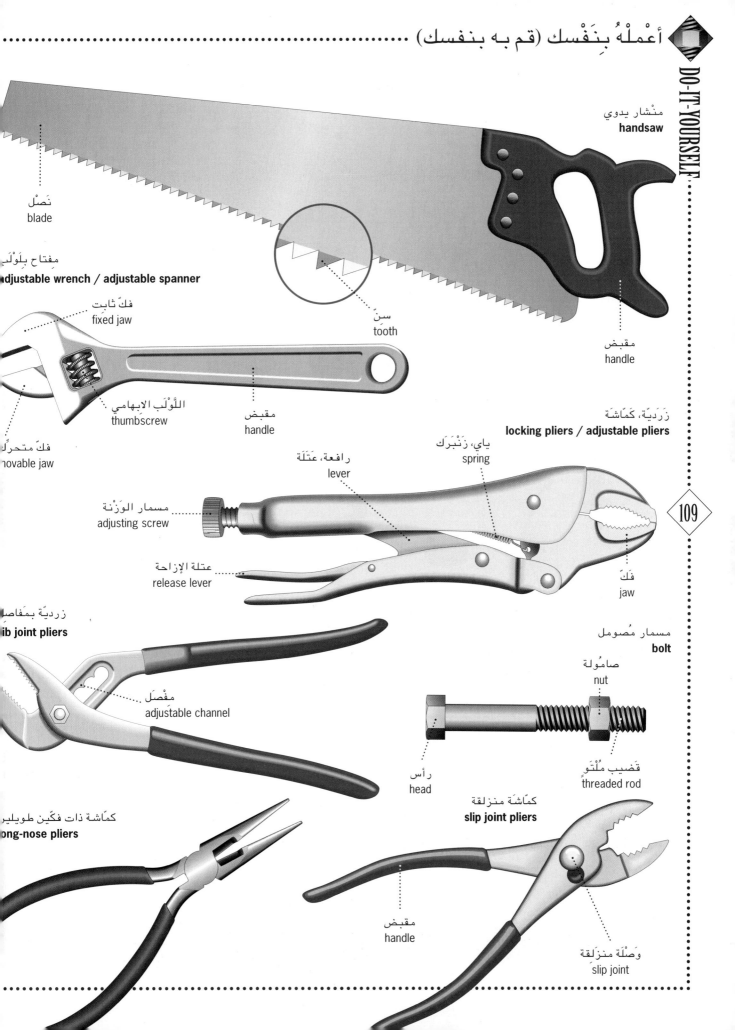

منشار يدوي
handsaw

نَصْل
blade

مِفْتاح بِلَوْلَب
djustable wrench / adjustable spanner

فكّ ثابِت
fixed jaw

سِنّ
tooth

مقبض
handle

اللَّوْلَب الابهامي
thumbscrew

مقبض
handle

فكّ متحرّك
novable jaw

زَرَدِيَّة، كَمَّاشَة
locking pliers / adjustable pliers

رافعة، عَتَلَة
lever

ياي، زَنْبَرَك
spring

مسمار الوَزْنة
adjusting screw

عتلة الإزاحة
release lever

فَكّ
jaw

109

زرديَّة بمَفاصِل
ib joint pliers

مفْصَل
adjustable channel

مسمار مُصومل
bolt

صامُولة
nut

رأس
head

قَضيب مُلْتَوٍ
threaded rod

كمّاشة ذات فكّين طويليـ
ong-nose pliers

كمّاشَة منزلقة
slip joint pliers

مقبض
handle

وَصْلَة منزَلقة
slip joint

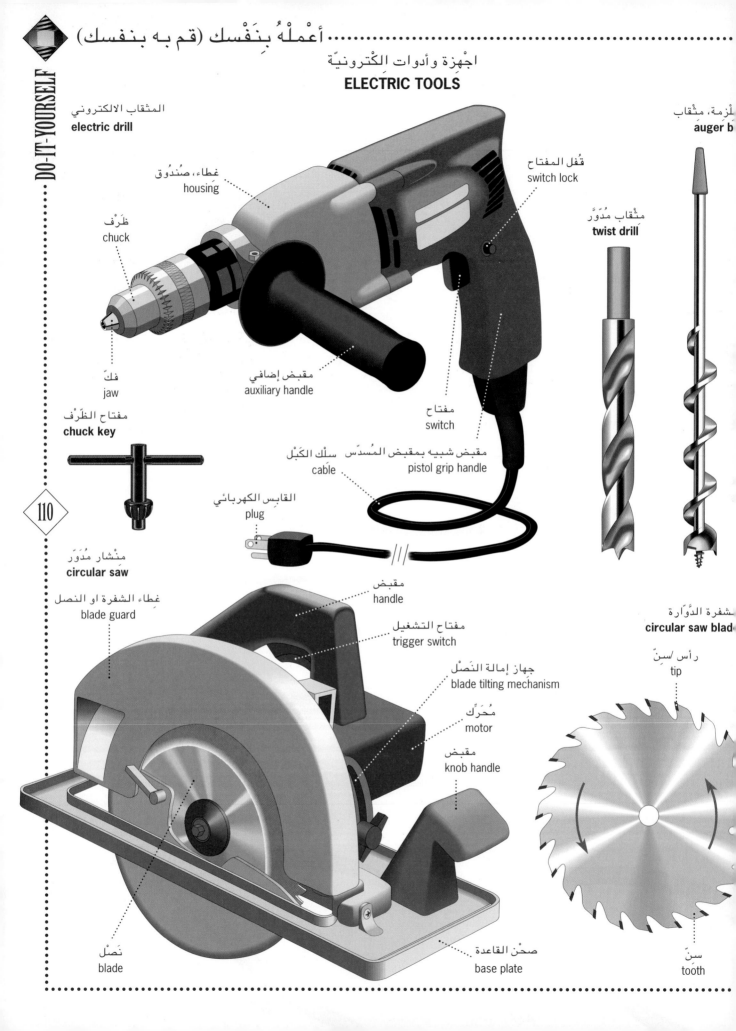
اجْهِزة وأَدوات الكْترونِيّة
ELECTRIC TOOLS

المثقاب الالكتروني
electric drill

غطاء، صُندُوق
housing

قُفل المفتاح
switch lock

ظَرْف
chuck

فكّ
jaw

مقبض إضافي
auxiliary handle

مفتاح
switch

مفتاح الظَّرْف
chuck key

مقبض شبيه بمقبض المُسدّس
pistol grip handle

سلْك الكَبْل
cable

القابِس الكهربائي
plug

لُزمة، مثْقاب
auger b

مثْقاب مُدَوَّر
twist drill

مِنْشار مُدَوَّر
circular saw

غِطاء الشفرة او النصل
blade guard

مقبض
handle

مفتاح التشغيل
trigger switch

جهاز إمالة النَصْل
blade tilting mechanism

مُحَرِّك
motor

مقبض
knob handle

نَصْل
blade

صحْن القاعدة
base plate

شفرة الدَّوَّارة
circular saw blad

رأس /سِنّ
tip

سِنّ
tooth

أدوات الطِّلاء
PAINTING UPKEEP

دحْرُوجة الطِّلاء
paint roller

صِينِيَّة
tray

كاشطة
scraper

نصْل
blade

السُّلَّم المُمَطَّ
extension ladder

هَيْكَل الدَّحْروجة
roller frame

فرْشاة
brush

مقبض
handle

غطاء الدَّحْروجة
roller cover

هُلْب الفرشاة
bristles

السِّيبِيَّة
stepladder

أحَد عمودي السلم
side rail

بكْرَة
pulley

أداة كابِحَة
locking device

111

دَرَجَة(من درجات السلم)
rung

سُلَّم ذو مِنَصَّة
platform ladder

حَبْل الرَّفْع والإنْزال
hoisting rope

مِسْنَد كابِح
anti-slip shoe

ملابِس رِجاليّة
MEN'S CLOTHING

قَميص
shirt

ياقَة
collar

طرَف الياقة
collar point

فتحة القميص
placket

جَيْب امامي
breast pocket

حمالة البنطلون
suspenders / brace

بكُرَة منزَلِقَة
adjustment slide

واجِهَة
front

زرارة، عُرْوَة
button loop

بكلَة حمالة البنطلون
suspender clip

طَيَّة، ثْنيَّة
cuff

زِرارة
button

حلقة النهاية(الجلدية)
leather end

طرف القميص
shirttail

رَبْطَة عنق
tie

وَزْرَة خلْفيَّة
rear apron

وَزْرَة عنق
neck end

أُنْشُوطة
loop

وَزْرَة أَماميَّة
front apron

رداء، بنطلون
pants / trousers

حزام الصلب
waistband

جيْب
pocket

لسان لتغطية ازرار الرِّداء
fly

حِزام
belt

إطار
frame

خُرم، ثُقْب
punch hole

خطّ(على حافة رجل الرِّداء)
crease

حامل الحزام
belt carrier

لسان
tongue

قميص داخلي
tank top; undershirt / vest

رداء
boxer shorts

مايوه
briefs

لِسان لتغطية ازرار الرِّداء
fly

مُتْشعَب
crotch

حزام الصلب
waistband

طيَّة
cuff

جاكيت مُزدوج الصَّدر
double-breasted jacket

ياقَة
collar

تبْطين
lining

الجيب المُسَيَّر
breast welt pocket

كُمّ
sleeve

جيب تحْتي
concealed pocket

غطاء الجيب، حاشية
flap

الجيب المُثبّت بالخياطة
patch pocket

الدَّفيل :سترْة من الصُّوف
duffle coat

غطاء الرأس والعنق
hood

عُرْوَة
frog

جَديلة زِرّارة
toggle fastening

قَلَنْسَوة، قاووق
cap

تاج
crown

حاشية مُسْتَدقَّة
peak

قلنْسَوة مخروطيَّة الشَّكْل
stocking cap / bobble hat

قلنسوة الصَّيد
hunting cap

غطاء الأذن
ear flap

جاكيت
jacket

كَبْسُولة
snap fastener

حِزام الوسط البلاستيكي
elastic waistband

سترَة قصيرة
windbreaker

حِزام الصلب
waistband

تكَّة
drawstring

WOMEN'S CLOTHING
ملابس نسائيّة

البلاكلافا: طاقية تُغطي الرأس
والأذنين معاً
balaclava

حاشية
peak

التُّوكَة
toque

قُبُّعَة محْبُوكَة
knitted hat

البِيريه
beret

بَدْلَة، طقْم
suit

جاكيت، سِترَة
jacket

بلَوزة
blouse

جاكيت مُزدوج الصّدر
double-breasted jacket

تَنُّورة
skirt

فُسْتان
dress

مِعْطَف
overcoat

البُنْش
poncho

114

جِينز
jeans

سِرْوال التَّزَلُّج
ski pants

شورت :سروال تحتي صغير
shorts

شورت برمودا
Bermuda shorts

عُصابة القَدَم
footstrap

تَنُّورة غير مُحَزَّزَة
straight skirt

كُوْلوت
culottes

تنُّورة ذات اطواق او ثنيات
pleated skirt

ملابِس نسائيّة
WOMEN'S CLOTHING

بيجاما
pajamas

صُديرية
bra

... سير الكَتِف
shoulder strap

كأس ....
cup

سروال
pants / briefs

تنُّورة داخلية
half-slip / waist slip

بُرْنس حمّام
bathrobe / dressing gown

السِّتْرات المُعرِّقَة (من الصوف غالباً)
SWEATERS

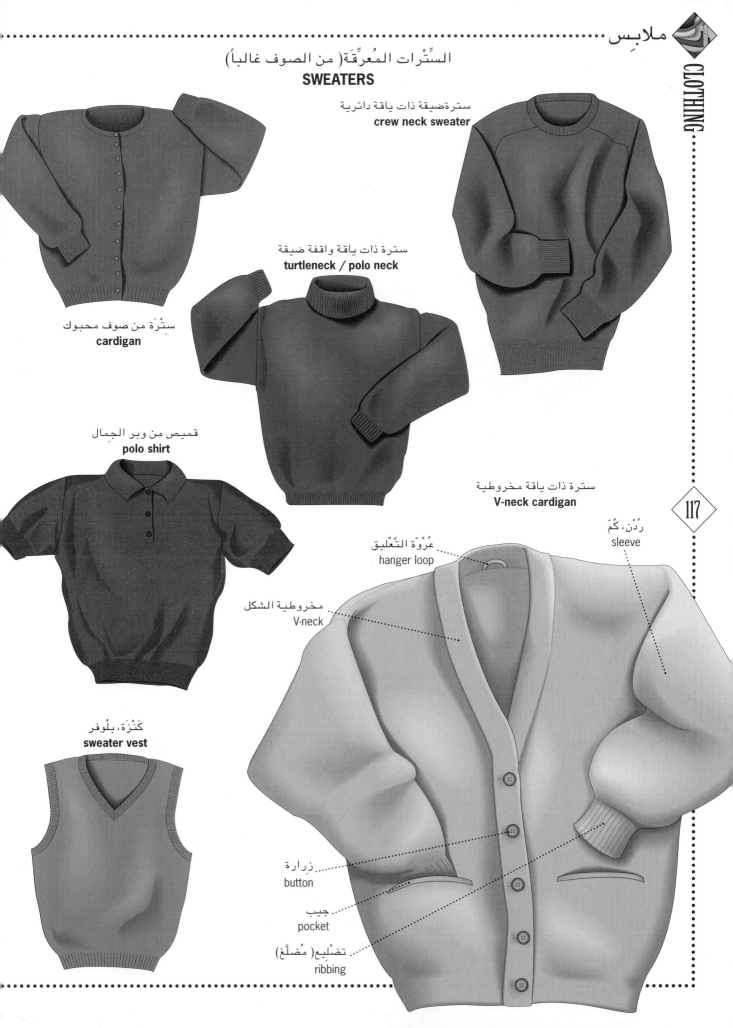

ستْرَة من صوف محبوك
cardigan

سترة ضيقة ذات ياقة دائرية
crew neck sweater

سترة ذات ياقة واقفة ضيقة
turtleneck / polo neck

قميص من وبر الجمال
polo shirt

سترة ذات ياقة مخروطية
V-neck cardigan

عُرْوَة التَّعْليق
hanger loop

مخروطية الشكل
V-neck

رُدْن، كُمّ
sleeve

كَنْزَة، بلُوفر
sweater vest

زِرارة
button

جيب
pocket

تضْليع (مُضلّع)
ribbing

القَفازات والجَوارب
GLOVES AND STOCKINGS

قفازات
gloves

جَوْرَب
sock

أُصبَع القفاز
glove finger

إبْهام
thumb

راحة
palm

كَبْسُولة
snap fastener

دَرْز، تطريز
stitching

الطَرَف المُضَلَّع
ribbed top

رِجل
leg

مشْط القدم
instep

كَعْب، عَقِب
heel

باطِن القدم، أخْمَص
sole

أُصيَع
toe

قفازات للسِّواقة
driving glove

قفاز
mitten

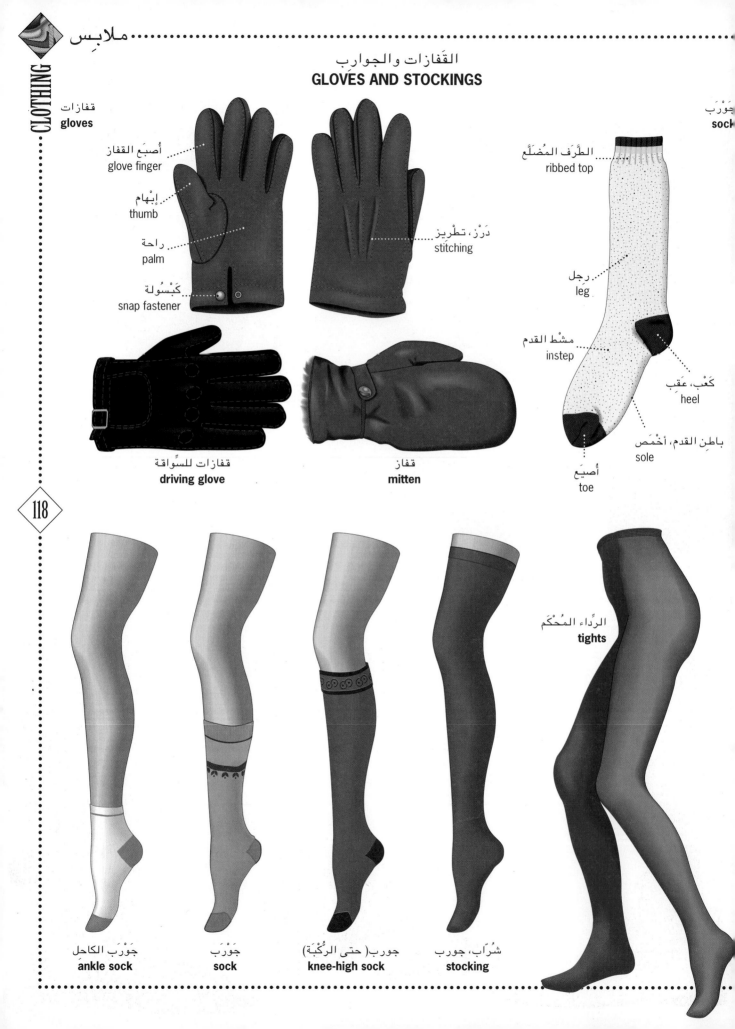

جَوْرَب الكاحِل
ankle sock

جَوْرَب
sock

جورب(حتى الرُكْبَة)
knee-high sock

شُرّاب، جورب
stocking

الرِّداء المُحْكَم
tights

الأَحْذِيّة
SHOES

حذاء للأشْغال الشّاقة
heavy duty boot / walking boot

حذاء لرَقص الباليه
ballerina / pump

صَنْدل
slingback

حِذاء طويل يغطي الفخذ
thigh-boot

الخُفّ ذو الكعب العالي
pump / court

حذاء التنس
tennis shoe

الاسْبَدريل :حذاء خفيض
قماشِي الفرعة، مرن النعل
espadrille

حذاء شبيه بالموكسان ذو كعب
loafer

قَبْقاب
sandal / mule

المُوكْسان
moccasin

حذاء، نَعْل، جَزْمَة
boot

حذاء الكاحل
ankle boot

119

ملابِس الرِّياضَة
SPORTSWEAR

ملابِس التمارين الرياضية
EXERCISE WEAR

فَنِلَة
tank top

مايوه السِّبَاحَة
swimsuit

لِباس الراقص او البَهْلَوان
leotard

زَيّ السِّباق، زيّ المِضْمار
TRACK SUIT

كَنْزَة فَضفاضَة
sweatshirt

سِترَة قصيرة
windbreaker / anorak

كنزة ذات غطاء للرأس
hooded sweatshirt

سِروْال، بنطلون
**pants /
waterproof
trousers**

سِروْال فَضفاض
sweatpants / jogging bottoms

ملابِس التمارين الرياضية
EXERCISE WEAR

مايوه السباحة
swimming trunks

رِداء مُحْكَم بلا اقدام
footless tights

مُدْفِئُ القدم
leg-warmer

رداء قصير(رداء الملاكَمَة)
boxer shorts

حذاء العَدْو
running shoe / trainer

121

قِطْعَة جلادية تحيط بمؤخِر الحذاء
counter

طوْق
collar

فَرْعَة
quarter

بِطانَة
lining

لِسان الفَرْعة
tongue

أنْف الفرعة
nose of the quarter

ثُقْب رِباط الحذاء
eyelet

القَيْدُوم
vamp

العَقْب
heel

مَخيط
stitching

النعْل الأوْسط
midsole

وُحْدة هوائية
air unit

طرَف لدائني معدني
tag

رِباط الحذاء
shoelace

حافة أخْمص النعل
outsole

مسمار تثبيت
stud

أشياء شخصية

(أدوات) العِناية بالأسْنان
DENTAL CARE

فُرْشَة أسنان
toothbrush

نُقطة معجون
stimulator tip

مقْبض
handle

هُلْب، أسْنان الفُرشة
bristles

مُشاقة
dental floss

رأس
head

مَعجُون أسنان
toothpaste

كَواقير
HAIRDRESSING

مُشْط ذو مقبض ذيْليّ
tail comb

مِّشط ذو أسْنان واسعة الفتحات
rake comb

سِيشوار
hair-dryer

مِرْوَحَة
fan

مِفتاح التَّحكُم في الحرارة
heat selector switch

ماسُورة، أُنْبوب
barrel

فرشاة الشَّعَر
hairbrush

الخلال
hair pick

مفتاح السُرْعَة
speed selector switch

مفتاح الكهْرُباء
on-off switch

شبكة منفذ الهواء
air-outlet grille

مُكثِّف الهواء
air concentrator

مقبض
handle

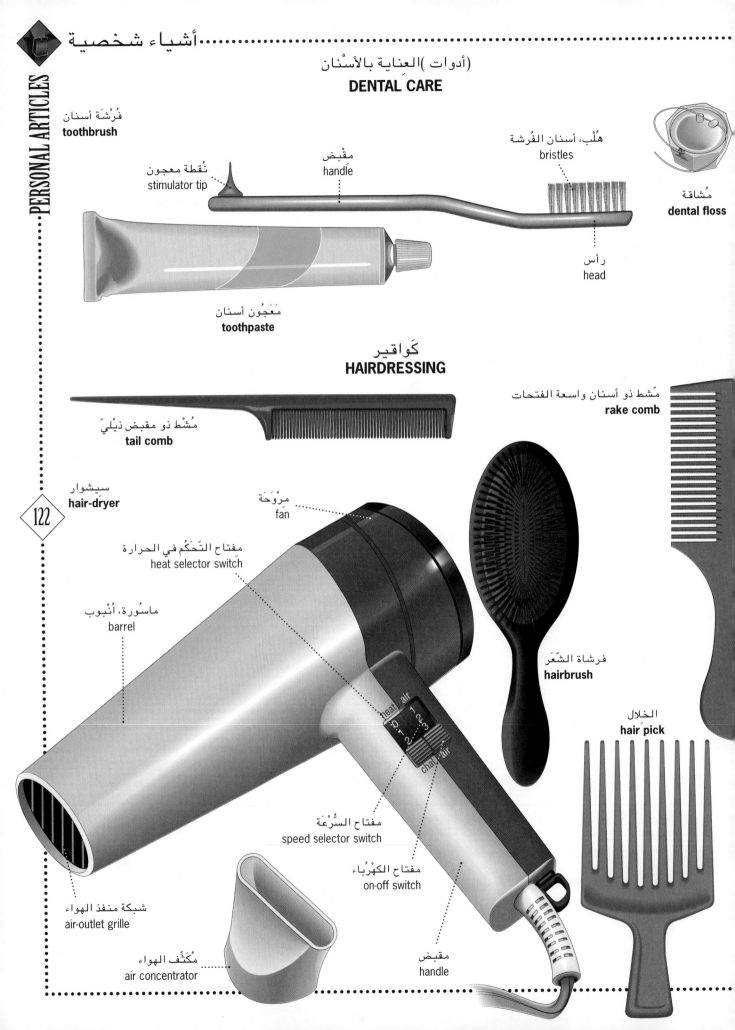

بَضائِع جِلْديّة
LEATHER GOODS

حَقيبة ذات تِكّة
drawstring bag

تِكّة، ساحِب
drawstring

حقيبة او شنْطة الظهر
knapsack

صُندوق المفاتيح
key case

مِحْفظة حيب
wallet

يدّ الشّنطة، سيْر الكَتف
shoulder strap

مِحْفَظَة، جُزْلان
purse

نَظارات
GLASSES

عَدَسة
glass lens

جِسر النّظارة
bridge

قَضيب
bar

إطار
rim

حَشيّة الأنْف
nose pad

ذُراع النّظارة
temple

جيْب أَمامي
front pocket

مِظلّة
UMBRELLA

قُبّة المظلّة
canopy

رأس، أسْلَة
tip

النّاشِرَة
spreader

طوْق، حَلَقَة
ring

رِباط، عُقْدة
tie

مظلّة تِليسكوبية
telescopic umbrella

ساق المقبض
shank

رافِدة، ضِلع
rib

عُرْوَة
tab

مِقبض
handle

غِطاء
cover

الاِتصالات

الاتصال بالهاتف(التليفون)
COMMUNICATION BY TELEPHONE

جِهاز هاتِف
telephone set

تليفون مُرَكَّب
handset

مايكرفُون الإرسال
mouthpiece

سَمَّاعة
earpiece

شاشَة
display

لوحة المفاتيح الوظيفيّة
function selectors

حَبْل التِّليفون المُرَكّب
handset cord

الهاتِف الأُتوماتيكيّ
automatic dialer

(الأزرار)الضاغِطة
push buttons

قائمة، مسرد
telephone index

جهاز تسْجيل الرسائل الصَّوتيّة
telephone answering machine

شريط الرسائل الصّوتية الموُجَّهة
outgoing announcement cassette

شريط الرسائل الصّوتية القادمة
incoming message cassette

ميكرفون
speaker

زرّ الاِستِماع
listen button

زرّ التّسْجيل
record announcement button

مفتاح ضَبْط الصَّوْت
volume control

مفاتيح تشغيل آلة التَّسْجيل
cassette player control

الهاتِف العام(هاتف الأُجْرَة)
pay phone

ثُقْب القِطَع المعْدَنيّة
coin slot

شاشة
display

(الأزرار)الضاغِطة
push buttons

تليفون مُرَكَّب
handset

قارِئ البِطاقات الالكترونية
card reader

فتحة الفلوس الراجعَة
coin return tray

هاتف ذو أزرار ضاغطة
push-button telephone

الهاتِف المحمول
portable cellular telephone

الهاتِف اللّاسِلكي
cordless telephone

124

التَّصوير الفُوتغرافيّ
PHOTOGRAPHY

كاميرا ذات عَدَسَة واحدة
single lens reflex (slr) camera

مقعد الإضافيات
accessory shoe

زرّ السحْب للوراء او الإرجاع
film rewind button

مِمْسَك
hot-shoe contact

زرّ السحب للأمام
film advance button

لوحّة التَّشغيل
control panel

زرّ التَّشغيل
control dial

زرّ أخْذ اللَقَطَات
exposure button

سُرْعَة الفيلم
film speed

زرّ التّشغيل من بُعْد
remote control terminal

هيكل الكاميرا
camera body

دائرة تعديل مَدَى التّصوير
focus setting ring

مفتاح مِصْراع الكاميرا
shutter release button

العَدَسَة الشَّيْئيَّة
objective lens

الكَشّاف
electronic flash

الأُنبوب الساطع
flashtube

ثُقوب السَّحْب
perforation

الكاسيت
cassette film

ساحِب الفيلم او الشريط
film leader

الكاميرا المُدْمَجَة
compact camera

خليّة كَهْروضَوئيّة
photoelectric cell

البلارويد
Polaroid® Land camera

مِشْبَك
mounting foot

كاميرا للجيب
pocket camera

فيلم اللَّفيفة
cartridge film

شريط
film pack

التليفزيون
TELEVISION

جِهاز التليفزيون
television set

صندوق ....
cabinet

شاشة
screen

جسّاس التشغيل من بُعد
remote control sensor

مِفتاح
on/off button

مُؤشِرات
indicators

أزرار التّشغيل
tuning controls

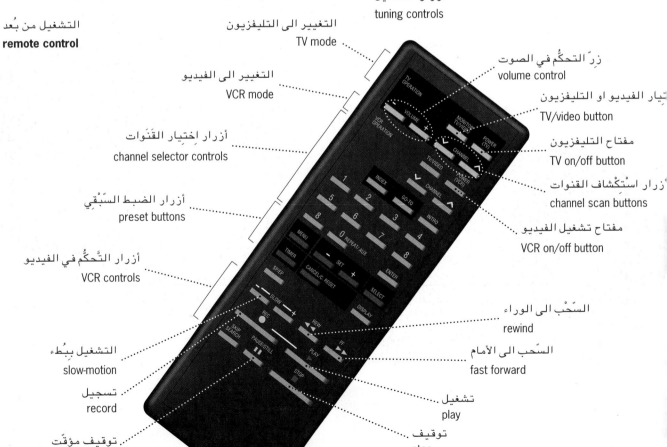

التشغيل من بُعد
remote control

التغيير الى التليفزيون
TV mode

التغيير الى الفيديو
VCR mode

أزرار اِختِيار القَنَوات
channel selector controls

أزرار الضبط السّبقِي
preset buttons

أزرار التَّحكُّم في الفيديو
VCR controls

التشغيل بِبُطء
slow-motion

تسجيل
record

توقيف مؤقّت
pause

زِرّ التحكُّم في الصوت
volume control

خِيار الفيديو او التليفزيون
TV/video button

مفتاح التليفزيون
TV on/off button

زِرّ اسْتِكْشاف القنوات
channel scan buttons

مفتاح تشغيل الفيديو
VCR on/off button

السّحْب الى الوراء
rewind

السّحب الى الأمام
fast forward

تشغيل
play

توقيف
stop

الفيديو
VIDEO

جهاز الفيديو
videocassette recorder

مفتاح
on/off button

شاشة المعلومات
data display

أزرار الضبط السَّبْقي
preset buttons

مفتاح إخْراج الكاسيت
cassette eject switch

خزانَة الكاسيت او الشريط
cassette compartment

أزرار التحكُّم
controls

كاميرة فيديو
video camera

مَقعد الإضافيات
accessory shoe

مفتاح التكبير او التصغير
power zoom button

جهاز ضبط المناظر
electronic viewfinder

عينيـة تسـدد للعْـنه
eyepiece

مفتاح إخْراج الكاسيت
cassette eject switch

أزرار تشغيل شريط الفيديو
videotape operation controls

مفاتيح ضبط وتعديل المناظِر
viewfinder adjustment keys

المايكرفون اللاّصِق
built-in microphone

البَطاريّة
battery

زرّ إخْراج البَطاريّة
battery eject switch

عدسة التَّزْويم
zoom lens

مفاتيح التحكم في التصوير وضبطه
shooting adjustment keys

خزانة الكاسيت
cassette compartment

شاشة المعلومات
data display

أزرار البحث والتحرير
edit/search buttons

127

جهاز الاِسْتِيريو
STEREO SYSTEM / HI-FI SYSTEM

أجزاء الجهاز
SYSTEM COMPONENTS

مِذْياع، راديو
tuner

هوائي ال اف ام
FM antenna

هوائي ال اى ام
AM antenna

القُرْص الدَّوّار
turntable

جهاز الأقراص الدّوّارة
compact disc player

مُفَخِّم الصَّوت
amplifier

جهاز اشرِطَة الكاسيت
cassette tape deck

المُوازِن البيّاني
graphic equalizer

مُكَبِّر الصَّوت
loudspeakers

القناة الشمالية
left channel

القناة اليُمْنَى
right channel

مُخَفِّض الصَّوت
tweeter

المدى المتوسط
midrange

سمّاعة الرأس، سمّاعة الأُذنين
headphone

حشيّة الأذن
ear cushion

عُصابة رأس
headband

مُكَبِّر
woofer

طَبْلَة المايكرفون
diaphragm; cone

شريط تعديل
adjusting band

مِسْماع
earphone

غطاء المايكرفون
speaker cover

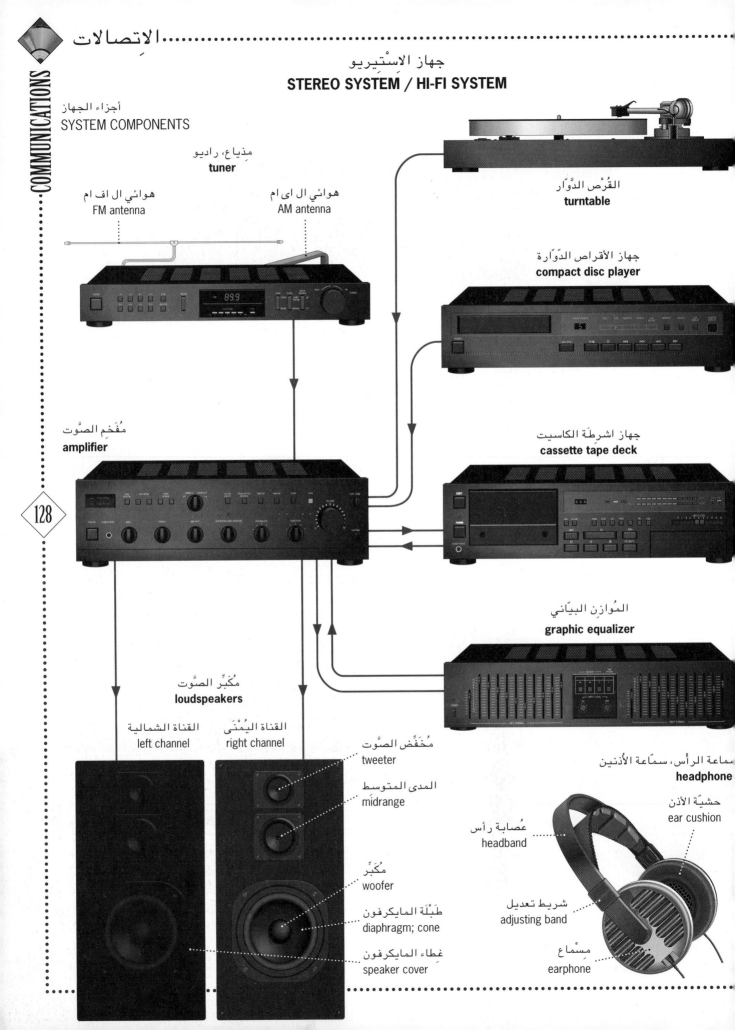

128

أجْهِزَة الصّوت المحمولة(المُتنقلة)
PORTABLE SOUND SYSTEMS

جهاز راديووتسْجيل مَحْمُول
portable CD AM/FM cassette recorder

مفتاح صوت وضابط صوت
on/off/volume control

اخْتيار نوع التّشْغيل
mode selectors

مُشغِّل القُرْص المدمج
compact disc player

هوائي
antenna

القُرْص المُدْمَج
compact disc

حمّالَة
handle

أزرار التّشْغيل
disc player controls

ضابط الاستيريو
stereo control

مقْبَس سماعة الرأ...
headphone jack

مِذْياع راديو
tuner

أزرار التّشْغيل
tuning control

مُشغِّل الكاسيت
cassette player

مايكرفون
speaker

كاسيت، شريط
cassette

أزرار تشغيل الكاسيت
cassette player controls

وُوكْمان
personal AM/FM cassette player; Walkman®

القُرْص المدمج
compact disc

كَبْل
cable

مُوصِّل سمّاعة الاذنين
headphone plug

سيْر الرأس
headband

جُزْء مَضْغوط
pressed area

مفتاح
on/off button

ضابط الصّوت
volume control

بداية القراءة
reading start

زرّ السّحب للوراء او الإرجا...
rewind button

أزرار التّشْغيل(ضبط الموجات)
tuning control

زرّ التشغيل
play button

سماعة الرأس، سمّاعة الأُذنين
headphones

شريط تخزين المعلومات الفنية
technical identification band

زرّ السّحب السّريع
fast-forward button

كاسيت، شريط
cassette

قُرْص مدوّر
record

زرّ الإرجاع الأُتوماتيكي
auto reverse

مُشغِّل الكاسيت
cassette player

أُحْفُور لوْلَبي مُتجه الى الداخل
spiral-in groove

غطاء، بيْت
housing

مِذْياع راديو
tuner

دائرة لوْلبيّة
spiral

كاسيت، شري...
...assette

البَكَرَة السّاحِبَة
take-up reel

سطح لولبي
band

شريط تسجيل
recording tape

أُحْفُور لوْلَبي مُتجه الى الخارج
tail-out groove

ممرّ الشّريط
tape guide

بِطاقَة
label

البَكَرَة المُتدَحْرِج...
...guide roller

شُبّاك التّشْغيل
playing window

المركَز
center hole

السَّيّارة، العَرَبَة
CAR

هَيْكَل السيارة، تصميم السيارة
body

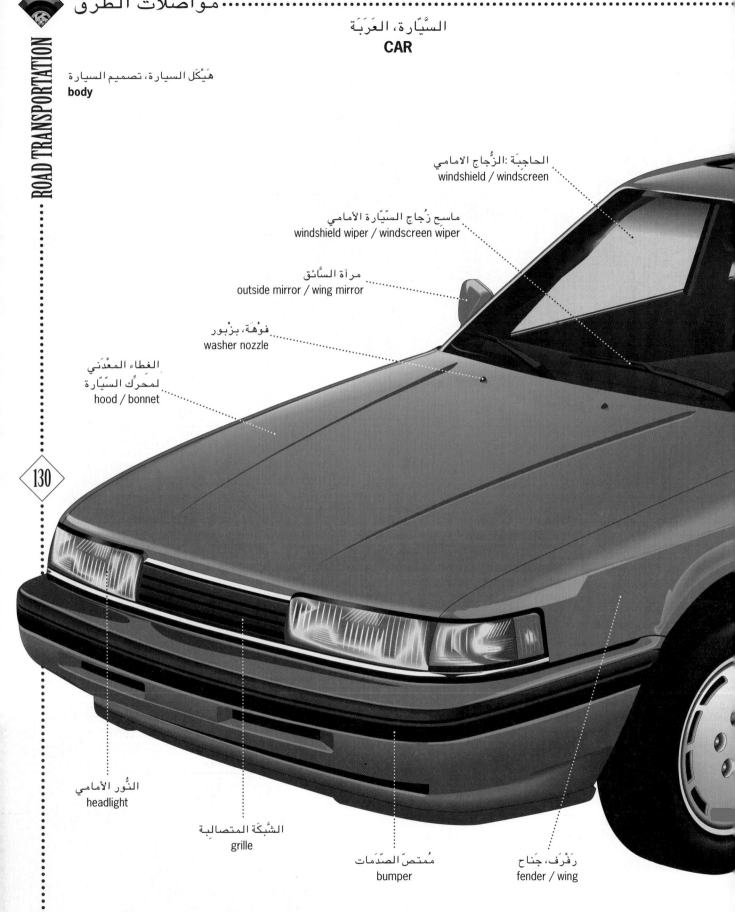

الحاجِبَة :الزُّجاج الامامي
windshield / windscreen

ماسِح زُجاج السّيّارة الأمامي
windshield wiper / windscreen wiper

مرآة السَّائِق
outside mirror / wing mirror

فوْهَة، بزْبُور
washer nozzle

الغطاء المعْدَني لمحرِّك السّيّارة
hood / bonnet

النُّور الأمامي
headlight

الشَّبَكة المتصالِبة
grille

مُمتصّ الصَّدَمات
bumper

رَفْرَف، جَنَاح
fender / wing

130

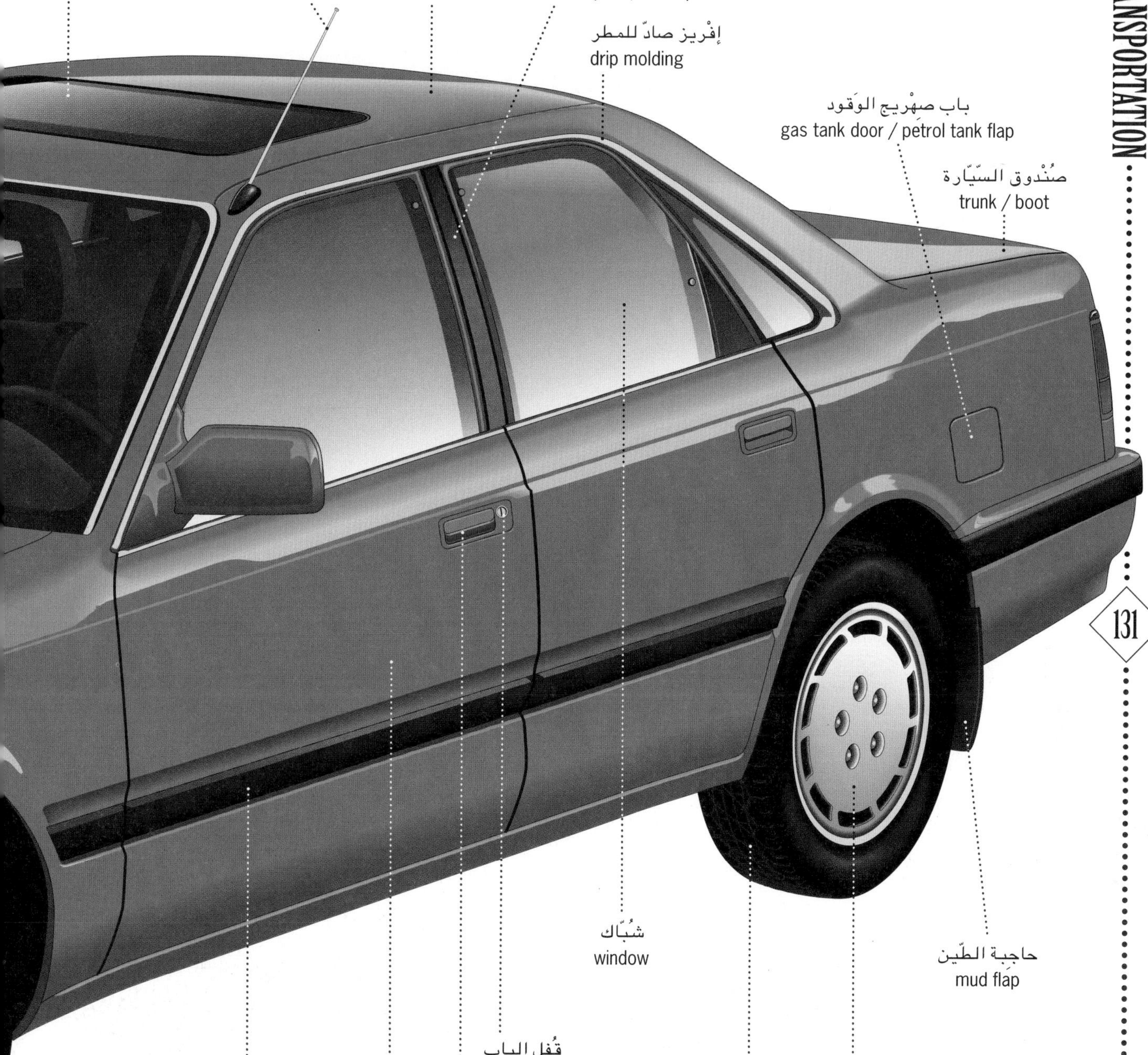

السَّطْح الشَّمْسي
sunroof

هوائي
antenna / aerial

سَقْف
roof

عمود او سارية وسط
center post / door pillar

إفْريز صادّ للمطر
drip molding

باب صهْريج الوَقود
gas tank door / petrol tank flap

صنْدوق السيّارة
trunk / boot

131

شُبّاك
window

حاجِبة الطّين
mud flap

قُفل الباب
door lock

غطاء العَجلَة
wheel cover / hub cap

إفريز جانبي
side molding / side panel

مقبض الباب
door handle

إطار
tire / tyre

باب
door

مواصلات الطُرُق

السيَّارة، العَرَبة
CAR

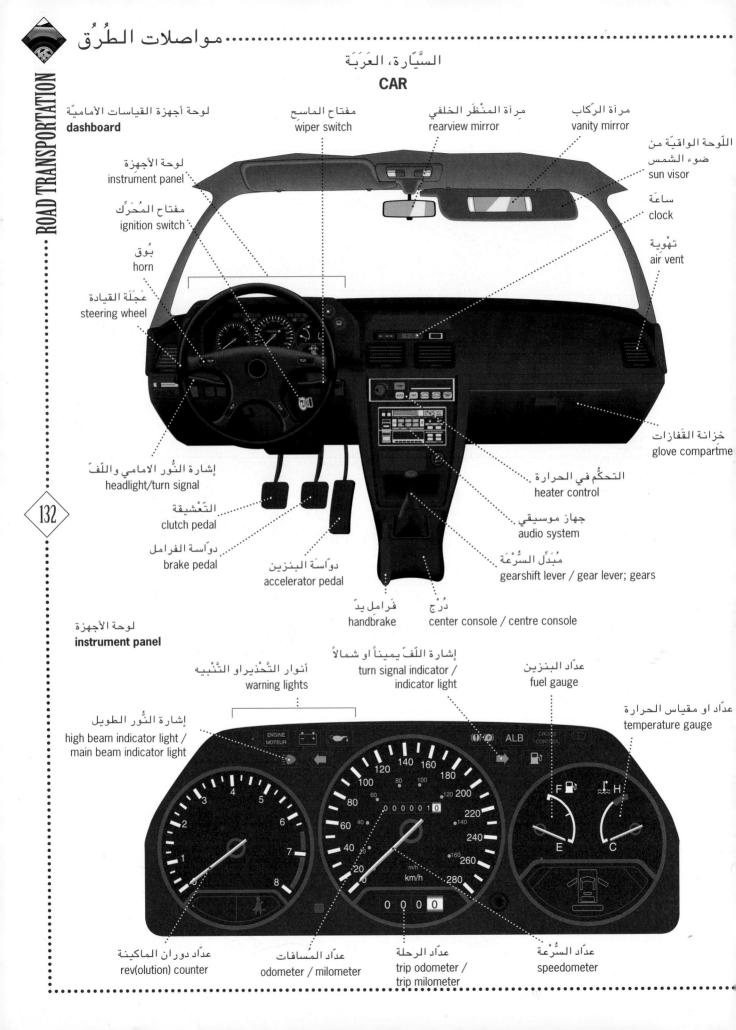

لوحة أجهزة القياسات الأماميّة
dashboard

مفتاح الماسِح
wiper switch

مِرآة المنظَر الخلفي
rearview mirror

مرآة الركّاب
vanity mirror

لوحة الأجهزة
instrument panel

اللّوحة الواقيّة من ضوء الشمس
sun visor

مفتاح المُحَرِّك
ignition switch

ساعَة
clock

بُوق
horn

تهْوية
air vent

عَجَلَة القيادة
steering wheel

خِزانة القَفازات
glove compartme

إشارة النُور الامامي واللَّف
headlight/turn signal

التحكُّم في الحرارة
heater control

التَّعْشيقة
clutch pedal

جهاز موسيقي
audio system

دوّاسَة الفرامل
brake pedal

دوّاسَة البنزين
accelerator pedal

فَرامِل يدّ
handbrake

دُرْج
center console / centre console

مُبَدِّل السُرْعَة
gearshift lever / gear lever; gears

لوحة الأجهزة
instrument panel

أنوار التَّحْذيراو التَّنْبيه
warning lights

إشارة اللَّفّ يميناً او شمالاً
turn signal indicator /
indicator light

عدّاد البنزين
fuel gauge

إشارة النُور الطويل
high beam indicator light /
main beam indicator light

عدّاد او مقياس الحرارة
temperature gauge

عدّاد دوران الماكينة
rev(olution) counter

عدّاد المَسافات
odometer / milometer

عدّاد الرحلة
trip odometer /
trip milometer

عدّاد السُرْعَة
speedometer

أنوار السيّارة
CAR LIGHTS

الأنوار الأماميّة
front lights

الأنوار الخلفيّة
rear lights

النُّور القصير
w beam / dipped headlights

إشارة
turn signal / indicator

الإشارة الجانبيّة
side light

النُّور الطّويل
eam / main beam headlights

نور الضّباب
fog light / fog lamp

نور لوحة السيّارة
license plate light / number plate light

نور الفرامل
brake light

إشارة
turn signal / indicator

النُّور الخلفي
tail light / rear light

الإشارة الجانبيّة
side light

نور الفرامل
brake light

نور الرُّجوع الى الخلف
backup light / reversing light

أنواع هياكل السيّارات
TYPES OF CAR BODIES

سيّارة رياضيّة
sports car

سيّارة ذات بابين
two-door sedan / coupe

سيّارة ذات باب خلفي كبير
hatchback

شاحنة خفيفة
pickup truck

سيّارة ذات غطاء قابل للطّي
convertible

حافلَة
station wagon / estate car

سيّارة ذات أرْبَعة أبواب
four-door sedan / four-door saloon

شاحنَة صغيرة مغْلَقَة
minivan / estate wagon

سيّرة مُتعَدِّدَة الأغراض
multipurpose vehicle

ليموزين
limousine

133

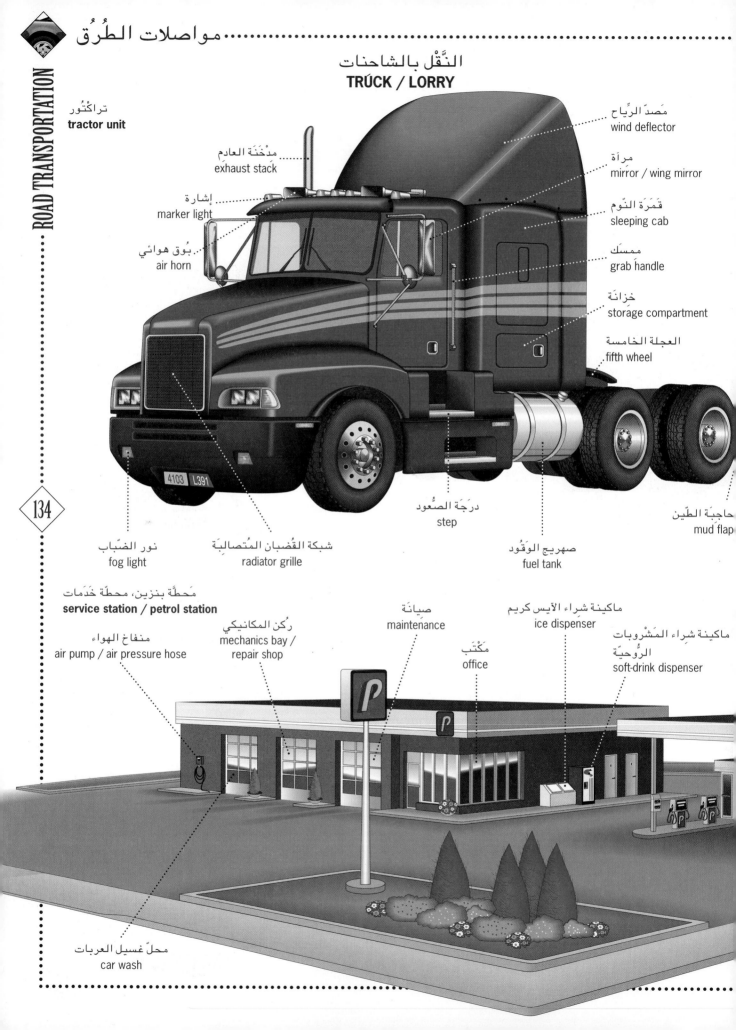

النَّقْل بالشاحنات
TRÚCK / LORRY

تراكْتُور
tractor unit

مِدْخَنَة العادِم
exhaust stack

إشارة
marker light

بُوق هوائي
air horn

مَصدّ الرِّياح
wind deflector

مِرآة
mirror / wing mirror

قَمَرَة النّوم
sleeping cab

مِمسَك
grab handle

خِزانَة
storage compartment

العجلة الخامسة
fifth wheel

درَجَة الصُّعود
step

صِهريج الوَقُود
fuel tank

حاجِبَة الطّين
mud flap

نور الضّباب
fog light

شبكة القُضبان المُتصالِبَة
radiator grille

134

مَحطَّة بنزين، محطَّة خَدَمات
service station / petrol station

منفاخ الهواء
air pump / air pressure hose

رُكن المكانيكي
mechanics bay /
repair shop

صيانَة
maintenance

مَكْتَب
office

ماكينة شِراء الآيسكريم
ice dispenser

ماكينة شِراء المَشْروبات
الرُّوحيّة
soft-drink dispenser

محلّ غسيل العُربات
car wash

دَرّاجَة ناريّة
MOTORCYCLE

حاجِز الرِّياح
windshield / windscreen

مِرآة
mirror

صهريج الوقود
fuel tank

النُّور الخلفي
tail light / rear light

ذُراع التَّعْشيقة
clutch lever

مقبض توجيه الدَّرّاجَة
handgrip

مَقْعد مُزْدوج
dual seat

إشارة
turn signal / indicator

لوحة المفاتيح وأجهزة القيا
dashboard

النُّور الأمامي
headlight

الرَّفْرَف الأمامي
front fender / front mudguard

الشُّعْبَة التلسْكوبيّة
telescopic front fork

مَوْطِئ القَدَم
footrest

ممتَصّ الصّدمات الخلفي
rear shock absorber

إطار مَعْدَني
rim

مِمْساك الفرامل
brake caliper

مُحرِّك
engine

مُرْتَكَز
stand

أُنبوب العادم
exhaust pipe / silencer

الفرامل القُرْصيّة
disc brake

بدّال التَّعْشيقة
gearchange pedal

135

دُكّان
kiosk

خُوذَة واقيّة
protective helmet / crash helmet

طُلُمْبَة جازولين
gasoline pump / petrol pump

الوِقاء المطاطي
bubble

قَيْدُوم الخُوذة
visor

حامي الذَّقْن
chin protector

طُلُمْبَة
pump island / forecourt

دَرّاجَة
BICYCLE

السَّرْج
saddle

عمود السَّرْج او المقعد
seat post

مِنْفاخ العَجل
tire pump / tyre pump

العاتِق
frame

حامِل
carrier

الفرامِل الخلفيّة
rear brake

مُوَلِّد، دينمو
generator / dynamo

مشْبَك زُجاجة الماء
water bottle clip

العاكِس
reflector

مُتحكِّم الدَّحْرَجَة الأمامي
front derailleur

النُّور الخلفي
rear light

زُجاجة ماء
water bottle

العجلة المزرودة او
المُتَرَّسَة
chain wheel

كَرَنْك
crank

مشْبَك
toe clip

بَدّال
pedal

مُوَجِّهَة السِّلْسِلَة
chain guide

مُتحكِّم الدَّحْرَجَة الخلفي
rear derailleur

السِّلْسِلة الدّافِعَة
drive chain

حاجز الطّين
mudguard

136

شنْطة الدّرّاجة
bicycle bag / pannier bag

قُفل
lock

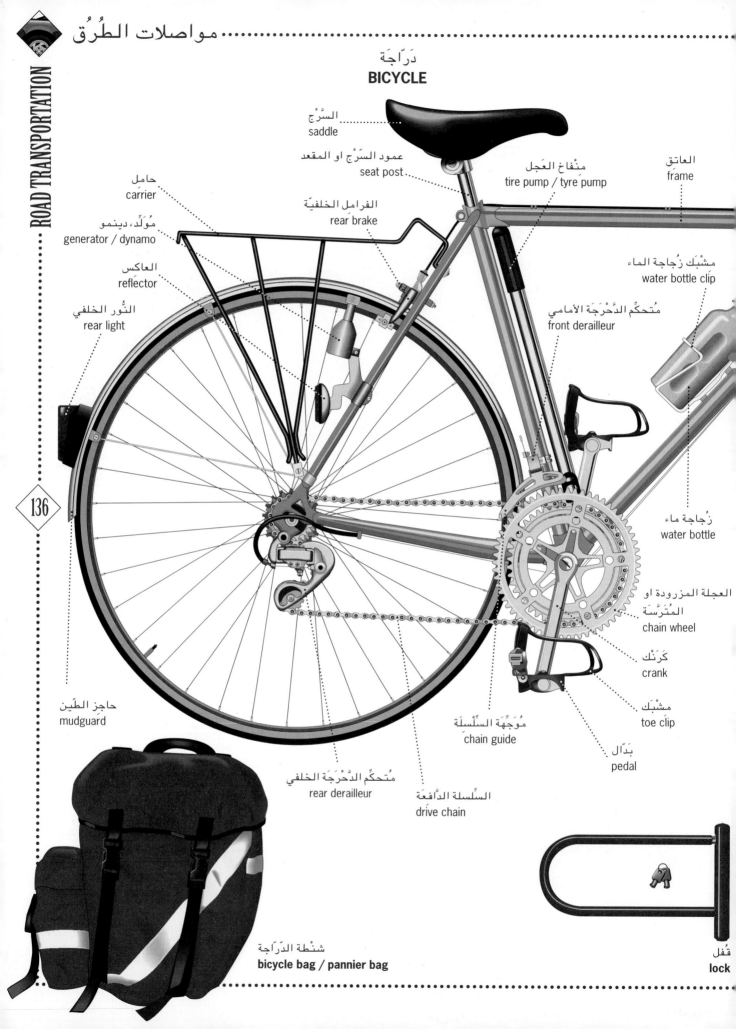

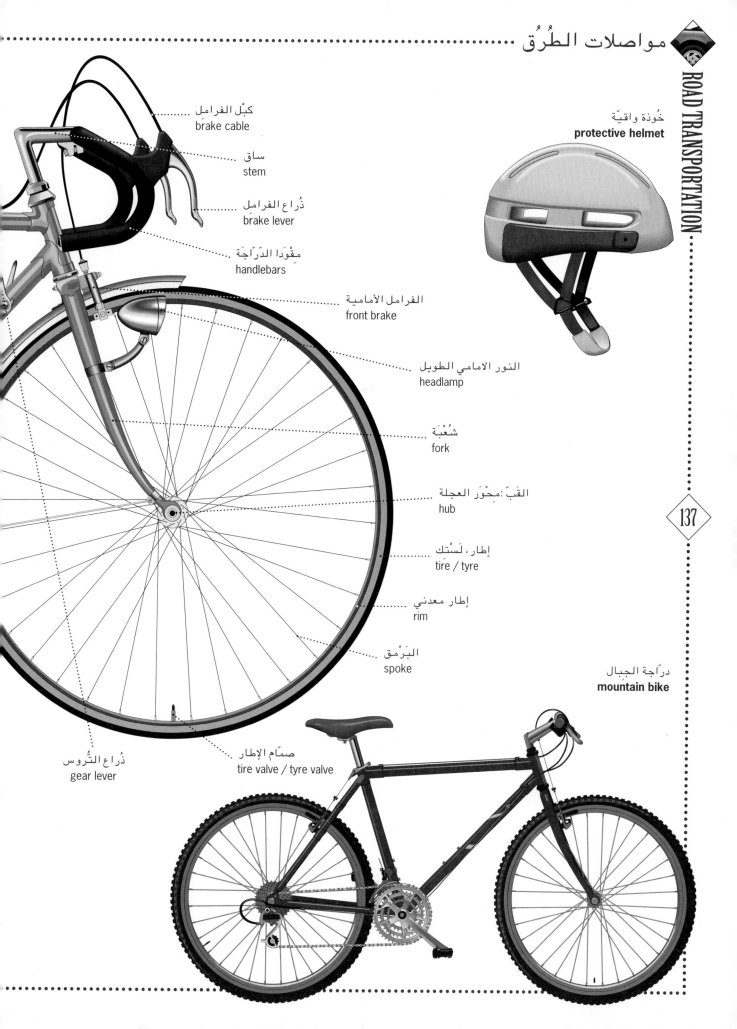

كبْل الفرامل
brake cable

ساق
stem

ذُراع الفرامل
brake lever

مقْوَدا الدّرّاجَة
handlebars

الفرامل الأمامية
front brake

النور الامامي الطويل
headlamp

شُعْبَة
fork

القَبّ: مِحْوَر العجلة
hub

إطار، لَسْتك
tire / tyre

إطار معدني
rim

البَرْمق
spoke

ذُراع التُّروس
gear lever

صمّام الإطار
tire valve / tyre valve

خُوذة واقيّة
protective helmet

137

درّاجة الجبال
mountain bike

قاطِرَة الدِّيزل الالكْترونيّة
DIESEL-ELECTRIC LOCOMOTIVE

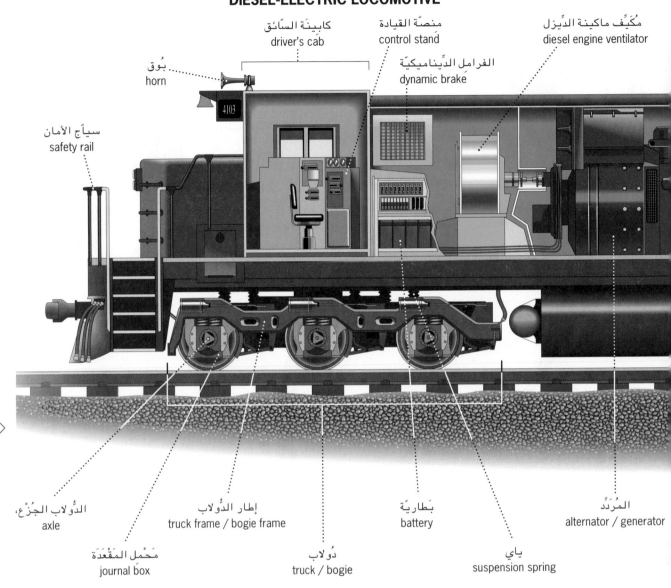

كابينَة السّائق
driver's cab

مُكَيِّف ماكينة الدِّيزل
diesel engine ventilator

منصّة القيادة
control stand

الفرامل الدّيناميكيّة
dynamic brake

بُوق
horn

سياَج الأمان
safety rail

الدُّولاب الجُزْع،
axle

مَحْمِل المَقْعَدَة
journal box

إطار الدُّولاب
truck frame / bogie frame

دُولاب
truck / bogie

بَطاريّة
battery

ياي
suspension spring

المُرَدِّد
alternator / generator

أنواع الناقلات
TYPES OF FREIGHT CARS

شاحنَة المَواشي
livestock car / livestock van

الشاحنة المُصرّفة
hopper car / hopper wagon

الشاحنة الصُّندوقيّة
box car / bogie wagon

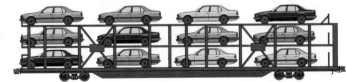

حاملة السيّارات
automobile car / bogie car-transporter wagon

الشاحنة الحاويّة
container car / container flat wagon

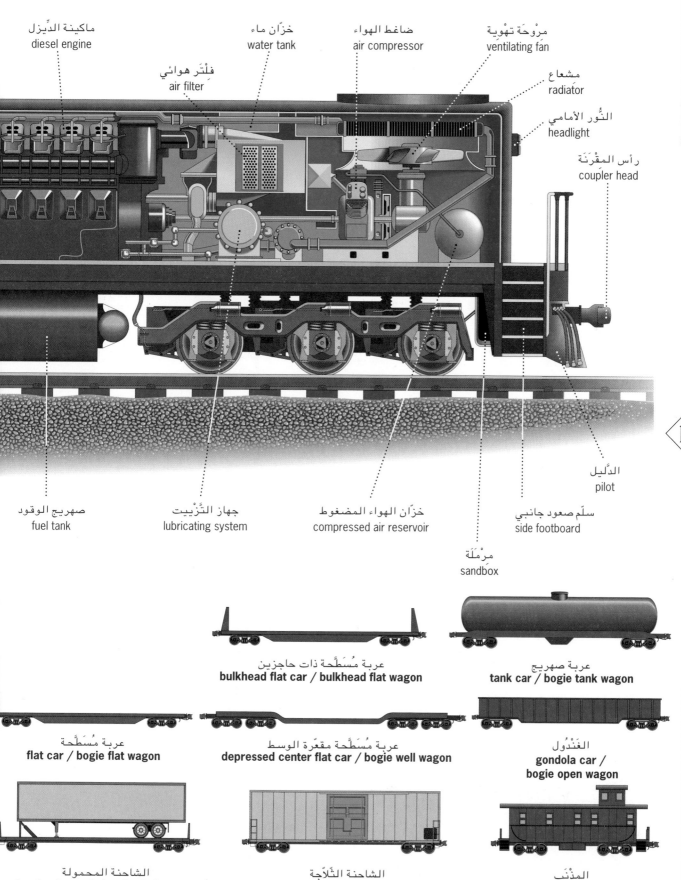

ماكينة الدِّيزل
diesel engine

فلْتَر هوائي
air filter

خزّان ماء
water tank

ضاغط الهواء
air compressor

مرْوحة تهْوية
ventilating fan

مشعاع
radiator

النُّور الأمامي
headlight

رأس المقْرنَة
coupler head

صهريج الوقود
fuel tank

جهاز التَّزْييت
lubricating system

خزّان الهواء المضغوط
compressed air reservoir

مرْمَلَة
sandbox

الدَّليل
pilot

سلَّم صعود جانبي
side footboard

عربة مُسطَّحة ذات حاجزين
bulkhead flat car / bulkhead flat wagon

عربة صهريج
tank car / bogie tank wagon

عربة مُسطَّحة
flat car / bogie flat wagon

عربة مُسطَّحة مقعَّرة الوسط
depressed center flat car / bogie well wagon

الغنْدُول
gondola car /
bogie open wagon

الشاحنة المحمولة
piggyback car / piggyback flat wagon

الشاحنة الثَّلاّجة
refrigerator car / refrigerator van

المذنَّب
caboose / brake van

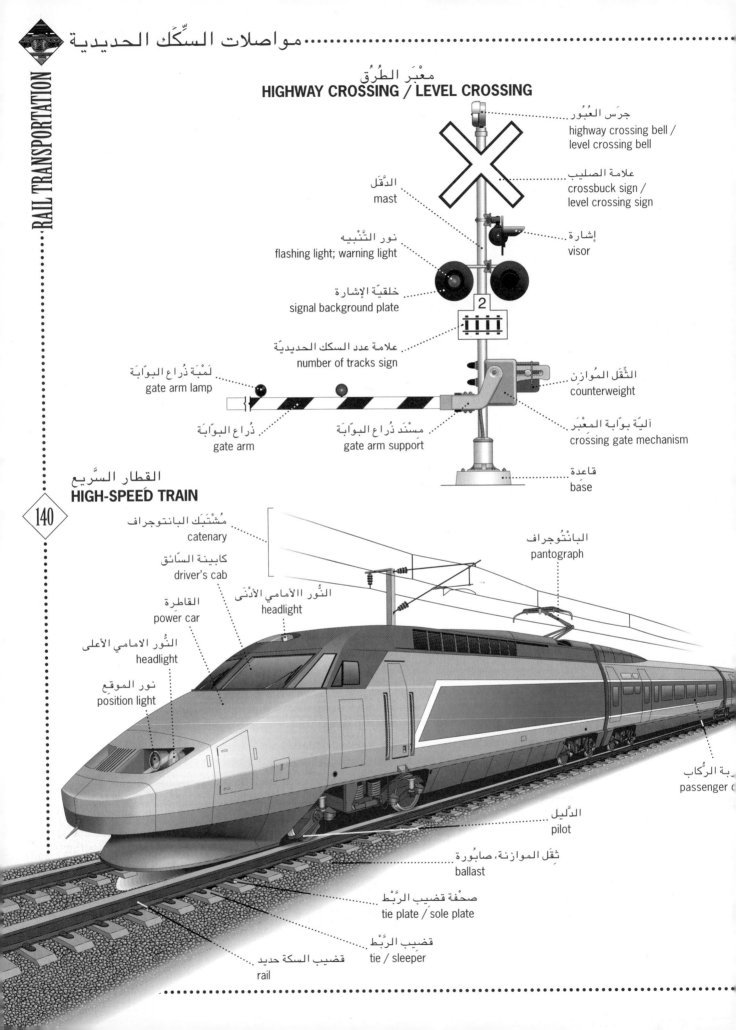

مواصلات السِّكَك الحديدية

معْبَر الطُرُق
HIGHWAY CROSSING / LEVEL CROSSING

جرَس العُبُور
highway crossing bell /
level crossing bell

علامة الصليب
crossbuck sign /
level crossing sign

الدَّقَل
mast

إشارة
visor

نور التَّنْبيه
flashing light; warning light

خلقيَّة الإشارة
signal background plate

علامة عدد السكك الحديديَّة
number of tracks sign

لَمْبَة ذُراع البوَّابَة
gate arm lamp

الثَّقَل المُوازِن
counterweight

ذُراع البوَّابَة
gate arm

مِسْنَد ذُراع البوَّابَة
gate arm support

آلِيَّة بوَّابة المعْبَر
crossing gate mechanism

قاعدة
base

القطار السَّريع
HIGH-SPEED TRAIN

مُشْتَبَك البانتوجراف
catenary

البانْتُوجراف
pantograph

كابينة السَّائق
driver's cab

القاطِرة
power car

النُور الأَمامي الأَدْنَى
headlight

النُّور الامامي الأَعلى
headlight

نور الموقِع
position light

ربة الرُكاب
passenger

الدَّليل
pilot

ثِقَل الموازنة، صابُورة
ballast

صحْفة قضيب الرَّبْط
tie plate / sole plate

قضيب الرَّبْط
tie / sleeper

قضيب السكة حديد
rail

سفينة رُباعيّة الصّواري
FOUR-MASTED BARK / FOUR MASTED BAROQUE

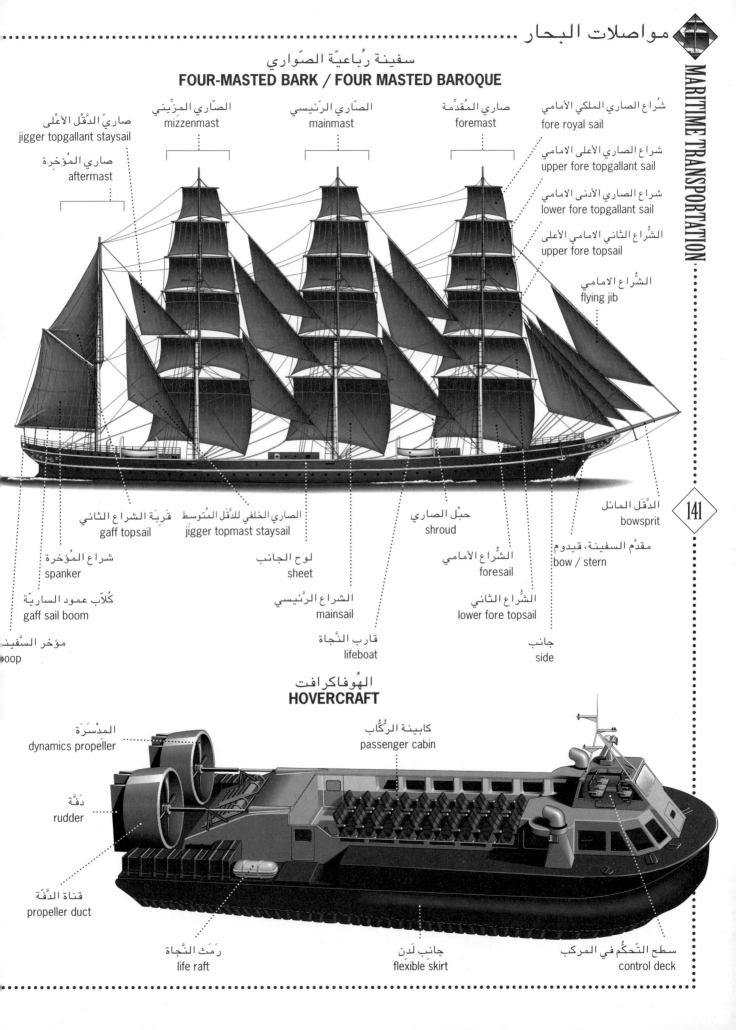

صاريّ الدَّقْل الأعْلى
jigger topgallant staysail

صاري المُؤخِرة
aftermast

الصّاري المِزّيني
mizzenmast

الصّاري الرّئيسي
mainmast

صاري المُقدِّمة
foremast

شُراع الصاري الملكي الأمامي
fore royal sail

شراع الصاري الأعلى الامامي
upper fore topgallant sail

شراع الصاري الأدنى الامامي
lower fore topgallant sail

الشُّراع الثاني الامامي الأعلى
upper fore topsail

الشُّراع الامامي
flying jib

قَربة الشراع الثاني
gaff topsail

الصاري الخلفي للدَّقَل المُتوسط
jigger topmast staysail

الشّراع الثاني
gaff topsail

حبْل الصاري
shroud

الدَّقَل المائل
bowsprit

مقدَّم السفينة، قيدوم
bow / stern

مؤخر السَّفين
oop

شراع المُؤخِرة
spanker

كُلّاب عمود الساريّة
gaff sail boom

لوح الجانب
sheet

الشراع الرّئيسي
mainsail

الشُّراع الأمامي
foresail

الشُّراع الثاني
lower fore topsail

جانب
side

قارب النّجاة
lifeboat

141

الهُوفاكرافت
HOVERCRAFT

المِدسَرَة
dynamics propeller

كابينة الرُّكّاب
passenger cabin

دَفَّة
rudder

قناة الدَّفَّة
propeller duct

رَمَث النّجاة
life raft

جانب لَدن
flexible skirt

سطح التَّحكُّم في المركب
control deck

الباخِرَة المُطوِّفَة
CRUISE LINER

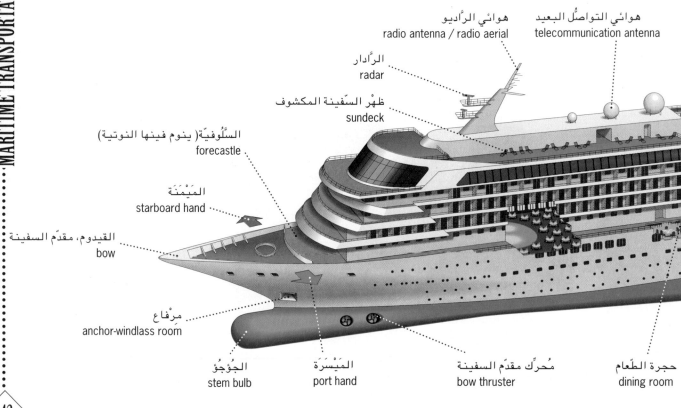

هوائي التواصُل البعيد
telecommunication antenna

هوائي الرَّاديو
radio antenna / radio aerial

الرَّادار
radar

ظهْر السَّفينة المكشوف
sundeck

السَّلُوفيَّة(ينوم فيِنها النوتية)
forecastle

المَيْمَنَة
starboard hand

القيدوم، مقدّم السفينة
bow

مِرْفاع
anchor-windlass room

الجُؤجُؤ
stem bulb

المَيْسَرَة
port hand

مُحرِّك مقدّم السفينة
bow thruster

حجرة الطَّعام
dining room

ميناء، مَرْفَأَ
HARBOR

رصيف الشحْن
bulk terminal

جسْر تحميل الحاويات
container-loading bridge

حوض السُّفُن الجاف، رصيف
dry dock

رَصيف، مرفأ
quay

رصيف الحبوب
grain terminal

مَسَدّ القنال
canal lock

السَّلوات(م سَلْوَة)
silos

الرَّافعة العائمَة
floating crane

ناقلة الحاويات
container ship

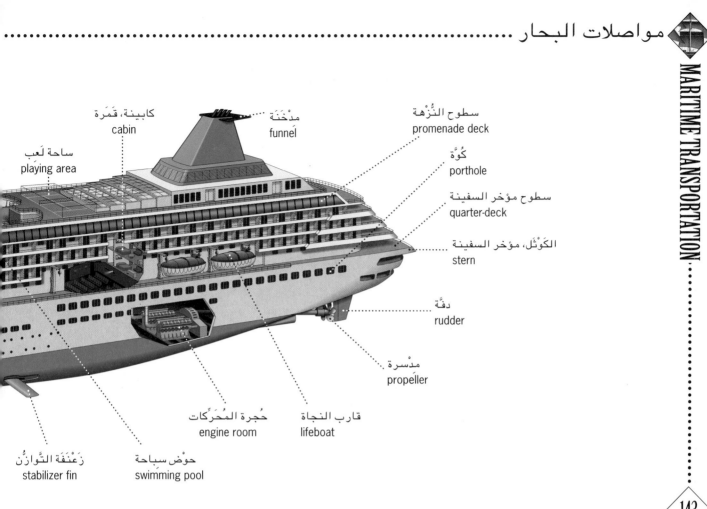

ساحة لَعِب
playing area

كابينة، قَمَرة
cabin

مِدْخَنَة
funnel

سطوح النُّزْهة
promenade deck

كُوَّة
porthole

سطوح مؤخر السفينة
quarter-deck

الكَوْثَل، مؤخر السفينة
stern

دفَّة
rudder

مِدْسرة
propeller

حُجرة المُحَرِّكات
engine room

قارب النجاة
lifeboat

زَعْنَفة التَّوازُن
stabilizer fin

حوْض سباحة
swimming pool

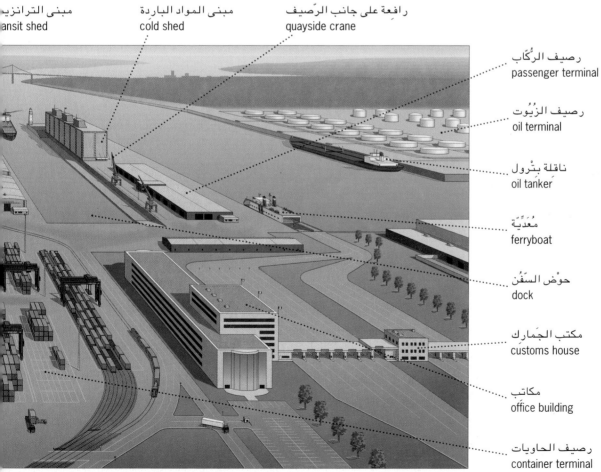

مبنى الترانزيت
transit shed

مبنى المواد الباردة
cold shed

رافِعة على جانب الرَّصيف
quayside crane

رصيف الرُّكَّاب
passenger terminal

رصيف الزُيُوت
oil terminal

ناقِلة بِتْرول
oil tanker

مُعَدِّيّة
ferryboat

حوْض السَّفُن
dock

مكتب الجَمَارك
customs house

مكاتِب
office building

رصيف الحاويات
container terminal

طائرة، طَيّارَة
PLANE

أنواع أجْنحَة الطيّارات
TYPES OF WING SHAPES

جناح عادي
straight wing

جناح مُتغيّر الأشكال
variable geometry wing

جناح مُرْتَد الى الوراء
swept-back wing

الجناح المُدَبَّب
tapered wing

الجناح المُثلّثي
delta wing

طائرة نفّاثة
long-range jet

زعْنَفة
fin

دفّة
rudder

مَجْمَعَة الذّيل
tail assembly

جسْم الطائرة
fuselage

ذنَب، ذيْل
tail

المُوازن الأفقي
horizontal stabilizer / tailplane

السّطْح الرّافع
elevator

الجُنَيْح
aileron

الحافّة الخلفيّة
trailing edge

حاجبة
spoiler

غطاء الحافة الخلفيّة
trailing edge flap

144

جُنَيْح
winglet

جناح
wing

ترْس الهُبوط الرّئيسي
main landing gear

نور الملاحَة
navigation light

وُصْلَة او شريحة الجناح
wing slat

الحافّة الامامية الرئيسية
leading edge

المحرّك النفّاث التُّربيني
turbojet engine

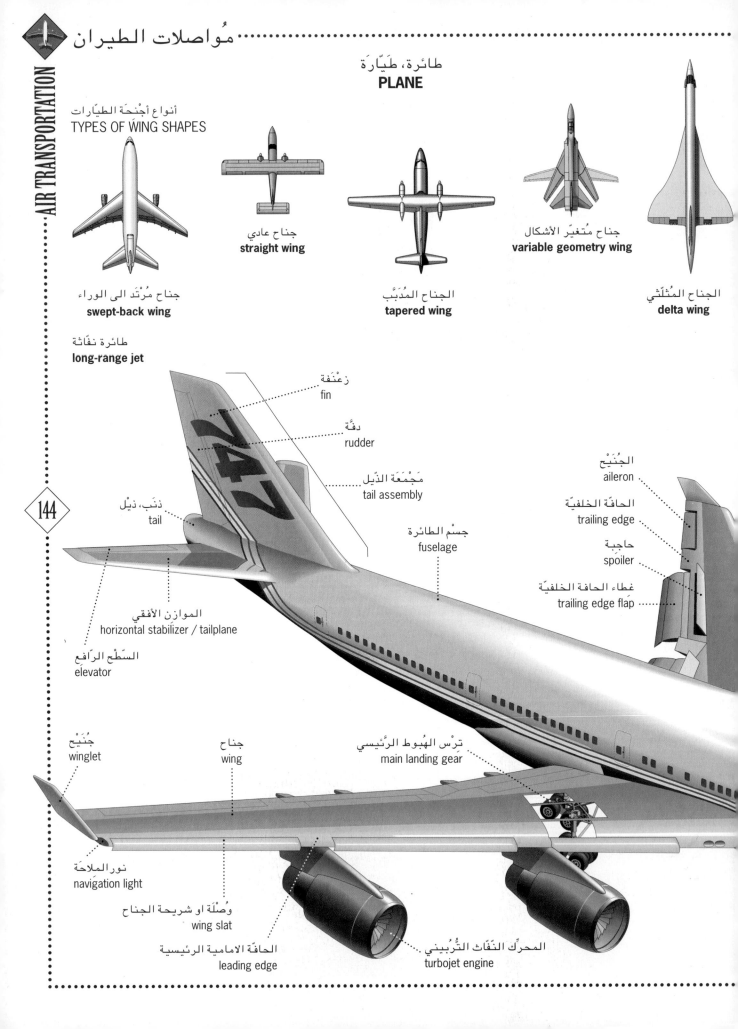

الطّائرة المرْوحيّة
HELICOPTER

زَعْنَفَة
fin

عزْم التَّدْوير، مروحة
anti-torque tail rotor

راحة الدّوّار
rotor blade

مِحْوَر الدّوّار
rotor hub

الموازن الأفقي
horizontal stabilizer / tailplane

صاريّ
mast

عاتق الطائرة، ذُراع الذّيْل
tail boom

رأس الدّوّار
rotor head

نور الموقع
position light

زَحَافَة الذّيْل
tail skid

كابينة الرُّبّان
cockpit

أُنْبوب العادِم
exhaust pipe

مخزن العَفَش
baggage compartment / luggage compartment

مدخَل الهواء
air inlet

هوائي
antenna / aerial

صهْريج الوَقُود
fuel tank

عصاة التّحكُّم، عجلة التّحكُّم
control stick

شُبّاك الهُبُوط
landing window

زحَافة
skid

كابينة الركّاب
passenger cabin

نور الهُبوط
landing light

درَجَة الصُّعُود
boarding step

أنواع أذْيال الطائرة
TYPES OF TAIL SHAPES

ذيل مَضْمُوم الى جسْم الطائرة
fuselage mounted tail unit

ذيل مَضْمُوم الى زَعْنَفَة الطائرة
fin-mounted tail unit

هوائي
antenna / aerial

غُرْفة القيّادة
flight deck

أنْف
nose

ذيل على شكل
T-tail unit

رادار الجوّ
weather radar

شُبّاك
window

ثُلاثي الأذناب
triple tail unit

تِرْس الهُبوط الأمامي
nose landing gear

145

مُواصلات الطيران

مَطار
AIRPORT

بُرْج المُراقَبَة
control tower

كابينة بُرْج المُراقَبَة
control tower cab

طريق وُصول
access road

مدرَّج الإقْلاع السَّريع
high-speed exit runway

مدَرَّج جانبي
by-pass runway

ساحة المطار
apron

ساحة المطار
apron

طريق الخدمات
service road

المُدَرَّج
runway

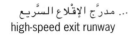

146

آلات وأجهزة المطار الأرضيّة
AIRPORT GROUND EQUIPMENT

العمود القاطِر
tow bar

التراكتُور القاطِر او الساحِب
tow tractor

منصَّة النقل والتحميل
container/pallet loader

سُلَّم الصعود الى الطائرة
universal step

مِسْحابَة العفش
baggage conveyor

127

ساندة العجلة، الكابِحة
wheel chock

حَظيرة التَّصليح
maintenance hangar

مَوْقِف
parking area

بُرْج الرُّكّاب
passenger terminal

مَمْشَى الصُّعود الى الطائرة
boarding walkway

موقع صعود الركاب النصف قطري
radial passenger loading area

المَجاز التِّلِسْكوبي
telescopic corridor

محطّة خدَمات
service area

خطّ المُدَرَّج
runway line

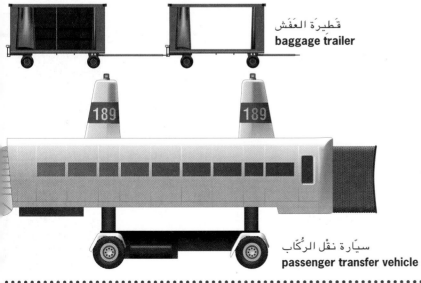

قَطيرَة العَفَش
baggage trailer

سيّارة نقْل الرُّكّاب
passenger transfer vehicle

التراكتُور القاطِر او الساحِب
tow tractor

مرْكِبَة خدمات الطعام
catering vehicle

سفينة فضائيّة، مكُوك الفضاء
SPACE SHUTTLE

سفينة الفضاء في لحظة الإقلاع
space shuttle at takeoff

صهريج خارجي
external tank

المظلّة المُعزِّزة
booster parachute

مكُوك الفضاء في فَلَكه
space shuttle in orbit

مُعزِّز الصّارُوخ
solid rocket booster

مكُوك الفضاء
shuttle

دفَّة
rudder

فوْهَة
nozzle

أجهزة علميّة
scientific instruments

بُويب
hatch

مُحرّك المُناوَرَة
maneuvering engine

شبّاك المُراقَبَة
observation window

المحرّكات الرئيسية
main engines

صهاريج الوقود
fuel tanks

رفْرَف جسْم المكوك
body flap

رفْرَف الجناح
elevon

معمل الفضاء
spacelab

ألواح عازلة
insulation tiles

جناح
wing

لوحة المشْعاع
radiator panel

باب مخزن العفش
cargo bay door

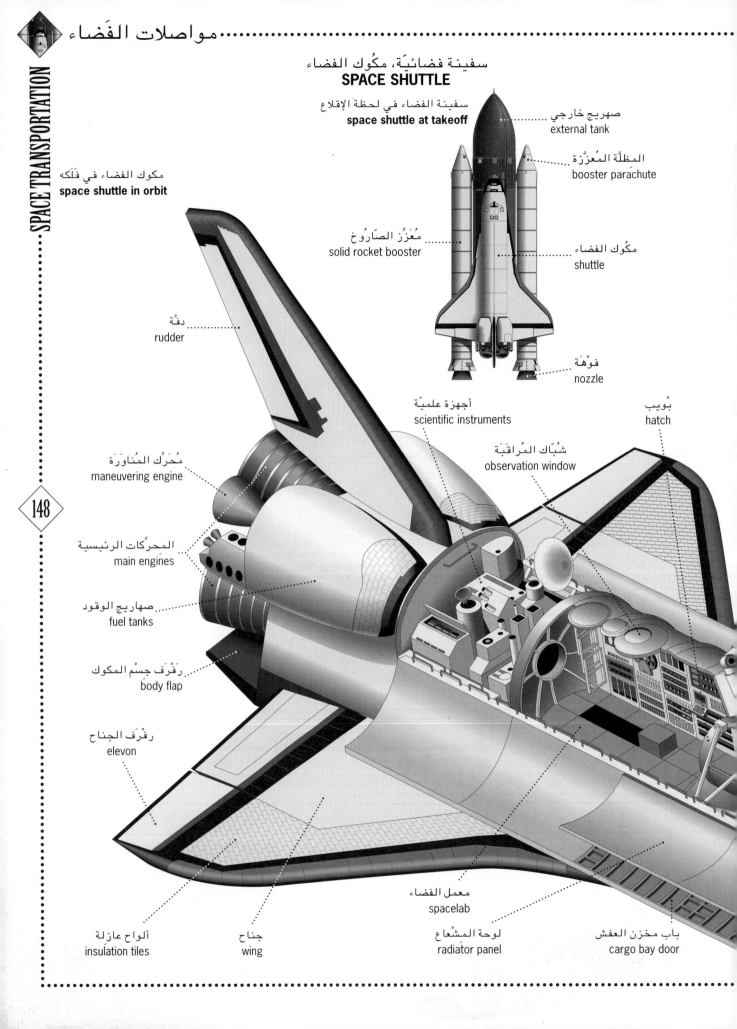

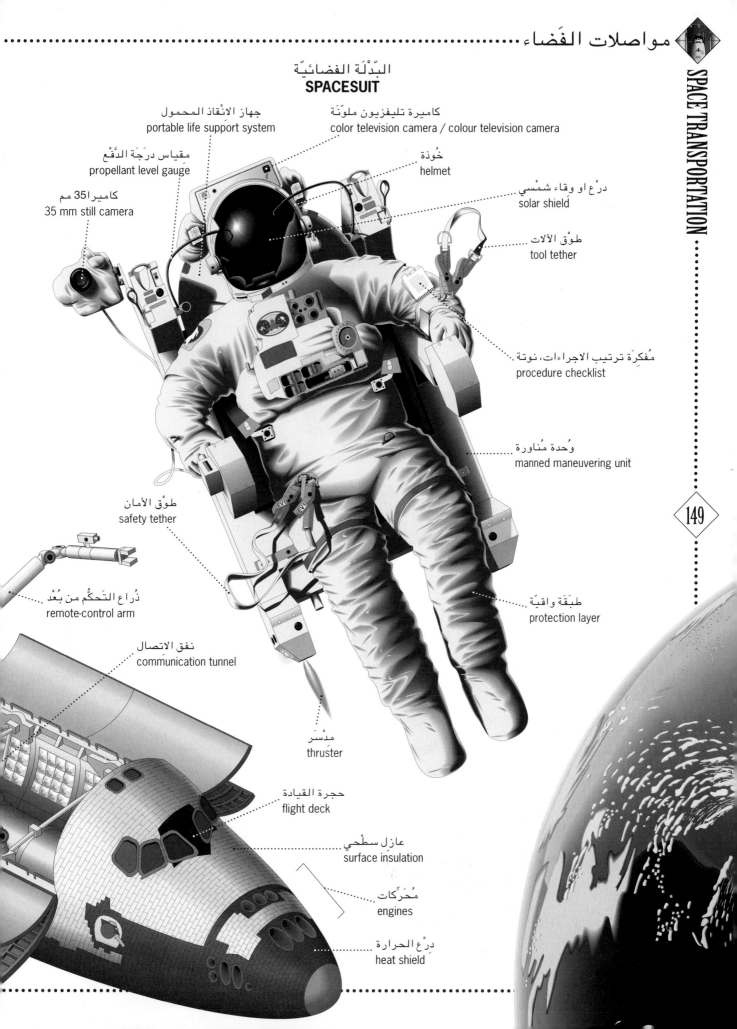

البَدْلَة الفَضائيّة
SPACESUIT

جهاز الانْقاذ المحمول
portable life support system

كاميرة تليفزيون ملوّنَة
color television camera / colour television camera

مقياس درَجَة الدَفْع
propellant level gauge

خُوذة
helmet

كاميرا35 مم
35 mm still camera

درْع او وقاء شمْسي
solar shield

طوْق الآلات
tool tether

مُفكِرَة ترتيب الاجراءات، نوتة
procedure checklist

وُحدة مُناورة
manned maneuvering unit

طوْق الأمان
safety tether

ذُراع التَحكُّم من بُعْد
remote-control arm

طبَقَة واقيّة
protection layer

نفق الاتصال
communication tunnel

مدْسَر
thruster

حجرة القيادة
flight deck

عازل سطْحي
surface insulation

مُحَرِّكات
engines

درْع الحرارة
heat shield

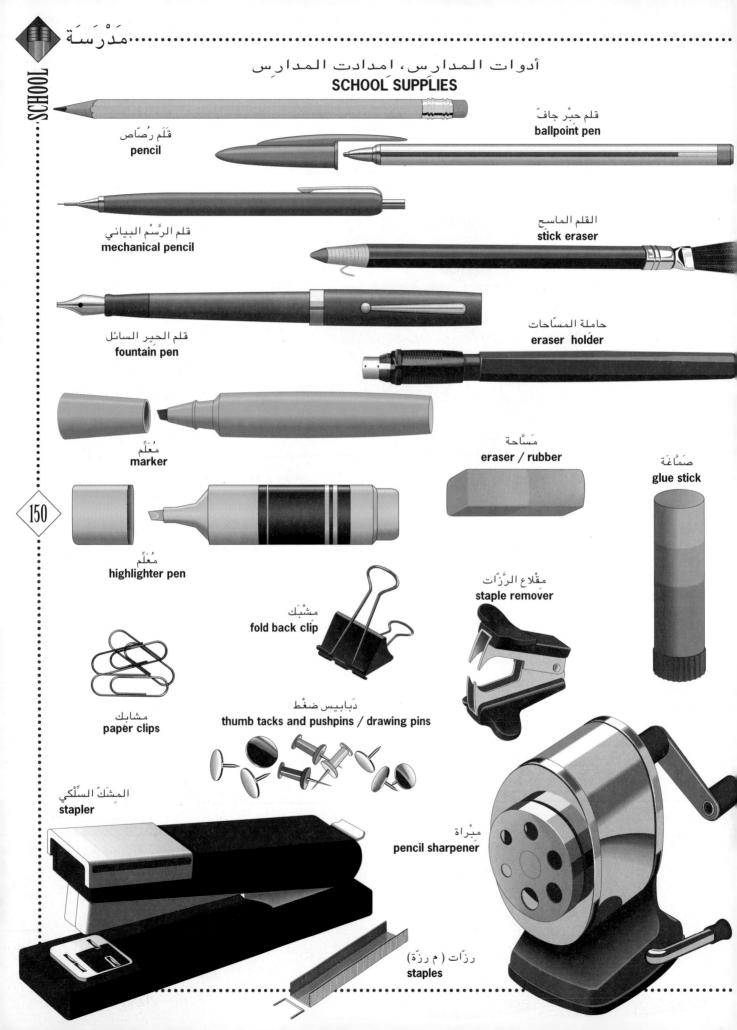

أدوات المدارس، امدادت المدارس
SCHOOL SUPPLIES

قلم حبْر جافّ
ballpoint pen

قَلَم رُصَاص
pencil

قلم الرَّسْم البياني
mechanical pencil

القلم الماسِح
stick eraser

قلم الحيِر السائل
fountain pen

حامِلة المسّاحات
eraser holder

مُعَلِّم
marker

مَسَّاحة
eraser / rubber

صَمَّاغَة
glue stick

مُعَلِّم
highlighter pen

مقْلاع الرَّزّات
staple remover

مشْبَك
fold back clip

مشابك
paper clips

دَبابيس ضغْط
thumb tacks and pushpins / drawing pins

المِشَكّ السِّلْكي
stapler

مِبْراة
pencil sharpener

رزّات (م رزّة)
staples

مَسْطَرَة
ruler

مِنْقَلَة
protractor

المَلَف الحلقي
ring binder

مُثَلَّث الرّسم
set square

حافظة الشّريط اللاّصقَة
tape dispenser

نوْتَة ذات تغليف حلزوني
spiral bound notebook

ورق غير مُجلَّد
loose-leaf paper

نوتة، كُراسَة
notebook

مُفكِّرَة، نوتة، دَفْتَر
notepad

شنْطَة
briefcase

شنْطة تُحمَل على الظّهْر
backpack / satchel

أدَوات المدارس
SCHOOL EQUIPMENT

سَبُّورة
blackboard

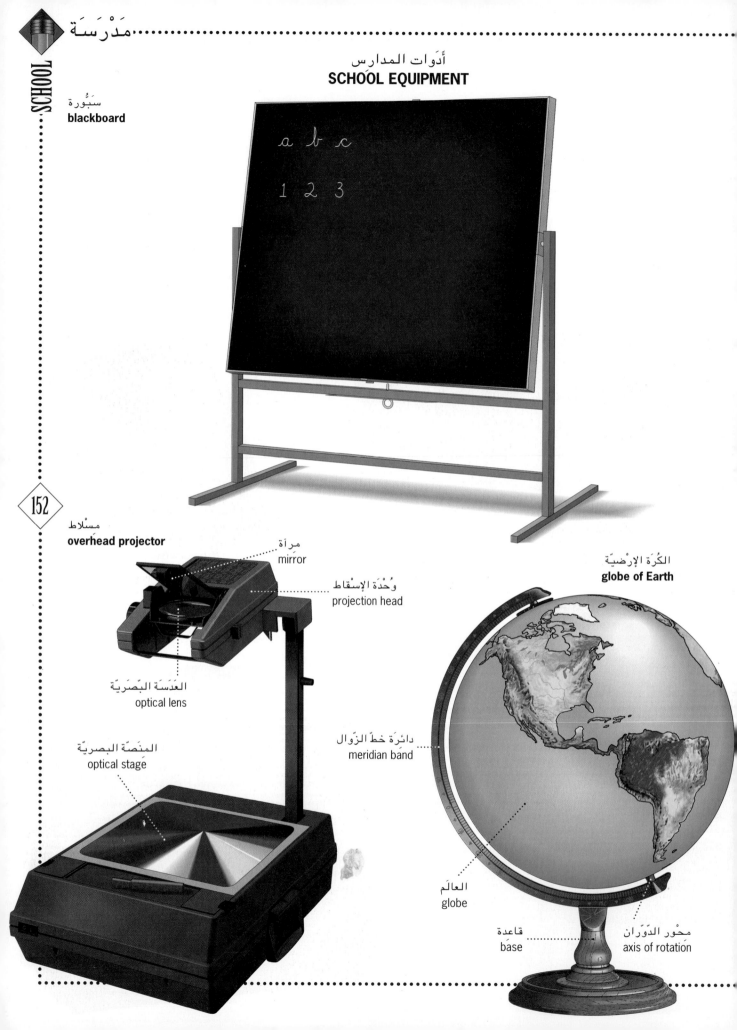

a b c

1 2 3

152

مِسْلاط
overhead projector

مِرآة
mirror

وُحْدَة الإسْقاط
projection head

العَدَسَة البَصَرِيّة
optical lens

المِنَصّة البَصريّة
optical stage

الكُرَة الإرْضيّة
globe of Earth

دائِرَة خطّ الزّوال
meridian band

العالَم
globe

قاعِدة
base

مِحْوَر الدَّوَران
axis of rotation

المِسْلاط المُنْزَلِق
slide projector

مفتاح تحريك الشّرائح للأمام
forward slide change

مفتاح
on/off switch

شَريحَة زُجاجيّة
slide

القُفل الحلقي
lock ring

خِزانة الشّرائح
slide tray

مخْزَن
storage compartment

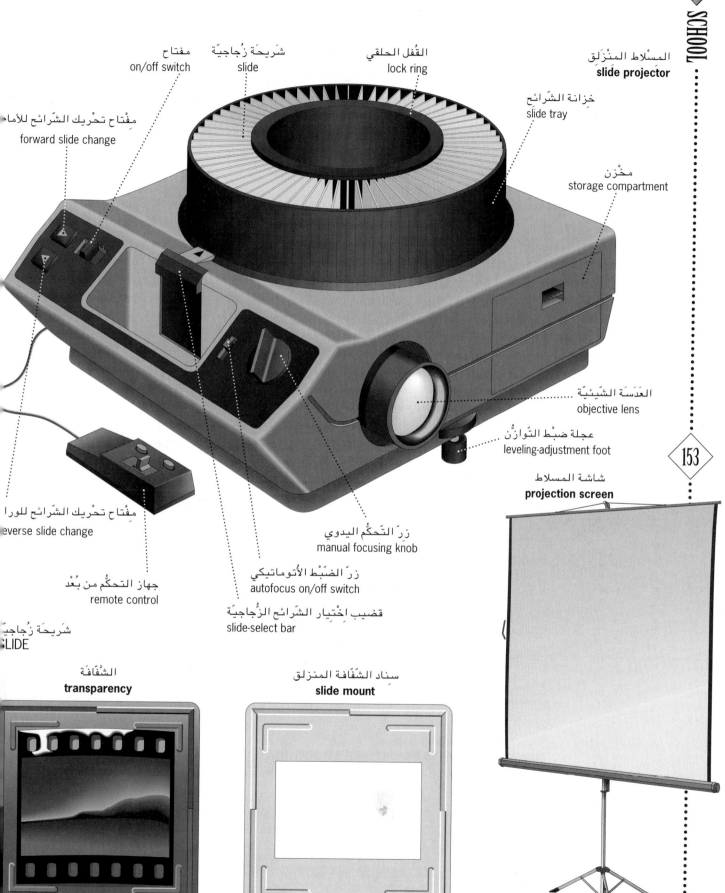

العَدَسَة الشَّيئيّة
objective lens

عجلة ضبْط التّوازُن
leveling-adjustment foot

شاشة المِسْلاط
projection screen

153

مفتاح تحريك الشّرائح للورا
reverse slide change

جهاز التحكُّم من بُعْد
remote control

شَريحَة زُجاجيّ
SLIDE

زرّ التّحكُّم اليدوي
manual focusing knob

زرّ الضّبْط الأتوماتيكي
autofocus on/off switch

قضيب اخْتيار الشّرائح الزُّجاجيّة
slide-select bar

الشّفّافَة
transparency

سناد الشّفّافة المنزلق
slide mount

أَدَوات المدارس
SCHOOL EQUIPMENT

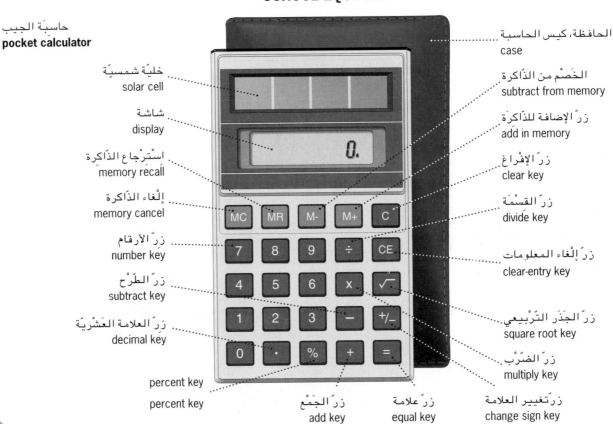

حاسبَة الجيب
pocket calculator

خليّة شمسيّة
solar cell

شاشة
display

اسْترْجاع الذّاكرة
memory recall

إلْغاء الذّاكرة
memory cancel

زرّ الأرقام
number key

زرّ الطّرْح
subtract key

زرّ العلامة العَشْريّة
decimal key

percent key

percent key

MC — MR — M- — M+ — C

7 8 9 ÷ CE

4 5 6 x √

1 2 3 − +/−

0 · % + =

الحافظة، كيس الحاسبة
case

الخَصْم من الذّاكرة
subtract from memory

زرّ الإضافة للذّاكرَة
add in memory

زرّ الإفْراغ
clear key

زرّ القسْمَة
divide key

زرّ إلْغاء المعلومات
clear-entry key

زرّ الجَذَر التّرْبيعي
square root key

زرّ الضّرْب
multiply key

زرّ تغيير العلامة
change sign key

زرّ الجَمْع
add key

زرّ علامة
equal key

154

الحاسُوب
personal computer

شاشة الحاسُوب
video monitor

المُعالج المركزي
central processing unit

كبْل لوْحة المفاتيح
keyboard cable

File Edit Arrange View Paint Type Window Graph

مادة مطْبوعَة
printed document;
printout

طابعَة
printer

القُرص الالكتروني
disk drive

شريط
disk

الفَأرَة
mouse

لوحة المفاتيح
keyboard

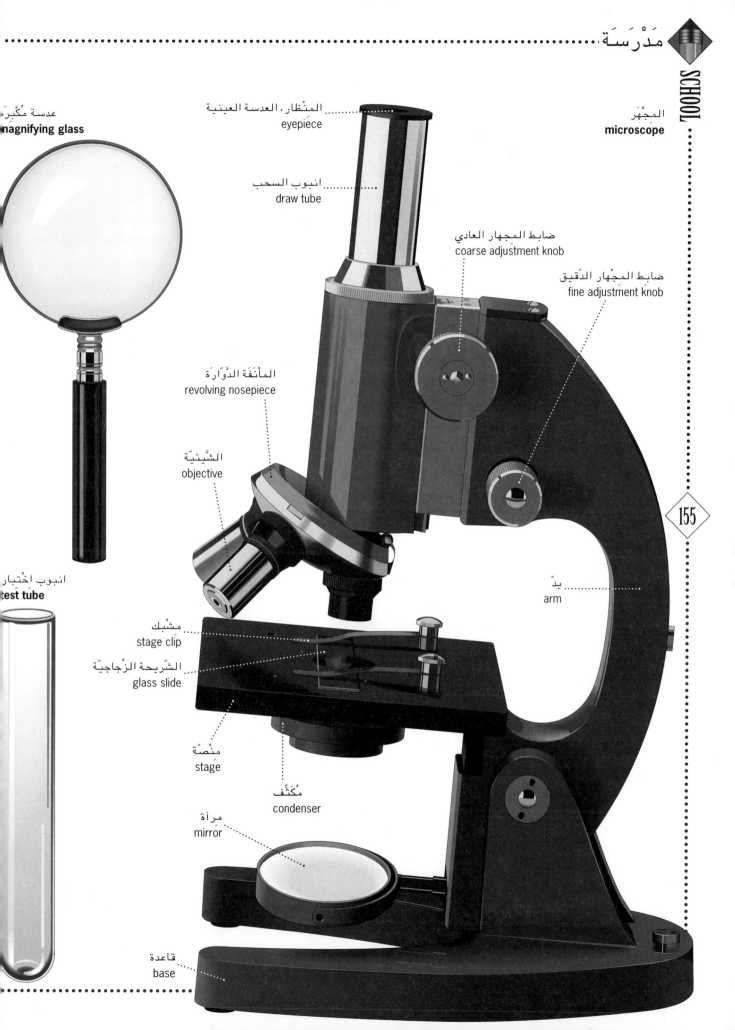

عدسة مُكَبِّرَة
magnifying glass

المِنْظار، العدسة العينية
eyepiece

المِجْهَر
microscope

انبوب السحب
draw tube

ضابط المجهار العادي
coarse adjustment knob

ضابط المِجْهار الدَّقيق
fine adjustment knob

المأْنَفَة الدَّوَّارَة
revolving nosepiece

الشَّيئِيَّة
objective

يَدّ
arm

انبوب اخْتِبار
test tube

مشْبك
stage clip

الشَّريحة الزُّجاجيّة
glass slide

مِنْصّة
stage

مُكَثَّف
condenser

مِرآة
mirror

قاعدة
base

أشْكال هنْدَسِيّة
GEOMETRY

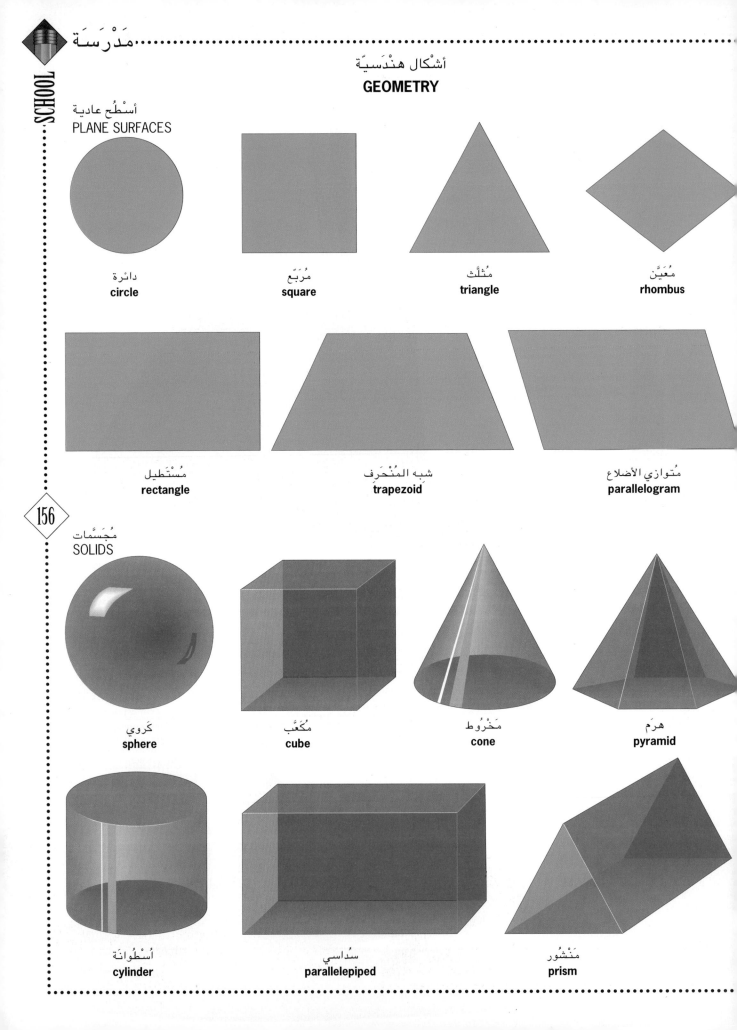

أسْطُح عادية
PLANE SURFACES

دائِرة
circle

مُرَبّع
square

مُثلّث
triangle

مُعَيَّن
rhombus

مُسْتَطيل
rectangle

شِبه المُنْحَرِف
trapezoid

مُتوازي الأضلاع
parallelogram

مُجَسَّمات
SOLIDS

كَروي
sphere

مُكَعّب
cube

مَخْرُوط
cone

هرَم
pyramid

أُسْطُوانَة
cylinder

سُداسي
parallelepiped

مَنْشُور
prism

156

رسم
DRAWING

الألوان الثانويّة
secondary colors

دائرة الألوان
COLOR CIRCLE / COLOUR CIRCLE

الألوان الأوّليّة
primary colors

الألوان الثُّلثيّة
tertiary colors

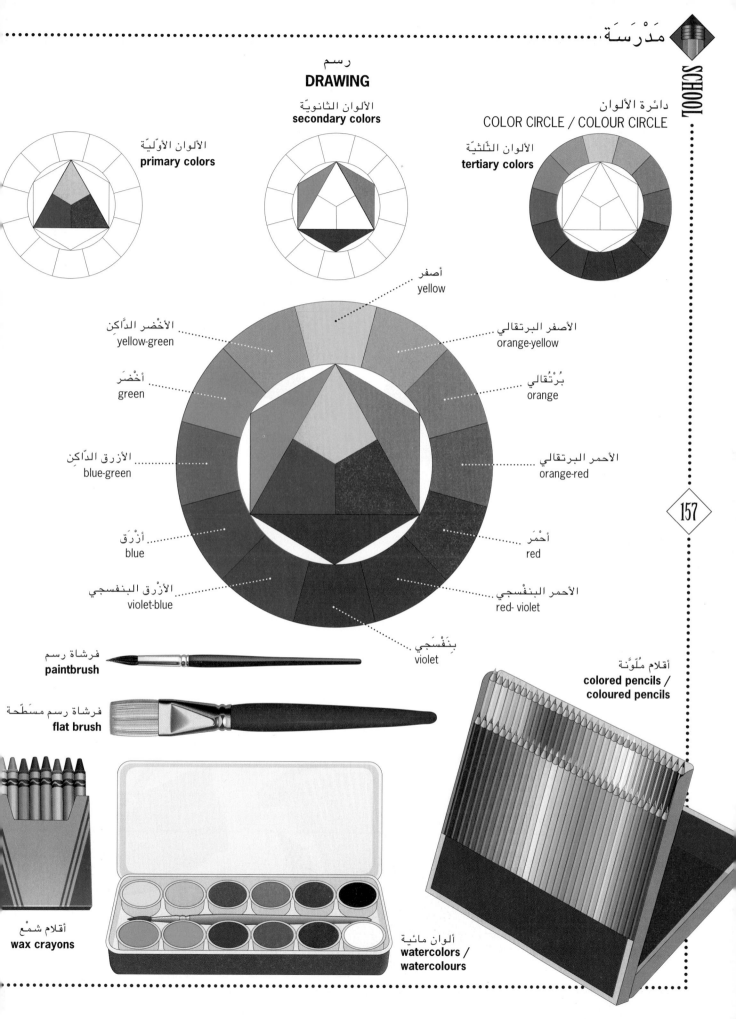

أصفر
yellow

الأخْضَر الدَّاكِن
yellow-green

الأصفر البرتقالي
orange-yellow

أخْضَر
green

بُرْتُقالي
orange

الأزرق الدَّاكِن
blue-green

الأحمر البرتقالي
orange-red

أزْرَق
blue

أحْمَر
red

الأزْرق البنفْسجي
violet-blue

الأحمر البنفْسجي
red- violet

بِنَفْسَجي
violet

فرشاة رسم
paintbrush

فرشاة رسم مسطّحة
flat brush

أقلام مُلَوَّنة
**colored pencils /
coloured pencils**

أقلام شمْع
wax crayons

ألوان مائية
**watercolors /
watercolours**

آلات موسيقية تقليديّة
TRADITIONAL MUSICAL INSTRUMENTS

البلالايكة
balalaika

ماندَلينة
mandolin

قانُون
zither

قيثارَة
lyre

اللّوحة المُصوَّتَة
soundboard

ثلاثي الشكل
triangular body

أوتار مفتوحة
open strings

أوْتار الميلودية
melody strings

مصْفار
panpipes

زمار القرْبَة
bagpipe

المنْفَخ
blowpipe; mouthpipe

انبوب مزمار القِربة
drone pipe

البانْجُو
banjo

مخروطي الشكل
pear-shaped body

دائري الشكل
circular body

هارْمونيكا
harmonica

158

منافيخ
bellows

أكورديون
accordion

لوحة مفاتيح النغمات
عاليّة الطّبقة
treble keyboard

لوحة مفاتيح نغمات الباصّ
bass keyboard

القرْبَة
windbag

ضبْط طيقات التنغيم العالي
treble register

ضبط طيقات تنغيم الباصّ
bass register

المُرنِّم
chanter

الأجهزة الموسيقيّة بلوحة مفاتيح
KEYBOARD INSTRUMENT

البيانو القائم
upright piano

لِباد كاتم الصوت
muffler felt

مطرقة
hammer

الدُّسَر، الدبابيس الرّنّانة (م دَبُوس)
tuning pin

جاجِز
hammer rail

قضيب الضّغْط
pressure bar

منصة الدّبابيس الرّنّانة
pin block

غِطاء
case

مفتاح(موسيقي)
key

لوحة مفاتيح
keyboard

كُرْسي المفاتيح
keybed

عمود البدّال
pedal rod

اللّوحة المُصوِّتَة
soundboard

مشط النبر العالي
treble bridge

بدّال ترْقيق الصوت
soft pedal

إطار معدني
metal frame

أوْتار
strings

بدّال كتْم الصوت
muffler pedal

مشط الباصّ
bass bridge

بدّال توْهين الصوت
damper pedal

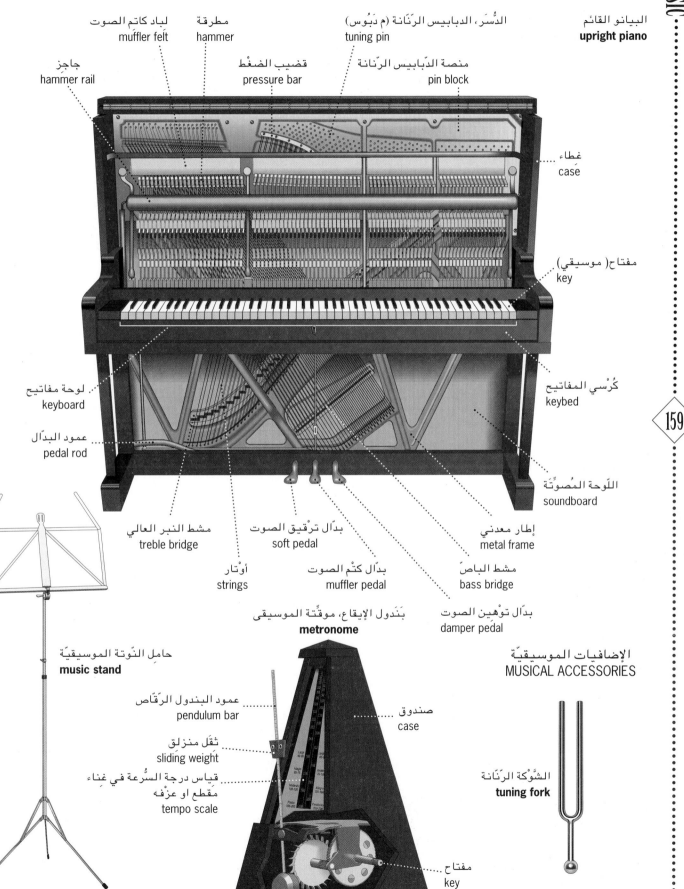

بَنَدول الإيقاع، موقِّتة الموسيقى
metronome

حامِل النّوتة الموسيقيّة
music stand

الإضافيات الموسيقيّة
MUSICAL ACCESSORIES

عمود البندول الرّقّاص
pendulum bar

صندوق
case

ثقَل منزلق
sliding weight

قياس درجة السُرْعة في غِناء مَقطع او عزْفه
tempo scale

الشّوْكة الرّنّانة
tuning fork

مفتاح
key

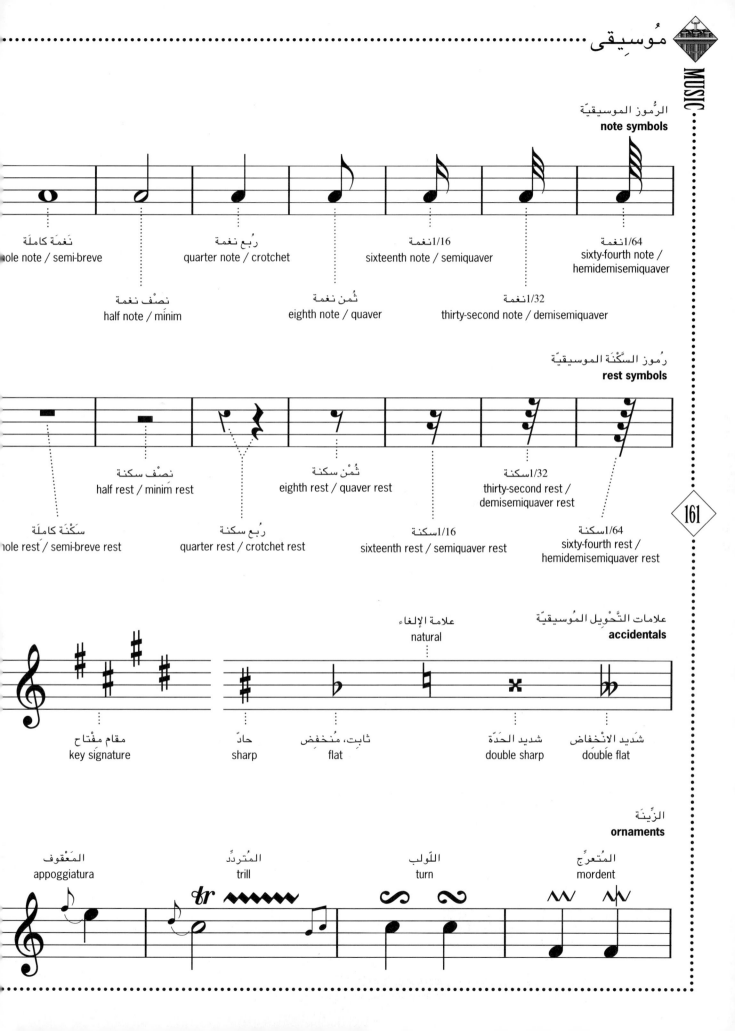

الآلات الوتريّة
STRINGED INSTRUMENTS

قوْس الكَمان
bow

كَمان
violin

الجيتار الصّوتيّ، الجيتار الجهير
acoustic guitar

مِلْوى التنغيم
tuning peg

رأس
head

الرأس المعْقوف
scroll

رأس
head

شعْرَة الوَتَر
hair

صندوق المِلْوَى
peg box

حَزَقَة
nut

مِلْوَى التّنْغيم
tuning peg

عتَب
fret

عصاة القوس
stick

مَلْعَب الأصابع
finger board

مُعَيِّن
position marker

اللّوحة المُصوِّتَة
soundboard

عُنق
neck

وتر
string

كعب
heel

خصْر، صُلْب
waist

المُشْط
bridge

القُرْص الوردي
rose

ثقب الصوت
sound hole

جسم، هيكل
body

وتر
handle

كعْب
heel

الذّيل العاجي
tailpiece

عُرْوَة
frog

المُشْط
bridge

مسمار
screw

اللّوحة المُصوِّتَة
soundboard

مسند الذّقْن
chin rest

عائلة الكمانات
VIOLIN FAMILY

زرّ النهايّة
end button / end pin

كَمان
violin

كَمَنْجَة كبيرة
cello

الكمان الأوسط
viola

الدّبُلْبِس
double bass

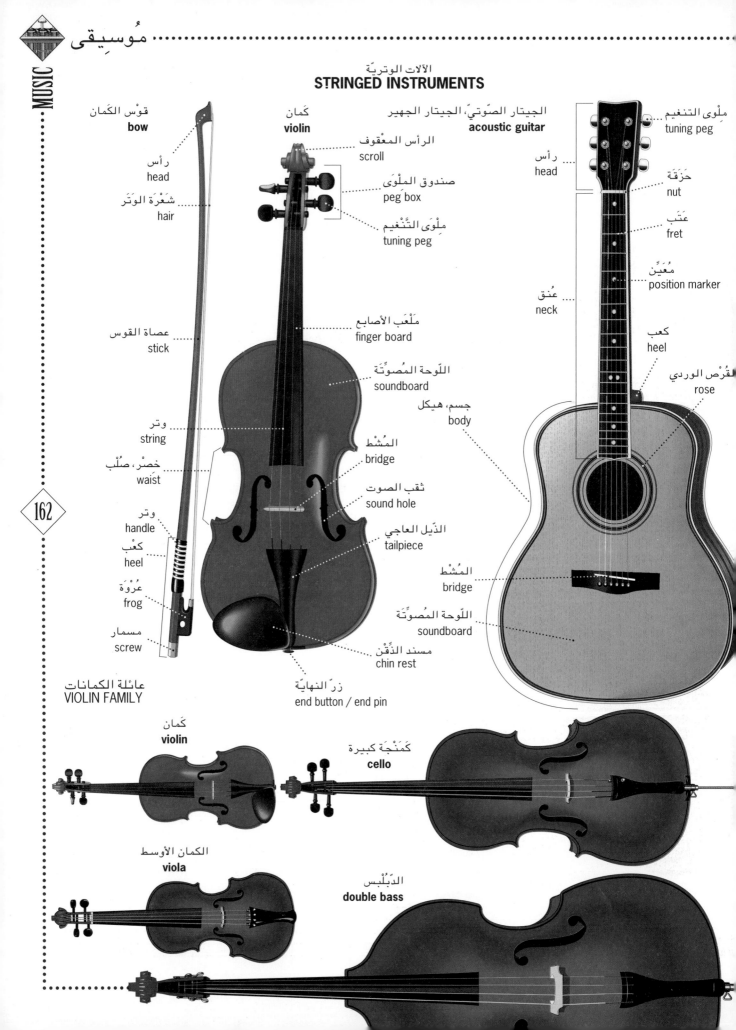

الجيتار الالكتروني
electric guitar

مُنغِّم النبْر العالي
treble pickup

مَجْمَعَة الأَمشاط
bridge assembly

مُنغِّم وسيط
midrange pickup

الجسم الصلْب
solid body

منغِّم الباصّ
bass pickup

مُعيِّن
position marker

عتَب
fret

ملعب الأَصابِع
finger board

ملْوَى التَّنْغيم
tuning peg

الواقي
pickguard

الذِّراع الهزّازة
vibrato arm

مُخْتار المُنغِّمات
pickup selector

التحكُّم في النغْم
tone controls

التحكُّم في الصوت
volume control

حَزَقَة
nut

رأس
head

عنق
neck

163

مقْبِس
output jack

جسم، هيكل
body

الباصّ جيتار
bass guitar

المُشْط
bridge

مُنغِّمات
pickups

نظام الشَّدّ
strap system

ملْوَى التَّنْغيم
tuning peg

حَزَقَة
nut

عتَب
fret

التحكُّم في تنغيم الباصّ
bass tone control

التحكم في تنغيم النبر العالي
treble tone control

ضابط الوَزْنَة
balancer

التحكُّم في الصوت
volume control

عنق
neck

مُعيِّن
position marker

ملعب الأَصابِع
finger board

رأس
head

الآلات الموسيقية الهوائيّة
WIND INSTRUMENTS

بُوق
trumpet

زِرّ الأصبع
finger button; piston valve

مشبك البُنْصُر
little finger hook

حلقة
ring

جَرَس
bell

البوق، المِنفاخ
mouthpiece

صمّام اسطوانة التنغيم المنزلقة
tuning slide

مشبك الإبهام
thumb hook

صمّام اسطوانة التنغيم الأوّل
first valve slide

صمّام اسطوانة التنغيم الثالِث
third valve slide

مفتاح الماء
water key

صمّام اسطوانة التنغيم الثاني
second valve slide

صمّام
valve

العائلة النِّحاسيّة
BRASS FAMILY

غطاء الصّمّام
valve casing

مخْفات
mute

بُوق
trumpet

بوق
cornet

بوق، ناقُور
bugle

النّفير، المُتردِّدة
trombone

التُّوبا
tuba

السّكْهورن
saxhorn

البوق الفرنسي
French horn

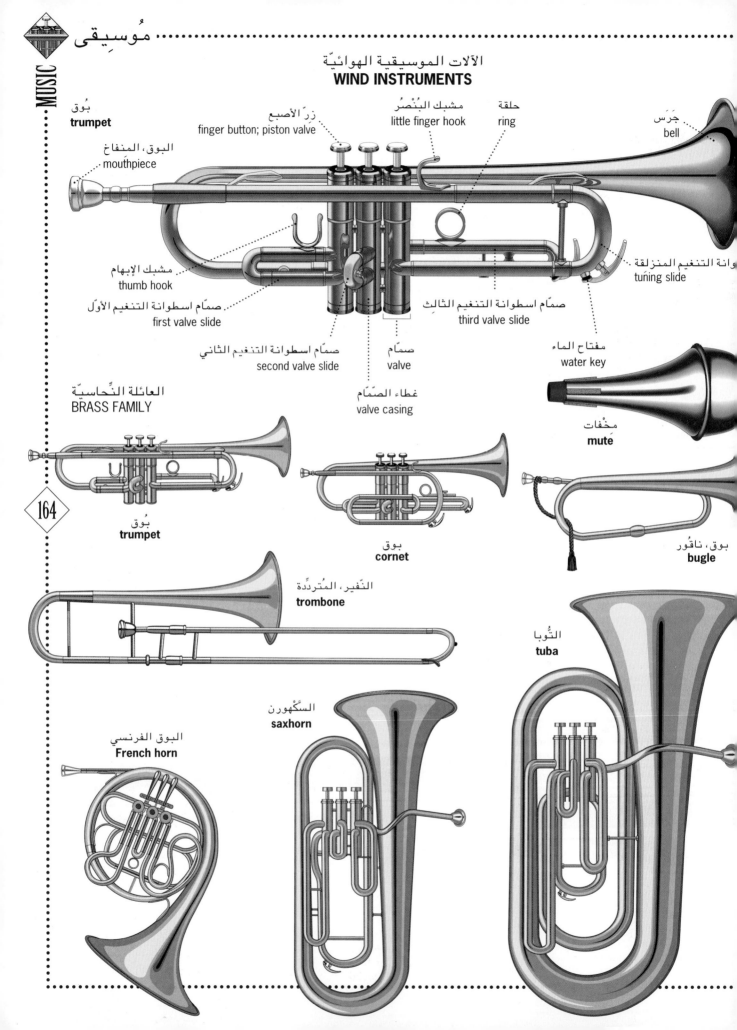

164

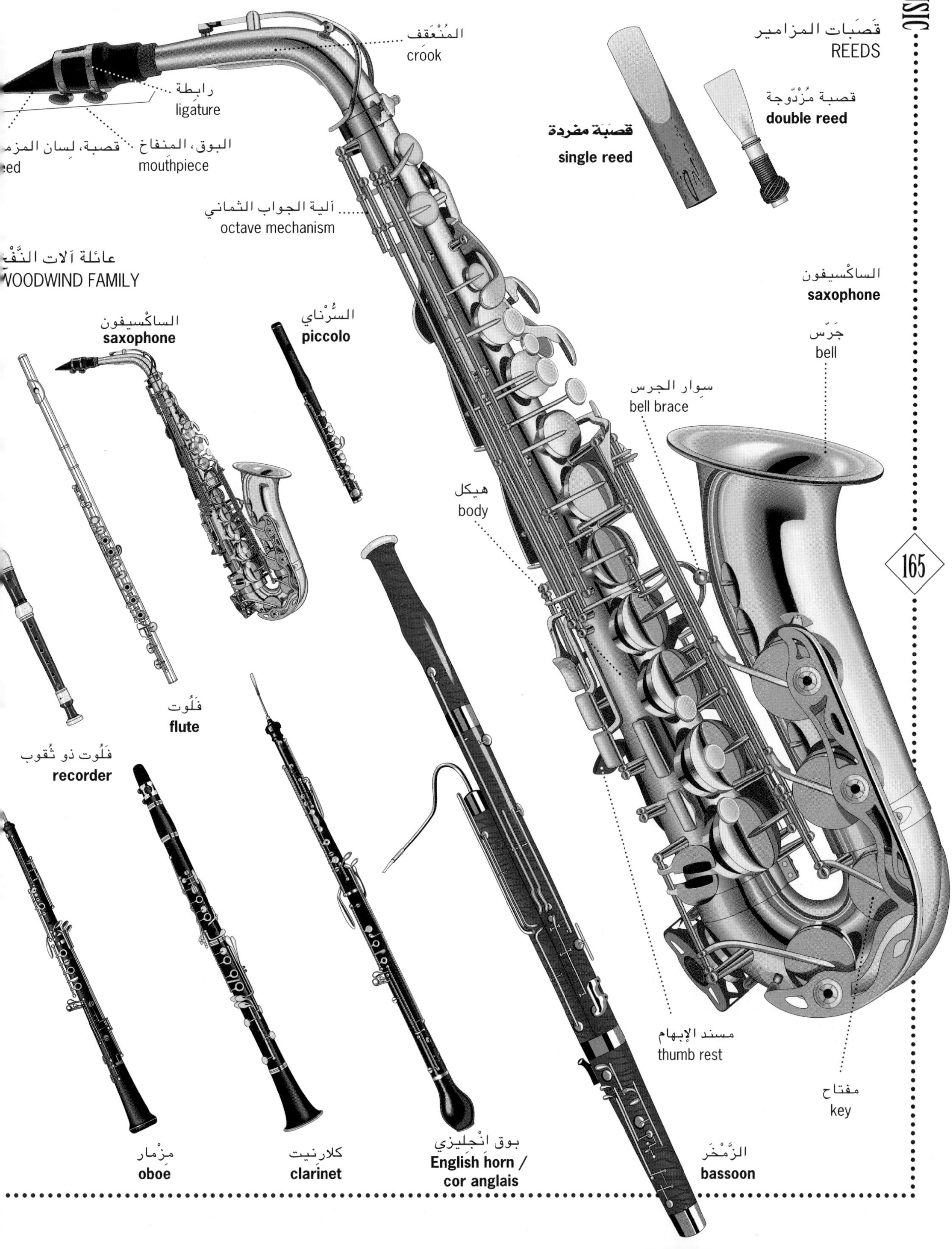

قَصَبات المزامير
REEDS

المُنْعَقَف
crook

رابِطة
ligature

قصَبة مُزْدَّوجة
double reed

البوق، المِنْفاخ، قصَبة، لِسان المزمار
mouthpiece

قصَبة مفردة
single reed

آلية الجواب الثماني
octave mechanism

الساكْسيفون
saxophone

عائلة آلات النَّفْخ
WOODWIND FAMILY

جَرَس
bell

الساكْسيفون
saxophone

السُّرْناي
piccolo

سِوار الجرس
bell brace

هيكل
body

فَلُوت
flute

فَلُوت ذو ثُقوب
recorder

مسند الإبهام
thumb rest

مفتاح
key

مِزْمار
oboe

كلارِنيت
clarinet

بوق إنْجليزي
English horn /
cor anglais

الزَّمْخَر
bassoon

165

آلات النَّقْر(القَرْع)
PERCUSSION INSTRUMENTS

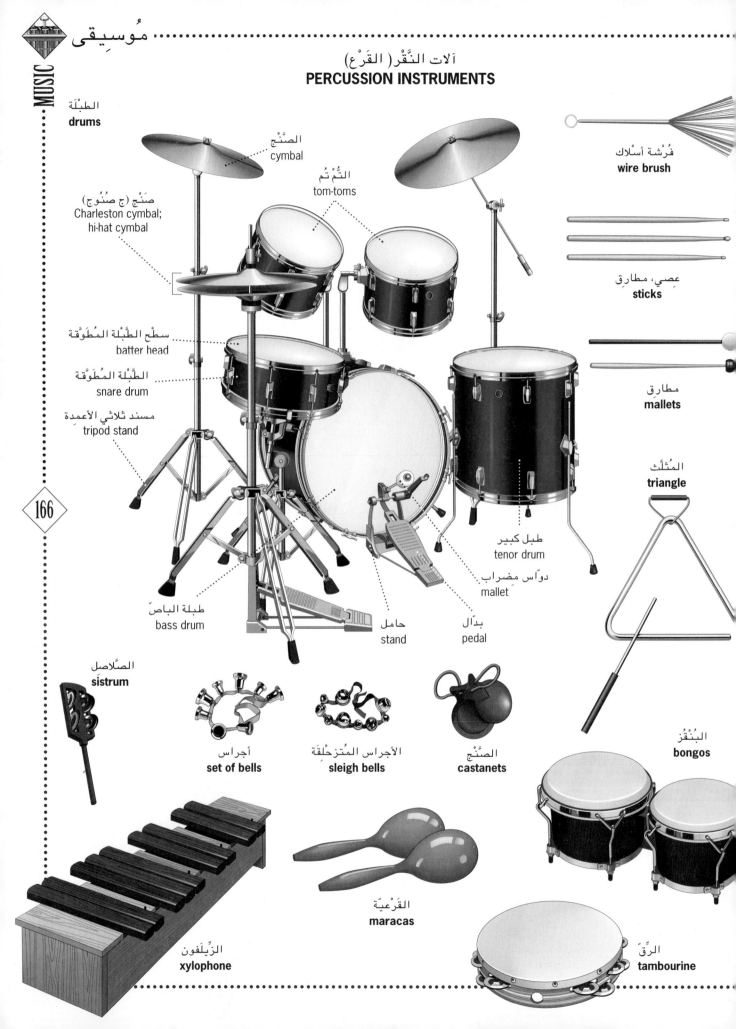

الطَّبْلَة
drums

الصَّنْج
cymbal

التُّمْتُم
tom-toms

فُرْشة أسْلاك
wire brush

صَنْج (ج صُنُوج)
Charleston cymbal;
hi-hat cymbal

عِصِي، مِطارِق
sticks

سطْح الطَّبْلة المُطَوَّقة
batter head

الطَّبْلة المُطَوَّقة
snare drum

مِطارِق
mallets

مسند ثلاثي الأعمدة
tripod stand

المُثلَّث
triangle

طبل كبير
tenor drum

دوّاس مِضراب
mallet

بدَال
pedal

طبلة الباصّ
bass drum

حامل
stand

الصَّلاصِل
sistrum

أجراس
set of bells

الأجراس المُتزحْلِقَة
sleigh bells

الصَّنْج
castanets

البُنْقُر
bongos

الزِّيلَفون
xylophone

القَرْعيّة
maracas

الرِّقّ
tambourine

اوركِسْترا السيمفونيّة
SYMPHONY ORCHESTRA

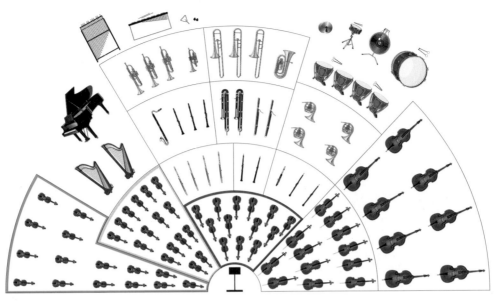

منصّة قائد الاوركسترا
conductor's podium

أجراس أُنبوبيّة
tubular bells

الزِّيلَفون
xylophone

طبلة الباصّ
bass drum

قيْثار
harp

بيانو
piano

فلوت
flute

مزمار
oboe

السُّرْناي
piccolo

بوق انْجليزي
English horn / cor anglais

الدَّبِلبس
double bass

كمان أوّل
first violin

كمان ثانٍ
second violin

كمان أوْسط
viola

كَمَنْجَة كبيرة
cello

الباصّ كلارنيه
bass clarinet

كلارنيه
clarinet

الكمان الجَهير
contrabassoon

الزَّمْخَر
bassoon

بوق فرنسي
French horn

البُوق
cornet

البوق
trumpet

النَّفير
trombone

التُّوبا
tuba

المثلث
triangle

الطبلة المطوَّقة
snare drum

الصنّج
cymbals

الصنّج
castanets

الطبلة النَّقاريّة
kettledrum

الجرس القُرْصي، النَّاقوس
gong

البايسبول
BASEBALL

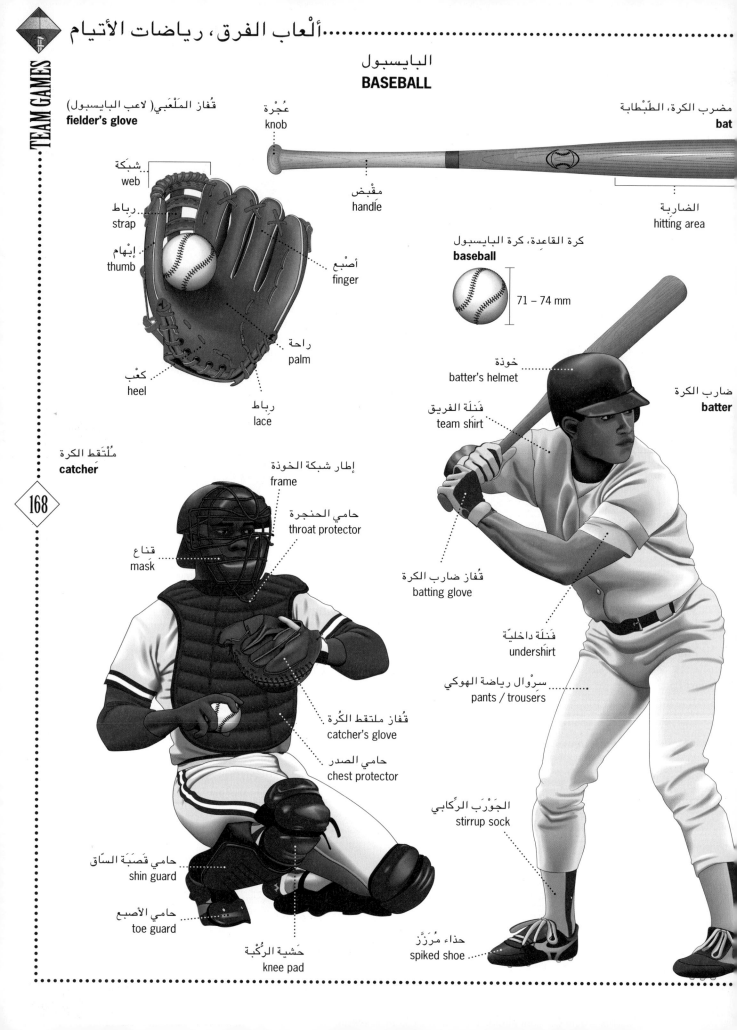

قُفاز المَلْعَبي(لاعب البايسبول)
fielder's glove

عُجْرة
knob

مضرب الكرة، الطَّبْطابة
bat

شبْكة
web

رباط
strap

إبْهام
thumb

أصْبع
finger

مقْبِض
handle

الضاربة
hitting area

راحة
palm

كعْب
heel

رباط
lace

كرة القاعِدة، كرة البايسبول
baseball

71 – 74 mm

خوذة
batter's helmet

فَنَلَة الفريق
team shirt

ضارب الكرة
batter

مُلْتَقط الكرة
catcher

إطار شبكة الخوذة
frame

حامي الحنجرة
throat protector

قناع
mask

قُفاز ضارب الكرة
batting glove

فَنَلَة داخليّة
undershirt

قُفاز ملتقط الكُرة
catcher's glove

حامي الصدر
chest protector

سرْوال رياضة الهوكي
pants / trousers

الجوْرَب الرِّكابي
stirrup sock

حامي قَصَبَة السّاق
shin guard

حامي الأصبع
toe guard

حَشية الرُكْبة
knee pad

حذاء مُرَزَّز
spiked shoe

168

ميدان، ملْعَب
field

الوقف
shortstop

الملعب الأوسط
center field

المَلْعَبي الشّمال
left fielder

المَلْعَبي الأوسط
center fielder

الهَدّاف الثّاني
second baseman

الملعب الشّمال
left field

مِضمار التّحذير
warning track

خطّ المُخالفات
foul line

المَلْعَبي اليمين
right fielder

الملعب الشّمال
right field

27,4 m

الهَدّاف الثّالث
third baseman

الهَدَف الثّالث
third base

مقْصُورة المُدرِّب
coach's box

الهدف الثّاني
second base

الدّائرة
on-deck circle

مقصورة اللاعبين
dugout

الهَدّاف الأوّل
first baseman

الهدف الأوّل
first base

الملعب الدّاخلي
infield

موقِع مسْتَقبِل الكرة
home plate

قاذف الكرة، الرامي
pitcher

موقِع قاذف الكرة
pitcher's plate

رابية قاذف الكرة
pitcher's mound

الضارب
batter

المُلْتَقط
catcher

حَكَم
home-plate umpire

ألْعاب الفرق، رياضات الأتيام

كُرة القدم الأمريكيّة
AMERICAN FOOTBALL

لاعب الكرة
American football player

خُوذة
helmet

رَقَم اللاّعب
player's number

رباط او طوق الذِّقن
chin strap

فَنلة الفريق
team shirt

عُصابة المِعْصَم
wristband

كُرَة
football

279-286مم
279 – 286 mm

أجْهزة وأدَوات واقيّة
protective equipment

خُوذة
helmet

قناع الوجه
face mask

حشْوَة الكَتف
shoulder pad

سِرْوال
pants / trousers

حامي الصَّدر
chest protector

حامي الذُّراع
arm guard

حامي الضُّلوع
rib pad

حشوة الكُوع
elbow pad

حشوة الوَرك
hip pad

حشوة القَطَن
lumbar pad

الكَأس الواقي
protective cup

شُرابات، جوارب
sock

حشوة الفَخذ
thigh pad

حذاء مُرزَّر
cleated shoe

حشوة الرُّكْبَة
knee pad

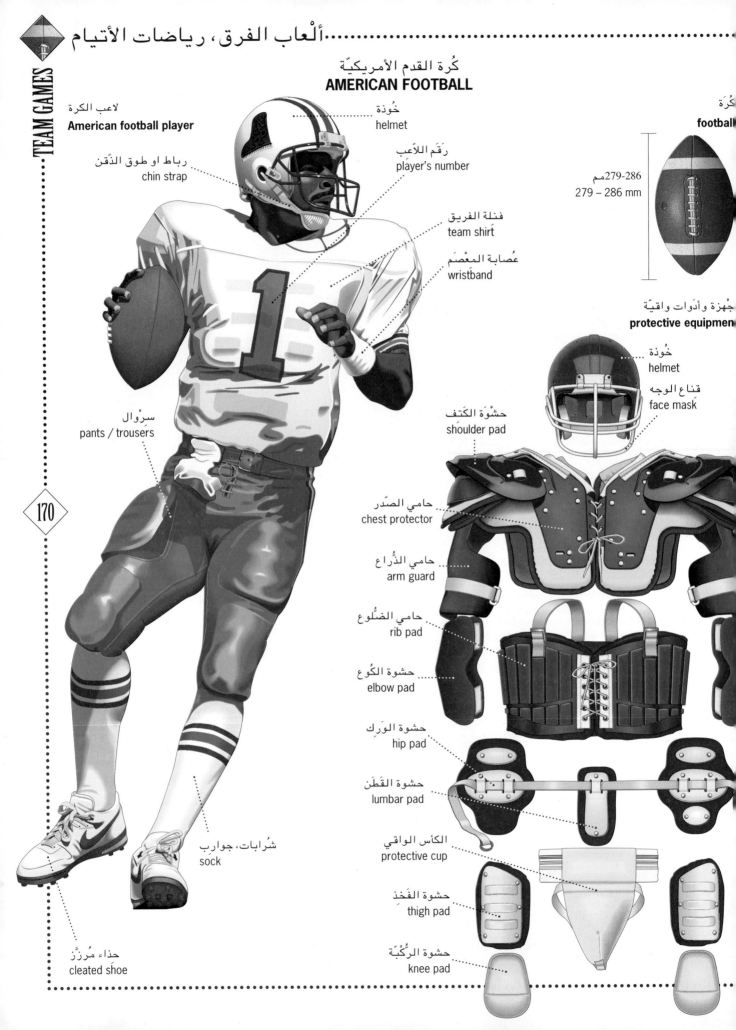

TEAM GAMES

معاركَة (مُواجَهَة) اللاعبين (من أجل استلام الكرة)
scrimmage

حكَم الخطّ
line judge

الهُجوم
OFFENSE

دِفاع
DEFENSE

مَنْطقَة الالتقاء
tight end

حكم الوسط
referee

خطّ الإمساك بالخصم الشّمال
left tackle

الظهير الشمال المتأخّر
left halfback

الحارس الشّمال
left guard

الظهير
fullback

الظهير المتقدّم
quarterback

الوسط
center

الظهير اليمين المُتأخّر
right halfback

الحارس اليمين
right guard

منطقة الإمساك بالخصم اليمين
right tackle

مَنْطقَة الافْتراق
split end

رجُل الخطّ
head linesman

منْطقة الوسط المحايدة
neutral zone

دفاع المنطقة الرُكنيّة الشّمال
right cornerback

دفاع الوَسط الجانبي
outside linebacker

لاعب تأمين الظهْر اليمين
right safety

الدّقاع اليمين
right defensive end

حكم
umpire

دفاع الوَسَط
middle linebacker

لاعب تأمين الظهْر الشّمال
left safety

حكم خط الظهْر
back judge

خطّ الإمساك بالخصم الدّفاعي اليمين
right defensive tackle

خطّ الإمساك بالخصم الدّفاعي الشّمال
left defensive tackle

دفاع الوَسط الجانبي
inside linebacker

الدّقاع الشّمال
left defensive end

خطّ المُعاركَة
line of scrimmage

ظهير الرُكْن الشّمال
left cornerback

خطّ الدّخول الى الملعب
inbound line

ملْعَب كرة القَدَم الامريكيّة
playing field for American football

خطّ المرمى
goal line

خطّ اليارِدة
yard line

خطّ النّهايَة
end line

هَدَف
goal

عارِضَة المَرْمى
goal post

خطّ مُنتصف الملعب
center line

نِطاق النّهايَة
end zone

مَقاعد اللاعبين
players' bench

خطّ جانبي
sideline

9,1م
9,1 m

91,4م
91,4 m

49م
49 m

171

TEAM GAMES

كُرة قَدَم
SOCCER

لاعِب كرة القدم
soccer player

كُرة
soccer ball

فنلة الفريق
team shirt

218م
218 mm

رداء
shorts

172

حامي الظُّنْبوب
shin guard

حذاء كرة القدم، كَدَّارة
soccer shoe / football boot

جَوايط، أوْتاد
interchangeable studs

مَلْعَب
playing field

الراية الرُّكْنِيَّة
corner flag

مَنْطقَة المرْمى
goal area

مَنْطقة الجَزاء
penalty area

حُدود منطقة الجَزاء
penalty area marking

نُقْطة ضَرْبَة الجزاء
penalty spot

دائرة المرمى
penalty arc

90 – 120 m

راية الوسَط
center flag / centre flag

الجَناح الأيْمَن
outside right

مَرْكَز دائرة مُنْتَصف الملعب
center spot / centre spot

مهاجم مُتَقَدِّم
center forward /
centre forward

مُهاجم
inside right

جناح متأخِّر
right half

خطّ التَّماس
touch line

رجُل الخطّ
linesman

ظَهير أيْمَن
right back

رُكْن الملعب
corner arc

حَكَم
referee

مَرْمى
goal

45 – 90 m

173

ظَهير أيْسَر
left back

حارس المَرْمى
goalkeeper

دائرة مُنْتَصف الملعب
center circle / centre circle

خطّ الوسَط
midfield line

مهاجم
inside left

قَلْب الدِّفاع
center back / centre back

الجناح الأيْسَر
outside left

جناح مُتأخِّر
left half

كريكيت
CRICKET

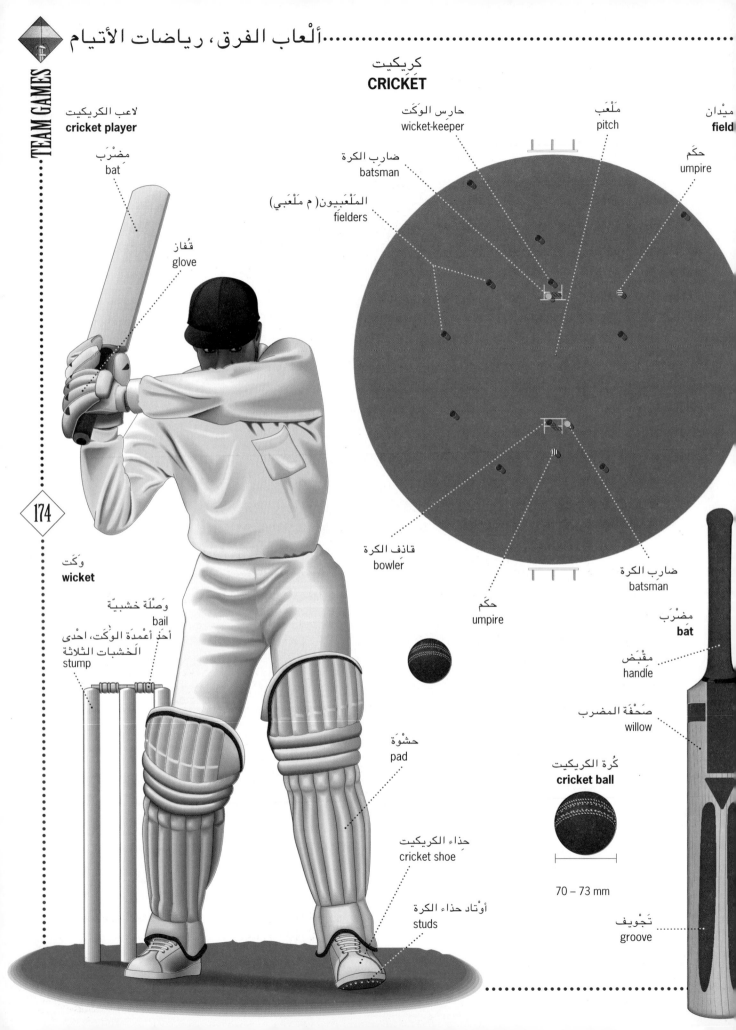

لاعب الكريكيت
cricket player

مِضْرَب
bat

قُفاز
glove

حارس الوَكَت
wicket-keeper

ضارب الكرة
batsman

المَلْعَبيون(م مَلْعَبي)
fielders

مَلْعَب
pitch

مِيْدان
field

حَكَم
umpire

قاذف الكرة
bowler

حَكَم
umpire

ضارِب الكرة
batsman

مِضْرَب
bat

مِقْبَض
handle

صَحْفَة المضرب
willow

وَكَت
wicket

وَصْلَة خشبيّة
bail

أحَدُ أعْمِدَة الوَكَت، احدى
الَخشبات الثلاثة
stump

حشْوَة
pad

كُرة الكريكيت
cricket ball

حذاء الكريكيت
cricket shoe

أوْتاد حذاء الكرة
studs

70 – 73 mm

تَجْويف
groove

174

هوكي الميدان
FIELD HOCKEY

ميدان الهوكي
playing field

54,9 m

الرايَة الرُّكْنيّة
corner flag

دائِرة المرمى
striking circle

22,9 metre line

خطّ جانِبي
sideline

خطّ الوسَط
center line / centre line

مُهاجِم مُتقدِّم
center forward /
centre forward

لاعِب الهُجُوم الشَّمال
left inner

لاعِب الهُجُوم اليمين
right inner

الجِناح الشَّمال
left wing

91,4 m

لاعِب الوسط الشَّمال
left half

الجِناح اليمين
right wing

الظَّهِير الشَّمال
left back

لاعِب الوسط اليمين
right half

حارِس المرمى
goalkeeper

لاعِب الوسَط
center half / centre half

مَرْمى
goal

الظَّهِير اليمين
right back

خطّ المرمى
goal line

كرة الهوكي
hockey ball

مِضْرَب الهوكي
hockey stick

66-7مم
66 – 74 mm

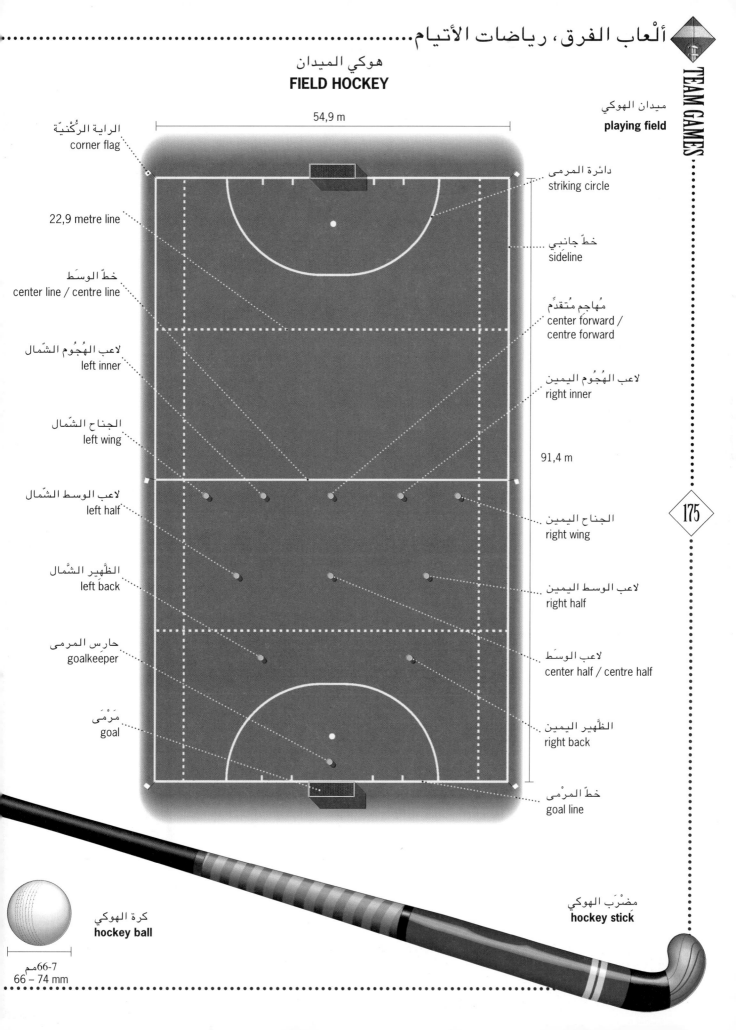

هوكي الجّليد
ICE HOCKEY

لبَكّ: قُرْص مطاطي
puck

26 – 30 m

25 mm

76 mm

المَزْلَجَة
rink

خطّ المرمى
goal line

ساحة المرمى
goal crease

دائرة المُواجَهَة
face-off circle

الخطّ الأزْرَق
blue line

ساحة محايدة
neutral zone

مقاعد الجَزاء(المخالفات)
penalty bench

مقاعد الحُكّام
officials' bench

جناح أيْسَر
left wing

وسَط
center / centre

الدِّفاع الشّمال
left defense

نطاق الدِّفاع
defending zone

لوْحات
boards

حكم المرمى
goal judge

مَرْمَى
goal

نُقْطة المواجَهَة
face-off spot

نطاق الهُجوم
attacking zone

حكَم
referee

خطّ الوسَط
center line / centre lin

61 m

مقاعد اللاعبين
players' bench

جناح يمين
right wing

رجُل الخطِّ
linesman

دائرة المواجهة الوُسْطى
center face-off circle /
centre face-off circle

الدِّفاع اليمين
right defense

حارس المرمى
goalkeeper

ركُن المزلجة
rink corner

مِضْرَب لاعِب الهوكي
player's stick

عَقِب المِضْرب
butt end

خُوذة
helmet

لاعِب هوكي الجليد
ice hockey player

حشِيَة الكوع
elbow pad

حشْوَة الكَتف
shoulder pad

مُطَوَّق المِعْصَم
cuff

حِزام واقي
protective girdle

قُفاز
glove

الكَأس الواقِيَّة
protective cup

حشِية الرُكْبة
knee pad

حشْوة الظُنبوب، حشِيَّة
shin pad

مِزْلَج
skate

جذْع او قَصَبَة المِضْرب
shaft

حارِس المَرْمَى
goalkeeper

قِناع الوجه
face mask

واقي الحِنجرة او الرقبة
throat protector

حشِية الذُراع
arm pad

حشْوة واقِية للصّدْر
body pad

حشْوَة الظَهْر
back pad

سِروال
pants

الحافّة
blade

قُفاز الإمساك بالكرة
catch glove

حشِية لحماية رِجلي حارس المرمى
goalkeeper's pad

مِزْلَج
skate

كعب
heel

الحافّة
blade

مِضْرب حارِس المرمى
goalkeeper's stick

كرة السَّلَّة
BASKETBALL

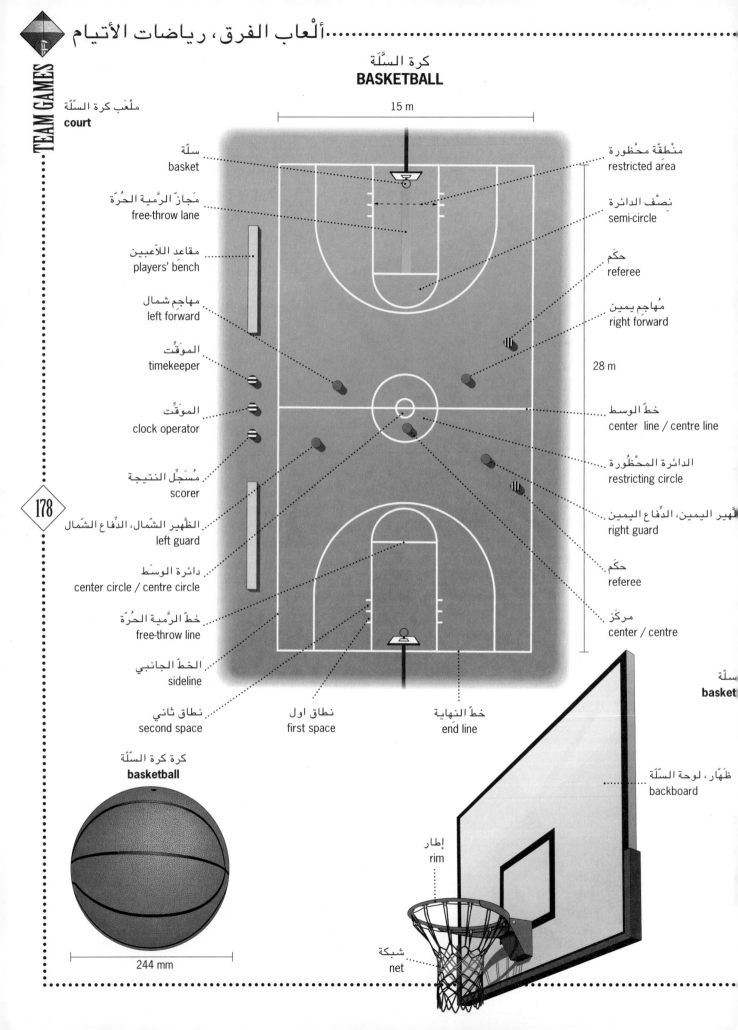

مَلْعَب كرة السَّلَّة
court

15 m

سلّة
basket

مَجازّ الرَّمية الحُرّة
free-throw lane

مقاعد اللاَّعبين
players' bench

مهاجم شمال
left forward

المُوَقِّت
timekeeper

المُوَقِّت
clock operator

مُسَجِّل النتيجة
scorer

الظَّهير الشّمال، الدِّفاع الشّمال
left guard

دائرة الوسَط
center circle / centre circle

خطّ الرَّمية الحُرّة
free-throw line

الخطّ الجانبي
sideline

منْطقة محْظورة
restricted area

نصْف الدائرة
semi-circle

حكَم
referee

مُهاجم يمين
right forward

28 m

خطّ الوسَط
center line / centre line

الدائرة المحْظُورة
restricting circle

الظَّهير اليمين، الدِّفاع اليمين
right guard

حكَم
referee

مركَز
center / centre

نطاق ثاني
second space

نطاق اول
first space

خطّ النهاية
end line

كرة السَّلَّة
basketball

244 mm

سلّة
basket

ظهّار، لوحة السَّلَّة
backboard

إطار
rim

شبكة
net

178

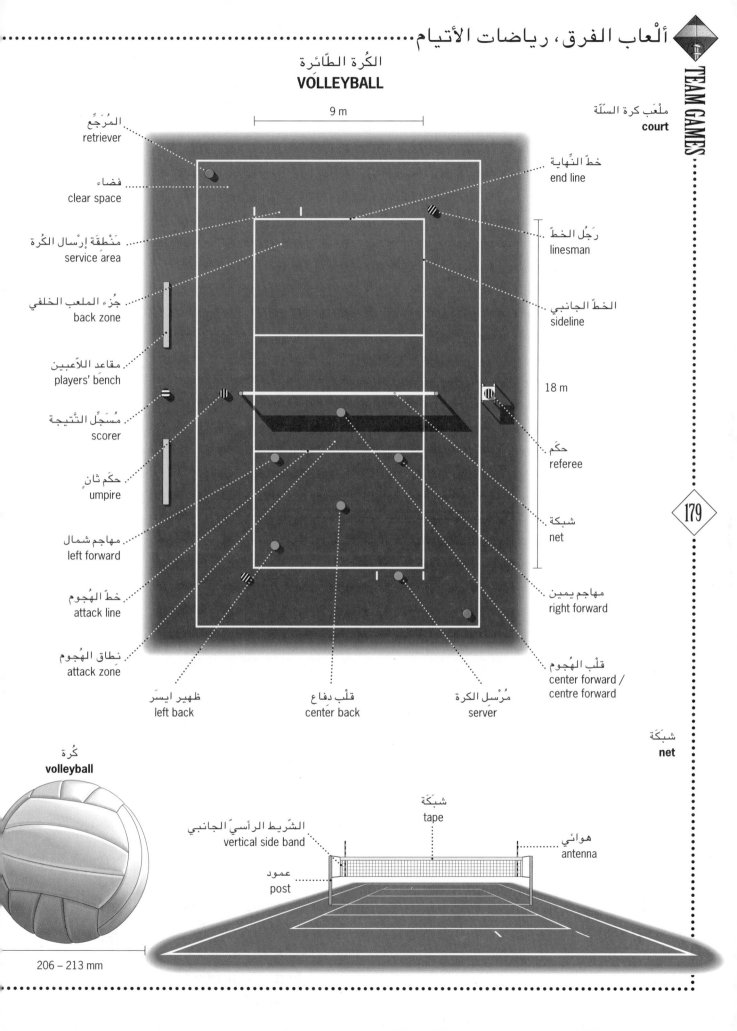

الكُرة الطّائِرة
VOLLEYBALL

9 m

ملْعَب كرة السلّة
court

المُرَجِّع
retriever

خطّ النِّهاية
end line

فضاء
clear space

رَجُل الخطّ
linesman

مَنْطِقة إرْسال الكُرة
service area

الخطّ الجانبي
sideline

جُزء المَلعب الخلفي
back zone

18 m

مقاعد اللاعبين
players' bench

مُسَجِّل التَّتيجة
scorer

حكَم ثانٍ
umpire

حكَم
referee

مهاجم شمال
left forward

شبَكة
net

خطّ الهُجوم
attack line

مهاجم يمين
right forward

نطاق الهُجوم
attack zone

ظهير ايسَر
left back

قلْب دفاع
center back

مُرْسِل الكرة
server

قلْب الهُجوم
center forward /
centre forward

كُرة
volleyball

الشّريط الرّأسيّ الجانبي
vertical side band

شبَكَة
tape

هوائي
antenna

عمود
post

206 – 213 mm

شبَكَة
net

كُرة المضْرَب، التَّنس
TENNIŚ

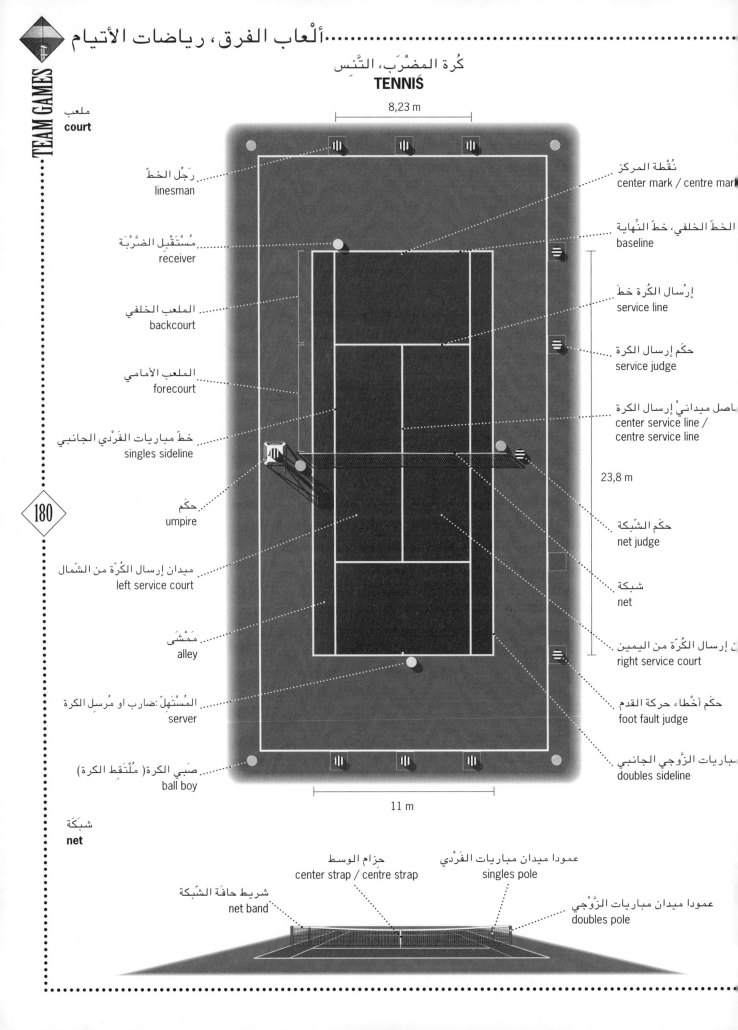

ملعب
court

8,23 m

رجُل الخطّ
linesman

نُقْطة المركز
center mark / centre mark

مُسْتَقْبِل الضَّرْبَة
receiver

الخطّ الخلفي، خطّ النِّهاية
baseline

الملعب الخلفي
backcourt

إرْسال الكُرة خطَ
service line

حكَم إرسال الكرة
service judge

الملعب الأمامي
forecourt

ـاصل ميداني إرْسال الكرة
center service line /
centre service line

خطّ مباريات الفَرْدي الجانبي
singles sideline

23,8 m

حكَم
umpire

حكَم الشّبّكة
net judge

ميدان إرْسال الكُرة من الشّمال
left service court

شبكة
net

مَمْشَى
alley

ن إرسال الكُرة من اليمين
right service court

المُسْتَهِلّ:ضارب او مُرسِل الكرة
server

حكَم أخْطاء حركة القدم
foot fault judge

ـباريات الزَّوْجي الجانبي
doubles sideline

صبي الكرة(مُلْتَقِط الكرة)
ball boy

11 m

شبكَة
net

حزام الوسط
center strap / centre strap

عمودا ميدان مباريات الفَرْدي
singles pole

شريط حافَة الشّبّكة
net band

عمودا ميدان مباريات الزَّوْجي
doubles pole

180

كُرة التَّنِس
tennis ball

64 – 68 mm

لاعِب كرة التَّنِس
tennis player

عُصابَة رأس
headband

قميص
polo shirt

عُصابة مِعْصَم
wristband

مِضْرَب كرة التَّنِس
tennis racket

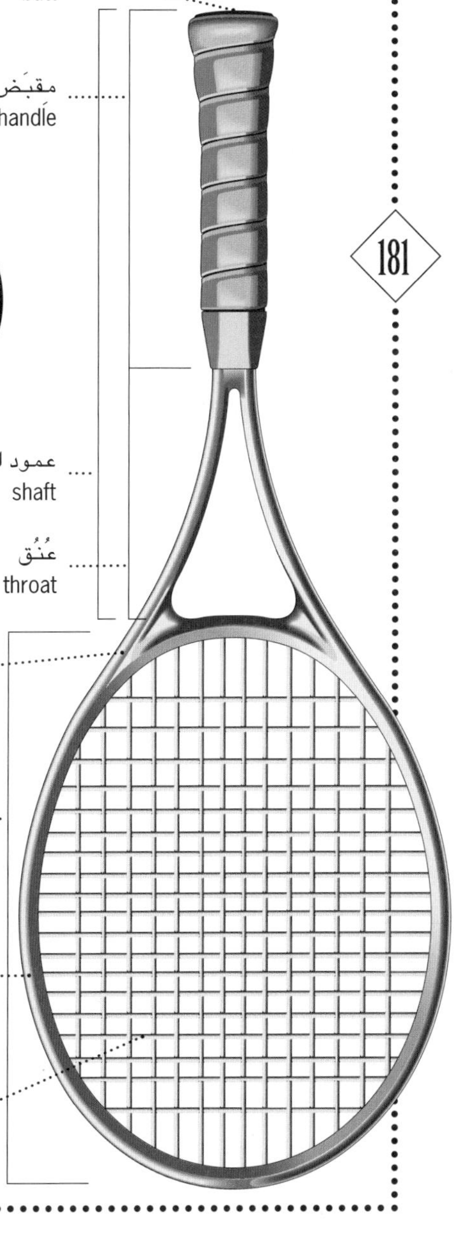

عَقِب المِضْرَب
butt

مقبَض
handle

رداء
skirt

عمود المقبض
shaft

عُنُق
throat

كَتِف
shoulder

رأس
head

إطار
frame

شَبَكَة
strings

حذاء التنس
tennis shoe

جَوْرَب
sock

181

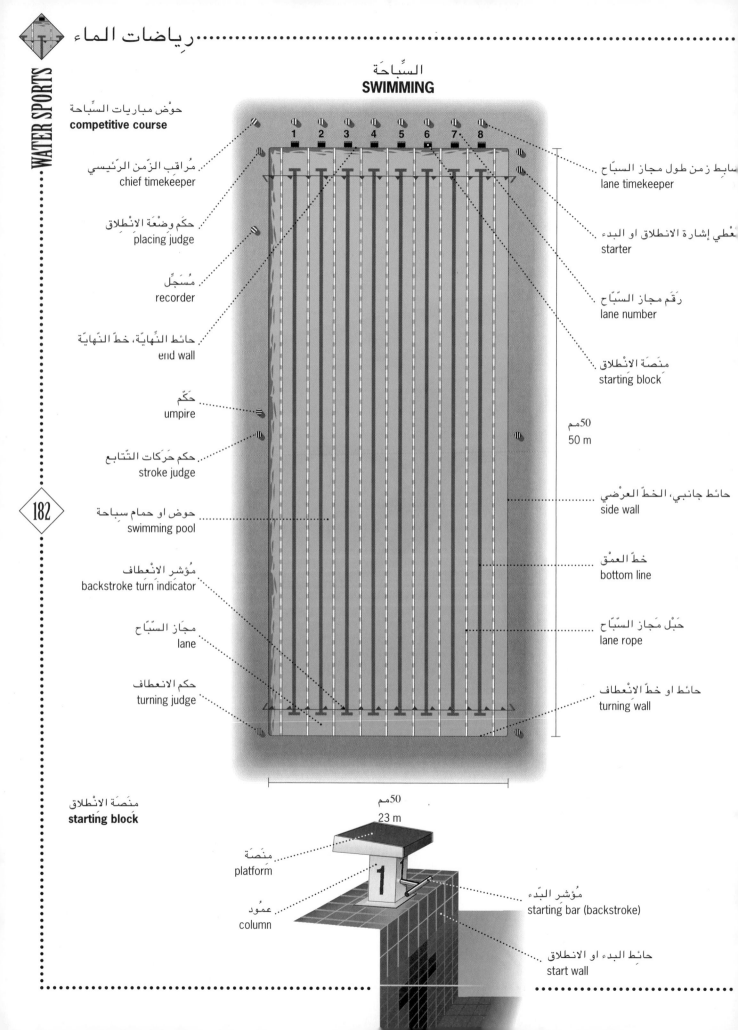

السِّباحَة
SWIMMING

حوْض مباريات السِّباحة
competitive course

مُراقِب الزّمن الرّئيسي
chief timekeeper

حَكَم وضْعَة الانْطلاق
placing judge

مُسَجِّل
recorder

حائط النِّهايَة، خطّ النِّهايّة
end wall

حَكَم
umpire

حكم حَرَكات التّتابع
stroke judge

حوض او حمام سباحة
swimming pool

مُؤشِر الانْعطاف
backstroke turn indicator

مَجاز السّبّاح
lane

حكم الانعطاف
turning judge

ضابِط زمن طول مجاز السّبّاح
lane timekeeper

يُعْطي إشارة الانطلاق او البدء
starter

رَقَم مجاز السّبّاح
lane number

مَنصَة الانْطلاق
starting block

حائط جانبي، الخطّ العرْضي
side wall

خطّ العمْق
bottom line

حَبْل مَجاز السّبّاح
lane rope

حائط او خطّ الانْعطاف
turning wall

50مم
50 m

مَنصَة الانْطلاق
starting block

50مم
23 m

مَنصَة
platform

عمُود
column

مُؤشر البّدء
starting bar (backstroke)

حائط البدء او الانطلاق
start wall

182

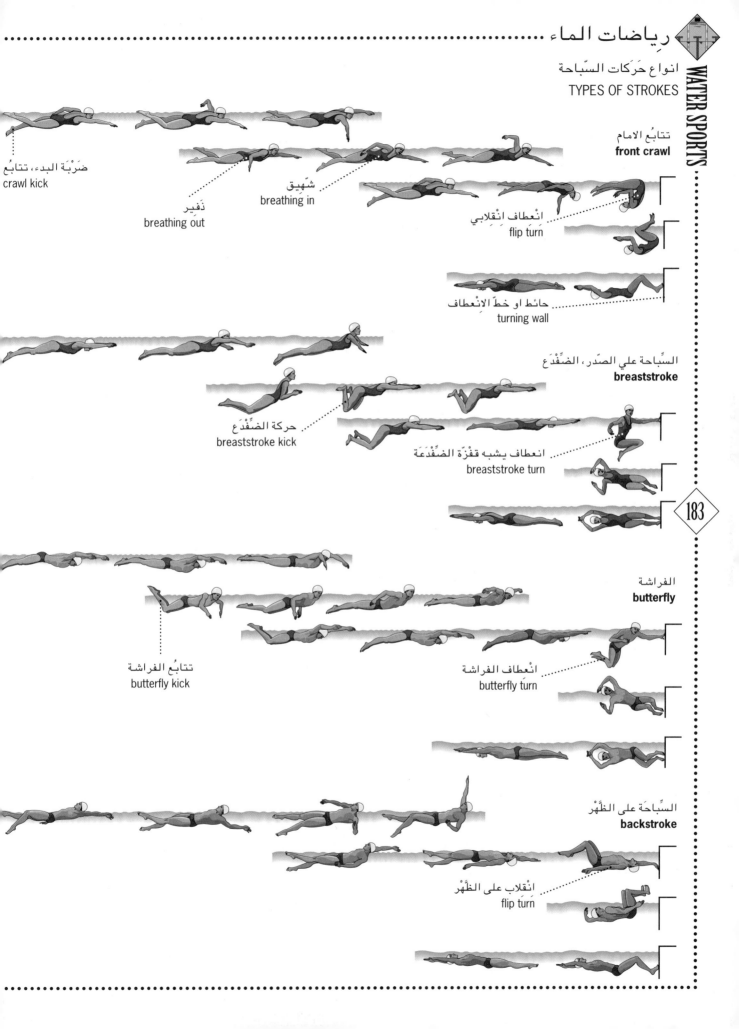

انواع حَرَكات السِّباحة
TYPES OF STROKES

تتابُع الامام
front crawl

ضَرْبَة البدء، تتابُع
crawl kick

دَفير
breathing out

شَهيق
breathing in

انْعِطاف انْقِلابي
flip turn

حائط او خطّ الانْعِطاف
turning wall

السِّباحة علي الصَّدر، الضِّفْدَع
breaststroke

حركة الضِّفْدَع
breaststroke kick

انعطاف يشبه قفْزة الضِّفْدَعَة
breaststroke turn

183

الفراشة
butterfly

تتابُع الفراشة
butterfly kick

انْعِطاف الفراشة
butterfly turn

السِّباحة على الظَهْر
backstroke

انْقِلاب على الظَهْر
flip turn

الشّراعيّة
SAILBOARD

شِراع
sail

أعْلَى الصّاري
masthead

جُلْبَة الصّاري
mast sleeve

حافّة الشّراع
luff

العارِضَة
batten

جيْب العارِضة
batten pocket

شبّاك
window

عمود مُنْحَني
wishbone boom

صاري
mast

مُغَيِّر الاتجاه
uphaul

زاوية الشّراع، حبْل
tack

أدْنى الصّاري
mast foot

اللّوح الرئيسي، لوح القصّ
board

مُقدَّم المركب
bow

الكظامَة
clew

مَشْبَك القدَم
foot strap

لوح شبيه بالخَنْجَر
daggerboard

مُؤخر رافِدة القصّ
skeg

الكَوْثَل
stern

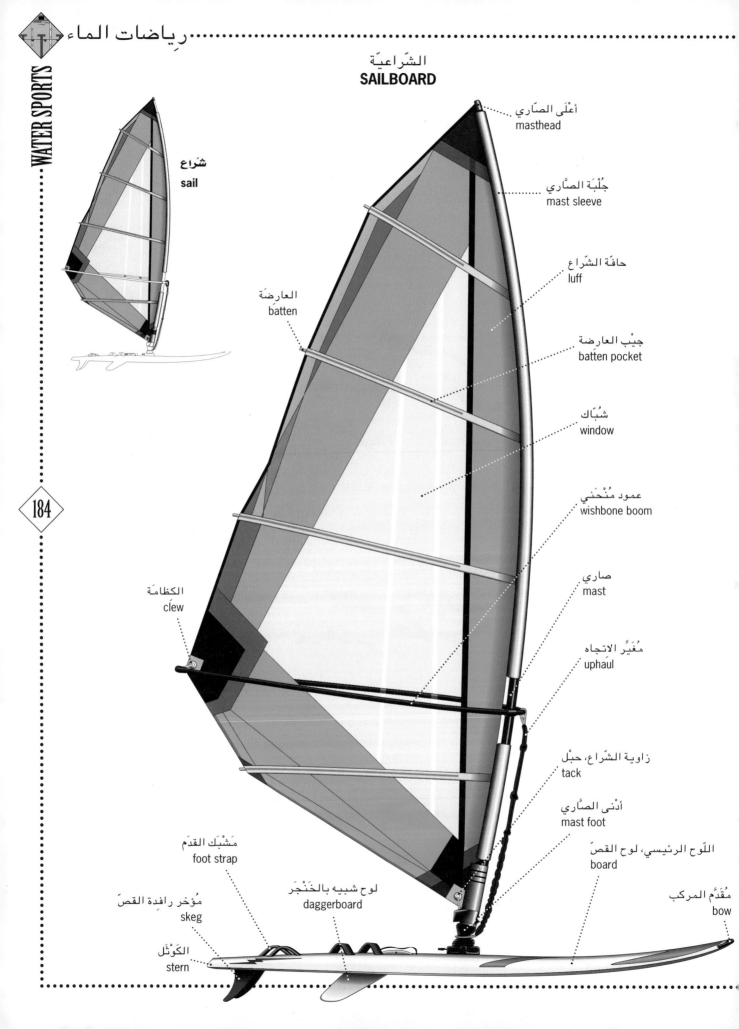

تَزَحْلُق، تَزَلُّج
SKATING

التَّزَلُّج السَّريع
speed skate

حذاء داخلي
inner boot

غطاء عُلْوي
upper shell

التَّزحْلُق بعجلات
in-line skate

حزام ضابط
adjusting buckle

حذاء
boot

مِزْلَج الهوكي
hockey skate

حامي الوَتَرَة
tendon guard

حذاء
boot

مِحْوَر
axle

عَجَلَة
wheel

دولاب الحذاء
truck

كابح
heel stop

التَّزَلُّج الرّاقص
figure skate

لِسان
tongue

زِرّ
hook

شِكال
backstay

ثُقْب رِباط الحذاء
eyelet

حذاء
boot

رِباط الحذاء
lace

صندوق الأصابع
toe box

طَرَف
point

سِناد قائِم
stanchion

حافة المِزْلَج
blade

مِشبك المِزلاج
skate guard

حافّة
edge

حافة المِزْلَج
blade

باطن نَعْل الحذاء
sole

مقدَّم المِزْلَج
toe pick

185

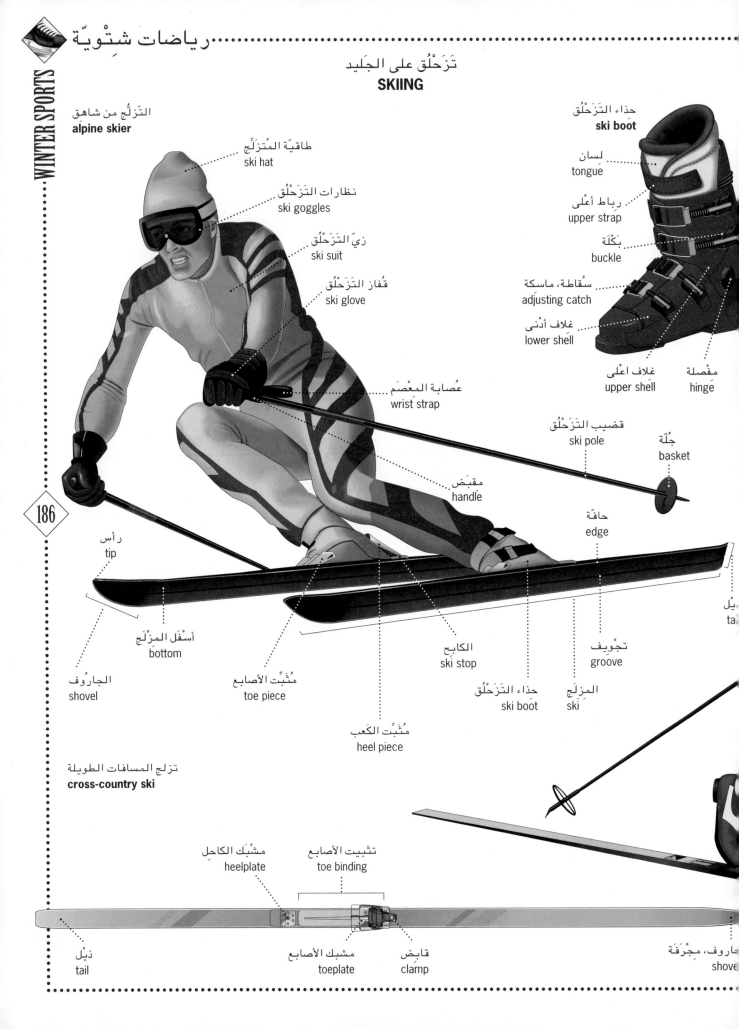

رياضات شِتْوِيّة

تَزَحْلُق على الجَلِيد
SKIING

التَزَلُّج من شاهِق
alpine skier

طاقِيّة المُتَزَلِّج
ski hat

نظارات التَزَحْلُق
ski goggles

زيّ التَزَحْلُق
ski suit

قُفاز التَزَحْلُق
ski glove

عُصابة المِعْصَم
wrist strap

مِقبَض
handle

حذاء التَزَحْلُق
ski boot

لِسان
tongue

رباط أعْلى
upper strap

بَكْلَة
buckle

سُقّاطة، ماسكة
adjusting catch

غلاف أدْنى
lower shell

غلاف اعْلى
upper shell

مِفصلة
hinge

قضيب التَزَحْلُق
ski pole

جُلّة
basket

حافّة
edge

رأس
tip

أسْفَل المِزلَج
bottom

الجاروف
shovel

مُثَبِّت الأصابِع
toe piece

مُثَبِّت الكَعب
heel piece

الكابِح
ski stop

حذاء التَزَحْلُق
ski boot

المِزلَج
ski

تجوِيف
groove

يْل
ta

تزلج المسافات الطويلة
cross-country ski

مشْبَك الكاحِل
heelplate

تثبيت الأصابع
toe binding

ذيّل
tail

مشبك الأصابع
toeplate

قابِض
clamp

اروف، مِجرَفَة
shove

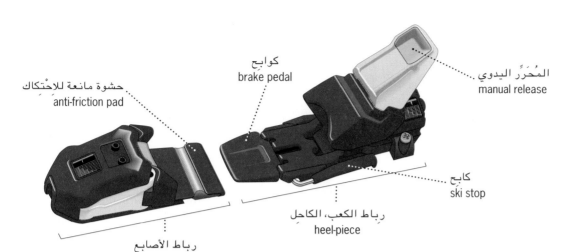

رِباط الأمان
safety binding

كوابح
brake pedal

حشوة مانعة للاِحْتكاك
anti-friction pad

المُحَرِّر اليدوي
manual release

كابِح
ski stop

رِباط الكعب، الكاحِل
heel-piece

رِباط الأصابِع
toe-piece

المُتزلِّج عبْر الدُوَل
cross-country skier

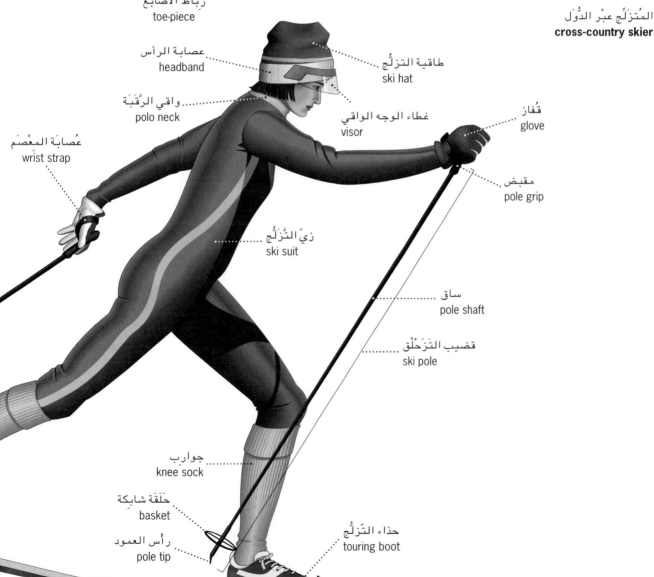

عصابة الرأس
headband

طاقية التزلُّج
ski hat

واقي الرَّقَبَة
polo neck

غطاء الوجه الواقي
visor

قُفاز
glove

عُصابَة المِعْصَم
wrist strap

مقبض
pole grip

زيّ التَّزَلُّج
ski suit

ساق
pole shaft

قضيب التَزحْلُق
ski pole

جوارب
knee sock

حَلَقَة شابكة
basket

رأْس العمود
pole tip

حذاء التّزلُّج
touring boot

التَّزَلُّج عبْر الدُوَل، التَّزَلُّج بعيد المدَى
cross-country ski

الجُمْباز

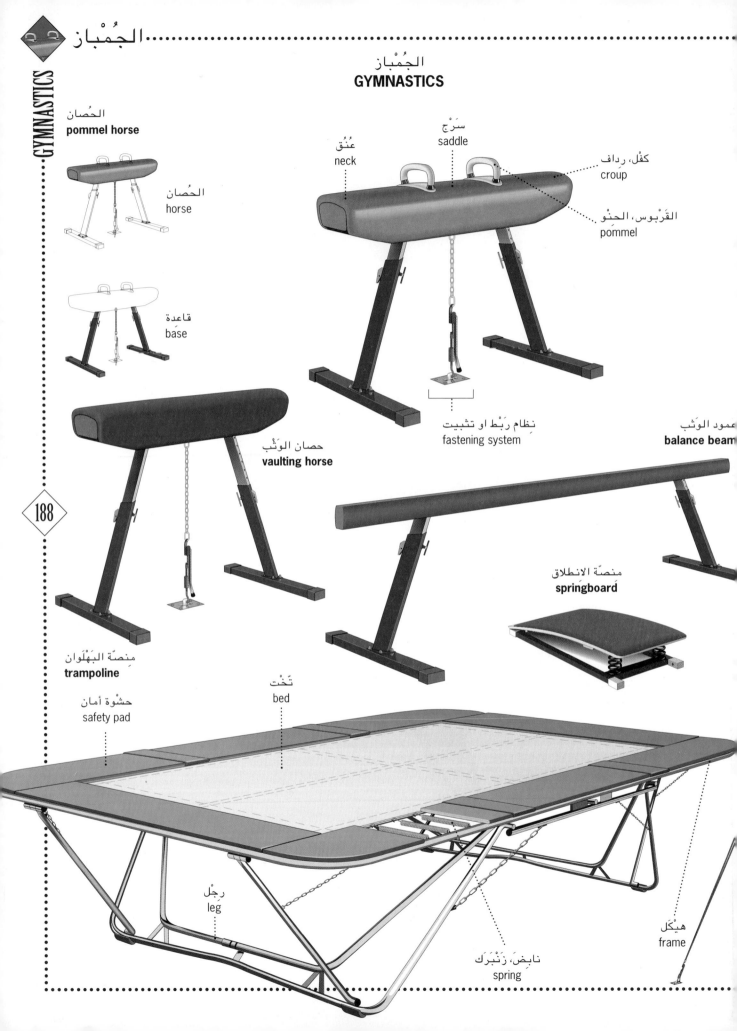

الحُصان
pommel horse

الحُصان
horse

قاعدة
base

عُنُق
neck

سَرْج
saddle

كفْل، رِداف
croup

القَرْبوس، الحِنْو
pommel

نِظام رَبْط او تثبيت
fastening system

حصان الوَثْب
vaulting horse

عمود الوَثْب
balance beam

مِنصّة الانطلاق
springboard

مِنصّة البَهْلَوان
trampoline

حشْوة أمان
safety pad

تَّخْت
bed

رِجْل
leg

هَيكَل
frame

نابِض، زَنْبَرَك
spring

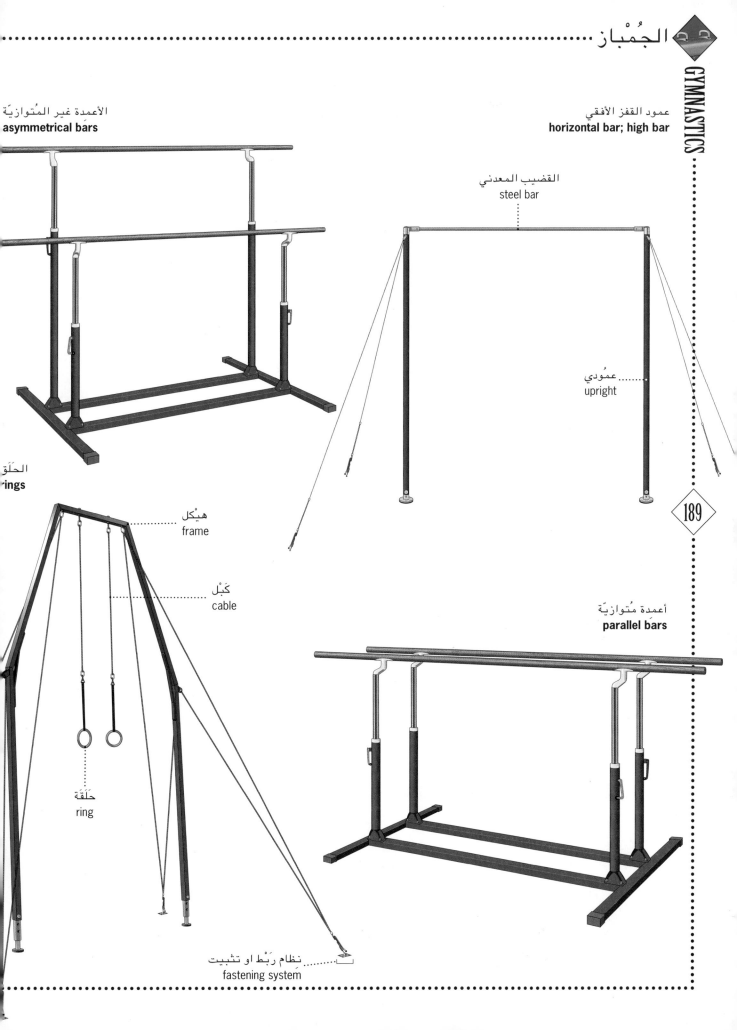

الأعمدة غير المُتوازيّة
asymmetrical bars

عمود القفز الأفقي
horizontal bar; high bar

القضيب المعدني
steel bar

عمُودي
upright

الحَلَق
rings

هيْكل
frame

كَبْل
cable

أعمدة مُتوازيّة
parallel bars

حَلَقَة
ring

نظام رَبْط او تثبيت
fastening system

التَّخْيِيم :الإقامة في معسكر او خِيام

خِيام (م خَيْمَة)
TENTS

خَيْمَة لشخْصين
two-person tent

ر المطر :طرْف الخيمة يسيل منّه المطر
rainfly / flysheet

باب
door

ظلَّة :لِسان باب الخيمة
awning

الشدَّادة
guy line / guy rope

وتِد
stake / tent pe,

مَشَدّ
strainer

زمام مُنْزِّلق
zipper / zip

خَيْمَة داخليَّة
inner tent

أنْواع الخيام الرئيسية
MAJOR TYPES OF TENTS

خَيْمَة كبيرة
wagon tent

خيمة حائط، خيمة
مسْتَطيلة
wall tent

خيمة الجرو :خيمة كندية صغيرة
pup tent / ridge tent

خيمة مُقبَّبة
dome tent

الخيْمَة القُبِّيَّة
pop-up tent

خيمة للعائلة :ذات حُجَرات
family tent

خيمة لشخص واحد
one-person tent

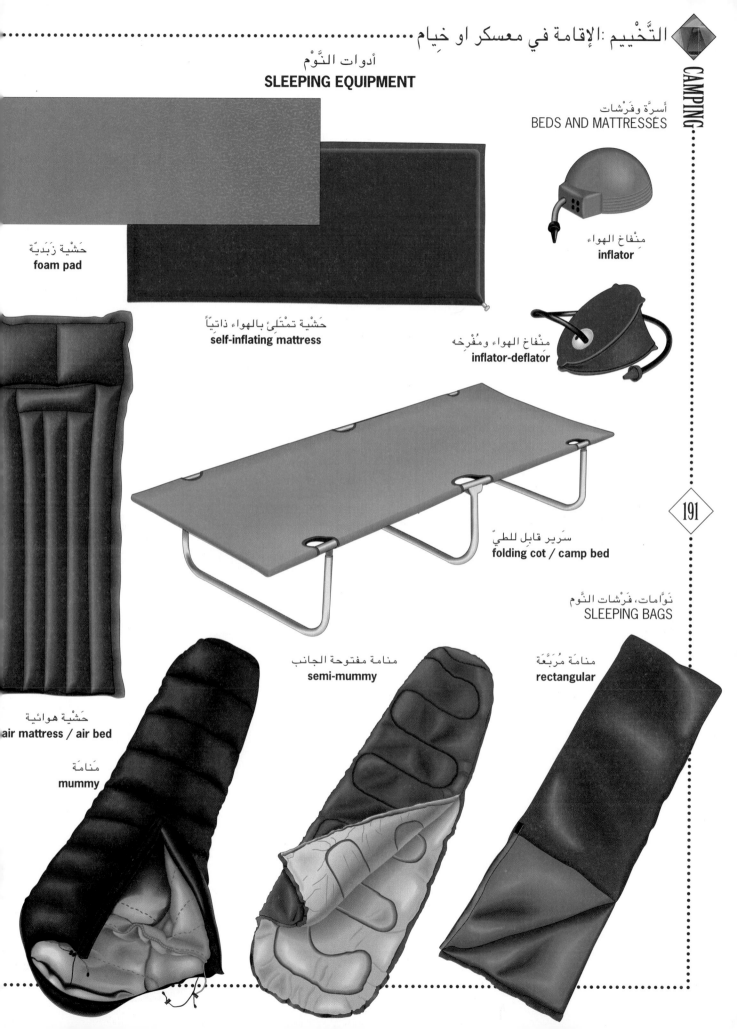

أدوات النَّوْم
SLEEPING EQUIPMENT

أَسِرَّة وفَرْشات
BEDS AND MATTRESSES

مِنْفاخ الهواء
inflator

مِنْفاخ الهواء ومُفْرِخه
inflator-deflator

حَشْية زَبَدِيّة
foam pad

حَشْية تمْتَلِئ بالهواء ذاتيّاً
self-inflating mattress

سَرير قابِل للطيّ
folding cot / camp bed

191

نَوّامات، فَرْشات النَّوْم
SLEEPING BAGS

منامة مفتوحة الجانب
semi-mummy

منامَة مُرَبَّعَة
rectangular

حَشْية هوائية
air mattress / air bed

مَنامَة
mummy

أجهزة وأدَوات المُعَسْكَر
CAMPING EQUIPMENT

سِكِّين الجُنْدي السُّويسريّة
Swiss army knife

مقصّ
scissors

مِسْطَرَة
ruler

مقْشَرَة السَّمَك
fish scaler

مِنْشار
file

مُكَبِّر
magnifier

مفَكّ نَجْمَة
cross-tip screwdriver

نَصْل صغير
small blade

مفَكّ
screwdriver

مفْتاح الزُّجاجات
bottle opener

مفَكّ
screwdriver

نَصْل كبير
large blade

حَزّاز الأظافر
nail nick

مِخْرَز
awl

مِبْرام
corkscrew

مفْتاح العُلَب
can opener /
tin opener

غمْد جِلْديّ
leather sheath

سكّين
knife

غمْد
sheath

بَطاريّة، كَشّافة
**flashlight /
pocket torch**

فأْس قصيرة اليَد، البُلَيْطَة
hatchet / axe

مجموعة آلات طبْخ
COOKING SET

رَكْوَة قَهْوَة
coffee pot

صحْن، طَبَق
plate

طَوَّة
frying pan

كَوْب
cup

حافظَة الماء
canteen

مقبض
handle

كَفْت
saucepan

192

حقيبة ظهْر، شَنْطة ظهْر
backpack / rucksack

الغطاء الأعلى المُتَدَلّي
top flap

الكَتفيّة
shoulder strap

الرِّباط المِحْزام الجانبي
side compression strap

الشّكل الدّاخلي
internal frame

حزام الوَسَط
waist belt

اِبزيم للشَدّ
tightening buckle

عُرْوة الرِّباط او الشَّريط
strap loop

الرِّباط المِحْزام الأمامي
front compression strap

إسْعافات أوّليّة
first aid kit

بوصَلة
magnetic compass

غطاء
cover

مَنْظَر
sight

مرآة المناظر
sighting mirror

خطّ النَّظَر
sighting line

إبرَة مَغْنَطيسية
magnetic needle

مِحْوَر
pivot

مِقْياس
scale

حافّة
edge

قُرْص البوصَلة
compass card

القُرْص المُدَرّج
graduated dial

شريط لاصق
adhesive tape / plaster tape

مَحْلُول مُطَهِّر
antiseptic lotion

مُطَهِّر
antiseptic

مِلْقاط صغير
tweezers

جَبيرة
splint

شاش مَلْفوف
gauze roller bandage

زُجاجة متعدِّدة الأغْراض
multipurpose bottle /
multipurpose flask

لَفّة قُطْن
cotton roll

مقَصّ
scissors

ضمادَة صغيرة
small bandage / plaster

قطَع غِيار مُعَقَّم
sterile dressing

رِياضات (ألْعاب) داخِل القاعات

ألْعات الورق
CARD GAMES

الكَوْبَة، الهارْت
heart

الدِّناريّ
diamond

الاسْباتيّ
club

البَسْتُونيّ
spade

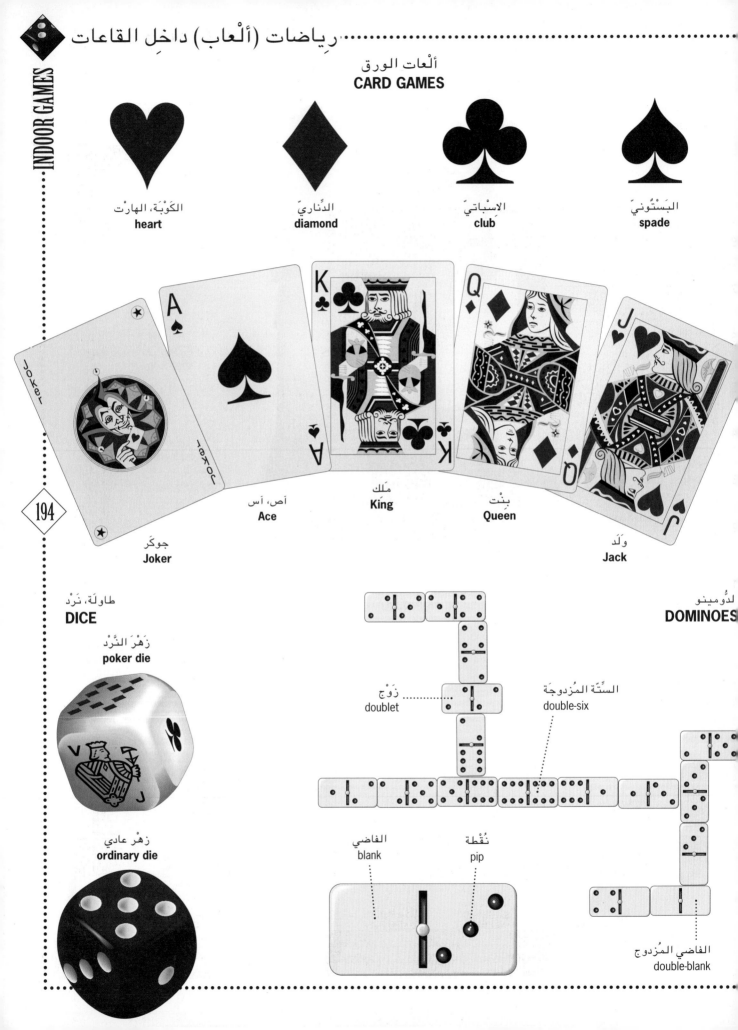

جوكَر
Joker

آص، آس
Ace

مَلك
King

بِنْت
Queen

وَلَد
Jack

194

طاولَة، نَرْد
DICE

زَهْرَ النَّرْد
poker die

زهْر عادي
ordinary die

لدُّومينو
DOMINOES

زَوْج
doublet

السِّتّة المُزدوجَة
double-six

الفاضي
blank

نُقْطة
pip

الفاضي المُزدوج
double-blank

الشَّطْرَنج
CHESS

قِطَع(م قِطْعَة)
MEN

رُقْعَة الشَّطْرَنج
chessboard

جانب الوزير
Queen's side

جانب المَلِك
King's side

أَسْوَد
Black

مُرَبَّع أَبْيَض
white square

مُرَبَّع أَسْوَد
black square

أَبْيَض
White

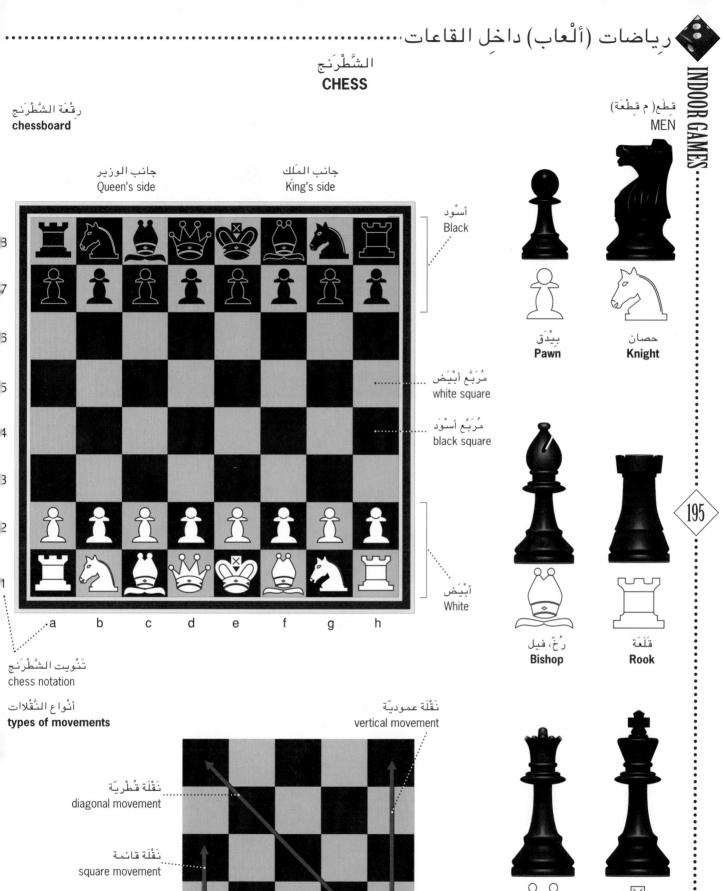

بَيْدَق
Pawn

حصان
Knight

رُخّ، فيل
Bishop

قَلَعَة
Rook

تَنْويت الشَّطْرَنج
chess notation

أَنْواع النَّقَلات
types of movements

نَقْلَة عموديّة
vertical movement

نَقْلَة قُطْريّة
diagonal movement

نَقْلَة قائمة
square movement

نَقْلَة أُفقيّة
horizontal movement

وَزير
Queen

مَلِك
King

رِياضات (ألْعاب) داخِل القاعات

طاوِلة، نَرْد
BACKGAMMON

أحْمَر
Red

الطَّاولة الخارجيّة
outer table

الطَّاولة الدّاخليّة
inner table

كوْب الزّهْر
dice cup

زهْر مُزْدَوج او ثنائي
doubling die

زهْر
die

خانَة
point

أبْيَض
White

حاجِز
bar

دُمي
men

دُميّة متقدِّمَة
runner

الدّاما
CHECKERS / DRAUGHTS

حَجَر
checker / draughtsman

رقْعَة الدّاما
checkerboard / draughtsboard

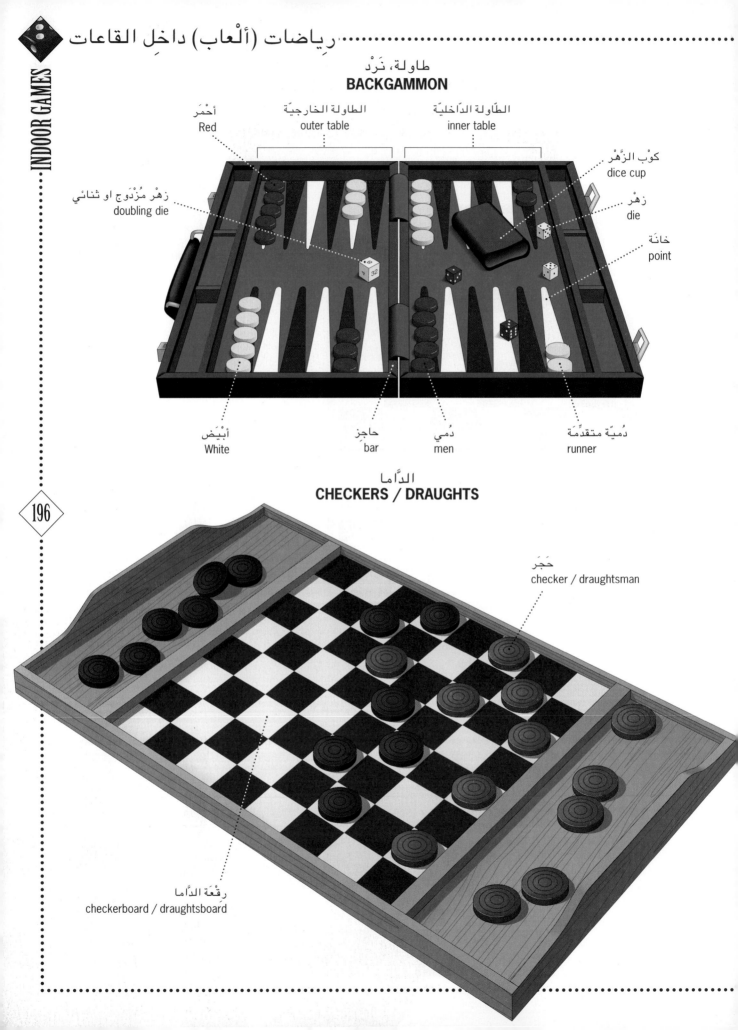

196

جِهاز التَّرْويح المَرئي
VIDEO ENTERTAINMENT SYSTEM

شاشة
visual display

اللَّفيفة
game cartridge

جِهاز التَّحَكُّم
control deck

مفتاح وَظيفيّ
function button

لَوْح ضَبْط التَّشْغيل
control pad

سَهْم مُرَيَّش
dart

لَعْبَة السِّهام المُرَيَّشة
GAME OF DARTS

اللَّوْحة
dartboard

مُؤخِر السَّهْم
flight

النِّقاط المُحْرَزَة في القِطاع
segment score number

دائرة النِّقاط المُزْدَوِجة
double ring

قَصَبَة السهم
shaft

دائرة النِّقاط المُثلَّثَة
triple ring

نُقْطة الهدف
bull's-eye

ماسورة
barrel

قِطاع الـ25
25 ring

رأس، أسْلَة
point

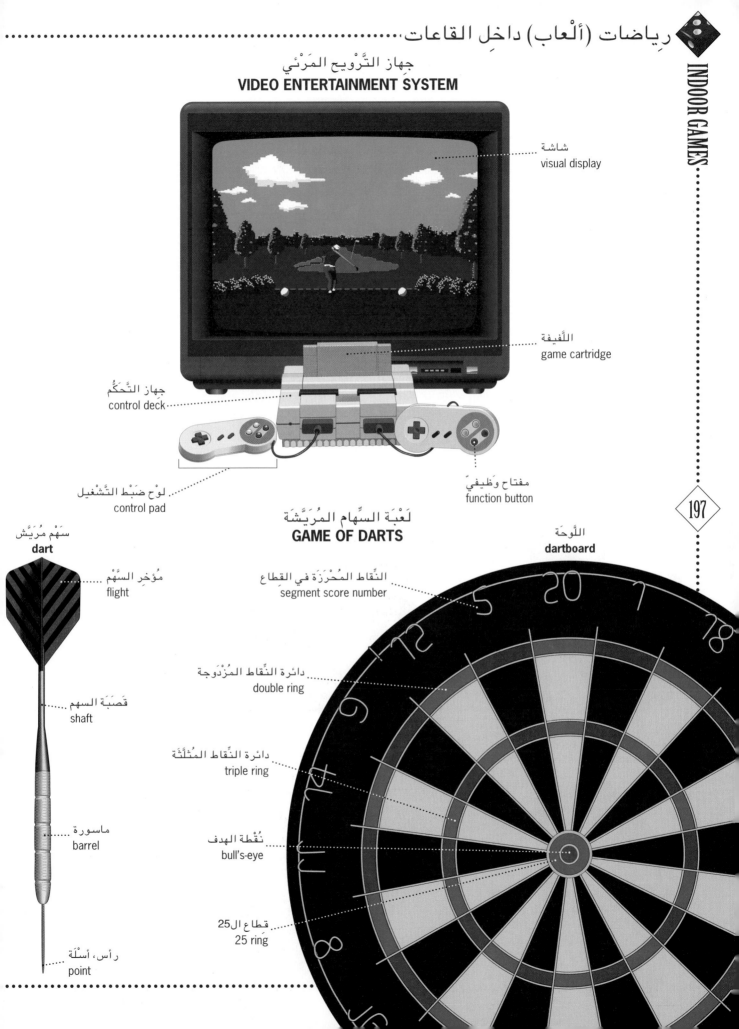

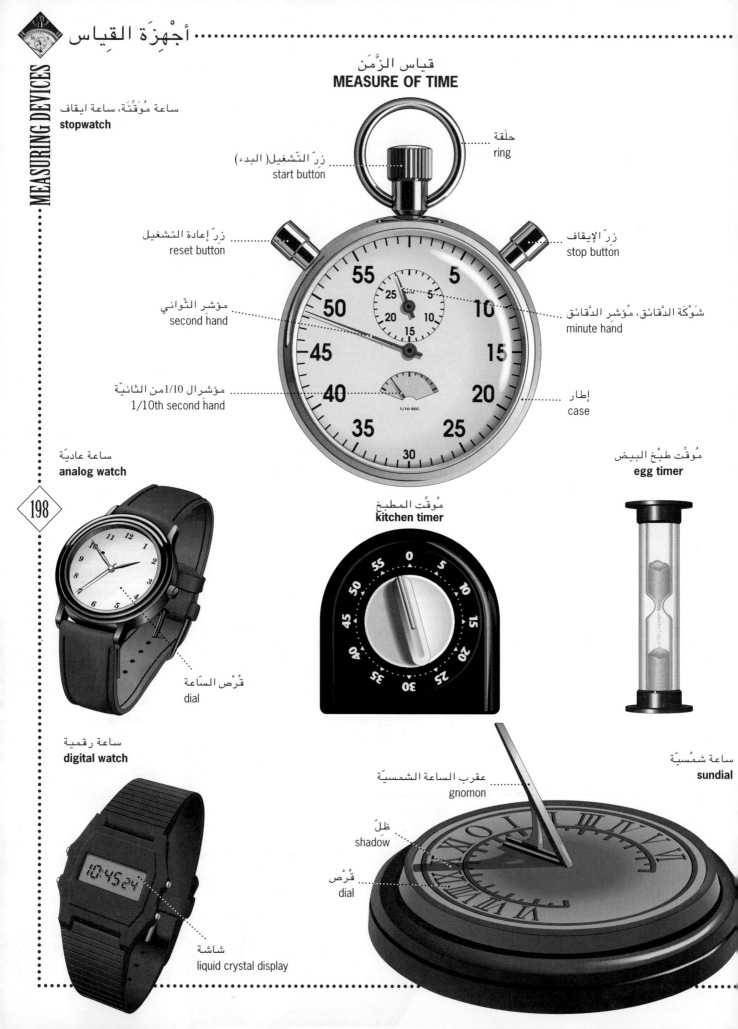

قِياس الزَّمَن
MEASURE OF TIME

ساعة مُوَقَّتَة، ساعة ايقاف
stopwatch

حلَقة
ring

زرّ التَّشغيل(البدء)
start button

زرّ الإيقاف
stop button

زرّ إعادة التشغيل
reset button

مؤشر الثَّواني
second hand

شَوْكَة الدَّقائق، مُؤشر الدَّقائق
minute hand

مؤشرال1/10 من الثانيّة
1/10th second hand

إطار
case

1/10 SEC

ساعة عاديّة
analog watch

مُوَقِّت طبْخ البيض
egg timer

مُوَقِّت المطبخ
kitchen timer

قُرْص السَّاعة
dial

ساعة رقمية
digital watch

ساعة شمْسيّة
sundial

عقرب الساعة الشمسيّة
gnomon

ظلّ
shadow

قُرْص
dial

شاشة
liquid crystal display

مقياس درجة الحرارة
MEASURE OF TEMPERATURE

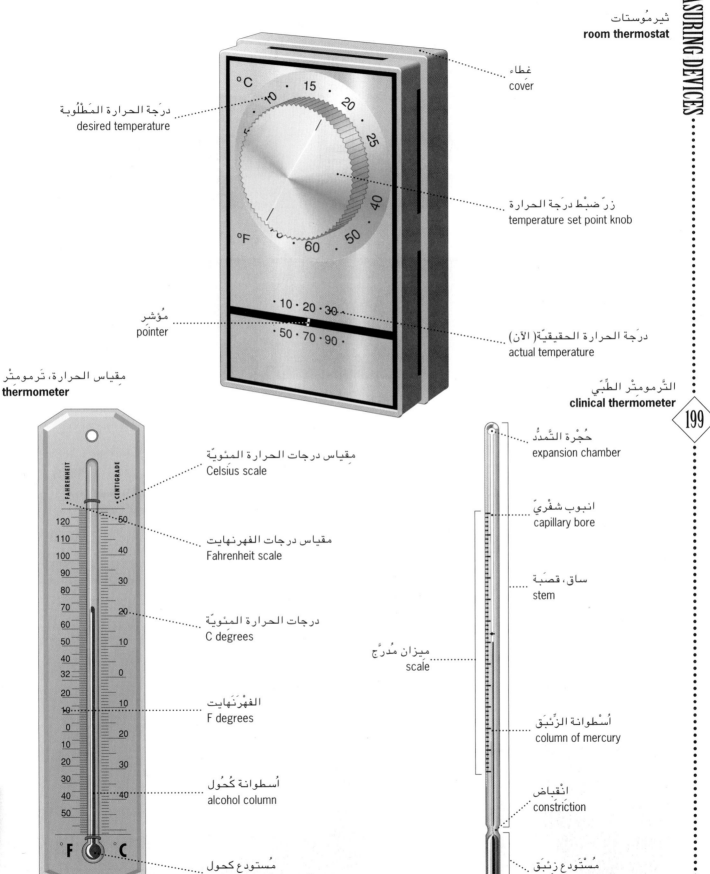

ثيرموستات
room thermostat

غِطاء
cover

درَجة الحرارة المَطْلُوبة
desired temperature

زرّ ضبْط درَجة الحرارة
temperature set point knob

مُؤشِر
pointer

درَجة الحرارة الحقيقيّة (الآن)
actual temperature

مِقياس الحرارة، تَرمومِتْر
thermometer

مِقياس درجات الحرارة المئويّة
Celsius scale

مقياس درجات الفهرنهايت
Fahrenheit scale

درجات الحرارة المئويّة
C degrees

الفهْرَنَهايت
F degrees

أُسطوانة كُحُول
alcohol column

مُستودع كحول
alcohol bulb

التَّرمومِتْر الطِّبِّي
clinical thermometer

حُجْرة التَّمَدُّد
expansion chamber

انبوب شفْريّ
capillary bore

ساق، قصَبَة
stem

ميزان مُدرَّج
scale

أُسْطوانة الزِّئبَق
column of mercury

انْقِباض
constriction

مُسْتَودع زِئبَق
mercury bulb

قِياس الوَزْن
MEASURE OF WEIGHT

مِيزان
balance

قُرص مُدَرَّج
dial

مُؤشِر
pointer

وزْن، عِيار
weight

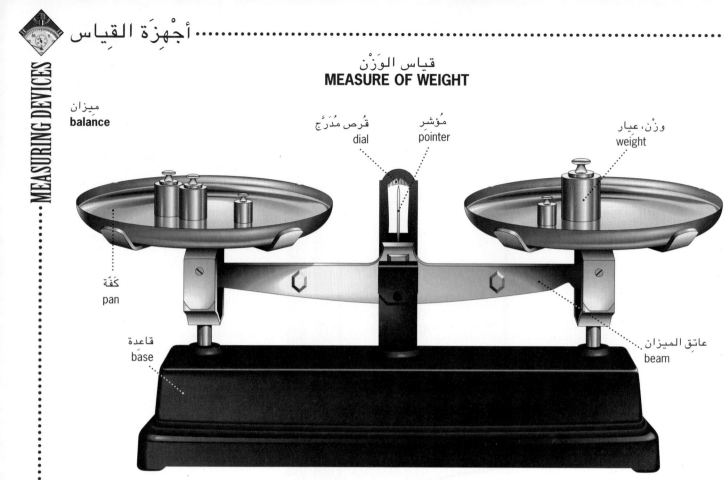

كَفّة
pan

قاعدة
base

عاتِق الميزان
beam

200

المِيزان القبّاني
steelyard

عِيار مُنْزَلِق
sliding weight

درَجة
notch

الورْنيّة
vernier scale

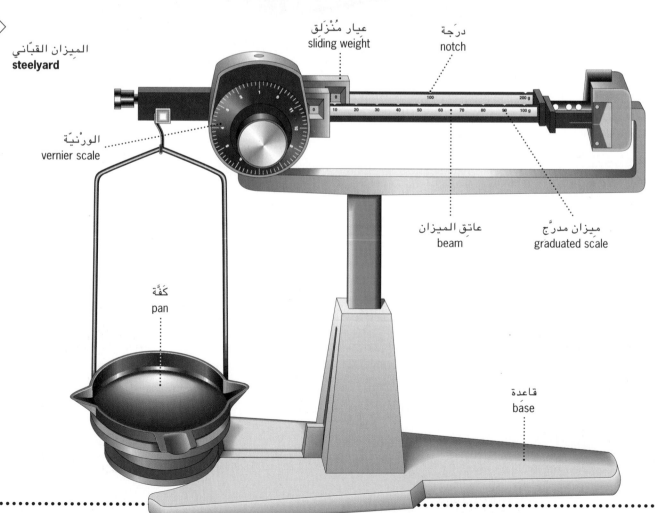

عاتِق الميزان
beam

مِيزان مدرَّج
graduated scale

كَفّة
pan

قاعدة
base

ميزان زَنْبَرَكي
spring balance

حلقة
ring

مُؤشِّر
pointer

مِيزان مدرَّج
graduated scale

كُلَّاب
hook

كَفَّة، طَبْلية
platform

أرْقام السِّلَع المُشَفَرة
product code

لوحة المفاتيح
numeric keyboard

مِيزان الحمّام
bathroom scale

ميزان الكتروني
electronic scale

مقْدار الوَزْن
weight

سعْر الوُحْدَة
unit price

شاشة العرْض
display

إجمالي القيمة
total

مادة مطْبُوعة(فاتورة)
printout

مفاتيح وظيفيّة
function keys

مِيزان المطبَخ
kitchen scale

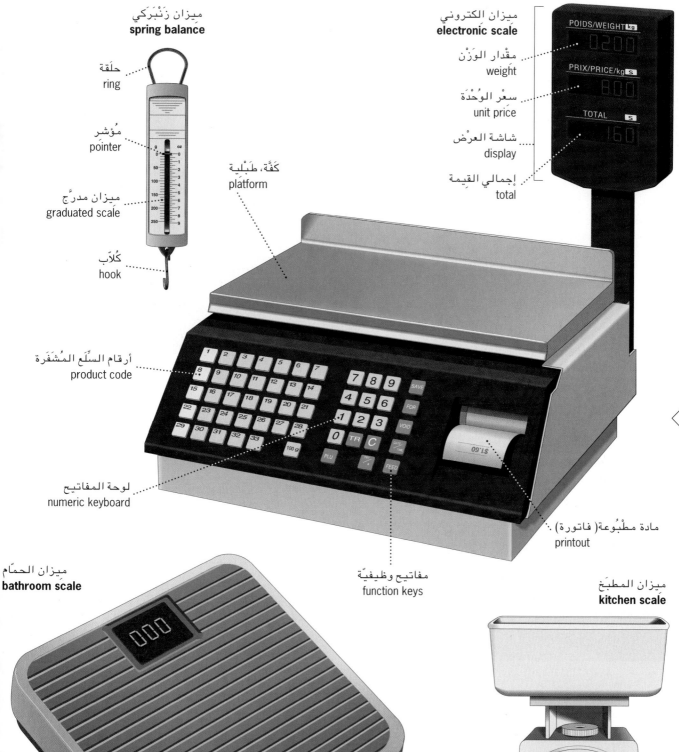

POIDS/WEIGHT kg
0200

PRIX/PRICE/kg $
8.00

TOTAL $
160

النَّفْط، البِتْرول
OIL

النَّقْل البَرِّي
GROUND TRANSPORT

انبوب او خطّ بترول
pipeline

التَّنْقيب
PROSPECTING

حفْر
DRILLING

التَّنْقيب في البرّ
surface prospecting

حَفَّارة
drilling rig

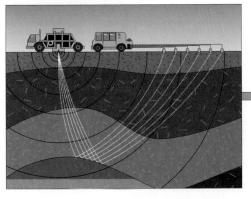

قَطيرة النفط
tank trailer / road trailer

202

التَّنْقيب في البحْر
offshore prospecting / offshore drilling

محطّة انْتاج او توليد
production platform

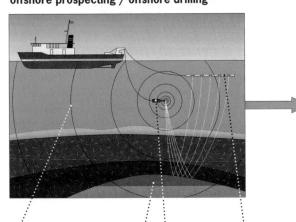

النَّقْل البحريّ
MARITIME TRANSPORT

موج الصّدْمة
shock wave

تسْجيل الانْفِجار الزِّلْزالي
seismographic recording

خطّ بترول جوفي
submarine pipeline

مِحْبَس بِترول
petroleum trap

شُحْنَة ناسفة
blasting charge

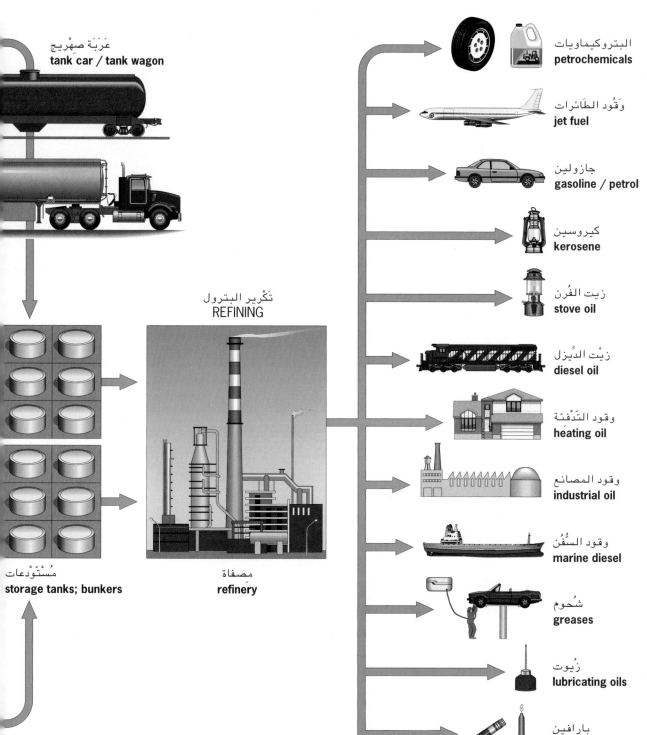

مُنْتجات مصفاة البترول
REFINERY PRODUCTS

عَرَبَة صِهْريج
tank car / tank wagon

تَكْرير البترول
REFINING

مُسْتَوْدعات
storage tanks; bunkers

مصفاة
refinery

ناقِلَة بترول
oil tanker

البتروكيماويات
petrochemicals

وَقُود الطَّائِرات
jet fuel

جازولين
gasoline / petrol

كيروسين
kerosene

زيت الفُرن
stove oil

زيْت الدِّيزل
diesel oil

وقود التّدْفِئَة
heating oil

وقود المصانع
industrial oil

وقود السُّفُن
marine diesel

شُحوم
greases

زُيوت
lubricating oils

بارافين
paraffins

أَسْفَلَت
asphalt

الطّاقة الكهرومائيّة
HYDROELECTRIC ENERGY

مُجمَّع انتاج طاقة كهرومائيّة
hydroelectric complex

أعلى الخزّان
top of dam

خزّان، مُسْنودع
reservoir

ونْش، رافعة
gantry crane

خزّان
dam

انبوب اوقناة تِصرْيف
spillway

مدْخل الانبوب
spillway gate

انبوب مائِل لإنْزال المياه
log chute

بوّابة الخزّان
penstock

محطّة توليد الطاقة
الكهرومائيّة
powerhouse

مقطع عرضي لمحطّةتوليد الطّاقة الكهرومائيّة
cross section of hydroelectric power station

حُجرة الماكينة او المحرّك
machine hall

حُجرة التّشغيل
control room

ونْش، رافعة
gantry crane

مُحَوِّل
transformer

بِطانة معدَنيّة
bushing

بوّابة
gate

مُسْتودع
reservoir

حاجز مُنْخلي
screen

مَصَبّ او مَسْرَب
المياه
water intake

مَصَدّ الصَواعق
lightning arrester /
lightning conductor

الرّافعة المُتحرِّكة
traveling crane

حُجرة الماكينة او المحرِّك
machine hall

المُوَلِّد الكهربي
generator unit

قناة سُفْلَى
tailrace

بوّابة الخزّان
penstock

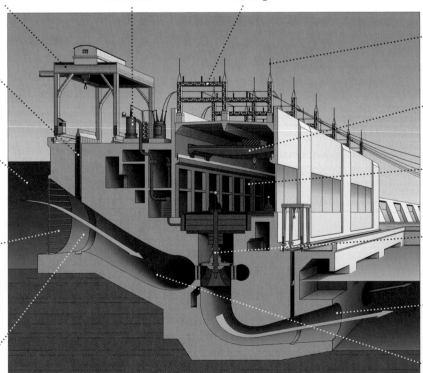

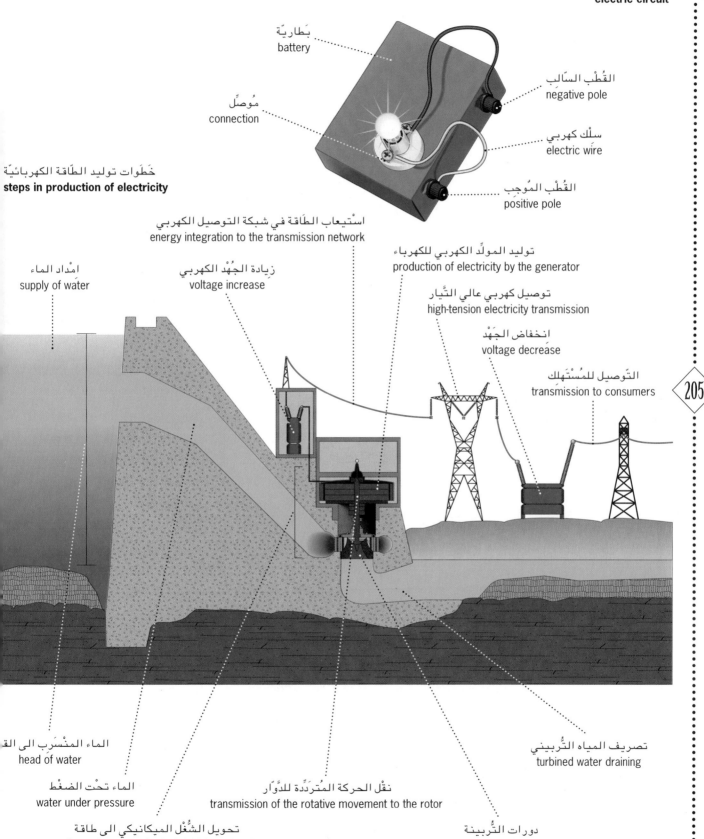

دائرة كهربيّة
electric circuit

بَطاريّة
battery

القُطْب السّالِب
negative pole

مُوصِّل
connection

سلْك كهربي
electric wire

القُطْب المُوجِب
positive pole

خَطَوات توليد الطّاقة الكهربائيّة
steps in production of electricity

اسْتيعاب الطّاقة في شبكة التوصيل الكهربي
energy integration to the transmission network

توليد المولِّد الكهربي للكهرباء
production of electricity by the generator

امْداد الماء
supply of water

زيادة الجُهْد الكهربي
voltage increase

توصيل كهربي عالي التّيّار
high-tension electricity transmission

انخفاض الجَهْد
voltage decrease

التّوصيل للمُسْتَهلك
transmission to consumers

الماء المنْسَرِب الى الق...
head of water

تصريف المياه التُّربيني
turbined water draining

الماء تحْت الضغْط
water under pressure

نقْل الحركة المُتَرَدِّدة للدّوّار
transmission of the rotative movement to the rotor

تحويل الشُّغْل الميكانيكي الى طاقة
transformation of mechanical work into electricity

دورات التُّربينة
rotation of the turbine

الطّاقَة النَّوويّة
NUCLEAR ENERGY

محطّة (توليد) طاقة نوويّة
nuclear power station

صمّام الماء الناتج
dousing water valve

صهريج الماء الناتج
dousing water tank

مولِّد بُخار
steam generator

مضخّة نقل الحرارة
heat transport pump

مبْنى المُفاعل
reactor building

خزّان الوقود المُستهلَك
spent fuel storage bay

المُفاعِل الذَّرِّي
reactor

خزّان الوَقود النافد
spent fuel discharge bay

مَبْنى التُّربينات
turbine building

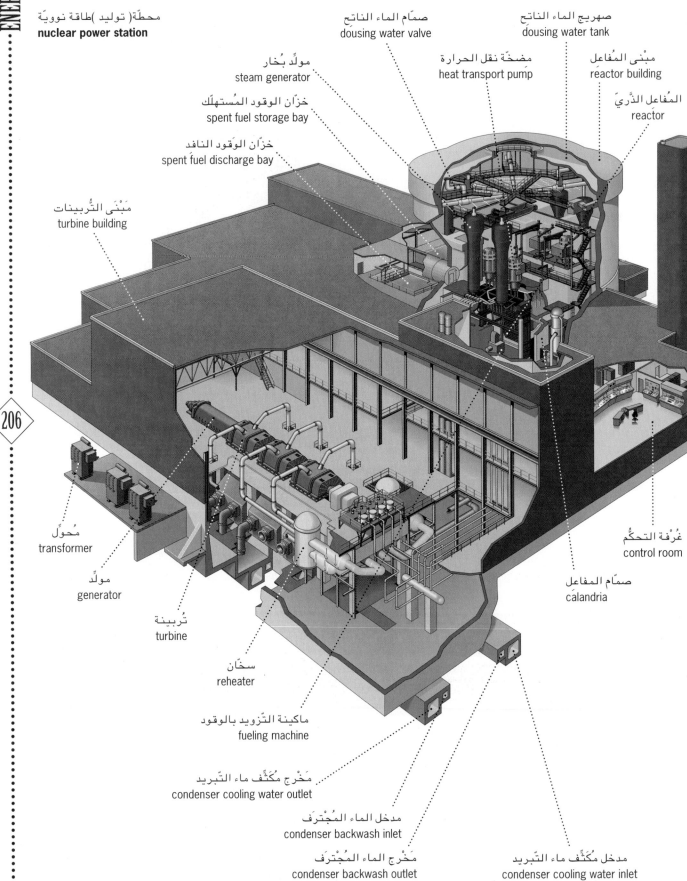

مُحوِّل
transformer

مولِّد
generator

تُربينة
turbine

سخّان
reheater

ماكينة التّزويد بالوقود
fueling machine

مَخْرج مُكثَّف ماء التّبريد
condenser cooling water outlet

مدخل الماء المُجترَف
condenser backwash inlet

مَخْرج الماء المُجترَف
condenser backwash outlet

غرْفة التحكُّم
control room

صمّام المفاعل
calandria

مدخل مُكثَّف ماء التّبريد
condenser cooling water inlet

توليد الطَّاقة من الطَّاقة النوويّ
production of electricity from nuclear energy

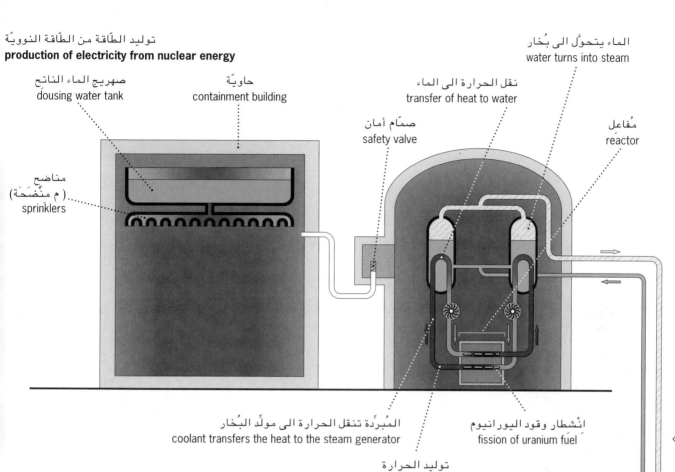

صهريج الماء النّاتج
dousing water tank

حاويّة
containment building

الماء يتحوَّل الى بُخار
water turns into steam

نقل الحرارة الى الماء
transfer of heat to water

مُفاعل
reactor

صمّام أمان
safety valve

مناضِح (م مِنْضَحَة)
sprinklers

المُبرِّدة تنقل الحرارة الى مولِّد البُخار
coolant transfers the heat to the steam generator

انْشطار وقود اليورانيوم
fission of uranium fuel

توليد الحرارة
heat production

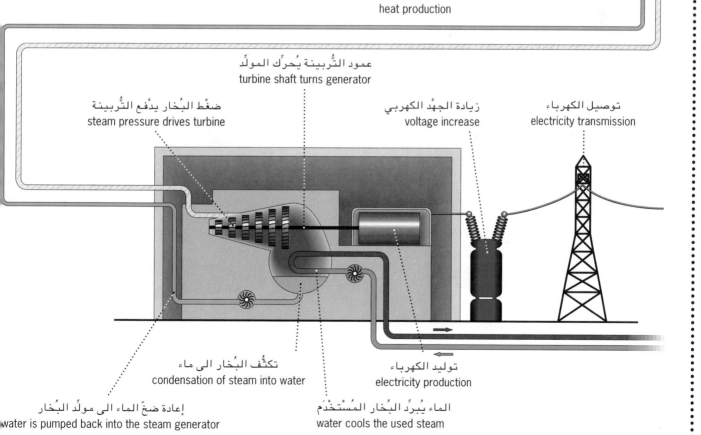

عمود التُّربينة يُحرّك المولِّد
turbine shaft turns generator

ضغْط البُخار يدْفع التُّربينة
steam pressure drives turbine

زيادة الجهْد الكهربي
voltage increase

توصيل الكهرباء
electricity transmission

تكثُّف البُخار الى ماء
condensation of steam into water

توليد الكهرباء
electricity production

إعادة ضخّ الماء الى مولِّد البُخار
water is pumped back into the steam generator

الماء يُبرِّد البُخار المُسْتخْدَم
water cools the used steam

الطّاقَة

الطاقة الشّمسيّة
SOLAR ENERGY

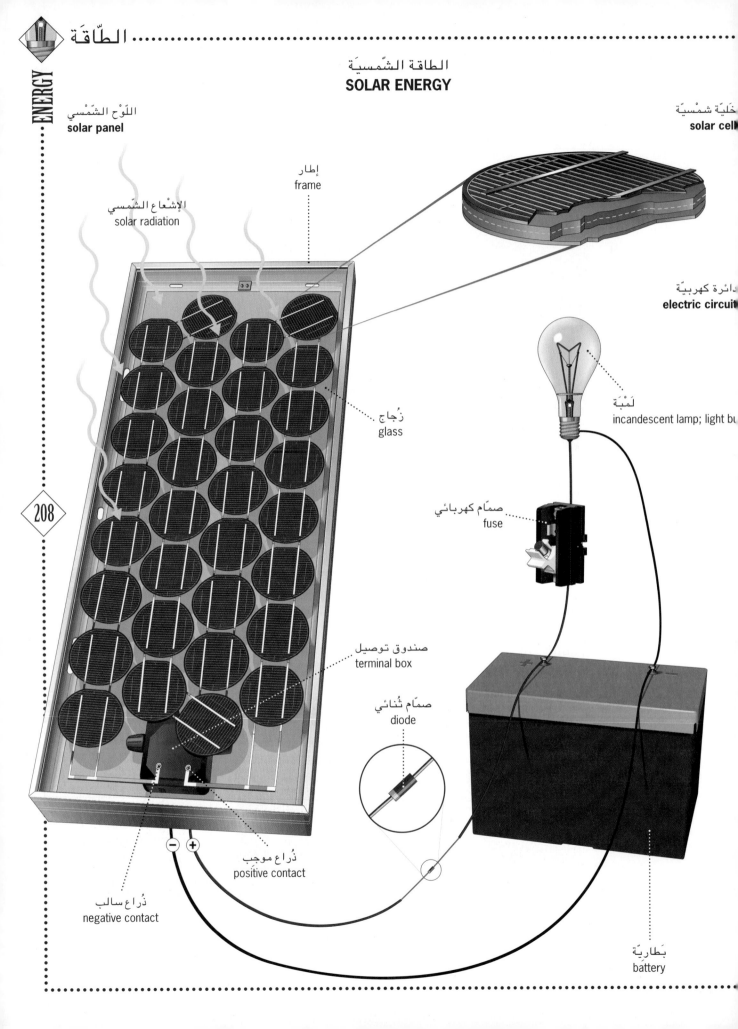

اللّوْح الشّمْسي
solar panel

خَلِيّة شمْسيّة
solar cell

إطار
frame

الإشْعاع الشّمسي
solar radiation

دائرة كهربيّة
electric circuit

لَمْبَة
incandescent lamp; light bulb

زُجاج
glass

صمّام كهربائي
fuse

صندوق توصيل
terminal box

صمّام ثُنائي
diode

ذُراع موجب
positive contact

ذُراع سالب
negative contact

بَطاريّة
battery

طاقة هوائيّة
WIND ENERGY

تُربينة رياح ذات مِحْوَر أفقي
horizontal-axis wind turbine

دَوّار
hub

كِنَّة المحرِّك، الباسِنة
nacelle

عارِضة، سِناد
stock

قماش الشِّراع
sail cloth

طاحونة هوائيّة
windmill

عمود الشِّراع
sailbar

ذيْل المروحة
fantail

مِرْوَحَة
blade

عمود إدارة
windshaft

بُرْج
tower

شِراع
sail

بُرْج
tower

تُربينة رياح ذات مِحْوَر رأْسي
vertical-axis wind turbine

مِرْوَحَة
blade

شكال
strut

دَوّار
rotor

كابح ايرودينامي
aerodynamic brake

العمود الرّئيسي المركَزي
central column

قاعِدة
base

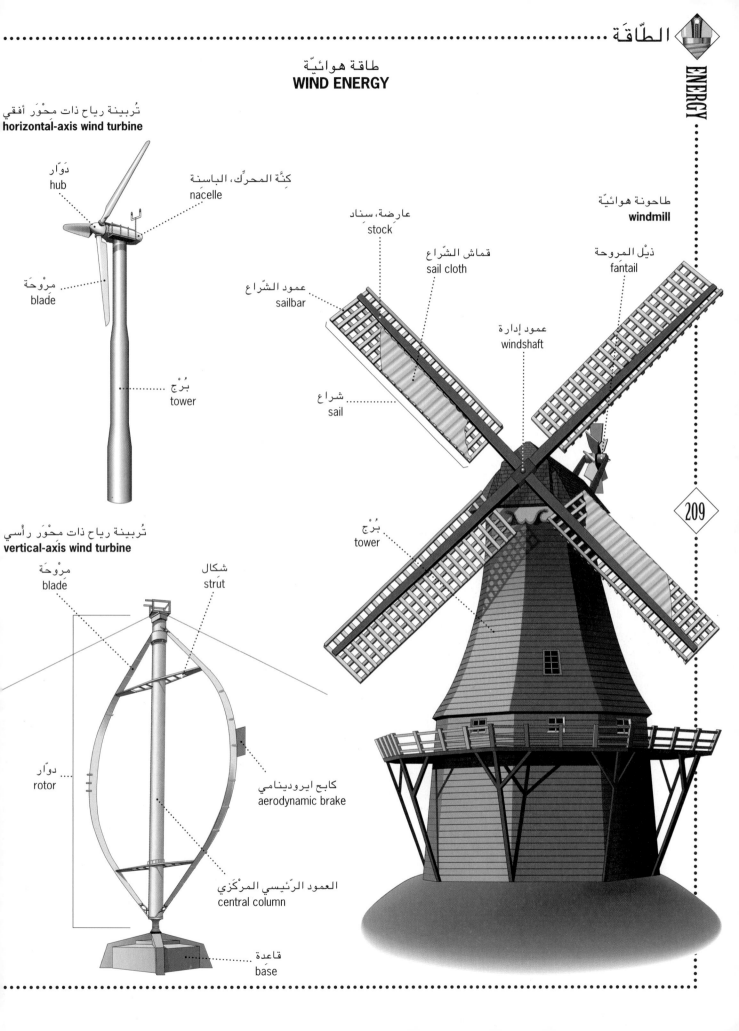

مَطافِئ
FIRE PREVENTION

خَرَطوش مياه
fire hose

المطفاة المحمولة
portable fire extinguisher

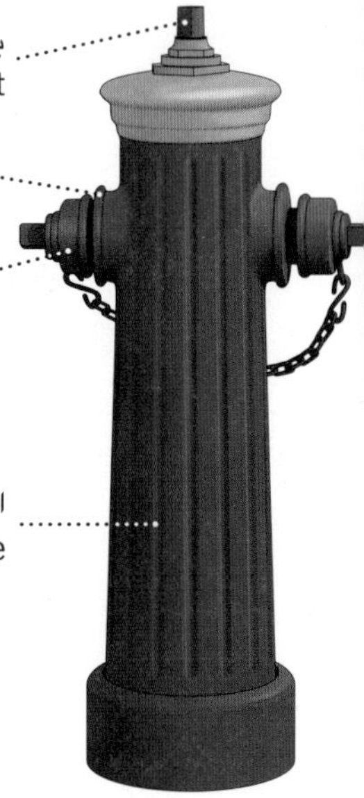

صُنْبور الإطْفاء
fire hydrant

بروش او زرّ التشغيل
operating nut

امداد الماء
water supply point

الغطاء الكأْسيّ
cap

انبوب قائم
upright pipe

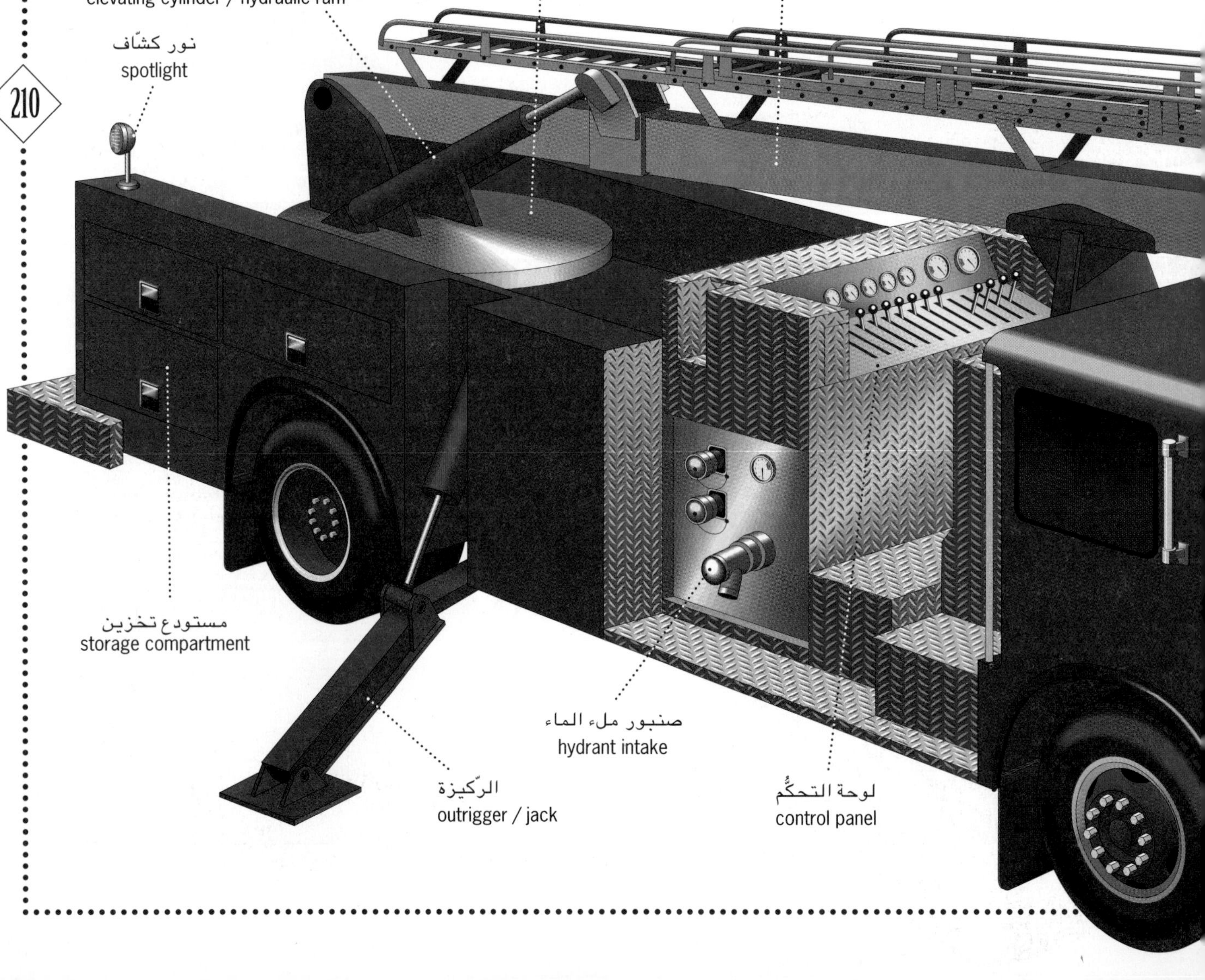

عرَبَة مطافِئ
fire engine

اسْطُوانة رافعة
elevating cylinder / hydraulic ram

صحْن دوّار
turntable mounting

عمود تليسكوبي
telescopic boom

نور كشّاف
spotlight

مستودع تخزين
storage compartment

صنبور ملء الماء
hydrant intake

الرّكيزة
outrigger / jack

لوحة التحكُّم
control panel

كراكي
pike pole

رَجُل مطافئ
fire-fighter

اسطوانة الهواء المضْغُوط
compressed-air cylinder

فأس
fire-fighter's hatchet / fireman's axe

خُوذة
helmet

قِناع كامل للوجه
full face mask

جهاز تنفُس تلقائي
self-contained breathing apparatus

سُلّم
tower ladder

انبوب التّزوُّد بالهواء
air-supply tube

نور وهّاج
flashing light

السُّلّم الأعلى
top ladder

علامة او اداة تحذير
warning device

صنبُور الماسورة
ladder pipe nozzle

ملابس واقية من البلل والنار
fireproof and waterproof garment

حذاء مصنوع من المطاط
rubber boot

الشّاحنات الثّقيلة
HEAVY VEHICLES

الشّاحنة
loader

أجهزة تشغيل الجاروف الخلفي
back-hoe controls

ذراع
arm

عمود او قضيب
boom

ماسورة الذُّراع
arm cylinder / hydraulic ram

جارُوف
bucket

الشاحن الأمامي
front-end loader

تراكتور بعجلات
wheel tractor

ذُراع الرّافعة
lift arm

محرّك الدّيزل
diesel engine

الجاروف او الدّلُو الخلفي
backward bucket

مسْمار المفْصَلَة
bucket hinge pin

الجاروف الخلْفي
back-hoe

212

بُلدوزر
bulldozer

محرّك الدّيزل
diesel engine

فلْتَر الهواء
air filter

انبوب العادم
exhaust pipe

كابينة
cab

اسطُوانة رفْع الجاروف
blade lift cylinder

جارُوف
blade

راحة او كفّة المجْراف
blade

الطَّرَف القاطِع
cutting edge

ضاغط الهيكل
frame push

الجنزير
track

سنّ المجْراف
ripper tooth

التراكتور الدّبّابة
crawler tractor

المشْقاق
ripper

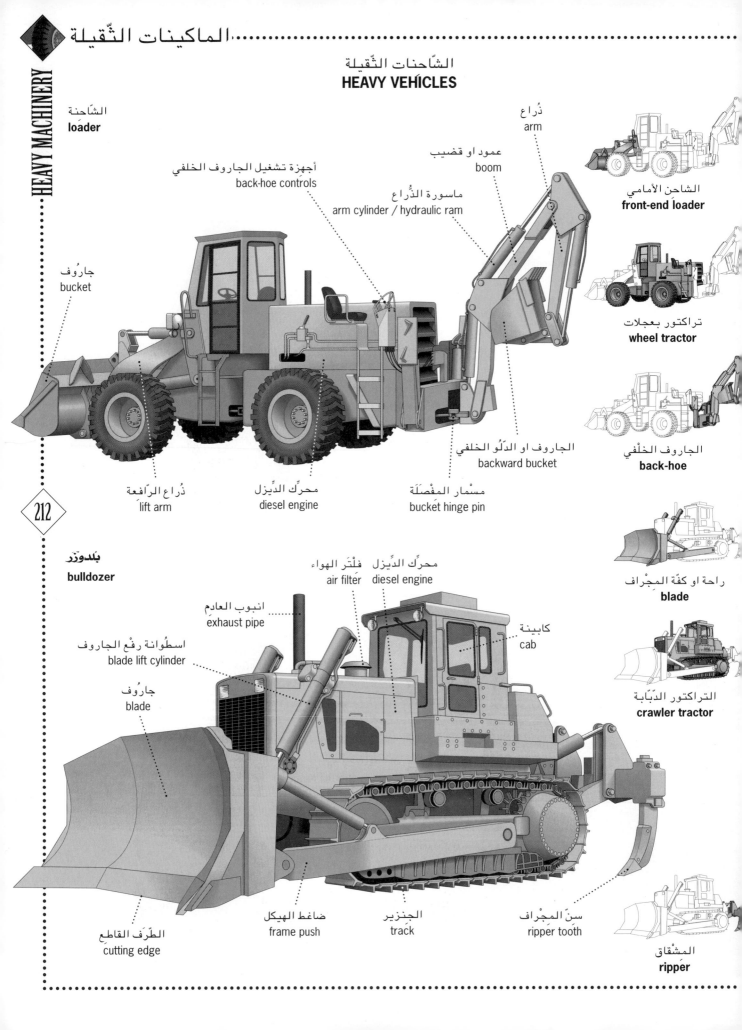

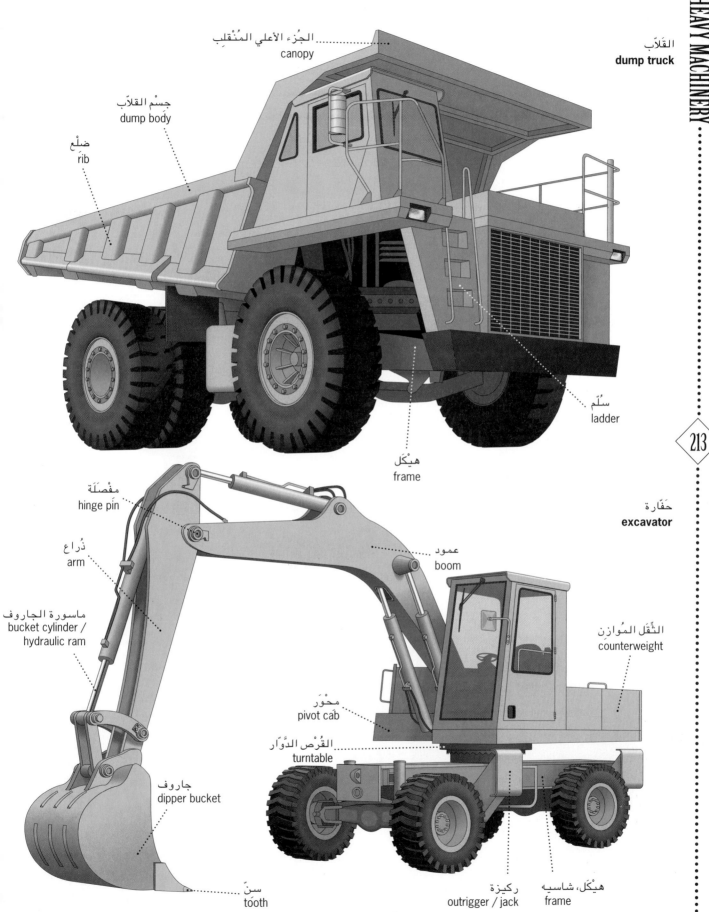

القَلّاب
dump truck

الجُزء الأعلى المُنْقلب
canopy

جسْم القلّاب
dump body

ضلْع
rib

سُلّم
ladder

هيْكَل
frame

حَفّارة
excavator

مفْصَلَة
hinge pin

ذُراع
arm

ماسورة الجاروف
bucket cylinder /
hydraulic ram

عمود
boom

الثّقَل المُوازِن
counterweight

مِحْوَر
pivot cab

القُرْص الدّوّار
turntable

جاروف
dipper bucket

سنّ
tooth

ركيزة
outrigger / jack

هيْكَل، شاسيّه
frame

الشّاحنات الثّقيلة
HEAVY VEHICLES

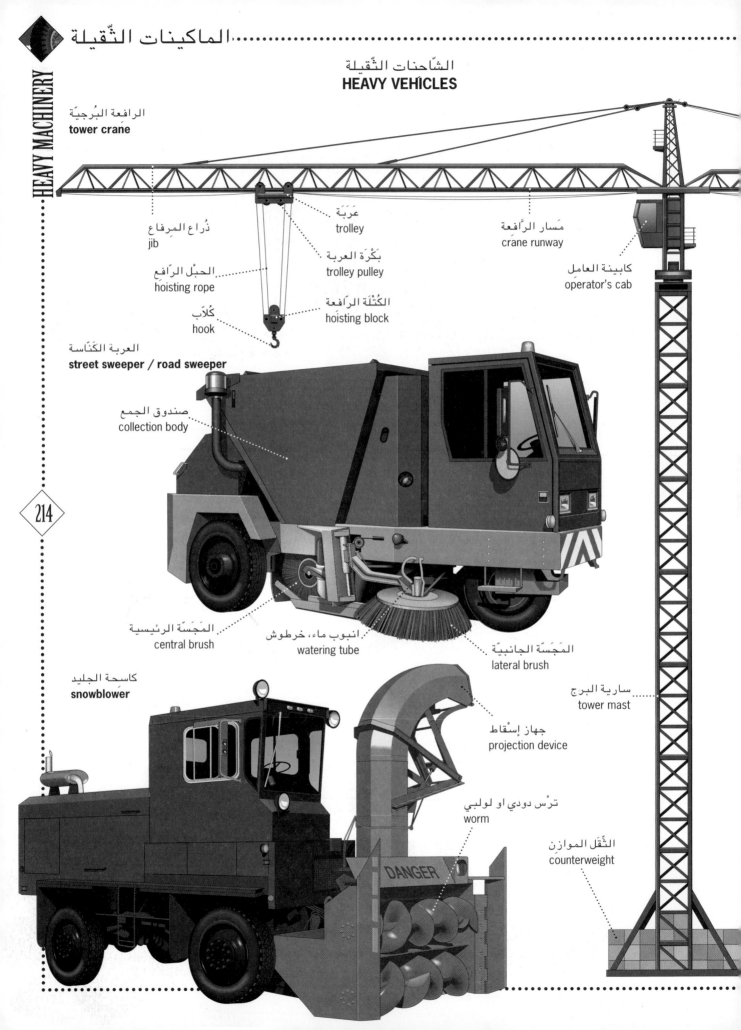

الرافعة البُرجيّة
tower crane

ذُراع المِرفاع
jib

عَرَبَة
trolley

مَسار الرَّافِعة
crane runway

بَكْرة العربة
trolley pulley

الحَبْل الرّافِع
hoisting rope

كابينة العامِل
operator's cab

الكُتْلة الرّافِعة
hoisting block

كُلّاب
hook

العربة الكَنّاسة
street sweeper / road sweeper

صندوق الجمع
collection body

المَجَسّة الرئيسية
central brush

انبوب ماء، خرطوش
watering tube

المَجَسّة الجانبيّة
lateral brush

سارية البرج
tower mast

كاسِحة الجليد
snowblower

جهاز إسْقاط
projection device

تَرْس دودي او لولبي
worm

الثِّقَل الموازِن
counterweight

DANGER

214

رابِط ذراع المرفاع
jib tie

ثقَل المُوازَنَة: صابورة
counterjib ballast

جسْم الكَبْس
packer body

سيارة نقْل الأوساخ
sanitation truck / refuse lorry

مُوازِن ذراع المرفاع
counterjib

جهاز التحميل
loading hopper

عمود تليسكوبيّ
telescopic boom

اسطوانة الرَّفْع
elevating cylinder / hydraulic ram

وِنْش العربة
truck crane / mobile crane

215

ركيزة
outrigger / jack

عمود او قضيب
boom

اسْطُوانة رافعة
elévating cylinder /
hydraulic ram

وِنْش
winch

العربة القاطِرة
tow truck / recovery lorry

كَبْل
cable

مِشْبَك
hook

جهاز قَطْر
towing device

جهاز التحكُّم في الوِنْش
winch controls

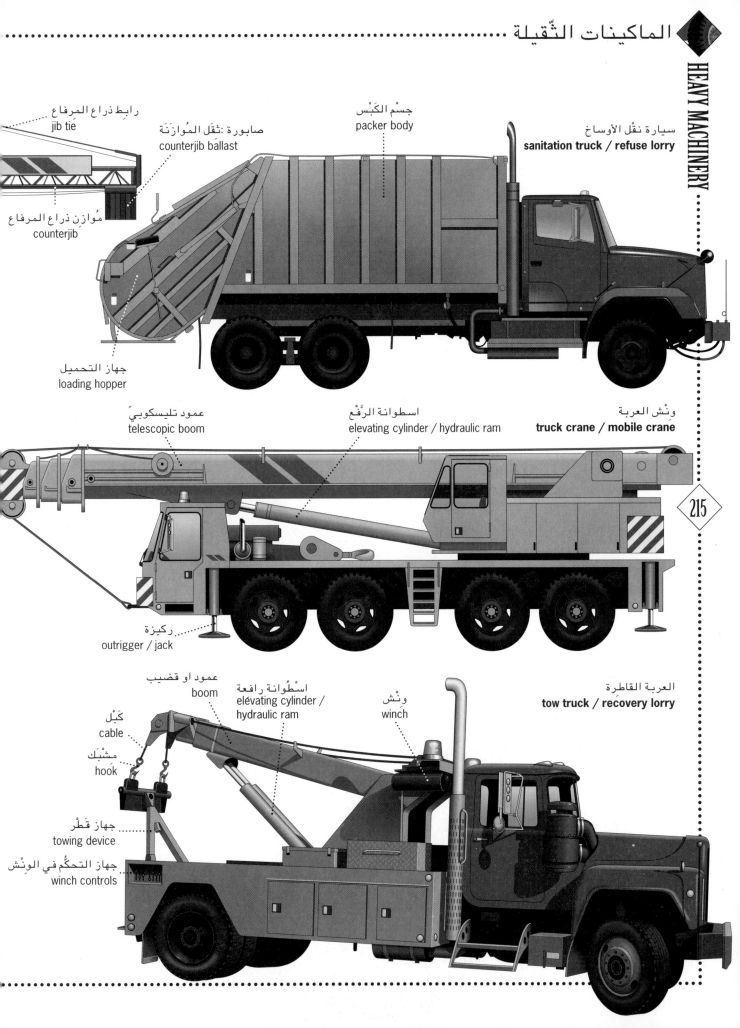

رُموز عامة
COMMON SYMBOLS

دَوْرة مياه للنِّساء
women's rest room /
women's toilet

دَوْرة مياه للرِّجال
men's rest room /
men's toilet

دَوْرة مياه للمُعوَّقين
wheelchair access

مُسْتَشفى
hospital

هاتف، تليفون
telephone

ممنوع التَّدْخين
no smoking

مُعَسْكَر
camping (tent)

ممنوع المعسكرات
camping prohibited

قِفْ عند التَّقاطُع
stop at intersection

رُموز الأمان والسَّلامة
SAFETY SYMBOLS

تآكُل
corrosive

خطَر كهرباء!
electrical hazard

قابل للانْفِجار
explosive

قابل للاشْتِعال
flammable

مواد مُشِعَّة
radioactive

سامّ
poisonous

الوقاية او الحماية
PROTECTION

وقاية للعين
eye protection

وقاية للأُذْن
ear protection

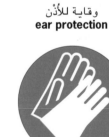

وقاية للرأْس
head protection

وقاية لليدِّ
hand protection

وقاية للقَدَم
foot protection

وقاية للجهاز التَّنفُّسي
respiratory system
protection

216

1/10th second hand 198.
25 ring, dartboard 197.
35 mm still camera 149.

A

a 160.
abdomen 61.
abdomen 57, 59, 74.
ablutions fountain 87.
absorbed heat 28.
accelerator pedal 132.
access road 146.
accessory shoe 125, 127.
accidentals, musical notation 161.
accordion 158.
Ace 194.
achene 44.
acid precipitation 31.
acid rain 32, 33.
acoustic guitar 162.
action of wind 31.
actual temperature 199.
Adam's apple 78.
add in memory 154.
add key 154.
adhesive tape/plaster tape 193.
adjustable channel 109.
adjustable wrench/adjustable spanner 109.
adjustable pliers 109.
adjusting band 128.
adjusting buckle 185.
adjusting catch 186.
adjusting screw 109.
adjustment slide 112.
aerial 131, 145.
aerodynamic brake 209.
aerosol 29.
Africa 19.
aftermast 141.
aileron 144.
air bed 191.
air compressor 139.
air concentrator 122.
air conditioner 29.
air filter 139, 212.
air horn 134.
air inlet 145.
air mattress/air bed 191.
air pressure hose 134
air pressure, measure 23.
air pump/air pressure hose 134.
air space 75.
air unit 121.
air vent 132.
air-outlet grille 122.
air-supply tube 211.
AIRPORT 146.
airport 27.
airport ground equipment 146.
ala 84.
albumen 75.
alcohol bulb 199.
alcohol column 199.
alighting board 59.
alley 180.
almond 45.
alpine skier 186.
alternator/generator 138.
altitude clamp 11.
altitude fine adjustment 11.
AM antenna 128.
ambulatory 89.
AMPHIBIANS 60.
amphibians 60.
amplifier 128.
anal fin 63.
analog watch 198.

anchor-windlass room 142.
anemometer 23.
ankle 78.
ankle boot 119.
ankle sock 118.
annual ring 40.
annular eclipse 10.
anorak 120.
ant 56.
Antarctic Circle 12.
Antarctica 18.
antenna 57, 58, 61, 129, 174.
antenna/aerial 131, 145.
antennule 61.
anther 38.
anti-friction pad 187.
anti-slip shoe 111.
anti-torque tail rotor 145.
antiseptic 193.
antiseptic lotion 193.
aortic arch 81.
appendix 81.
apple 46.
appoggiatura, musical notation 161.
apricot 45.
apron 97, 146.
aquatic bird 74.
Arabian camel 73.
archipelago 26.
Arctic 18.
Arctic Circle 12, 24.
Arctic Ocean 19.
arm 67, 79, 97, 155, 212, 213.
arm guard 170.
arm pad 177.
armchair 96, 97.
armpit 78.
arterial blood 81.
artery, anterior tibial 81.
artery, common carotid 81.
artery, femoral 81.
artichoke 49.
artichoke, Jerusalem 51.
ash layer 15.
Asia 19.
asparagus 52.
asphalt 203.
asteroid belt 6.
Atlantic Ocean 18.
atmosphere 12, 20.
atmospheric pollution 30.
attack line 174.
attack on human beings 31.
attack on nature 31.
attack zone 174.
attacking zone 176.
audio system 132.
auditory canal 83.
auditory nerve 83.
auditory ossicles 83.
auger bit 110.
auricle 83.
Australia 19.
auto reverse 129.
autofocus on/off switch 153.
automatic dialer 124.
automatic drip coffee maker/
automatic filter coffee maker 105.
automobile car/bogie car-transporter wagon 138.
autumn 20.
autumn squash 49.
autumnal equinox 20.
auxiliary handle 110.
avocado 48.
awl 192.
awning 190.
axe 192.
axillary bud 36.
axis of rotation 152.
axle 138, 185.
azimuth clamp 11.
azimuth fine adjustment 11.

B

b 160.
back 66, 67, 75, 79, 97, 101.
back judge 171.
back zone 174.
back, left 175.
back, right 175.
back-hoe 212.
back-hoe controls 212.
backboard 179.
backboard support 179.
backcourt 180.
BACKGAMMON 196.
backguard 107.
backpack/satchel 151.
backpack/rucksack 193.
backstay 185.
backstroke 183.
backstroke turn indicator 182.
backup light/reversing light 133.
backward bucket 212.
bag, drawstring 123.
baggage compartment/luggage compartment 145.
baggage conveyor 146.
baggage trailer 147.
bagpipes 158.
bailey 88.
balaclava 114.
balalaika 158.
balance 200.
balance beam 188.
balancer 163.
ball boy 180.
ballast 140.
ballerina/pump 119.
ballpoint pen 150.
banana 48.
band 129.
banjo 158.
bar 123, 196.
bar line 160.
bar stool 96.
BARK, FOUR-MASTED 141.
bark, inner 40.
bark, outer 40.
barograph 23.
barrel 122, 197.
base 99, 140, 152, 155, 188, 200, 209.
base plate 110.
BASEBALL 168.
baseball 168.
baseball, field 169.
baseline 180.
baseman, first 169.
baseman, second 169.
baseman, third 169.
basement 93.
basement window 93.
basic source of food 28.
basket 179.
basket 105, 178, 186, 187.
BASKETBALL 178.
basketball 179.
basketball 179.
basketball player 179.
basketball, court 178.
bass bridge 159.
bass clarinet 167.
bass drum 166, 167.
bass guitar 163.
bass keyboard 158.
bass pickup 163.
bass register 158.
bass tone control 163.
bassoon 165.
bassoon 167.
bat 168.
bathrobe/dressing gown 116.
bathroom scales 201.

The terms in **bold type** correspond to an illustration; those in CAPITALS indicate a title.

217

batten 184.
batten pocket 184.
batter 168.
batter 169.
batter head 166.
batter's helmet 168.
battery 127, 138, 205, 208.
battery eject switch 127.
batting glove 168.
battlement 88.
bay 9, 26.
bay window 93.
bayonet base 99.
beach 14.
beam 200.
bean sprouts 52.
beater 105.
beater ejector 105.
beaver 70.
BED 95.
bed 188, 191.
bedrock 34.
beer mug 100.
beet 51.
begonia 38.
belfry 89.
bell 164, 165.
bell brace 165.
bell tower 89.
bellows 158.
belly 67.
belt 112.
belt carrier 112.
belt highway 27.
bench 96.
beret 114.
Bering Sea 19.
Bermuda shorts 115.
berries, major types 44.
BERRY FRUITS 44.
berry, section 44.
BICYCLE 136.
bicycle bag/pannier bag 136.
bile duct 81.
bill 74.
bills, principal types 74.
birch 42.
BIRD 74.
bird feeder 75.
bird of prey 74.
bird's nest 75.
bird, morphology 74.
birdhouse 75.
BIRDS, EXAMPLES 76.
Bishop 195.
bitter taste 84.
Black 195.
black bass 63.
black currant 44.
Black Sea 19.
black square 195.
blackboard 152.
bladder 81.
blade 212.
blade 36, 101, 109, 110, 111, 177, 185, 209, 212.
blade guard 110.
blade tilting mechanism 110.
blank 194.
blanket 95.
blasting charge 202.
blastodisc 75.
blender 105.
blocker 177.
blouse 114.
blow pipe 158.
blue 157.
blue line 176.
blue-green 157.
blueberry 44.
board 184.
boarding step 145.
boarding walkway 147.

boards 176.
bobble hat 113.
bodies, types 133.
body 130.
body 162, 163, 165.
body flap 148.
body pad 177.
bogie 138.
bogie car-transporter wagon 138.
bogie flat wagon 139
bogie frame 138.
bogie open wagon 139.
bogie tank wagon 139.
bogie wagon 138.
bolster 95.
bolt 109.
bongos 166.
bonnet 130.
book bag 151.
boom 212, 213, 215.
booster parachute 148.
boot 119.
boot 131, 185.
bottle opener 102.
bottle opener 192.
bottom 186.
bottom line 182.
boulevard/high street 90.
bow 162.
bow/stern 142, 184.
bow thruster 142.
bow window 92.
bowl 101.
bowsprit 141.
box car/bogie wagon 138.
box spring 95.
boxer shorts 112.
bra 116.
braces 112.
brake cable 137.
brake caliper 135.
brake lever 137.
brake light 133.
brake pedal 132, 187.
brake van 139.
branch 43.
branch 40.
branches 40.
brass family 164.
brassiere cup 116.
brattice 88.
bread and butter plate 100.
breast 74.
breast pocket 112.
breast welt pocket 113.
breaststroke 183.
breaststroke kick 183.
breaststroke turn 183.
breathing in 183.
breathing out 183.
bridge 123, 162, 163.
bridge assembly 163.
briefcase 151.
briefs 112, 116.
bristles 111, 122.
broad beans 52.
broccoli 49.
brush 111.
Brussels sprouts 53.
bubble 135.
bucket 212.
bucket hinge pin 212.
buckle 186.
bud 50.
bud, flower 36.
bud, terminal 34, 36.
bugle 164.
built-in microphone 127.
bulb 99.
bulb 99.
bulb vegetables 50.
bulb, energy saving 97.

bulbil 50.
bulk terminal 142.
bulkhead flat car/bulkhead flat wagon 139.
bulkhead flat wagon 139.
bull's-eye 197.
bulldozer 212.
bumper 130.
bunkers 203.
burner 104, 107.
bushing 204.
butt 181.
butt end 177.
butter compartment 106.
butter dish 100.
butter knife 101.
BUTTERFLY 57.
butterfly kick 183.
butterfly stroke 183.
butterfly turn 183.
butterfly, hind leg 57, 59.
button 112, 117.
button loop 112.
by-pass runway 146.

C

c 160.
C clef 160.
C-clamp 108.
cab 212.
cabbage lettuce 53.
cabin 143.
cabinet 126.
cable 110, 129, 189, 215.
caboose/brake van 139.
calandria 206.
calculator, pocket 154.
calf 68.
calf 79.
Callisto 6.
calyx 38.
cambium 40.
camera body 125.
camera, 35 mm still 149.
camera, pocket 125.
camera, single lens reflex 125.
camera, video 127.
camp bed 191.
camping (tent) 216.
CAMPING EQUIPMENT 192.
camping prohibited 216.
can opener/tin opener 102.
can opener/tin opener 192.
canal lock 142.
canine 70, 85.
cannon 67.
canopy 123, 213.
cantaloupe 49.
canteen 192.
cap 113.
cap 35, 210.
cape 26.
capillary bore 199.
capital 26.
CAR 130, 132.
car lights 133.
car park 91.
car wash 134.
carafe 100.
carafe 105.
carapace 61, 64.
carbon dioxide 33.
CARD GAMES 194.
card reader 124.
cardigan 117.
cardoon 52.
cargo bay door 148.
Caribbean Sea 18.
carnassial 70.

The terms in **bold type** correspond to an illustration; those in CAPITALS indicate a title.

carnation 39.
carnivore's jaw 70.
carnivores 29, 33.
CARPENTRY TOOLS 108.
carpus 80.
carrier 136.
carrot 51.
CARTOGRAPHY 24, 26.
cartridge film 125.
case 108, 154, 159, 198.
casement window 94.
casement window (inward opening) 94.
casing 54.
Caspian Sea 19.
casserole 104.
cassette 129.
cassette 129.
cassette compartment 127.
cassette eject switch 127.
cassette film 125.
cassette player 129.
cassette player controls 124, 129.
cassette tape deck 128.
castanets 166.
castanets 167.
CASTLE 88.
castle 88.
CAT 66.
catcher 168.
catcher 169.
catcher's glove 168.
catching glove 177.
catenary 140.
catering vehicle 147.
caterpillar 57.
caterpillar 57.
cathedral 90.
CATHEDRAL, GOTHIC 89.
caudal fin 63.
cauliflower 49.
CAVE 13.
cave 14.
ceiling fixture 98.
celeriac 51.
celery 52.
cell 57, 59.
cello 162.
cello 167.
Celsius scale 199.
center/centre 171, 176, 178.
center back/centre back 173, 174.
center circle/centre circle 173, 178.
center console/centre console 132.
center face-off circle/centre face-off circle 176.
center field/ centre field 169.
center fielder/centre fielder 169.
center flag/centre flag 173.
center forward/centre forward 173, 174, 175.
center half/centre half 175.
center hole/centre hole 129.
center line/centre line 171, 175, 176, 178.
center mark/centre mark 180.
center post/door pillar 131.
center service line/centre service line 180.
center spot/centre spot 173.
center strap/centre strap 180.
Central America 18.
central brush 214.
central column 209.
central incisor 85.
central nave 87.
central processing unit 154.
cephalothorax 61.
cereal bowl 100.
chain guide 136.
chain wheel 136.
CHAIRS 97.
chaise longue 96.
chameleon 65.
champagne flute 100.
champagne glass 100.
change sign key 154.
channel scan buttons 126.

channel selector controls 126.
chanter 158.
chapel 88.
chapel, Lady 89.
chapel, side 89.
Charleston cymbal 166.
Charon 7.
checker/draughtsman 196.
checkerboard/draughtsboard 196.
CHECKERS/DRAUGHTS 196.
cheek 66, 78.
cheese knife 101.
cherimoya 48.
cherry 45.
CHESS 195.
chess notation 195.
chessboard 195.
chest 67, 78.
chest protector 168, 170.
chestnut 67.
chevet 89.
chick 68.
chick peas 52.
chicory 53.
chief timekeeper 182.
chilli 49.
chimney 93.
chin 74, 78.
chin protector 135.
chin rest 162.
chin strap 170.
China Sea 19.
Chinese cabbage 53.
chives 50.
choir 89.
chrysalis 57.
chrysalis 59.
chuck 110.
chuck key 110.
church 91.
ciliate 37.
circle 156.
circular body 158.
circular saw 110.
circular saw blade 110.
cirque 9.
cirque, glacial 16.
citrus fruit, section 47.
CITRUS FRUITS 47.
citrus fruits, major types 47.
city 26.
clamp 186.
clarinet 165.
clarinet 167.
clavicle 80.
claw 57, 61, 64, 66, 75, 108.
clear key 154.
clear space 174.
clear-entry key 154.
cleated shoe 170.
clefs 160.
clew 184.
cliff 9, 14, 17.
CLIMATES OF THE WORLD 21.
clinical thermometer 199.
clip 150.
clock 132.
clock operator 178.
clock timer 107.
cloud 22.
cloud of volcanic ash 15.
club 194.
clutch lever 135.
clutch pedal 132.
coach's box 169.
coarse adjustment knob 155.
COASTAL FEATURES 14.
cob 52.
cobra 64.
coccyx 80.
cochlea 83.
cock 68.

cockpit 145.
cod 63.
coffee cup 100.
coffee plunger 100.
coffee pot 192.
coffee spoon 101.
coin return tray 124.
coin slot 124.
colander 103.
cold shed 143.
collar 36, 112, 113, 121.
collar point 112.
collecting funnel 23.
collecting vessel 23.
collection body 214.
color circle/colour circle 157.
color television camera/colour television camera 149.
colored pencils/coloured pencils 157.
colour circle. 157.
coloured pencils 157.
column 13, 182.
column of mercury 199.
coma 10.
COMET 10.
comforter/eiderdown 95.
commercial premises 91.
commissure of lips 84.
COMMON SYMBOLS 216.
COMMUNICATION BY TELEPHONE 124.
communication tunnel 149.
compact camera 125.
compact disk 129.
compact disk 129.
compact disk player 128.
compact disk player 129.
COMPASS CARD 27.
compass card 193.
compass, magnetic 193.
compost bin 55.
compound eye 57, 58.
compound leaves 36.
compressed air reservoir 139.
compressed-air cylinder 211.
computer, personal 154.
concealed pocket 113.
concentration of gases 29.
condensation 31.
condensation of steam into water 207.
condenser 155.
condenser backwash inlet 206.
condenser backwash outlet 206.
condenser cooling water inlet 206.
condenser cooling water outlet 206.
conductor's podium 167.
cone 14, 43, 156.
cone 128.
CONFIGURATION OF THE CONTINENTS 18.
conical projection 25.
CONIFER 43.
coniferous forest 20.
connection 205.
constriction 199.
contact 99.
container 23, 105.
container car/container flat wagon 138.
container ship 142.
container terminal 143.
container-loading bridge 142.
container/pallet loader 146.
containment building 207.
container flat wagon 138.
continental climates 21.
CONTINENTS, CONFIGURATION 18.
contrabassoon 167.
control deck 141, 197.
control dial 125.
control knob 107.
control pad 197.
control panel 107, 125, 210.
control room 204, 206.
control stand 138.
control stick 145.

The terms in **bold type** correspond to an illustration; those in CAPITALS indicate a title.

219

control tower 146.
control tower cab 146.
controls 127.
convection zone 8.
convention center 90.
conventional door 92.
convertible 133.
COOKING APPLIANCES 107.
cooking set 192.
COOKING UTENSILS 104.
cooktop/hob 107.
coolant transfers the heat to the steam generator 207.
cor anglais 165, 167.
cordless telephone 124.
core 8, 46.
corkscrew 192.
corkscrew, lever 102.
corn salad 53.
corner arc 173.
corner flag 173, 175.
corner tower 88.
cornerback, left 171.
cornerback, right 171.
cornet 164.
cornet 167.
cornice 92, 93.
corolla 38.
corona 8.
coronet 67.
corrosive 216.
cotton roll 193.
cotyledons 34.
counter 121.
counterjib 215.
counterjib ballast 215.
counterweight 11, 140, 213, 214.
country 26.
coupe 133.
coupler head 139.
courgette 49.
court 119.
courtyard 87.
cover 99, 123, 193, 199.
covered parapet walk 88.
cow 68.
crab 61.
cradle 11.
cranberry 44.
crane runway 214.
crane, floating 142.
crane, gantry 204.
crane, quayside 143.
crane, tower 214.
crank 136.
crash helmet 135.
crater 9, 15.
crawl kick 183.
crawler tractor 212.
crayfish 61.
crayons 157.
creamer 100.
crease 112.
crenate 37.
crenel 88.
crest 17.
crevasse 16.
crew neck sweater 117.
crisper 106.
crocodile 64.
crocus 39.
crook 165.
cross-country ski 186.
cross-country ski 187.
cross-country skier 187.
cross-tip screwdriver 192.
crossbuck sign/level crossing sign 140.
crossing 89.
crossing gate mechanism 140.
crosspiece 97.
crotch 112.
crotchet 161.
crotchet rest 161.

croup 67, 188.
crow 76.
crown 40, 74, 85, 113.
CRUISE LINER 142.
CRUSTACEANS 61.
cube 156.
cucumber 49.
cuff 112, 177.
culottes 115.
cultivated mushroom 35.
cup 100, 192.
curly endive 53.
curly kale 53.
curtain wall 88.
customs house 143.
cutting blade 105.
cutting edge 101, 212.
cylinder 156.
cylinder 75, 212, 213, 215.
cylindrical projection 25.
cymbal 166.
cymbals 167.
cypress scalelike leaves 43.

D

d 160.
daffodil 39.
daggerboard 184.
dairy compartment 106.
dairy products 33.
dam 204.
damper pedal 159.
dandelion 53.
dart 197.
dartboard 197.
dashboard 132.
dashboard 135.
data display 127.
date 45.
dead bolt 93.
deadly mushroom 35.
decanter 100.
deciduous forest 20.
decimal key 154.
declination setting scale 11.
decomposers 29.
deer, white-tailed 73.
defending zone 176.
defense 171.
deflector 54.
deforestation 29.
degrees, C 199.
degrees, F 199.
Deimos 6.
delivery ramp 90.
delta wing 144.
demisemiquaver 161.
demisemiquaver rest 161.
DENTAL CARE 122.
dental floss 122.
dentate 37.
dentin 85.
depressed center flat car/bogie well wagon 139.
depth of focus 13.
desert 21.
desired temperature 199.
destroying angel 35.
dew 22.
dew shield 11.
dewclaw 66.
diagonal movement 195.
dial 198, 200.
diamond 194.
diaphragm 81, 128.
diastema 70.
DICE 194.
dice cup 196.
die 196.

diesel engine 139, 212.
diesel engine ventilator 138.
diesel oil 203.
diesel, marine 203.
DIESEL-ELECTRIC LOCOMOTIVE 138.
digit 60.
digital pad 66.
digital watch 198.
dining room 142.
dinner fork 101.
dinner knife 101.
dinner plate 100.
DINNERWARE 100.
diode 208.
dipped headlights 133.
dipper bucket 213.
direct-reading rain gauge 23.
direction of Mecca 87.
disk 154.
disk brake 135.
disk drive 154.
disk player controls 129.
dispersed heat 29.
display 124, 154, 201.
divide key 154.
dock 143.
DOG 66.
dog's forepaw 66.
dog, morphology 66.
dolphin 72.
dome tent 190.
DOMINOES 194.
door 93.
door 87, 107, 131, 145, 190.
door handle 93, 131.
door lock 131.
door pillar 131.
doors, types 92.
dormant volcano 14.
dorsum of nose 84.
double bass 162.
double bass 167.
double boiler 104.
double flat, musical notation 161.
double reed 165.
double ring 197.
double sharp, musical notation 161.
double-blank 194.
double-breasted jacket 113, 114.
double-six 194.
doubles pole 180.
doubles sideline 180.
doublet 194.
doubling die 196.
dousing water tank 206, 207.
dousing water valve 206.
DOWNTOWN 90.
dragonfly 56.
drainpipe 92.
DRAUGHTS 196.
draughtsboard 196.
draughtsman 196.
draw tube 155.
drawbridge 88.
drawer 97, 107.
DRAWING 157.
drawing pins 150.
drawstring 113, 123.
drawstring bag 123.
dress 114.
dressing gown 116.
drilling 202.
drilling rig 202.
drip molding 131.
drive chain 136.
driver's cab 138, 140.
driveway 92.
driving glove 118.
dromedary 73.
drone pipe 158.
drone, honey-bee 58.
drop-leaf 97.

The terms in **bold type** correspond to an illustration; those in CAPITALS indicate a title.

drums 166.
drupelet 44.
dry continental - arid 21.
dry continental - semiarid 21.
dry dock 142.
dry gallery 13.
dry subtropical 21.
dual-carriageway 90.
dual seat 135.
duck 68.
duffle coat 113.
dugout 169.
dump body 213.
dump truck 213.
dune 14.
duodenum 81.
dust 30, 31.
dust tail 10.
dynamo 136
dynamic brake 138.
dynamics propeller 141.

E

e 160.
EAR 83.
ear 78, 97.
ear cushion 128.
ear drum 83.
ear flap 113.
ear protection 216.
ear, parts 83.
eardrum 60, 64.
earphone 128.
earpiece 124.
Earth 6, 10.
EARTH COORDINATE SYSTEM 12.
Earth's crust 12, 13.
EARTHQUAKE 13.
East 27.
East-northeast 27.
East-southeast 27.
Eastern hemisphere 24.
Eastern meridian 24.
eclipse, annular 10.
eclipse, partial 10.
ECLIPSE, SOLAR 10.
eclipse, total 10.
ECOLOGY 28, 30, 32.
edge 185, 186, 193.
edible crustaceans 61.
edible mushroom 35.
edit/search buttons 127.
eel 63.
egg 75.
egg 59.
egg beater 102.
egg timer 198.
egg tray 106.
eggplant 49.
eggs 60.
eiderdown 95.
eighth note/quaver 161.
eighth rest/quaver rest 161.
elastic 95.
elastic waistband 113.
elbow 66, 67, 79.
elbow pad 170, 177.
electric circuit 205, 208.
electric cooker 107.
electric drill 110.
electric guitar 163.
electric range/electric cooker 107.
ELECTRIC TOOLS 110.
electric wire 205.
electrical hazard 216.
electricity production 207.
electricity transmission 207.
electronic flash 125.

electronic scale 201.
electronic viewfinder 127.
elephant 73.
elevating cylinder/hydraulic ram 210, 215.
ELEVATION ZONES AND VEGETATION 20.
elevator 144.
elevon 148.
enamel 85.
end button/end pin 162.
end line 171, 174.
end pin 162.
end wall 182.
end zone 171.
endive, broad-leaved 53.
endocarp 45, 46.
energy integration to the transmission network 205.
ENERGY, HYDROELECTRIC 204.
ENERGY, NUCLEAR 206.
ENERGY, SOLAR 208.
energy, solar 28.
ENERGY, WIND 209.
engine 135.
engine room 143.
engines 149.
English horn/cor anglais 165.
English horn/cor anglais 167.
entire 37.
entrance 59.
entrance slide 59.
epicenter 13.
equal key 154.
Equator 12, 24.
equinox, autumnal 20.
eraser/rubber 150.
eraser holder 150.
escutcheon 93.
espadrille 119.
estate car 133.
estate wagon 133.
Eurasia 19.
Europa 6.
Europe 19.
Eustachian tube 83.
evaporation 30, 31.
excavator 213.
exercise wear 120, 121.
exhaust pipe/silencer 135, 145, 212.
exhaust stack 134.
exit cone 59.
exocarp 44, 45, 46.
expansion chamber 199.
explosive 216.
exposure button 125.
extension ladder 111.
exterior of a house 92.
external ear 83.
external gills 60.
external tank 148.
EYE 82.
eye 61, 64, 74, 78.
eye protection 216.
eye, compound 57, 58.
eye, simple 57.
eyeball 60.
eyebrow 82.
eyelash 82.
eyelashes 66.
eyelet 121, 185.
eyelid 64.
eyepiece 11, 127, 155.
eyepiece holder 11.

F

f 160.
f clef 160.
facade 89.
face 78, 108.
face mask 170, 177.

face-off circle 176.
face-off spot 176.
Fahrenheit scale 199.
fallout 31.
family tent 190.
fan 122.
fang 64.
fantail 209.
FARM ANIMALS 68.
farm animals 29.
farm pollution 32.
fast forward 126.
fast-forward button 129.
fastening system 188, 189.
fauces 84.
fault 13.
feet, principal types 74.
female cone 43.
femur 80.
fender/wing 130.
fennel 52.
ferryboat 143.
fertilizers 29, 32.
fetlock 67.
fetlock joint 67.
fibula 80.
FIELD HOCKEY 175.
fielder's glove 168.
fielder, left 169.
fielder, right 169.
fifth wheel 134.
fifth, musical interval 160.
fig 48.
figure skate 185.
filament 38, 99.
file 192.
film advance button 125.
film leader 125.
film pack 125.
film rewind button 125.
film speed 125.
fin 144, 145.
fin, anal 63.
fin, caudal 63.
fin, pectoral 62.
fin, pelvic 62.
fin, second dorsal 63.
fin-mounted tail unit 145.
finderscope 11.
fine adjustment knob 155.
finger 168.
finger board 162, 163.
finger button 164.
finger, little 82.
finger, middle 82.
finger, third 82.
fingernail 82.
fir needles 43.
fire engine 210.
fire extinguisher 210.
fire fighter 211.
fire fighter's hatchet/fireman's axe 211.
fire hose 210.
fire hydrant 210.
FIRE PREVENTION 210.
fireman's axe 211.
fireproof and waterproof garment 211.
firn 16.
first aid kit 193.
first base 169.
first baseman 169.
first dorsal fin 62.
first floor 92.
first leaves 34.
first molar 85.
first premolar 85.
first quarter 9.
first space 178.
first valve slide 164.
first violin 167.
FISH 62.
fish scaler 192.

221

The terms in **bold type** correspond to an illustration; those in CAPITALS indicate a title.

fishes, morphology 62.
fission of uranium fuel 207.
fixed jaw 109.
flamingo 76.
flammable 216.
flank 67, 75.
flanking tower 88.
flap 113.
flare 8.
flashing light 140, 211.
flashlight/pocket torch 192.
flashtube 125.
flat-boarder pillowcase 95.
flat brush 157.
flat car/bogie flat wagon 139.
flat mirror 11.
flat, musical notation 161.
flesh 44, 45, 46.
FLESHY FRUITS 44, 47.
fleshy leaves 50.
FLESHY POME FRUITS 46.
FLESHY STONE FRUITS 45.
flews 66.
flexible skirt 141.
flight 197.
flight deck 145, 149.
flip turn 183.
floating crane 142.
floating rib 80.
floor lamp 98.
flounder 63.
flower 36.
flower bud 36.
FLOWERS 38.
flowers, examples 38.
fluorescent tube 99.
fluorescent tube 99.
flute 165.
flute 167.
fly 56.
fly 112.
fly agaric 35.
flying buttress 89.
flying jib 141.
flysheet 190.
FM antenna 128.
foam pad 191.
focus 13.
focus setting ring 125.
focusing knob 11.
fog 22.
fog light/fog lamp 133, 134.
folding chair 96.
folding cot/camp bed 191.
folding door 92.
foliage 40.
fondue fork 101.
fondue pot 104.
fondue set 104.
food chain 28.
food pollution in water 32.
food pollution on ground 32.
foot 75, 78, 79.
foot fault judge 180.
foot protection 216.
foot strap 184.
FOOTBALL 170.
football 170.
football boot 172.
football player 170.
football, playing field 171.
footboard 95.
footbridge 88.
footless tights 121.
footrest 135.
footstool 96.
footstrap 115.
fore royal sail 141.
forearm 66, 79.
forecastle 142.
forecourt 134, 135, 180.
forehead 74, 78.

foreleg 57, 58.
forelimb 60.
forelock 67.
foremast 141.
foresail 141.
forest 17.
forest, coniferous 20.
forest, deciduous 20.
forest, tropical 20.
forewing 57.
fork 55, 101.
fork 11, 137.
forked tongue 64.
forks, types 101.
fortified wall 87.
forward slide change 153.
forward, left 178.
forward, right 178.
fossil fuels 28.
foul line 169.
fountain pen 150.
four-door sedan/four-door saloon 133.
four-four time 160.
FOUR-MASTED BARK/FOUR MASTED BAROQUE 141.
four-toed hoof 71.
fourth, musical interval 160.
frame 94, 112, 136, 168, 181, 188, 189, 208, 213.
frame push 212.
framing square 108.
free-throw lane 178.
free-throw line 178.
freeway/dual-carriageway 90.
freezer compartment 106.
FREIGHT CARS, TYPES 138.
French horn 164.
French horn 167.
fret 162, 163.
frog 60.
frog 113, 162.
frog, life cycle 60.
front 112.
front apron 112.
front brake 137.
front compression strap 193.
front crawl 183.
front derailleur 136.
front fender/front mudguard 135.
front lights 133.
front mudguard 135.
front pocket 123.
front steps 92.
front-end loader 212.
fruit vegetables 49.
frying pan 104, 192.
fuel gauge 132.
fuel tank 134, 135, 139, 145.
fuel tanks 148.
fueling machine 206.
full face mask 211.
full Moon 9.
fullback 171.
fumarole 14.
function button 197.
function keys 201.
function selectors 124.
funnel 103.
funnel 143.
fuse 208.
fuselage 144.
fuselage mounted tail unit 145.

G
••••••••••••••••••••••••••••••

g 160.
g clef 160.
gable 93.
gaff sail boom 141.
gaff topsail 141.
gall bladder 81.

gallery 89.
game cartridge 197.
GAME OF DARTS 197.
gantry crane 204.
Ganymede 6.
garage 92.
garden sorrel 53.
GARDENING 54.
garlic 50.
gas 30, 31, 99.
gas tail 10.
gas tank door/petrol tank flap 131.
gaskin 67.
gasoline/petrol 203.
gasoline pump/petrol pump 135.
gate 204.
gate arm 140.
gate arm lamp 140.
gate arm support 140.
gauze roller bandage 193.
gear lever 137.
gear lever; gears 132.
gearchange pedal 135.
gearshift lever/gear lever; gears 132.
generator/dynamo 136, 206.
generator 138.
generator unit 204.
GEOMETRY 156.
germ 34.
GERMINATION 34.
geyser 15.
gill 35.
gills 62.
gills, external 60.
giraffe 72.
glacial cirque 16.
GLACIER 16.
glacier 20.
glacier tongue 16.
glass 100.
glass 208.
glass cover 106.
glass lens 123.
glass slide 155.
GLASSES 123.
GLASSWARE 100.
glazed frost 22.
globe 152.
globe of Earth 152.
glottis 64.
glove 177, 187.
glove compartment 132.
glove finger 118.
GLOVES 118.
gloves 118.
glue stick 150.
gnomon 198.
goal 171, 173, 175, 176.
goal area 173.
goal crease 176.
goal judge 176.
goal line 171, 175, 176.
goal post 171.
goalkeeper 177.
goalkeeper 173, 175, 176.
goalkeeper's pad 177.
goalkeeper's stick 177.
goat 69.
gondola car/bogie open wagon 139.
gong 167.
goose 68.
gooseberry 44.
gorge 13.
GOTHIC CATHEDRAL 89.
gour 13.
grab handle 134.
graduated dial 193.
graduated scale 200, 201.
grain terminal 142.
granivorous bird 74.
grape 44.
grapefruit 47.

The terms in **bold type** correspond to an illustration; those in CAPITALS indicate a title.

graphic equalizer 128.
grassbox 54.
grasshopper 56.
grater 103.
greases 203.
green 157.
green bean 49.
green cabbage 53.
green peas 52.
green pepper 49.
greenhouse effect 28.
greenhouse gases 29.
Greenland Sea 18.
grid system 24.
grille 130.
groove 186.
ground moraine 16.
ground transport 202.
grounding terminal 99.
guard rail 106.
guard, left 178.
guard, right 178.
guardhouse 88.
guava 48.
guide roller 129.
gulf 26.
gum 84, 85.
gutter 92.
guy line/guy rope 190.
GYMNASTICS 188-189.

H

hair 79, 162.
hair pick 122.
hair-dryer 122.
hairbrush 122.
HAIRDRESSING 122.
half note/minim 161.
half rest/minim rest 161.
half, left 175.
half, right 175.
half-slip/waist slip 116.
halfback, left 171.
halfback, right 171.
hammer 159.
hammer rail 159.
hammer, carpenter's 108.
hammer, claw 108.
HAND 82.
hand 79.
hand blender 105.
hand cultivator 54.
hand fork 54.
hand mixer 105.
hand protection 216.
handbrake 132.
handgrip 135.
handle 54, 95, 101, 108, 109, 110, 111, 122, 123, 129, 162, 168, 181, 186, 192.
handlebars 137.
handsaw 109.
handset 124.
handset cord 124.
hanger loop 117.
hanging glacier 16.
hanging pendant 98.
HARBOR 142.
harmonica 158.
harp 167.
hatch 148.
hatchback 133.
hatchet/axe 192.
head 10, 57, 58, 79, 108, 109, 122, 162, 163, 181.
head linesman 171.
head of water 205.
head protection 216.
headband 128, 129, 181, 187.

headboard 95.
header 93.
headlamp 137.
headland 14.
headlight 130, 135, 139, 140.
headlight/turn signal 132.
headphone 129.
headphone jack 129.
headphone plug 129.
headphones 128.
heart 194.
heart 81.
heartwood 40.
heat production 207.
heat selector switch 122.
heat shield 149.
heat transport pump 206.
heater control 132.
heating oil 203.
heavy duty boot/walking boot 119.
HEAVY MACHINERY 214.
HEAVY VEHICLES 212.
heel 79, 118, 121, 162, 168, 177.
heel piece 186.
heel stop 185.
heel-piece 187.
heelplate 186.
HELICOPTER 145.
helix 83.
helmet 149, 170, 177, 211.
hemidemisemiquaver 161.
hemidemisemiquaver rest 161.
hemispheres 24.
hen 68.
herbivore's jaw 70.
herbivores 29, 33.
hi-hat cymbal 166.
Hi-Fi system 128
high bar 189.
high beam/main beam headlights 133.
high beam indicator light/main beam indicator light 132.
high-rise apartment/high rise block 91.
high rise block 91.
high-speed exit runway 146.
HIGH-SPEED TRAIN 140.
high street 90.
high-tension electricity transmission 205.
highland climates 21.
highland climates 21.
highlighter pen 150.
highway 27.
HIGHWAY CROSSING/LEVEL CROSSING 140.
highway crossing bell/level crossing bell 140.
highway number 27.
hill 17.
hind leg, butterfly 57, 59.
hind limb 60.
hind toe 75.
hind wing 57.
hinge 93, 186.
hinge pin 213.
hip 79.
hip pad 170.
hitting area 168.
hive 59.
hive body 59.
hob 107.
hock 66, 67.
hockey ball 175.
hockey skate 185.
hockey stick 175.
hockey, playing field 175.
hoisting block 214.
hoisting rope 111, 214.
home plate 169.
home-plate umpire 169.
honey cell 59.
HONEYBEE 58.
honeycomb 59.
honeycomb section 59.
hood 113.
hood/bonnet 130.

hooded sweat shirt 120.
hoof 67.
HOOFS, TYPES 71.
hook 94, 108, 185, 201, 214, 215.
hopper car/hopper wagon 138.
horizontal bar 189.
horizontal movement 195.
horizontal pivoting window 94.
horizontal stabilizer/tailplane 144, 145.
horizontal-axis wind turbine 209.
horn 132, 138.
horns of giraffe 71.
horns of mouflon 71.
horns of rhinoceros 71.
HORNS, MAJOR TYPES 71.
horny beak 64.
HORSE 67.
horse 70.
horse 188.
horseradish 51.
hospital 216.
hot pepper 49.
hot-shoe contact 125.
hotel 91.
HOUSE 92.
house on stilts 86.
house, exterior 92.
HOUSES, TRADITIONAL 86.
housing 99, 110, 129.
HOVERCRAFT 141.
hub 137, 209.
hub cap 131.
huckleberry 44.
HUMAN ANATOMY 81.
HUMAN BODY 78, 79.
HUMAN DENTURE 85.
humerus 80.
humid - long summer 21.
humid - short summer 21.
humid subtropical 21.
humidity, measure 23.
hummingbird 77.
hunting cap 113.
husk 52.
hut 87.
hydrant 210.
hydrant intake 210.
hydraulic ram 210, 215.
hydroelectric complex 204.
HYDROELECTRIC ENERGY 204.
hydroelectric power station, cross section 204.
hydrosphere 20.
hygrograph 23.

I

ice 30.
ice cream scoop 103.
ice cube tray 106.
ice dispenser 134.
ICE HOCKEY 176.
ice hockey player 177.
ice hockey, rink 176.
igloo 86.
ignition key 54.
ignition switch 132.
ilium 80.
in-line skate 185.
inbound line 171.
incandescent lamp 99.
incandescent lamp 208.
incisor 70.
incisors 85.
incoming message cassette 124.
index finger 82.
Indian fig 48.
Indian Ocean 19.
indicators 126, 133, 135.
indicator light 132.

223

The terms in **bold type** correspond to an illustration; those in CAPITALS indicate a title.

industrial oil 203.
industrial pollution 32, 33.
inert gas 99.
infield 169.
infiltration 30.
inflator 191.
inflator-deflator 191.
inflorescent vegetables 49.
inner bark 40.
inner boot 185.
inner core 12.
inner table 196.
inner tent 190.
inner, left 175.
inner, right 175.
inorganic matter 29.
insectivores 29.
insectivorous bird 74.
INSECTS 56.
inside 101.
inside left 173.
inside linebacker 171.
inside right 173.
instep 118.
instrument panel 132.
instrument panel 132.
instrument shelter 23.
insulation tiles 148.
interchangeable studs 172.
internal boundary 26.
internal ear 83.
internal frame 193.
international boundary 26.
internode 36.
interrupted projection 25.
intervals 160.
Io 6.
iris 82.
island 26.
isthmus 26.

J

Jack 194, 210, 213, 215.
jacket 113.
jacket 114.
jalousie 94.
jamb 93.
Japanese persimmon 48.
Japanese plum 46.
jaw 109, 110.
jaw, carnivore's 70.
jaw, herbivore's 70.
jaw, rodent's 70.
JAWS, TYPES 70.
jay 77.
jeans 115.
Jerusalem artichoke 51.
jet fuel 203.
jib 214.
jib tie 215.
jib, flying 141.
jigger topgallant staysail 141.
jigger topmast staysail 141.
Joker 194.
jogging bottoms 120.
journal box 138.
Jupiter 6.

K

kangaroo 73.
keep 88.
kernel 52.
kerosene 203.
kettle 105.

kettledrum 167.
key 159, 165.
key case 123.
key signature, musical notation 161.
keybed 159.
keyboard 154, 159.
keyboard cable 154.
KEYBOARD INSTRUMENT 159.
King 194, 195.
King's side 195.
kiosk 135.
KITCHEN APPLIANCES 105.
kitchen scale 201.
kitchen timer 198.
KITCHEN UTENSILS 102.
kiwi 48.
knapsack 123.
knee 67, 78.
knee pad 168, 170, 177.
knee sock 187.
knee-high sock 118.
knife 101, 192.
Knight 195.
knitted hat 114.
knives, types 101.
knob 97, 168.
knob handle 110.
knuckle 82.
kohlrabi 51.

L

label 129.
labial palp 57.
lace 168, 185.
ladder 213.
ladder pipe nozzle 211.
ladle 102.
Lady chapel 89.
ladybug 56.
lagoon 14.
lake 9, 17, 26.
lamb 69.
lanceolate 37.
Land camera, Polaroid® 125.
landing light 145.
landing window 145.
lane 182.
lane number 182.
lane rope 182.
lane timekeeper 182.
larch 43.
large blade 192.
large intestine 81.
last quarter 9.
latch 107.
latch bolt 93.
lateral brush 214.
lateral incisor 85.
lateral moraine 17.
latitude 12.
latitude, lines 24.
lava flow 15.
lava layer 15.
lawn rake 55.
lawnmower 54.
lead-in wire 99.
leading edge 144.
leaf 37.
leaf 34, 36.
leaf axil 37.
leaf margins 37.
leaf node 36.
leaf vegetables 53.
leather end 112.
LEATHER GOODS 123.
leather sheath 192.
leaves, compound 36.
leaves, simple 37.

leaves, types 43.
ledger line 160.
leek 50.
left back 173, 174, 175.
left channel 128.
left cornerback 171.
left defense 176.
left defensive end 171.
left defensive tackle 171.
left field 169.
left fielder 169.
left forward 174, 178.
left guard 171, 178.
left half 173, 175.
left halfback 171.
left inner 175.
left safety 171.
left service court 180.
left tackle 171.
left wing 175, 176.
leg 64, 79, 95, 97, 118, 188.
leg-warmer 121.
lemon 47.
lemon squeezer 103.
lentils 52.
leotard 120.
level 108.
LEVEL CROSSING 140.
level crossing bell 140.
level crossing sign 140.
leveling-adjustment foot 153.
lever 105, 109.
license plate light/number plate light 133.
life raft 141.
lifeboat 141, 143.
lift arm 212.
ligature 165.
light 11.
light bulb 208.
LIGHTING 99.
lightning 22.
lightning conductor 204.
lightning arrester/lightning conductor 204.
lightning rod 93.
LIGHTS 98.
lily 39.
lily of the valley 39.
limb 40.
limo 47.
limousine 133.
line 160.
line judge 171.
line of scrimmage 171.
linear 37.
linebacker, inside 171.
linebacker, middle 171.
linebacker, outside 171.
linen 95.
lines of latitude 24.
lines of longitude 24.
linesman 173, 174, 176, 180.
linesman, head 171.
lining 113, 121.
lion 70, 72.
lip 66, 67.
liquid crystal display 198.
listen button 124.
litchi 48.
lithosphere 20.
little finger hook 164.
liver 81.
livestock car/livestock van 138.
lizard 65.
loader 212.
loading hopper 215.
loafer 119.
lobate 37.
lobate toe 74.
lobe 74, 83.
lobster 61.
lock 93, 136.
lock 93.

The terms in **bold type** correspond to an illustration; those in CAPITALS indicate a title.

lock ring 153.
locking device 111.
locking pliers/adjustable pliers 109.
LOCOMOTIVE, DIESEL-ELECTRIC 138.
log cabin 86.
log chute 204.
loin 67.
long-nose pliers 109.
long-range jet 144.
longitude 12.
longitude, lines 24.
loop 112.
loophole 88.
loose-leaf paper 151.
lorry 134.
loudspeakers 128.
louver-board 89.
louvred window 94.
loveseat/settee 96.
low beam/dipped headlights 133.
lower eyelid 60, 66, 82.
lower fore topgallant sail 141.
lower fore topsail 141.
lower lip 84.
lower mantle 12.
lower shell 186.
lubricating oils 203.
lubricating system 139.
luff 184.
luggage compartment 145.
lumbar pad 170.
LUNAR ECLIPSE 10.
lunar eclipses, types 10.
lunar features 9.
lung, left 81.
lung, right 81.
lunula 82.
lyre 158.

M

machicolation 88.
machine hall 204.
magma 15.
magma chamber 15.
magnetic compass 193.
magnetic needle 193.
magnifier 192.
magnifying glass 155.
main beam indicator light 132.
main beam headlights 133.
main engines 148.
main landing gear 144.
main mirror 11.
main tube 11.
main vent 15.
mainmast 141.
mainsail 141.
maintenance 134.
maintenance hangar 147.
male cone 43.
mallet 108.
mallet 166.
mallets 166.
mandarin 47.
mandible 57, 58, 62, 80.
mandolin 158.
mane 67.
maneuvering engine 148.
mango 45.
manned maneuvering unit 149.
manual focusing knob 153.
manual release 187.
map projections 25.
maple 41.
maracas 166.
margin 36.
marine 21.
marine diesel 203.

maritime transport 202.
marker 150.
marker light 134.
Mars 6.
mask 168.
mast 140, 145, 184.
mast foot 184.
mast sleeve 184.
masthead 184.
mattress 95, 191.
mattress cover 95.
maxilla 62, 80.
maxillary bone 85.
maxillipeds 61.
maximum thermometer 23.
measure of air pressure 23.
measure of humidity 23.
measure of rainfall 23.
measure of temperature 23.
MEASURE OF WEIGHT 200.
measure of wind direction 23.
measure of wind strength 23.
measuring spoons 102.
measuring tube 23.
meat 33.
meat tray 106.
mechanical pencil 150.
mechanics bay/repair shop 134.
medial moraine 16.
median strip 90.
Mediterranean Sea 19.
Mediterranean subtropical 21.
melody strings 158.
meltwater 17.
memory cancel 154.
memory recall 154.
men 195, 196.
MEN'S CLOTHING 112.
men's rest room/men's toilet 216.
Mercury 6.
mercury barometer 23.
mercury bulb 199.
meridian band 152.
merlon 88.
mesocarp 44, 45, 46, 47.
metacarpus 80.
metal frame 159.
metals 33.
metatarsus 80.
METEOROLOGICAL MEASURING INSTRUMENTS 23.
metronome 159.
microscope 155.
microwave oven 107.
middle ear 83.
middle leg 57, 58.
middle linebacker 171.
middle panel 93.
middle toe 74.
midfield line 173.
midrange 128.
midrange pickup 163.
midrib 37.
midsole 121.
Mihrab dome 87.
milometer 132.
minim 161.
minim rest 161.
minaret 87.
minimum thermometer 23.
minivan/estate wagon 133.
minute hand 198.
mirror/wing mirror 134.
mirror 135, 152, 155.
mist 22.
mitten 118.
mixed forest 20.
mizzenmast 141.
moat 88.
mobile crane 215.
moccasin 119.
mode selectors 129.
moisture in the air 30.

molar 70.
molar, cross section 85.
molars 85.
monkey 72.
MOON 9.
Moon 6, 10.
Moon's orbit 10.
moons 6.
moraine, ground 16.
moraine, lateral 17.
moraine, medial 16.
moraine, terminal 17.
mordent, musical notation 161.
MOSQUE 87.
motor 54, 110.
MOTORCYCLE 135.
MOUNTAIN 17.
mountain bike 137.
mountain range 9, 26.
mountain slope 17.
mountain torrent 17.
mounting foot 125.
mouse 154.
MOUTH 84.
mouth 60, 78.
mouthpiece 124, 164, 165.
mouthpipe 158.
movable jaw 109.
movable maxillary 64.
movements, chess 195.
mud flap 131, 134.
mud hut 86.
mudguard 136.
muffler felt 159.
muffler pedal 159.
mug 100.
mule 119.
multiply key 154.
mult-purpose flask 193.
multipurpose bottle/multi-purpose flask 193.
multipurpose vehicle 133.
mummy 191.
muntin 94.
museum 91.
MUSHROOM 35.
mushroom, structure 35.
music stand 159.
musical accessories 159.
MUSICAL INSTRUMENTS, TRADITIONAL 158.
MUSICAL NOTATION 160.
musical scale 160.
muskmelon 49.
mute 164.
muzzle 66, 67.
mycelium 35.

N

nacelle 209.
nail 108.
nail nick 192.
nape 75, 79.
nasal septum 84.
national park 27.
natural arch 14.
natural, musical notation 161.
nave 89.
navel 78.
navigation light 144.
neck 64, 67, 78, 79, 85, 162, 163, 188.
neck end 112.
nectarine 45.
negative contact 208.
negative pole 205.
Neptune 7.
net 174, 180.
net 174, 179, 180.
net band 180.
net judge 180.

225

The terms in **bold type** correspond to an illustration; those in CAPITALS indicate a title.

neutral zone 171, 176.
new crescent 9.
new Moon 9.
nictitating membrane 66.
nightingale 77.
no smoking 216.
North 27.
North America 18.
North Pole 12.
North Sea 19.
North-northeast 27.
North-northwest 27.
Northeast 27.
Northern hemisphere 12, 24.
Northwest 27.
NOSE 84.
nose 67, 78, 145.
nose landing gear 145.
nose leather 66.
nose of the quarter 121.
nose pad 123.
nostril 60, 62, 67, 84.
notch 200.
note symbols, musical notation 161.
notebook 151.
notepad 151.
nozzle 148.
NUCLEAR ENERGY 206.
nuclear power station 206.
nucleus 10.
number 179.
number key 154.
number of tracks sign 140.
number plate light 133.
numeric keyboard 201.
nut 109, 162, 163.
nutcracker 102.

oak 41.
objective 155.
objective lens 11, 125, 153.
oboe 165.
oboe 167.
observation window 148.
ocean 9, 26, 31.
Oceania 19.
octave 160.
octave mechanism 165.
odometer/milometer 132.
offense 171.
office 134.
office building 91, 143.
office tower 90.
officials' bench 176.
offshore drilling 203.
offshore prospecting/offshore drilling 202.
OIL 202.
oil tanker 203.
oil tanker 143.
oil terminal 143.
oil, diesel 203.
oil, heating 203.
oils, lubricating 203.
okra 49.
old crescent 9.
olive 45.
omnivores 28.
on-deck circle 169.
on-off switch 105, 122.
on/off button 126, 129.
on/off switch 153.
on/off/volume control 129.
one-person tent 190.
one-toe hoof 71.
onion, pickling 50.
onion, yellow 50.
open strings 158.

operating nut 210.
operator's cab 214.
operculum 60.
optical lens 152.
optical stage 152.
orange 47.
orange 157.
orange-red 157.
orange-yellow 157.
orbiculate 37.
orbits of the planets 6.
orchid 38.
ordinary die 194.
ORGAN OF HEARING 83.
ORGAN OF SIGHT 82.
ORGAN OF SMELL 84.
ORGAN OF TASTE 84.
ORGAN OF TOUCH 82.
ornaments, musical notation 161.
ostrich 76.
outer bark 40.
outer core 12.
outer table 196.
outer toe 74.
outgoing announcement cassette 124.
outlet 99.
output jack 163.
outrigger/jack 210, 213, 215.
outside left 173.
outside linebacker 171.
outside mirror/wing mirror 130.
outside right 173.
outsole 121.
outwash plain 17.
ovary 38.
oven 107.
oven control knob 107.
overcoat 114.
overhead projector 152.
overtrousers 120.
ovule 38.
owl 77.
ox 69.
ozone layer 29.

Pacific Ocean 18.
packer body 215.
padded pants 177.
paint roller 111.
paintbrush 157.
PAINTING UPKEEP 111.
pajamas 116.
pallet loader 146.
palm 82, 118, 168.
palm tree 42.
palmar pad 66.
palmate 36.
pan 200.
pane 94.
panel 93.
pannier bag 136.
panpipes 158.
pantograph 140.
pants/briefs 112, 116.
pants/trousers 120, 168, 170, 177.
papaya 48.
paper clips 150.
paraffins 203.
parallel 24.
parallel bars 189.
parallelepiped 156.
parallelogram 156.
park 90.
parking area 147.
parking lot/car park 91.
parrot 76.
parsnip 51.

partial eclipse 10.
parts 95.
pass 17.
passenger cabin 141, 145.
passenger car 140.
passenger terminal 143, 147.
passenger transfer vehicle 147.
pastern 67.
patch pocket 113.
patella 80.
pause 126.
Pawn 195.
pay phone 124.
peach 45.
peacock 77.
peak 17, 113, 114.
pear 46.
pear-shaped body 158.
pectoral fin 62.
pedal 136, 166.
pedal rod 159.
pedicel 38, 44, 45, 46.
peeler 102.
peg box 162.
pelvic fin 62.
pen, ballpoint 150.
pen, fountain 150.
pen, highlighter 150.
penalty arc 173.
penalty area 173.
penalty area marking 173.
penalty bench 176.
penalty spot 173.
pencil 150.
pencil sharpener 150.
pendulum bar 159.
peninsula 26.
penstock 204.
penumbra shadow 10.
pepper shaker 100.
percent key 154.
perch 75.
perching bird 74.
PERCUSSION INSTRUMENTS 166.
perforation 125.
pericarp 47.
perpetual snows 17.
personal AM-FM cassette player 129.
personal computer 154.
pesticides 32.
petal 38.
petiole 37.
petrochemicals 203.
petroleum trap 202.
petrol 203.
petrol pump 134, 135.
petrol station 134, 135.
petrol tank flap 131.
phalanges 80.
phases of the Moon 9.
philtrum 84.
Phobos 6.
phosphorescent coating 99.
photoelectric cell 125.
PHOTOGRAPHY 125.
physical map 26.
piano 167.
piccolo 165.
piccolo 167.
pickguard 163.
pickling onion 50.
pickup selector 163.
pickup truck 133.
pickups 163.
pig 69.
piggyback car/piggyback flat wagon 139.
pike 63.
pike pole 211.
pillar 89.
pillow 95.
pillow protector 95.
pillowcase 95.

The terms in **bold type** correspond to an illustration; those in CAPITALS indicate a title.

pilot 139, 140.
pin 99.
pin base 99.
pin block 159.
pine needles 43.
pine seeds 43.
pineapple 48.
pinnatifid 36.
pip 44, 46, 47, 194.
pipeline 202.
pistil 38.
pistol grip handle 110.
pitcher 169.
pitcher's mound 169.
pitcher's plate 169.
pith 40.
pivot 193.
pivot cab 213.
placing judge 182.
placket 112.
plain 26.
PLANE 144.
plane projection 25.
plane surfaces 156.
planetarium 90.
planets 6.
planets, orbits 6.
PLANT AND SOIL 34.
plant litter 34.
plaster 193.
plaster tape 193.
plastron 64.
plate 192.
plateau 17, 26.
platform 182, 201.
platform ladder 111.
play 126.
play button 129.
player's number 170.
player's stick 177.
players' bench 171, 176, 174, 178.
playing area 143.
playing window 129.
pleated skirt 115.
plexus of blood vessels 85.
plexus of nerves 85.
plug 110.
plug, American 99.
plug, European 99.
plum 45.
Pluto 7.
pocket 112, 117.
pocket calculator 154.
pocket camera 125.
pocket torch 192.
point 101, 185, 196, 197.
point of interest 27.
pointer 199, 200, 201.
poisonous 216.
poisonous mushroom 35.
poker die 194.
polar bear 72.
polar climates 21.
polar ice cap 21.
polar tundra 21.
Polaroid® Land camera 125.
pole grip 187.
pole pads 179.
pole shaft 187.
pole tip 187.
political map 26.
pollen basket 58.
pollen cell 59.
pollution, atmospheric 30.
pollution, food 32.
pollution, industrial 33.
polo neck 117, 187.
polo shirt 117.
polo shirt 181.
pome fruit, section 46.
pome fruits, major types 46.
pomegranate 48.

pommel 188.
pommel horse 188.
poncho 114.
poop 141.
pop-up tent 190.
poplar 41.
poppy 38.
port hand 142.
portable CD AM/FM cassette recorder 129.
portable cellular telephone 124.
portable fire extinguisher 210.
portable life support system 149.
PORTABLE SOUND SYSTEMS 129.
portal 89.
porthole 143.
position light 140, 145.
position marker 162, 163.
positive contact 208.
positive pole 205.
post 174.
potato 51.
potato masher 102.
power button 127.
power car 140.
power zoom button 127.
powerhouse 204.
prairie 26.
prayer hall 87.
precipitation 30, 31.
premolar 70.
premolars 85.
preset buttons 126, 127.
pressed area 129.
pressure bar 159.
pressure cooker 104.
pressure regulator 104.
primary colors 157.
primary root 34, 36.
prime meridian 24.
printed document 154.
printer 154.
printout 154, 201.
prism 156.
proboscis 57.
procedure checklist 149.
product code 201.
production of electricity by the generator 205.
production of electricity from nuclear energy 207.
production of electricity, steps 205.
production platform 202.
projection device 214.
projection head 152.
projection screen 153.
projector, overhead 152.
proleg 57.
promenade deck 143.
prominence 8.
propellant level gauge 149.
propeller 143.
propeller duct 141.
prospecting 202.
PROTECTION 216.
protection layer 149.
protective cup 170, 177.
protective equipment 170.
protective helmet, crash helmet 135, 137.
protractor 151.
province 26.
pruning shears 54.
puck 176.
pulley 111.
pulp 47, 85.
pump 119.
pump/court 119.
pump island/forecourt 135.
pumpkin 49.
punch hole 112.
pup tent/ridge rent 190.
pupil 66, 82.
purse 123.
push button 105.
push buttons 124.

push-button telephone 124.
pushpins/drawing pins 150.
pyramid 156.

Q

Qibla wall 87.
quarter 121.
quarter note/crotchet 161.
quarter rest/crotchet rest 161.
quarter-deck 143.
quarterback 171.
quay 142.
quayside crane 143.
quaver 161.
quaver rest 161.
Queen 194, 195.
queen cell 59.
Queen's side 195.
queen, honey-bee 58.
quince 46.

R

rack 107.
radar 142.
radial passenger loading area 147.
radiation zone 8.
radiator 139.
radiator grille 134.
radiator panel 148.
radicle 34, 36, 40.
radio antenna/radio aerial 142.
radioactive 216.
radish 51.
radius 80.
rail 93, 97, 140.
railroad 90.
railroad station 90.
rain 22.
rain forest, tropical 21.
rain gauge recorder 23.
rain gauge, direct-reading 23.
rainbow 22.
raindrop 22.
rainfall, measure 23.
rainfly/flysheet 190.
rake 55.
rake comb 122.
rampart 88.
rangefinder 125.
raspberry, section 44.
rattlesnake 65.
reactor 206, 207.
reactor building 206.
reading start 129.
rear apron 112.
rear brake 136.
rear derailleur 136.
rear light 136.
rear lights 133.
rear shock absorber 135.
rearview mirror 132.
receiver 180.
receptacle 38, 44.
record 129.
record 126.
record announcement button 124.
recorder 165.
recorder 182.
recording tape 129.
recording unit 23.
recovery lorry 215.
rectangle 156.
rectangular 191.
red 157.

227

Red 196.
red currant 44.
Red Sea 19.
red wine glass 100.
red- violet 157.
reed 165.
reeds 165.
referee 171, 173, 176, 174, 178.
refinery 203.
refinery products 203.
refining 203.
reflected heat 28.
reflected ultraviolet rays 28.
REFLECTING TELESCOPE 11.
reflecting telescope, cross section 11.
reflector 136.
REFRACTING TELESCOPE 11.
refracting telescope, cross section 11.
REFRIGERATOR 106.
refrigerator 29.
refrigerator car/refrigerator van 139.
refrigerator compartment 106.
refuse lorry 215.
reheater 206.
release lever 109.
remote control 126.
remote control 153.
remote control sensor 126.
remote control terminal 125.
remote-control arm 149.
repair shop 134.
repeat mark 160.
REPTILES 64.
reservoir 105, 204.
reset button 198.
respiratory system protection 216.
rest area 27.
rest symbols, musical notation 161.
restaurant 91.
restraining circle 178.
restricted area 178.
retriever 174.
rev(olution) counter 132.
reversing light 133.
reverse slide change 153.
revolving nosepiece 155.
rewind 126.
rewind button 120.
rhinoceros 73.
rhombus 156.
rhubarb 52.
rib 123, 213.
rib joint pliers 109.
rib pad 170.
ribbed top 118.
ribbing 117.
ribs 80.
ridge 17.
ridge rent 190.
right ascension setting scale 11.
right back 173, 175.
right channel 128.
right cornerback 171.
right defense 176.
right defensive end 171.
right defensive tackle 171.
right field 169.
right fielder 169.
right forward 174, 178.
right guard 171, 178.
right half 173, 175.
right halfback 171.
right inner 175.
right safety 171.
right service court 180.
right tackle 171.
right wing 175, 176.
rim 123, 135, 137, 179.
rind 47.
ring 35, 123, 164, 189, 198, 201.
ring binder 151.
rings 189.

rink 176.
rink corner 176.
ripper 212.
ripper tooth 212.
river 26.
river estuary 14, 26.
road 27.
road map 27.
road number 27.
road sweeper 214.
road trailer 202.
roasting pans 104.
robin 77.
rock 14.
rocking chair 96.
rodent's jaw 70.
roller cover 111.
roller frame 111.
rolling pin 102.
romaine lettuce 53.
roof 59, 92, 131.
Rook 195.
room thermostat 199.
rooster 68.
root 50, 85.
root canal 85.
root cap 36.
root hairs 34, 36.
root of nose 84.
root system 36.
root vegetables 51.
root, primary 34, 36.
root, secondary 34, 36.
root-hair zone 40.
rose 38.
rose 162.
rose window 89.
rotation of the turbine 205.
rotor 209.
rotor blade 145.
rotor head 145.
rotor hub 145.
rubber 150.
rubber boot 211.
rucksack 193.
rudder 141, 143, 144, 148.
ruler 151.
ruler 192.
rump 75.
rung 111.
runner 196.
running shoe/trainer 121.
runway 146.
runway line 147.
rutabaga 51.

S
•••••••••••••••••••••••••••••••••••

sacrum 80.
saddle 188.
safety binding 187.
safety handle 54.
safety pad 188.
safety rail 138.
SAFETY SYMBOLS 216.
safety tether 149.
safety valve 104, 207.
sail 184.
sail 209.
sail cloth 209.
sail, fore royal 141.
sail, lower fore topgallant 141.
sail, upper fore topgallant 141.
sailbar 209.
SAILBOARD 184.
salad bowl 100.
salad dish 100.
salad plate 100.
salad spinner 103.
salamander 60.

salsify 51.
salt marsh 14.
salt shaker 100.
salty taste 84.
sand island 14.
sandal 119.
sandbox 139.
sanitation truck/refuse lorry 215.
sapwood 40.
sash window 94.
Saturn 7.
satchel 151.
saucepan 104, 192.
sauté pan 104.
saxhorn 164.
saxophone 165.
scale 63, 64, 74, 108, 193, 199.
scale leaf 50.
scale, musical 160.
scales, bathroom 201.
scales, electronic 201.
scales, kitchen 201.
scallion 50.
scampi 61.
scapula 80.
scenic route 27.
SCHOOL EQUIPMENT 152, 154.
SCHOOL SUPPLIES 150.
scientific instruments 148.
scissors 192, 193.
sclera 82.
scorer 174, 178.
scraper 111.
screen 126, 204.
screw 108.
screw 162.
screw base 99.
screwdriver 108.
screwdriver 192.
screwdriver, cross-tip 192.
scrimmage 171.
scroll 162.
sea 9, 26.
sea horse 62.
sealed cell 59.
SEASONS OF THE YEAR 20.
seat 97, 136.
seat post 136.
3EAT3 90.
second base 169.
second baseman 169.
second dorsal fin 63.
second floor 92.
second hand 198.
second molar 85.
second premolar 85.
second space 178.
second valve slide 164.
second violin 167.
second, musical interval 160.
secondary colors 157.
secondary road 27.
secondary root 34, 36.
section of a bulb 50.
seed 34, 44, 45, 46, 47.
seed leaf 36.
seed vegetables 52.
seeds 75.
segment 47.
segment score number 197.
seismic wave 13.
seismographic recording 202.
self-contained breathing apparatus 211.
self-inflating mattress 191.
semi-breve 161.
semi-breve rest 161.
semi-circle 178.
semi-mummy 191.
semicircular canals 83.
semiquaver 161.
semiquaver rest 161.
sensor probe 107.

228

The terms in **bold type** correspond to an illustration; those in CAPITALS indicate a title.

sepal 38, 44.
serac 16.
server 174, 180.
service area 27, 147, 174.
service court, left 180.
service court, right 180.
service judge 180.
service line 180.
service road 146.
service station/petrol station 134.
set of bells 166.
set square 151.
settee 96
seventh, musical interval 160.
shade 98.
shadow 198.
shadow, penumbra 10.
shadow, umbra 10.
shady arcades 87.
shaft 177, 181, 197.
shallot 50.
shallow root 40.
sham/flat-border pillowcase 95.
shank 108, 123.
shark 63.
sharp, musical notation 161.
sheath 192.
sheath 37, 66, 67.
sheep 69.
sheet 141.
sheet, fitted 95.
sheet, flat 95.
shelf 106.
shell 64.
shell 75.
shield 65.
shin guard 168, 172.
shin pad 177.
shirt 112.
shirt 179.
shirttail 112.
shock wave 202.
shoelace 121.
SHOES 119.
shoot 36, 40.
shooting adjustment keys 127.
shorts 115, 121.
shorts 172, 179.
shortstop 169.
shoulder 66, 67, 78, 181.
shoulder blade 79.
shoulder pad 170, 177.
shoulder strap 116, 123, 193.
shovel 55.
shovel 186.
shrimp 61.
shroud 141.
shutter 94.
shutter release button 125.
shuttle 148.
side 141.
side chair 97.
side chapel 89.
side compression strap 193.
side footboard 139.
side light 133.
side molding/side panel 131.
side plate 100.
side panel 131.
side rail 111.
side vent 15.
side wall 182.
sideline 171, 175, 174, 178.
sight 193.
sighting line 193.
sighting mirror 193.
signal background plate 140.
signal lamp 107.
silencer 135.
silk 52.
silos 142.
SILVERWARE 101.

simple eye 57, 58.
simple leaves 37.
single lens reflex (slr) camera 125.
single reed 165.
singles pole 180.
singles sideline 180.
sink-hole 13.
siphon 13.
sistrum 166.
sixteenth note/semiquaver 161.
sixteenth rest/semiquaver rest 161.
sixth, musical interval 160.
sixty-fourth note/hemidemisemiquaver 161.
sixty-fourth rest/hemidemisemiquaver rest 161.
skate 177.
skate guard 185.
SKATING 185.
skeg 184.
SKELETON 80.
ski 186.
ski boot 186.
ski boot 186.
ski glove 186.
ski goggles 186.
ski hat 186, 187.
ski pants 115.
ski pole 186, 187.
ski stop 186, 187.
ski suit 186, 187.
skid 145.
SKIING 186.
skin 44, 45, 46, 60.
skirt 114, 181.
skull 78, 80.
skylight 92.
skyscraper 91.
sleeper 140.
sleeping bags 191.
sleeping cab 134.
SLEEPING EQUIPMENT 191.
sleeve 113, 117.
sleigh bells 166.
slide 153.
slide mount 153.
slide projector 153.
slide tray 153.
slide-select bar 153.
sliding door 93.
sliding folding door 92.
sliding folding window 94.
sliding weight 159, 200.
sliding window 94.
slingback 119.
slip joint 109.
slip joint pliers 109.
slot 105.
slow-motion 126.
small bandage/plaster 193.
small blade 192.
small intestine 81.
snap fastener 113, 118.
snare drum 166, 167.
sneakers 179.
snout 60.
snow 30.
snowblower 214.
SOCCER 172.
soccer ball 172.
soccer player 172.
soccer shoe/football boot 172.
soccer, playing field 173.
sock 118.
sock 170, 181.
sofa/settee 96.
soft palate 84.
soft pedal 159.
soft-drink dispenser 134.
SOIL PROFILE 34.
soleplate 140.
solar cell 208.
solar cell 154.
SOLAR ECLIPSE 10.

solar eclipses, types 10.
SOLAR ENERGY 208.
solar energy 28.
solar panel 208.
solar radiation 208.
solar shield 149.
SOLAR SYSTEM 6.
sole 118, 185.
solid body 163.
solid rocket booster 148.
solids 156.
sound hole 162.
sound reproducing system, components 128.
soundboard 158, 159, 162.
soup bowl 100.
soup spoon 101.
soup tureen 100.
sour taste 84.
sources of gases 29.
sources of pollution 30.
South 27.
South America 18.
South Pole 12.
South-southeast 27.
South-southwest 27.
Southeast 27.
Southern hemisphere 12, 24.
Southwest 27.
sow 69.
soybeans 52.
space 160.
SPACE SHUTTLE 148.
space shuttle at takeoff 148.
space shuttle in orbit 148.
spacelab 148.
SPACESUIT 149.
spade 55, 194.
spaghetti tongs 103.
spanker 141.
spatula 102.
speaker 124, 129.
speaker cover 128.
speed control 54, 105.
speed selector switch 122.
speed skate 185.
speedometer 132.
spent fuel discharge bay 206.
spent fuel storage bay 206.
sphere 156.
SPIDER 56.
spider 56.
spiked shoe 168.
spillway 204.
spillway gate 204.
spinach 53.
spindle 97.
spiny lobster 61.
spiral 129.
spiral bound notebook 151.
spiral-in groove 129.
spire 89.
spit 14.
spleen 81.
splint 193.
split end 171.
spoiler 144.
spoke 137.
spoon 101.
spoons, types 101.
spores 35.
sports car 133.
SPORTSWEAR 120.
spotlight 210.
spreader 123.
spring 20, 109, 188.
spring balance 201.
spring equinox 20.
springboard 188.
sprinklers 207.
spur 17.
square 156.
square 90.

229

The terms in **bold type** correspond to an illustration; those in CAPITALS indicate a title.

square movement 195.
square root key 154.
stabilizer fin 143.
stack 14.
stacking chairs 96.
stadium 91.
staff 160.
stage 155.
stage clip 155.
stake/tent peg 190.
stalactite 13.
stalagmite 13.
stalk 44, 45, 46.
stalk vegetables 52.
stamen 38.
stanchion 185.
stand 98, 135, 166.
staple remover 150.
stapler 150.
staples 150.
star diagonal 11.
starboard hand 142.
start button 198.
start wall 182.
starter 54, 182.
starting bar (backstroke) 182.
starting block 182.
starting block 182.
state 26.
station wagon/estate car 133.
staysail, jigger topgallant 141.
staysail, jigger topmast 141.
steak knife 101.
steam generator 206.
steam pressure drives turbine 207.
steel bar 189.
steelyard 200.
steering wheel 132.
stem 35, 36, 137, 141, 199.
stem bulb 142.
step 134.
stepladder 111.
steppe 21.
stereo control 129.
STEREO SYSTEM/HI-FI SYSTEM 128.
sterile dressing 193.
stern 142, 184.
sternum 80.
stick 162.
stick eraser 150.
sticks 166.
stigma 38.
stile 93, 97.
stimulator tip 122.
stinger 59.
stipule 37.
stirrup sock 168.
stitching 118, 121.
stock 209.
stock pot 104.
stockade 88.
stocking 118.
stocking cap/bobble hat 113.
STOCKINGS 118.
stomach 81.
stone 45.
stone fruit, section 45.
stone fruits, major types 45.
stool 96.
stop 66, 126.
stop at intersection 216.
stop button 198.
stopwatch 198.
storage compartment 134, 153, 210.
storage door 106.
storage tanks 203.
stork 76.
stormy sky 22.
stove oil 203.
straight skirt 115.
straight wing 144.
strainer 103.

strainer 190.
strait 26.
strap 168.
strap loop 193.
strap system 163.
stratosphere 28.
strawberry, section 44.
street 90.
street lamp 91.
street sweeper/road sweeper 214.
striking circle 175.
string 162.
STRINGED INSTRUMENTS 162.
strings 159, 181.
stroke judge 182.
strokes, types 183.
structure of a flower 38.
STRUCTURE OF A PLANT 36.
STRUCTURE OF THE BIOSPHERE 20.
STRUCTURE OF THE EARTH 12.
strut 209.
stud 121.
stump 40.
style 38.
subarctic climates 21.
subarctic climates 21.
sublimation 30.
submarine pipeline 202.
subsoil 34.
subterranean stream 13.
subtract from memory 154.
subtract key 154.
subtropical climates 21.
sugar bowl 100.
suit 114.
summer 20.
summer solstice 20.
summer squash 49.
summit 17.
SUN 8.
Sun 6, 10, 28.
sun visor 132.
Sun's surface 8.
Sun, structure 8.
sundeck 142.
sundial 198.
sunflower 39.
sunlight 28.
sunroof 131.
sunspot 8.
super 59.
supply of water 205.
support 11, 23, 97.
surface insulation 149.
surface prospecting 202.
surface runoff 30, 32.
suspender clip 112.
suspenders/braces 112.
suspension spring 138.
swallow 76.
swallow hole 13.
sweater vest 117.
SWEATERS 117.
sweatpants/jogging bottoms 120.
sweatshirt 120.
sweet corn 52.
sweet peas 52.
sweet pepper 49.
sweet potato 51.
sweet taste 84.
swept-back wing 144.
swimmerets 61.
SWIMMING 182.
swimming pool 143, 182.
swimming trunks 121.
swimming, competitive course 182.
swimsuit 120.
Swiss army knife 192.
Swiss chard 52.
switch 99.
switch 110.
switch lock 110.

swordfish 62.
SYMBOLS, COMMON 216.
SYMBOLS, SAFETY 216.
SYMPHONY ORCHESTRA 167.

T

T-tail unit 145.
tab 123.
TABLE 97.
table 97.
table lamp 98.
tack 184.
tadpole 60.
tag 121.
tail 61.
tail 65, 66, 67, 75, 144, 186.
tail assembly 144.
tail boom 145.
tail comb 122.
tail light/rear light 133, 135
tail shapes, types 145.
tail skid 145.
tail-out groove 129.
tailpiece 162.
tailplane 144, 145.
tailrace 204.
take-up reel 129.
talon 74.
tambourine 166.
tank car/bogie tank wagon 139, 203.
tank car/tank wagon 202.
tank top 120.
tank trailer/road trailer 202.
tape 108, 174.
tape dispenser 151.
tape guide 129.
tape lock 108.
tape measure 108.
tapered wing 144.
taproot 40.
target rectangle 179.
tarsus 80.
taste sensations 84.
team shirt 168, 170, 172.
teapot 100.
teaspoon 101.
technical identification band 129.
technical terms 44, 45, 46, 47.
telecommunication antenna 142.
telephone 216.
telephone answering machine 124.
telephone index 124.
telephone set 124.
telephone, cordless 124.
telephone, portable cellular 124.
TELESCOPE, REFLECTING 11.
TELESCOPE, REFRACTING 11.
telescopic boom 210, 215.
telescopic corridor 147.
telescopic front fork 135.
telescopic umbrella 123.
TELEVISION 126.
television set 126.
temperate climates 21.
temperature control 105.
temperature gauge 132.
temperature set point knob 199.
TEMPERATURE, MEASURE 199.
temperature, measure 23.
temple 78, 123.
tempo scale 159.
tendon guard 185.
TENNIS 180.
tennis ball 181.
tennis player 181.
tennis racket 181.
tennis shoe 119.
tennis shoe 181.

The terms in **bold type** correspond to an illustration; those in CAPITALS indicate a title.

tennis, court 180.
tenor drum 166.
TENTS 190.
tents, major types 190.
tent peg 190.
tepee 86.
terminal box 208.
terminal bud 34, 36.
terminal moraine 17.
tertiary colors 157.
test tube 155.
thermometer 199.
thermometer, clinical 199.
thermostat control 106.
thigh 66, 67, 79.
thigh pad 170.
thigh-boot 119.
third base 169.
third baseman 169.
third valve slide 164.
third, musical interval 160.
thirty-second note/demisemiquaver 161.
thirty-second rest/demisemiquaver rest 161.
thoracic legs 61.
thorax 57, 58.
thread 108.
threaded rod 109.
three-four time 160.
three-toed hoof 71.
threshold 93.
throat 74, 181.
throat protector 168, 177.
thruster 149.
thumb 82, 118, 168.
thumb hook 164.
thumb rest 165.
thumb tacks/drawing pins 150.
thumbscrew 109.
tibia 80.
tie 112.
tie/sleeper 123, 140.
tie plate/soleplate 140.
tight end 171.
tightening band 23.
tightening buckle 193.
tights 118.
time signatures 160.
TIME, MEASURE 198.
timekeeper 178.
tin opener 192.
tine 101.
tip 36, 108, 110, 123, 186.
tip of nose 84.
tire/tyre 131, 137.
tire pump/tyre pump 136.
tire valve/tyre valve 137.
Titan 7.
toad 60.
toaster 105.
toe 66, 74, 78, 118.
toe binding 186.
toe box 185.
toe clip 136.
toe guard 168.
toe pick 185.
toe piece 186.
toe-piece 187.
toeplate 186.
toggle fastening 113.
tom-toms 166.
tomato 49.
tone controls 163.
tongue 84, 112, 121, 185, 186.
tongue sheath 64.
tonsil 84.
tool tether 149.
TOOLS, CARPENTRY 108.
tooth 64, 84, 109, 110, 213.
toothbrush 122.
toothpaste 122.
top 40, 97.
top flap 193.

top ladder 211.
top of dam 204.
top rail 94.
topsail, gaff 141.
topsail, lower fore 141.
topsail, upper fore 141.
topsoil 34.
toque 114.
total 201.
total eclipse 10.
touch line 173.
touring boot 187.
tourist route 27.
tow bar 146.
tow tractor 146, 147.
tow truck/recovery lorry 215.
tower 89, 209.
tower crane 214.
tower ladder 211.
tower mast 214.
towing device 215.
track 98, 212.
track lighting 98.
track suit 120.
tractor unit 134.
tractor, crawler 212.
TRADITIONAL MUSICAL INSTRUMENTS 158.
traffic island 90.
trailing edge 144.
trailing edge flap 144.
trainer 121.
trampoline 188.
transept 89.
transept spire 89.
transfer of heat to water 207.
transformation of mechanical work into electricity 205.
transformer 98, 204, 206.
transit shed 143.
transmission of the rotative movement to the rotor 205.
transmission to consumers 205.
transparency 153.
transpiration 31.
trapezoid 156.
trapped heat 29.
traveling crane 204.
tray 111.
treble bridge 159.
treble keyboard 158.
treble pickup 163.
treble register 158.
treble tone control 163.
TREE 40.
tree frog 60.
tree, structure 40.
trees, examples 41.
triangle 156, 166.
triangle 167.
triangular body 158.
trifoliolate 36.
trigger switch 110.
trill, musical notation 161.
trip odometer/trip milometer 132.
triple ring 197.
triple tail unit 145.
tripod 11.
tripod accessories shelf 11.
tripod stand 166.
Triton 7.
trolley 214.
trolley pulley 214.
trombone 164.
trombone 167.
tropic of Cancer 12, 24.
tropic of Capricorn 12, 24.
tropical climates 21.
tropical forest 20.
TROPICAL FRUITS 48.
tropical fruits, major types 48.
tropical rain forest 21.
tropical savanna 21.
troposphere 28.
trousers 112, 120, 168, 170.

trout 62.
trowel 54.
TRUCK/LORRY 134.
truck/bogie 138, 185.
truck crane/mobile crane 215.
truck frame/bogie frame 138.
trumpet 164.
trumpet 167.
trunk 40, 79.
trunk/boot 131.
trunk, cross section 40.
tuba 164.
tuba 167.
tuber vegetables 51.
tubular bells 167.
tulip 38.
tumbler 100.
tuna 62.
tundra 20.
tuner 128.
tuner 129.
tungsten-halogen lamp 99.
tuning control 129.
tuning controls 126.
tuning fork 159.
tuning peg 162, 163.
tuning pin 159.
tuning slide 164.
turbine 206.
turbine building 206.
turbine shaft turns generator 207.
turbined water draining 205.
turbojet engine 144.
turkey 68.
turn signal/indicator 133, 135.
turn signal indicator/indicator light 132.
turn, musical notation 161.
turning judge 182.
turning wall 182, 183.
turnip 51.
turntable 128.
turntable 213.
turntable mounting 210.
turret 88.
turtle 64.
turtleneck/polo neck 117.
tusks of elephant 71.
tusks of walrus 71.
tusks of wart hog 71.
TUSKS, MAJOR TYPES 71.
TV mode 126.
TV on/off button 126.
TV/video button 126.
tweeter 128.
tweezers 193.
twig 36, 40.
twist drill 110.
two-door sedan/coupe 133.
two-person tent 190.
two-toed hoof 71.
two-two time 160.
tympanum 89.
tyre 131. 136, 137.
tyre pump 136, 137.
tyre valve 136, 137.

U

ulna 80.
umbra shadow 10.
UMBRELLA 123.
umbrella pine 43.
umbrella, telescopic 123.
umpire 171, 174, 180, 182.
under tail covert 75.
underground flow 31, 32.
underground stem 50.
undershirt 112.
undershirt/vest 168.

The terms in **bold type** correspond to an illustration; those in CAPITALS indicate a title.

231

uneven bars 189.
unison, musical interval 160.
unit price 201.
universal step 146.
uphaul 184.
upper eyelid 60, 66, 82.
upper fore topgallant sail 141.
upper fore topsail 141.
upper lip 84.
upper mantle 12.
upper shell 185, 186.
upper strap 186.
upper tail covert 75.
upright 189.
upright piano 159.
upright pipe 210.
Uranus 7.
usual terms 44, 45, 46, 47.
UTENSILS, KITCHEN 102.
uvula 84.

V

V-neck 117.
V-neck cardigan 117.
valley 17.
valve 164.
valve casing 164.
vamp 121.
vanity mirror 132.
variable geometry wing 144.
vault 188.
VCR controls 126.
VCR mode 126.
VCR on/off button 126.
vegetable steamer 104.
VEGETABLES 49, 50, 52.
vegetables 33.
vein 37.
vein, femoral 81.
vein, subclavian 81.
venom canal 64.
venom gland 64.
venom-conducting tube 64.
venomous snake's head 64.
venous blood 81.
vent, main 15.
vent, side 15.
ventilating fan 139.
Venus 6.
vernal equinox 20.
vernier scale 200.
vertebral column 80.
vertical movement 195.
vertical pivoting window 94.
vertical side band 174.
vertical-axis wind turbine 209.
vest 112.
vibrato arm 163.
VIDEO 127.
video camera 127.
VIDEO ENTERTAINMENT SYSTEM 197.
video monitor 154.
videocassette recorder 127.
videotape operation controls 127.
viewfinder adjustment keys 127.
vine leaf 53.
viola 162.
viola 167.
violet 38.
violet 157.
violet-blue 157.
violin 162.
violin family 162.
visor 135, 140, 187.
visual display 197.
volcanic bomb 15.
VOLCANO 15.
volcano 28.

VOLLEYBALL 174.
volleyball 174.
volleyball, court 174.
voltage decrease 205.
voltage increase 205, 207.
volume control 124, 126, 129, 163.
volva 35.

W

wading bird 74.
wagon tent 190.
waist 79, 162.
waist belt 193.
waistband 112, 113.
waist slip 116.
walking boot 119.
walking leg 57.
Walkman® 129.
wall 9, 47.
wall fixture 98.
wall tent 190.
wallet 123.
waning gibbous Moon 9.
warming plate 105.
warning device 211.
warning light 140.
warning lights 132.
warning track 169.
washer nozzle 130.
watch, digital 198.
water bottle 136.
water bottle clip 136.
water colours 157.
water cools the used steam 207.
water cycle 30.
water intake 204.
water is pumped back into the steam generator 207.
water key 164.
water pitcher 100.
water supply point 210.
water table 13.
water tank 139.
water turns into steam 207.
water under pressure 205.
watercolors/water colours 157.
watercress 53.
waterfall 17.
watering can 54.
watering tube 214.
watermelon 49.
waxing gibbous Moon 9.
WEATHER 22.
weather radar 145.
web 60, 74, 168.
webbed foot 60.
webbed toe 74.
weeping willow 42.
weight 200, 201.
WEIGHT, MEASURE 200.
West 27.
West-northwest 27.
West-southwest 27.
Western hemisphere 24.
Western meridian 24.
whale 72.
wheel 185.
wheel chock 146.
wheel cover/hub cap 131.
wheel tractor 212.
wheelbarrow 55.
wheelchair access 216.
whisk 102.
whiskers 66.
White 195, 196.
white cabbage 53.
white of eye 82.
white square 195.
white wine glass 100.

whole note/semi-breve 161.
whole rest/semi-breve rest 161.
wigwam 86.
WILD ANIMALS 72.
winch 215.
winch controls 215.
wind deflector 134.
wind direction, measure 23.
WIND ENERGY 209.
WIND INSTRUMENTS 164.
wind strength, measure 23.
wind vane 23.
windbag 158.
windbreaker/anorak 113, 120.
windmill 209.
WINDOW 94.
window 107, 131, 145, 184.
windows, types 94.
windscreen 130, 135.
windscreen wiper 130.
windshaft 209.
windshield/windscreen 130, 135.
windshield wiper/windscreen wiper 130.
wing 75, 144, 148.
wing 130.
wing mirror 130, 134.
wing shapes, types 144.
wing slat 144.
wing vein 57.
wing, left 175, 176.
wing, right 175, 176.
winglet 144.
winter 20.
winter solstice 20.
wiper switch 132.
wire brush 166.
wisdom tooth 85.
wishbone boom 184.
withers 66, 67.
wok 104.
WOMEN'S CLOTHING 114, 116.
women's rest room/women's toilet 216.
woodwind family 165.
woofer 128.
worker, honey-bee 58.
worm 214.
wrist 66, 79, 82.
wrist strap 186, 187.
wristband 170, 181.

X

xylophone 166.
xylophone 167.

Y

yard line 171.
yellow 157.
yellow onion 50.
yellow-green 157.
yolk 75.
yurt 87.

Z

zebra 73.
zest 47.
zipper/zip 190.
zither 158.
zoom lens 127.
zucchini/courgette 49.

The terms in **bold type** correspond to an illustration; those in CAPITALS indicate a title.